FITZGERALD'S CRAFT OF SHORT FICTION

FITZGERALD'S

CRAFT *of* SHORT FICTION

THE COLLECTED STORIES 1920–1935

Alice Hall Petry

THE UNIVERSITY OF ALABAMA PRESS
TUSCALOOSA AND LONDON

Library of Congress Cataloging-in-Publication Data

Petry, Alice Hall, 1951–
    Fitzgerald's craft of short fiction : the collected stories, 1920–
    1935 / Alice Hall Petry
        p.   cm.
    Includes bibliographical references and index.
    ISBN 0-8173-0547-5 (alk. paper)
        1.   Fitzgerald, F. Scott (Francis Scott), 1896–1940—
    Criticism and interpretation. 2. Short story.   I. Title.
    PS3511.I9Z814   1991   91–8642
    813'.52—dc20   CIP

British Library Cataloguing-in-Publication Data available

For
Grace Hall Slater
and in loving memory of
Peter J. Slater

Contents

Acknowledgments

It is always a pleasure to thank publicly the groups and individuals that have been instrumental in the creation of one's book. For providing me with the time and funding to pursue my work on Fitzgerald, I wish to thank the American Council of Learned Societies and the National Endowment for the Humanities for a 1987–1988 ACLS Senior Postdoctoral Fellowship. I am also deeply grateful to the Rhode Island School of Design—and in particular to Paul Nash, Vice President for Academic Affairs, and to Edward Dwyer, Chairman of the Liberal Arts Division—for arranging for me to have a full-year sabbatical leave in conjunction with my grant.

For their help in obtaining the necessary books, articles, and reviews, I wish to thank the Rockefeller Library of Brown University, the Providence Public Library, the Providence College Library, the Rhode Island College Library, and the Providence Athenaeum. I also thank Edgar A. Dryden, Editor of *Arizona Quarterly,* for permission to reprint (in slightly modified form) my 1983 essay on Fitzgerald's story "The Jelly-Bean."

I am especially grateful to four scholars who have been unstinting in their support of my work: George Monteiro of Brown University; Alan Gribben of the University of Texas; Jackson R. Bryer of the University of Maryland; and Milton R. Stern of the University of Connecticut. Their help, advice, and friendship have made all the difference.

Finally, I wish to thank the staff of the UMI Research Press, and in particular Christine B. Hammes, Barbara K. Timmons, Brad Taylor, Marilyn Meeker, and Louise Washburne; and the staff of The University of Alabama Press, especially Malcolm M. MacDonald and Nicole Mitchell.

Short Titles

Afternoon of an Author	F. Scott Fitzgerald, *Afternoon of an Author,* ed. Arthur Mizener (New York: Charles Scribner's, 1958)
Allen, *Candles and Carnival Lights*	Joan M. Allen, *Candles and Carnival Lights: The Catholic Sensibility of F. Scott Fitzgerald* (New York: New York University Press, 1978)
Bruccoli, *As Ever*	Matthew J. Bruccoli, ed., assisted by Jennifer M. Atkinson, *As Ever, Scott Fitz—: Letters between F. Scott Fitzgerald and His Literary Agent Harold Ober, 1919–1940* (Philadelphia and New York: J.B. Lippincott, 1972)
Bruccoli, *Correspondence*	Matthew J. Bruccoli and Margaret M. Duggan, eds., assisted by Susan Walker, *Correspondence of F. Scott Fitzgerald* (New York: Random House, 1980)
Bruccoli, *Epic Grandeur*	Matthew J. Bruccoli, *Some Sort of Epic Grandeur: The Life of F. Scott Fitzgerald* (New York: Harcourt Brace Jovanovich, 1981)
Bruccoli and Bryer, *A Miscellany*	Matthew J. Bruccoli and Jackson R. Bryer, eds., *F. Scott Fitzgerald in His Own Time: A Miscellany* (Kent, Ohio: Kent State University Press, 1971)

Bryer, *Critical Reception*

Jackson R. Bryer, ed., *F. Scott Fitzgerald: The Critical Reception* (New York: Burt Franklin and Co., 1978)

Bryer, *New Approaches*

Jackson R. Bryer, ed., *The Short Stories of F. Scott Fitzgerald: New Approaches in Criticism* (Madison: University of Wisconsin Press, 1982)

Cross, *F. Scott Fitzgerald*

K. G. W. Cross, *F. Scott Fitzgerald* (New York: Capricorn Books, 1971)

Donaldson, *Fool for Love*

Scott Donaldson, *Fool for Love: F. Scott Fitzgerald* (New York: Congdon & Weed, 1983)

Dear Scott/Dear Max

John Kuehl and Jackson R. Bryer, eds., *Dear Scott/Dear Max: The Fitzgerald-Perkins Correspondence* (New York: Charles Scribner's Sons, 1971)

Eble, *F. Scott Fitzgerald*

Kenneth Eble, *F. Scott Fitzgerald*, rev. ed. (Boston: Twayne, 1977)

Gallo, *F. Scott Fitzgerald*

Rose Adrienne Gallo, *F. Scott Fitzgerald* (New York: Frederick Ungar, 1978)

Geismar, *Last of the Provincials*

Maxwell Geismar, "F. Scott Fitzgerald: Orestes at the Ritz," in *The Last of the Provincials: The American Novel, 1915–1925* (Boston: Houghton Mifflin, 1947)

Higgins, *A Study*

John A. Higgins, *F. Scott Fitzgerald: A Study of the Stories* (Jamaica, New York: St. John's University Press, 1971)

Kazin, ed., *F. Scott Fitzgerald*

Alfred Kazin, ed., *F. Scott Fitzgerald: The Man and His Work* (New York: Collier Books, 1962)

Kuehl, *Apprentice Fiction*

John Kuehl, ed., *The Apprentice Fiction of F. Scott Fitzgerald: 1909–1917* (New Brunswick, New Jersey: Rutgers University Press, 1965)

Lehan, *Craft of Fiction*

Richard D. Lehan, *F. Scott Fitzgerald and the Craft of Fiction* (Carbondale: Southern Illinois University Press, 1966)

LeVot, *F. Scott Fitzgerald*

André LeVot, *F. Scott Fitzgerald: A Biography,* trans. William Byron (Garden City, New York: Doubleday, 1983)

Mellow, *Invented Lives*

James R. Mellow, *Invented Lives: F. Scott & Zelda Fitzgerald* (New York: Ballantine Books, 1984)

Milford, *Zelda*

Nancy Milford, *Zelda* (New York: Avon, 1970)

Mizener, *The Far Side*

Arthur Mizener, *The Far Side of Paradise: A Biography of F. Scott Fitzgerald,* 2d ed. (Boston: Houghton Mifflin, 1965)

Notebooks

Matthew J. Bruccoli, ed., *The Notebooks of F. Scott Fitzgerald* (New York: Harcourt Brace Jovanovich/Bruccoli Clark, 1978)

Perosa, *The Art of*
  F. Scott Fitzgerald

Sergio Perosa, *The Art of F. Scott Fitzgerald,* trans. Charles Matz and Sergio Perosa (Ann Arbor: University of Michigan Press, 1965)

Piper, *Critical Portrait*

Henry Dan Piper, *F. Scott Fitzgerald: A Critical Portrait* (New York: Holt, Rinehart and Winston, 1965)

Sklar, *The Last Laocoön*

Robert Sklar, *F. Scott Fitzgerald: The Last Laocoön* (New York: Oxford University Press, 1967)

Stavola, *Crisis in an
American Identity*

Thomas J. Stavola, *Scott Fitzgerald: Crisis
in an American Identity* (New York: Barnes
and Noble, 1979)

Stern, *The Golden Moment*

Milton R. Stern, *The Golden Moment: The
Novels of F. Scott Fitzgerald* (Urbana: University of Illinois Press, 1970)

Turnbull, *Letters*

Andrew Turnbull, ed., *The Letters of F.
Scott Fitzgerald* (New York: Dell, 1963)

Turnbull, *Scott Fitzgerald*

Andrew Turnbull, *Scott Fitzgerald* (New
York: Charles Scribner's Sons, 1962)

Introduction

To judge from the current state of scholarship, one would hardly surmise that short stories loomed large in the literary career of F. Scott Fitzgerald. Every year much is written about his four completed novels, in particular *The Great Gatsby*, while a handful of essays appear dealing with at least one of the half-dozen Fitzgerald stories that are the mainstay of so many college anthologies. But this bibliographical record would not lead one to suspect that he wrote nearly 180—yes, 180—short stories.[1] Perhaps the sheer immensity of Fitzgerald's short-story canon is simply too intimidating for most potential commentators. Or perhaps the neglect of these stories is due to their unavailability for so many years—an argument which has lost considerable ground since the appearance in the 1970s of two serviceable miscellanies, *Bits of Paradise* (1973) and *The Price Was High* (1979). And few of even the most dedicated Fitzgerald scholars are willing to dust off the back issues of *Liberty* and *Esquire* for a look at "The Passionate Eskimo" or "Shaggy's Morning," efforts so sorry that even the miscellanies exclude them. Perhaps indeed the real reason for the lack of attention paid to Fitzgerald's short fiction is that a large number of these stories simply are not very good. Many, in fact, richly warrant Fitzgerald's own appraisal of them as "trash." Many—but not all.

Fitzgerald himself from the very beginning of his career took great pride in his work as a writer of short fiction. True, he often stated publicly a preference for novels over short fiction, and late in his career he turned out for quick money a series of stories so poor that some, including "I'd Die For You" and "The Pearl and the Fur," remain only in typescript to this day. But quite early in his career he began differentiating carefully between his quality stories and the "trash," and no one knew better than he that some of his short fiction is absolutely first-rate, including the perennially anthologized "Babylon Revisited," "The Rich Boy," "The Diamond as Big as the Ritz," "May Day," "The Ice Palace," "Crazy Sunday," "The Last of the Belles," and "Winter Dreams." But this situation should not blind us to the fact that he wrote a series of other excellent stories which inexplicably have been ignored or dismissed lightly by

Fitzgerald scholars, and that the cream of his achievement as a writer of short fiction was presented to the public in four increasingly impressive authorized collections: *Flappers and Philosophers* (1920), *Tales of the Jazz Age* (1922), *All the Sad Young Men* (1926), and *Taps at Reveille* (1935). Fitzgerald took seriously the production of these collections, carefully selecting the stories he wished to include, revising their texts (all had appeared previously in periodicals), correcting proofs, choosing typeface, suggesting appropriate jacket illustrations, even composing his own "blurbs" for the public relations staff at Scribners, which published each of the collections. To Fitzgerald, these four authorized collections were works of art, to be crafted with the sort of care he devoted to his better-known novels; and further, he used them as repositories for the finest short fiction he had produced during a series of key periods in his career. Indeed, Fitzgerald perceived them as essentially the first four of seven volumes of short fiction which he planned to include in his projected seventeen-volume "Collected Works."[2] The four authorized story collections are, in fine, the permanent record of what Fitzgerald felt was a vital aspect of his work as a writer.

All this is not to say, however, that neither Fitzgerald nor Scribners appreciated the commercial possibilities of the four collections. These books were frankly intended by Scribners to cash in on the popularity of the four Fitzgerald novels that had been published shortly before each collection: *This Side of Paradise* (1920), *The Beautiful and Damned* (1922), *The Great Gatsby* (1925), and *Tender Is the Night* (1934). It proved to be a sound marketing strategy, for the story collections—with the notable exception of *Taps at Reveille,* published in the middle of the Depression—sold well. But the strategy had a high artistic price for Fitzgerald, for it meant that he had to produce at least eight quality stories at virtually the same time he was struggling with the novels. This was not a problem when he and Scribners editor Maxwell Perkins settled on the stories to be included in *Flappers and Philosophers,*[3] for all had been written in rapid succession in a burst of creativity in 1919–20, the result of the acceptance for publication of *This Side of Paradise* and the concomitant realization that it was, in fact, possible for him to pursue a career as a professional writer. But the plan posed serious problems with his next collection, *Tales of the Jazz Age.* Its companion novel, *The Beautiful and Damned,* had been difficult to write. At 450 pages, it is a swollen and often over-written book, with its two protagonists, who spend the entire novel wasting their lives and hurting each other as they await an inheritance, coming across as children rather than as the dynamic, colorful individuals Fitzgerald had intended. The composition of *The Beautiful and Damned* had been prolonged and painful, including several false starts, and by the time he finished it Fitzgerald was simply not ready to follow it up with a quality collection of short stories. That lack of readiness is apparent in the very selection of material for *Tales of the Jazz Age.* "Tarquin of

Cheapside" and "Jemina" are barely revised sketches from Fitzgerald's undergraduate days at Princeton, while "Mr. Icky" and "Porcelain and Pink" are not stories at all, but rather short plays. In addition, the two best stories in the collection, "May Day" and "The Jelly-Bean," properly belong in *Flappers and Philosophers* since they were written during that burst of creativity in 1919–20, and were not included in the first collection only because they had not yet seen magazine publication. There was an unfortunate aptness in calling the second collection *Tales of the Jazz Age,* a title which even Fitzgerald regarded as dated: these were basically old stories.

Having to resurrect college sketches was bad enough, but there was not even the consolation of critical appreciation for the more recent efforts. One of the newer stories, "The Diamond as Big as the Ritz" (written in October 1921) was very good indeed, but Fitzgerald had experienced repeated rejection in marketing it and eventually had to settle for publication in *The Smart Set.* Further, whatever pride he may have derived from the achievement of "Diamond" was qualified by the response to stories such as "The Camel's Back" (written in January 1920), a sorry farce that attracted far more critical and popular acclaim than the later, far better tale. Whatever financial success and popularity it may have enjoyed, *Tales of the Jazz Age* did not betoken the polishing of craft and the honing of judgment that Fitzgerald, acutely self-conscious of being a beginning author, would have wished to see between 1920 and 1922. Despite its occasional riches, *Tales of the Jazz Age* shows no progress in Fitzgerald's evolution as a writer of short fiction.

Part of the problem, of course, was that Fitzgerald was still quite young when he wrote the stories of *Flappers and Philosophers* and *Tales of the Jazz Age.* His literary apprenticeship, although long, had involved writing plays for a children's drama club in his hometown of St. Paul, or sketches and poems for his prep school's in-house literary magazine, or burlesques and musical comedies for a not always discriminating audience of Princeton undergraduates. By the early 1920s he had a writer's bag full of technical and stylistic tricks, but he did not yet have the professional experience or the critical acumen to be selective, to transmute those chosen elements into the mutually enriching components of a purposeful, aesthetically sound work of literary art. Consequently even the strongest efforts in these two early volumes are marred by inappropriate metaphors, vague descriptions, misleading details, and sophomoric asides. Fitzgerald is particularly liable to intrude clumsily into the stories: "To me the interesting thing about Ardita is the courage that will tarnish with her youth and beauty" ("The Offshore Pirate," *F&P,* 39). Or he injects details or asides that showcase his knowledge or amuse his fellow Princetonians while contributing little to the story: "the monastery trees were older than the monastery which, by true monastic standards, wasn't very old at all. And, as a matter of fact, it wasn't technically a monastery, but only a seminary; nevertheless it shall be a monastery here" ("Benediction," *F&P,* 142). Or he provides an essayistic or chatty opening that establishes a tone inappropriate for the story that follows (see "The Jelly-Bean," *TJA*). Or he introduces a provocative story line and then drops it, such as Horace Tarbox's Skinnerian childhood, "an experiment in precocity" engineered by his father, a Princeton professor ("Head and Shoulders," *F&P,* 76). Even two of the most fundamental elements of fictional art—maintaining an appropriate narrative voice and gauging the relationship between length of text and complexity of plot—often fall by the wayside as the young Fitzgerald lets the raw energy of boyish self-confidence, doubled with the thrill of fictional experimentation, outrun his fledgling artistic sense. Even so, one should not discount that raw energy, which lends a vigor to such technically weak stories as "The Offshore Pirate," "Tarquin of Cheapside," and "Head and Shoulders"; nor should one underestimate his artistic judgment, which was beginning to sharpen in the process of writing these stories. But the fact remains that Fitzgerald's lack of professional experience in the late teens and early 1920s had a serious negative impact on the quality of the stories in *Flappers and Philosophers* and *Tales of the Jazz Age.*

And yet that is only part of the picture, for at the same time that he was learning his fictional craft, Fitzgerald was beginning to use his writing to probe a spectrum of increasingly serious personal problems. True, most authors draw upon their own experiences and feelings when they write, but Fitzgerald did so to an extreme degree. With the possible exception of Emily Dickinson, whose poetic achievement is largely meaningless without some awareness of her personal feelings for the Rev. Charles Wadsworth, Fitzgerald is arguably the most dramatic example in American literary history of an author whose private life is reflected, consciously or otherwise, in virtually everything he wrote. This is not simply what Andrew Turnbull identifies as Fitzgerald's adherence to "the Renaissance and Romantic conception of the writer as a man of action who experiences his material at first hand," that "perilous doctrine" which may help explain his restless and often self-destructive lifestyle.[4] It was, perhaps more importantly, Fitzgerald's compulsion to probe his innermost thoughts, feelings, and fears in his fiction. As Richard Foster states the case, "self and art were so inextricably intertwined in the fabric of Fitzgerald's life that the acquisition of *self*-knowledge was virtually synonymous with the acquisition of knowledge about his art."[5]

It would appear, then, that a heightened awareness of Fitzgerald's personal life and feelings is a valuable key to appreciating their impact, for good or ill, on his achievement and development as a writer from the very dawn of his career—a career that coincided almost exactly with his marriage to Zelda Sayre. Beginning with their wedding in April 1920—indeed, even from the last days of their engagement—Fitzgerald was faced with financial over-extension, escalating alcoholism, and the increasingly evident emotional problems of Zelda.

Early in the 1920s these concerns were effectively controlling the selection of his themes and characters, as well as affecting—usually for the worse—his fictional technique and style. A striking example is *The Beautiful and Damned*. As Fitzgerald's contemporaries recognized, Anthony and Gloria Patch are modeled upon Scott and Zelda Fitzgerald.[6] Using his novel to probe the tension in his own marriage, Fitzgerald worked hard to impose an artificial sense of order (three sections of three chapters each) on the experiences of the Patches that was lacking in his troubled relationship with Zelda. Further, as he himself recognized early on, the meaning of the novel is obscure: sidestepping large issues and the implications of the Patches' situation for his own marriage, Fitzgerald overcompensated by focusing on attractive (but often irrelevant) details,[7] an evasion that reveals far more than he himself probably realized.

The personal problems that so affected the artistry of *The Beautiful and Damned* are evident likewise in the stories of *Flappers and Philosophers* and *Tales of the Jazz Age*. As the following chapters argue, their composition was in many cases apparently meant to be cathartic, enabling him to channel his fears and frustrations into the "safe" medium of art, but even so, the violence and bitterness that underlie even the farces argue that the stories could not permit him to deny or defuse them completely. The bitter worst-case scenarios of "Head and Shoulders" (*F&P*) and "The Lees of Happiness" (*TJA*) are ideal examples of how Fitzgerald apparently attempted at some level to use his short stories to explore his misgivings about his career and marriage. The stories were the medium enabling him to face his misgivings, if not always to articulate or resolve them.

Not surprisingly, there is an aura of hesitancy or even fear in even the most superficially polished or farcical early stories; and yet the record suggests that Fitzgerald did try to deal with his artistic and personal challenges. As he grew into both a seasoned professional author and a mature human being, Fitzgerald became increasingly capable of using his writing not just for airing his complaints and dramatizing his fears, but for drawing upon his own experiences and feelings—including his own culpability—to speak to the human condition through stories of terrible beauty. This achievement came relatively late in his career, in the mid-1920s and the 1930s, and the results are evident in the last two collections, *All the Sad Young Men* and *Taps at Reveille*.

Consider *All the Sad Young Men*, published in 1926. Although far from perfect, the writing in this collection is consistently tighter, both technically and stylistically, than in the previous two volumes. Moreover, the voice, the outlook—even in a farce like "Rags Martin-Jones and the Pr–nce of W–les"—is steadier, more controlled. This improvement is probably related to the same factors that enabled Fitzgerald to make the quantum leap from the bloated and confusing *The Beautiful and Damned* to his taut and graceful masterpiece, *The Great Gatsby* (1925). James E. Miller, Jr., in *F. Scott Fitzgerald: His Art and*

His Technique, argues persuasively that Fitzgerald's startling improvement as a writer in the mid-1920s was due to his decision to reject the Wellsian novel of saturation in favor of the Jamesian novel of selection, coupled with a new awareness of the possibilities of the Conradian participant-narrator. Of course, virtually by definition a short story is a work of selection, its limited canvas nurturing concision while short-circuiting the kind of chattiness to which Fitzgerald was temperamentally inclined, and his early interest in writing short fiction would suggest that he was receptive to fictional "selection" long before the Wells/James controversy. But if he had not always practiced selection in *Flappers and Philosophers* and *Tales of the Jazz Age,* he was certainly, by the time he worked on *All the Sad Young Men,* putting to good use what he had been assimilating through the study of other authors and learning from the infelicities of the first two collections.

And yet, as Milton Stern has observed, the dramatic improvement of *The Great Gatsby* over *The Beautiful and Damned* cannot be attributed solely to study and professional experience.[8] It was these elements, working in concert with a broader vision and greater maturity (as evidenced by a willingness to acknowledge his personal misgivings to Maxwell Perkins, his trusted editor and confidant at Scribner's; to his agent, Harold Ober; and to friends like Edmund Wilson) that enabled him to grow as an artist. The most dramatic instance of this was his attitude toward his wife, Zelda. His early infatuation with her had been tinged with an increasing awareness of her potential for destructiveness, although he had attempted to deny this by projecting her onto female characters in fantasies ("The Offshore Pirate," *F&P*) or farces ("Head and Shoulders," *F&P*). But he could not produce such psychologically complex *femmes fatales* as Judy Jones ("Winter Dreams," *ASYM*) or Ailie Calhoun ("The Last of the Belles," *TAR*) until he could admit freely to Edmund Wilson that "the most enormous influence on me in the four and a half years since I met her has been the complete, fine and full-hearted selfishness and chill-mindedness of Zelda."[9] And when her series of breakdowns, beginning in April 1930, effectively removed her from his daily life, he began to write sensitive, generally non-self-pitying stories about men without wives, including "Family in the Wind," "The Fiend," and "Babylon Revisited" (all from *Taps at Reveille*). Clearly, Fitzgerald's changing perception of his wife and his increasingly astute understanding of his own responsibility for their troubled relationship had a direct and immediate impact on his art.

Both *All the Sad Young Men* and *Taps at Reveille* are consistently insightful and satisfying volumes, with each containing a series of high-quality stories: "The Rich Boy," "Winter Dreams," "The Baby Party," and "Absolution" (all in *ASYM*), plus "Crazy Sunday," "The Last of the Belles," "Babylon Revisited," "Family in the Wind," "One Interne," and the best of the Basil and Josephine stories (all in *TAR*). There is in fact a disproportionate number of excellent stories in the last two collections; and were one to read all four of the authorized collections in succession, one would readily detect a kind of split between Fitzgerald's first and last two collections which is as palpable as the chasm between his first and last two completed novels. (*The Last Tycoon,* published posthumously, remains a glittering series of fragments.) It is because of this split that the present study approaches the four story collections through clusters of topics. There are two such clusters, each involving three concepts or series of related ideas. In the first cluster are (1) love, sex, and marriage, (2) self versus society, and (3) free will versus fate. In the second cluster are (1) dreams and disillusionment, (2) the historical sense, and (3) the idea of home. Clearly these topics are sometimes themes, sometimes motifs; clearly also they overlap considerably. But they do seem to be useful points of departure for probing the stories in the four authorized collections. The methodology is simply stated: the former cluster is the basis of the analyses of the first and third story collections, *Flappers and Philosophers* and *All the Sad Young Men.* The latter cluster performs the same function for the second and fourth collections, *Tales of the Jazz Age* and *Taps at Reveille.* As the result of changes in his marriage and career and of concomitant improvements in his artistry, Fitzgerald's handling of these clusters changed markedly after the split; but those changes would be obscured without the pairing-off of the early and late volumes.

The pairing-off of the four collections and the discussion of each collection in a separate chapter should also achieve another end: a reconsideration of the four volumes themselves as discrete works. The collections have, unfortunately, been long out of print, while in many instances the copies once available in public and research libraries have been discarded due to physical deterioration. As a result, few scholars have read all the stories in all four volumes in the order in which Fitzgerald himself arranged them. Further, though Malcolm Cowley performed an outstanding service in selecting tales from all four volumes for *The Stories of F. Scott Fitzgerald* (1951), that readily available anthology gives no sense of the four authorized collections as individual works, while the widespread practice of including just one or two stories in college anthologies draws readers even further away from the four volumes upon which Fitzgerald lavished so much energy, thought, and care.

Hence the present study. Based upon his copious personal correspondence, biographical studies, and all available criticism, *Fitzgerald's Craft of Short Fiction* probes at length how Fitzgerald perceived his four story collections from both artistic and commercial standpoints. Most of the study focuses upon the actual texts—that is, on the volumes as units and on the individual stories themselves. It is tempting, of course, to concentrate on the best-known and most widely analyzed stories; but although there are discussions of "May Day," "The Rich Boy," and the like, special effort has been made to take a fresh, objective look at stories that Fitzgerald scholars have never seemed to notice:

"Family in the Wind," "The Baby Party," "Benediction," "The Jelly-Bean," "Absolution," "The Curious Case of Benjamin Button," "One Interne"—all are worthy achievements about which little or nothing has been written. Further, there are literally dozens of other stories, including "'O Russet Witch!'" and "The Adjuster" which, although admittedly not of the first rank, are pleasant surprises that reveal much about the development of Fitzgerald's mind and art. Surely many students of Fitzgerald will be startled by the riches in these four collections, and perhaps this systematic reconsideration of these books will generate further interest in this undeservedly neglected aspect of Fitzgerald's career.

This study uses the texts of the first editions of the four collections as published by Charles Scribner's Sons, New York. All page numbers indicated parenthetically are to these editions.

Fitzgerald was a notoriously poor speller. Even the Scribners proofreaders were simply not able to catch all the obvious textual errors. However, this study rarely uses "[*sic*]" unless, as with unorthodox spellings of charactonyms, the reader may be confused. Likewise, no attempt has been made to correct the misspelled words and poor punctuation in Fitzgerald's private letters. Passages from the letters are presented exactly as they appear in the various editions of his correspondence.

Finally, so as to minimize editorial paraphernalia, short titles have been used as much as possible in the notes. See the List of Short Titles and the complete Bibliography for full documentation.

1

Flappers and Philosophers

In keeping with company policy, Scribners brought out the story collection *Flappers and Philosophers* in August 1920 so as to capitalize on the startling popular and critical acclaim accorded Fitzgerald's first novel, *This Side of Paradise,* which had been published in late March. By November 1922 there had been six printings of *Flappers and Philosophers* for a total of 15,325 copies—unusually high sales for a collection of short stories,[1] a literary form which traditionally does not fare well in the American marketplace. The popular success of *Flappers and Philosophers* was sweet to Fitzgerald. It brought him badly needed funds at a time when his unfortunate lifelong pattern of financial over-extension was already well established. (The $500 advance he had received for *Flappers and Philosophers* paled beside the $700 squirrel coat for which Zelda, like Gloria in *The Beautiful and Damned,* had campaigned so vigorously.)[2] And certainly it confirmed that the enormous success of *This Side of Paradise* was not a fluke. But there was a downside to the popularity of *Flappers and Philosophers,* the implications of which Fitzgerald would not begin to face squarely until after the publication of his second collection of stories, *Tales of the Jazz Age,* and his second novel, *The Beautiful and Damned:* although the popular response to *Flappers and Philosophers* was positive, the critical response was mixed, and often quite hostile. H. L. Mencken, the *Smart Set* editor whose favor Fitzgerald had curried and from whom he could have expected a laudatory review, pointed to the unevenness of the eight stories in *Flappers and Philosophers* in the strongest possible terms: "From 'Benediction' the leap to 'The Offshore Pirate' and other such confections is like the leap from the peaks of Darien to the slums of Colon. Here is thin and obvious stuff, cheap stuff—in brief, atrociously bad stuff."[3] When the critical reaction was more favorable, it was usually on the grounds that the stories were amusing, entertaining, pleasantly frothy; and often the sorriest efforts in the collection were singled out for the highest praise. Princeton president John Grier Hibben spoke for many when he praised "The Four Fists" for both its artistry ("admirably written") and its didacticism, its presentation of "a philosophy of life which I wish every young man of our country would feel and appreciate"; and even the usually reliable Max Perkins termed it "a very fine story told in an entirely independent way."[4] But still flushed with the fame engendered by *This Side of Paradise,* delighted with the popular response to *Flappers and Philosophers,* and buoyed by the fact that two of the stories in the collection, "The Offshore Pirate" and "Head and Shoulders," had been sold to Hollywood, Fitzgerald was sufficiently encouraged to continue pursuing his career as a writer of short fiction.

But one wishes that Fitzgerald had taken more to heart the various criticisms and misplaced praise garnered by *Flappers and Philosophers.* For a man motivated largely by a desire to improve as a writer (even Hollywood and the magazines had standards of competence), Fitzgerald would have done well to consider the implications of being praised for writing fluff and heavy-handed morality tales; he should have been more willing to take his cue from the dismayed reviewer in *The Nation* who urged him to wring "his art . . . free of all dross"—not to cultivate the dross for sale to the *Saturday Evening Post.*[5] But there was little that he could or would do at this stage. So as to confirm his status as a literary wunderkind, both in his own eyes and the public's, Fitzgerald was already immersed in the frustrating task of writing a second novel that would eventually become *The Beautiful and Damned.* (One of its false starts, "The Demon Lover," is mentioned in his correspondence as early as September 1919.) Deeply committed to a major project, Fitzgerald had little time or energy at this juncture to devote to the theory or craft of short fiction. Indeed, his next collection of stories, *Tales of the Jazz Age,* would have to be padded with sketches from his undergraduate days at Princeton, and many commentators would observe justly that this second volume was markedly poorer than the first.

All this is not to say that there was nothing of value in these collections, especially in *Flappers and Philosophers.* By most informed appraisals, "The Ice Palace" and "Bernice Bobs Her Hair" are excellent stories, and a strong case could be made for the little-known "Benediction," the sixth story in the collection. But there are difficulties in the conception and execution of these eight stories, all written between May 1919 and February 1920, which seem to stem from three broad concerns: his personal feelings regarding Zelda Sayre, whom he would marry on 3 April 1920 after a difficult engagement; his inability to reconcile the still-powerful notion of "romantic egotism" with the desire to be part of a group; and a faith in the power of the individual will that was challenged increasingly by his fear of forces that might intervene to check his career even as it began. These are substantial concerns, and it is not surprising that Fitzgerald, still in his early twenties, had barely begun to acknowledge them, let alone to resolve them. It is not surprising either that, as a writer of still-limited experience, he was unable to control the technical and stylistic infelicities engendered by his semiconscious grappling with these concerns. Not yet cognizant that his personal concerns, held in unresolved tension, could be exploited for dramatic effect (two happy exceptions being "Benediction" and "The Ice Palace"), Fitzgerald tended to gravitate between one position and its opposite, often within the same story, or to sublimate more intimidating concerns while focusing on the benign (see "The Offshore Pirate"). He likewise had not grasped the possibilities of ambiguity (which at this stage usually takes the form of unclear writing) or of irony: potentially ironic situations end up as O. Henryish reversals, while serious observations are punctured by strained humor and self-conscious inside jokes or, more dramatically, by denial: in "The Offshore Pirate," Ardita speaks for Fitzgerald ("All life is just a progression toward, and then a recession from, one phrase—'I love you'"), but then dismisses it with "It doesn't mean anything especially. It's just clever" (31). When Fitzgerald tries to deal with antithetical issues by forcing himself to adhere to one position, the result is clumsy, unconvincing, and often pedantic ("The Four Fists"). Worse yet, try as he may to maintain one position, the other intrudes willy-nilly into the story, often rendering a potentially powerful symbol an illogical or contradictory one (such as the punch bowl in "The Cut-Glass Bowl"). Small wonder that the tone of these stories is sometimes almost impossible to determine. Small wonder either that Fitzgerald himself, whether at the time of composition or from the vantage point of maturity, often makes totally contradictory appraisals of these stories. Consider "The Offshore Pirate." In a 1922 letter to Max Perkins he lauds the weak "Tarquin of Cheapside" by saying that "next to 'The Offshore Pirate' I like it better than any story I have ever written." But in 1925 he confessed in bewilderment that "my whole heart was in my first trash. I thought that 'The Offshore Pirate' was quite as good as 'Benediction.'" And yet in 1935 he selected "The Offshore Pirate," along with "Bernice Bobs Her Hair," "The Ice Palace," and "Benediction," for inclusion in a proposed collection of stories to be published in England by Chatto & Windus.[6] It is the kind of wavering that one would expect from a writer who, thinking he has written one sort of story, suddenly recognizes, with horror or awe, that he has produced something quite different. This frequent discrepancy between intention and creation renders *Flappers and Philosophers* an often fascinating and revealing document.

One of the most fundamental sources of tension or ambiguity in *Flappers and Philosophers* is Fitzgerald's inability to reconcile the generally sentimental notions of love and marriage that he had derived from his readings and imagination with the disappointment and insecurity he had experienced with romance thus far. He had always had a firm belief that lovers enjoy a special spiritual bond,[7] but this was challenged early on by his infatuation with sixteen-year-old Ginevra King, whom he had met in January 1915 during Christmas break from Princeton. As his biographers point out, Fitzgerald's first real affair of the heart was with this charming debutante from Lake Forest, Illinois, although she seems not to have felt so strongly about the matter. Miss King later calculated that they had been together for a grand total of fifteen hours over the three-and-a-half years he yearned for her, and Thomas J. Stavola credits the U.S. Post Office, which dutifully delivered Fitzgerald's voluminous correspondence to her, for whatever substance the relationship may have had.[8] But to Fitzgerald this was the first great passion of his life, and he apparently never quite got over it,[9] not even when she married a Yale man—a bitter blow to a Princetonian whose sophomoric attitudes toward other Ivy League colleges would endure throughout his life. Even Zelda could not at first erase the pain of Ginevra King.

As an army officer stationed at nearby Camp Sheridan, Fitzgerald had met Zelda Sayre at a dance in Montgomery, Alabama, in July 1918. He was essentially on the rebound from the soon-to-marry Ginevra, but even so he did not fall in love with Zelda until 7 September (according to the matter-of-fact notation in his *Ledger*), in the same month that Ginevra married Ensign William Hamilton Mitchell.[10] What attracted Fitzgerald to Zelda is for psychologists to decide, but the information provided by his biographers, as well as by Nancy Milford in *Zelda,* does offer some clues. They looked sufficiently alike to pass for siblings; they both were talented and imaginative, with a particular facility with words; they were rather selfish and inclined to exhibitionism; and they were frankly ambitious, each seeing the other as somehow able to facilitate the process of realizing their talents and attaining a wide audience for their achievements. But for Fitzgerald there was another aspect to their relationship: his love for Zelda was grounded in an awareness of her immense attractiveness to other men, be they fellow army officers or the gridiron heroes of Alabama and Georgia. Matthew J. Bruccoli is no doubt correct that "there had to be an element of competition" for Fitzgerald to be attracted to any woman,[11] and perhaps the most chillingly revealing remark Fitzgerald ever made about Zelda was "I wouldn't care if she died, but I couldn't stand to have anybody else marry her."[12] That stance would change markedly as he came to believe that, from both practical and psychological standpoints, Zelda was essential to his career success. From the very beginning she would serve as the prototype for many of his fictional heroines, perhaps most dramatically Nicole Diver in *Tender Is the Night;* and he used whole sections of her letters and diaries in his first two novels. But Fitzgerald also came quickly to recognize that Zelda was a sensitive and market-wise critic of his writing, as well as a reliable co-worker. (Throughout the 1920s they published under a double byline in *College Humor* a series of stories written by Zelda and revised by him.) As a practical man, Fitzgerald realized that it was helpful that Zelda be alive and near him; but he seems, in addition, to have acquired an almost superstitious conviction that he could not pursue his career without her. Certainly he bemoaned her absence when he was in St. Paul struggling to revise "The Romantic Egotist" into *This Side of Paradise,* but his attachment to Zelda seems to have moved quickly beyond a romantic desire for companionship to something fundamentally different. Nancy Milford surmises that Zelda had been reluctant to marry Fitzgerald out of the fear that, should he fail in his career, she would be blamed,[13] and as a beginning writer Fitzgerald might well have been looking for someone upon whom the burden of his own possible failure might be placed. And who better than this woman who, although admittedly useful at times, was essentially a spoiled extrovert whose orientation, especially early in their relationship, was toward partying and material goods—neither of which squares well with a career (like writing) that demands hard work, concentration, and sacrifice? Simultaneously the scapegoat for his failures and an important contributor to them, Zelda would prove to be a major negative factor in Fitzgerald's career, virtually since its inception.

Zelda's attitude toward Fitzgerald was only slightly less complex. Certainly she saw him as potentially the never-ending source of material goodies. During their engagement he had thrilled her with the gift of a $600 platinum-and-diamond wristwatch (it is mentioned briefly in "The Offshore Pirate"), which in 1927 she would throw out a train window in a fit of jealousy.[14] He was also her ticket out of sleepy Montgomery. And yet she derived a cruel pleasure out of discussing her other dates with him when he was away, and even sent him her photograph inscribed to another man.[15] Part narcissistic, part practical, and part cruel, their relationship on both sides was oddly self-serving and often callous. But perhaps the most obvious aspect of it was the economics involved. Whether one believes that Zelda married him only because of the publication of *This Side of Paradise,* literally ten days before the wedding; or because the sale of "Head and Shoulders" to Hollywood for $2,250 encouraged her to believe that by writing for the movies he could support her in the style for which she yearned; or because his self-confidence over his suddenly booming career was infectious, the fact remains that she had broken their engagement when it appeared that he would never be a financial success as a writer. Fitzgerald's famous 1920 telegram to Zelda—I HAVE SOLD THE MOVIE RIGHTS OF HEAD AND SHOULDERS TO THE METRO COMPANY FOR TWENTY FIVE HUNDRED DOLLARS I LOVE YOU DEAREST GIRL—bears eloquent testimony to the fact that "love and money became almost inextricably entangled in his mind."[16] Fitzgerald understood Zelda's reluctance to marry a man who could not support her, but he never quite forgave her for doing what he termed "the sensible thing," and he would often explore in his fiction this financial challenge to his belief in the fundamental spirituality of love. But this belief died hard: there is ample evidence that, despite the economics, selfishness, and callousness underlying their relationship, both Zelda and Fitzgerald felt they were deeply, genuinely in love, and they would maintain this stance for the duration of a mutually destructive marriage striated with alcoholism, insanity, infidelity, and attempted suicides. Throughout the stories of *Flappers and Phi-*

losophers, all written during the last months of their often troubled courtship, Fitzgerald's confusion and fear are palpable as he tries to reconcile his personal experience of love with the kind of romance that his own sentimental imagination and extensive juvenile readings had led him to believe was the norm.

Fitzgerald's handling of male/female relationships in *Flappers and Philosophers* reflects this ambivalence. Only "Dalyrimple Goes Wrong"—essentially a Dreiseresque study of free will, politics, and economics, and quite atypical of Fitzgerald's work—completely sidesteps the issues of love, sex, and marriage. The actual marriages depicted in these stories barely take shape, and the few treated at length are decidedly unpleasant. In "The Four Fists" we are told that Samuel Meredith has a wife and children with whom he would like to spend a week at the seashore (186), but since they never materialize—Fitzgerald in this very early story (written May 1919) tends to tell rather than show—it is obvious that they are a "plant," a bare technical device. If this noncorporeal family is intended to show that Meredith has a kindly heart, it doesn't work: the images of him as a bullying schoolboy in Part I of the story and a foppish undergraduate in Part II are too strong to be toppled with such a meager device. They may also have been intended to provide some dramatic tension in his decision to defy his powerful boss and sacrifice his job rather than steal all that oil land from those poor grizzled Texas ranchers. But since we know from the overlong, chatty opening of the tale that Meredith's is a "success story" (174), it is apparent that the noncorporeal family was not destined to starve: typical of the early Fitzgerald, the frame of the story undercuts rather than enhances it. The other marriage depicted in "The Four Fists" is that of the young Jersey City newlyweds in Part III. Meredith has a brief antiseptic fling with the wife, Marjorie, but this will end with a melodramatic scene capped with a punch from her husband:

> Every one has seen such scenes on the stage—seen them so often that when they actually happen people behave very much like actors. Samuel felt that he was playing a part and the lines came quite naturally: he announced that all had a right to lead their own lives and looked at Marjorie's husband menacingly, as if daring him to doubt it. Marjorie's husband spoke of the sanctity of the home, forgetting that it hadn't seemed very holy to him lately; Samuel continued along the line of 'the right to happiness'; Marjorie's husband mentioned firearms and divorce court. Then suddenly he stopped and scrutinized both of them—Marjorie in pitiful collapse on the sofa, Samuel haranguing the furniture in a consciously heroic pose. (182)

With no first-hand knowledge of marriage (the story was written a year before his wedding), Fitzgerald must resort to literary clichés to terminate Meredith's asexual affair with the simpering Marjorie. The open acknowledgment that he's dealing with clichéd material backfires on him. Instead of seeing Meredith and the newlyweds as impassioned people (hence the breathless snatches of indirect dialogue connected with semicolons), we see Fitzgerald as unoriginal; and although it may theoretically be a clever strategy to draw attention to one's lack of originality, in practice it almost never works—even in the hands of a writer more seasoned than young Fitzgerald.[17] The take-off on popular literature imparts a smirking "smartness" to the story, while the heavy-handed comedy actually undercuts what is meant to be a serious study of the education of a personage from infantile bully to benevolent tycoon.

The staginess of Fitzgerald's wronged husband in "The Four Fists" betokens a self-consciousness that he was able to keep in check in a later, more polished story, "Bernice Bobs Her Hair." In "Bernice" we get but a brief glimpse of the husband of the sensible Mrs. Harvey. He seems much more real than Marjorie's husband, even though Mr. Harvey exists in the story only to say "'Well, I'll be darned!' over and over in a hurt and faintly hostile tone" (138), thereby articulating the probable reactions of middle-aged *Post* readers to the bobbing of Bernice's hair.[18] Aiming very much to please as many readers as possible at this early stage of his career, Fitzgerald experimented shakily with point of view, often utilizing middle-aged men like Mr. Harvey as choruses responding to events in the stories; but such characters tend to be discarded when their purposes are served, and the cavalier briskness with which Fitzgerald extracts them from stories is partly responsible for the quality of hesitation or uncertainty which pervades his earliest professional efforts.

One finds a similar but more revealing problem in "The Cut-Glass Bowl." Although ostensibly a study of the part played by an enormous glass punch bowl in the ruin of the life of Evylyn Piper, much of the story traces the deterioration of her marriage to a prosperous hardware dealer whose business declines over the course of several years. Consider Harold Piper's seemingly open-minded response to Evylyn's brief early affair with Freddy Gedney:

> His attitude toward this Gedney matter was typical of all his attitudes. He had told Evylyn that he considered the subject closed and would never reproach her nor allude to it in any form; and he told himself that this was rather a big way of looking at it—that she was not a little impressed. Yet, like all men who are preoccupied with their own broadness, he was exceptionally narrow.(99)

Fitzgerald pursues the matter no further. Clearly Harold Piper has the potential to be a character of Jamesian complexity; one thinks immediately of Austin Sloper in *Washington Square,* whose apparent liberality likewise belies a cruel smugness. But to pursue the implications of Harold's part in the deterioration of his marriage and the litany of disasters that befall the Piper family would require the scope of a novel. Fitzgerald struggles with the excess of materials in "The Cut-Glass Bowl," trying to compress twenty difficult years of business failure, illness, and death into nineteen pages, with much of the text devoted to a needlessly detailed dinner party and most of the rest crammed into unconvincing summaries. Harold Piper is but one casualty (two others are the Piper children) of Fitzgerald's inability to gauge the relationship between length of text and complexity of plot. Yet clearly the psychological aspect of the husband intrigued him enough to wish to leave in this tantalizing but aborted analysis of his character. Several of the stories in *Flappers and Philosophers*—most notably "Benediction"—show Fitzgerald trying to put to good use his growing knowledge of Freudian psychology, in particular where love and/or marriage are concerned, but in "The Cut-Glass Bowl" he backs away from such concerns as soon as he introduces them.

A similar approach/avoidance strategy in "The Cut-Glass Bowl" involves the references to drinking. Harold Piper is clearly an alcoholic, so much so that it is a major factor in the ruin of his business and renders him ineffectual when his little girl nearly dies of blood poisoning. As "The Cut-Glass Bowl" begins to turn into a temperance tract, the ostensible focus of the story—the relationship between Evylyn and the punch bowl that is meant to be her personal symbol—is seriously blurred, and the impact of the story largely sacrificed in the confusion. There is a sense of Fitzgerald cutting his losses as he abandons the temperance issue that, left unchecked, would have run away with the entire story. But perhaps the most important consideration here is not artistic but personal: the whole matter of drinking probably hit too close to home for Fitzgerald to pursue willingly any further. Written in October 1919, "The Cut-Glass Bowl" was created by an incipient alcoholic[19] who was soon to wed a woman whose own excessive drinking was already public knowledge. Drinking was one matter he knew about from personal experience, even at this young age, but he could not, or would not, follow through with the implications for himself, his fiancée, or his forthcoming marriage. Potentially the most fascinating aspect of "The Cut-Glass Bowl," the Pipers' marriage instead becomes one of the must frustrating, as Fitzgerald steers clear of probing the toll that could be taken on a relationship by drinking, illicit sex, economic reversal, and unresolved psychological problems.

The one marriage which Fitzgerald examines at length in *Flappers and Philosophers* is that of Marcia Meadow and Horace Tarbox in "Head and Shoulders." Typical of the early Fitzgerald, the story seems to use farce as a kind of smoke screen that enables him to probe his concerns about his own imminent marriage and its possible impact on his career while simultaneously suggesting that none of it should be taken seriously. "Head and Shoulders" is a top-heavy story: John Higgins points out that two-thirds of it is devoted to the courtship of Marcia and Horace, as Fitzgerald's "efforts to write emotional and atmospheric college and young-love scenes . . . make him lose his sense of proportion."[20] Clearly, the engaged Fitzgerald was writing the most of what he knew best, college and young love; and however corny and sentimental the first two-thirds of the story may be, a case could be made that, in terms of the quality of writing, it surpasses the last third. For it is in the last third that Fitzgerald's misgivings about love and marriage seem to emerge, and begin to pull the story into directions that he apparently had not intended.

Of course, many of the excesses and infelicities of "Head and Shoulders" may be attributed to the story's sources and the conscious purposes for which it was written. It reads very much like an undergraduate sketch, a farcical fantasy in which a semiliterate vaudeville performer, lured by the promise of 5,000 Pall Mall cigarettes, seeks out one Horace Tarbox, boy prodigy, a Princetonian at thirteen and, at the time Marcia first arrives at his rooms, hard at work on his master's thesis at Yale. Marcia is a stock character who has much in common with Geraldine in *The Beautiful and Damned,* that "Shavian paragon of virtue from the lower classes,"[21] as well as with a long line of hookers with hearts of gold from turn-of-the-century melodramas, albeit Fitzgerald is quite careful to emphasize her bucolic wholesomeness (hence the surname "Meadow"). Horace is the stereotypical egg-headed Ivy Leaguer who knows of life only from the stuffy closure of his college rooms (hence "Tarbox"), who actually names his chairs "Berkeley" and "Hume," and who resents President Wilson "for allowing a brass band to play under his window on the night of the false armistice, causing him to leave three important sentences out of his thesis on 'German Idealism'"(72). Fitzgerald plays their courtship for laughs, with Horace staring pop-eyed at Marcia shimmying on the vaudeville stage (Robert Sklar suggests a comparison to *The Blue Angel*)[22] and Marcia oblivious to most of what Horace says. His proud announcement that "I am a realist of the School of Anton Laurier—with Bergsonian trimmings—and I'll be eighteen years old in two months" (77) leads to her suggestion that he see her show: "One of the characters is a Brazilian rice-planter. That might interest you" (77). The Bergsonian/Brazilian confusion is but one of an avalanche of malapropisms and lame collegiate inside jokes—Spencer is "Herb," Euclid is mistaken for a dead circus performer (88, 89)—which so striate "Head and Shoulders" that they quickly become predictable, and no doubt many college students enjoyed the fun poked at the historians, philosophers, and mathematicians most commonly studied by American undergraduates.

There is a very real anti-intellectualism and mistrust of college study evident in this story, but they have their sources in something far more personal than a theoretical understanding of American higher education: they seem to be tied directly to Fitzgerald's post-college misgivings about career and marriage. Fitzgerald never graduated from Princeton. He would articulate some of his frustration over this in a 1920 letter to Princeton president Hibben, claiming that *This Side of Paradise* was "written with the bitterness of my discovery that I had spent several years trying to fit in with a curriculum that is after all made for the average student,"[23] but this self-defensive posture barely concealed the real problem: Zelda's parents had cited his failure to finish college in an attempt to dissuade her from marrying him.[24] Further, the fact that the brilliant Horace Tarbox, M.A., is forced to assume a clerkship with a South American exporter—"his idea of the value of academic knowledge faded unmercifully" (86) during the job search—surely owes much to Fitzgerald's own abortive career as a ninety-dollar-a-month advertising copywriter with New York's Barron Collier agency, the only "literary" job he could find after leaving Princeton. (His chef d'oeuvre was a slogan for an Iowa laundry: "We keep you clean in Muscatine.")[25] Hence much of the bitterness and dismay underlying the comedy of Fitzgerald's presentation of Horace; and those emotions intensify during the last third of the story, when Horace is married to Marcia.

In terms of plot, the wedding occurs at the center of "Head and Shoulders," although its centrality is obscured by the top-heaviness caused by the extended comical courtship. Structurally, "Head and Shoulders" has the hourglass format cited by Percy Lubbock in reference to Henry James's *The Ambassadors*.[26] As "Head and Shoulders" opens, Horace is the very private intellectual (the mind) while Marcia is a very public actress/dancer (the body). With their marriage, Horace finds it necessary to become an acrobat (the body) while Marcia becomes a best-selling author (the mind). Hence the title "Head and Shoulders,"[27] an art term, the appropriateness of which is articulated by Marcia herself when too pregnant to dance any longer: "It's up to the old head [Horace] now. Shoulders is out of business" (90). Fitzgerald transparently labors to make the story take the 180° turn required by this type of role reversal: he has Marcia refer to her infamous dance as "only a sort of acrobatic stunt" (80); he reveals that Marcia had already been in print, when her crude thank-you letter to Peter Boyce Wendell appeared in his column (Wendell "said that 'the style was like Carlyle's, only more rugged, and that I ought to quit dancing and do North American literature' "[81]); and he even has Horace begin to speak like Marcia, including her signature statements "I hate these slot-machine people!" and "Oh, shut up!" (86). Fitzgerald also tries to undercut Horace's passivity and egocentric intellectualism by claiming that this sedentary scholar, who would change easy chairs "by way of exercise and variety" (73–74), had been seriously considered for the college gymnastics team (88). Even so, Horace's transformation is not to be believed, even by the notoriously flexible standards of farce.

But Fitzgerald was determined to play his hand through, and with good reason: Horace's situation evidently is an imaginative projection of what might happen to Fitzgerald himself. Giving him a job well below the dignity of an Ivy Leaguer suggests the Horace/Fitzgerald connection; less apparent is the fact that Fitzgerald literally believed that he, like Horace, was a prodigy.[28] For all the corny jokes leveled at poor Horace, there was a part of Fitzgerald that wanted him to channel all that genius and all those years of university study into something worthwhile, and that shuddered when Horace—as the direct result of an imprudent marriage and an unexpected pregnancy—was reduced to working as an acrobat in a circus. Horace is a fabulous success, popularly and financially, but he is simultaneously an increasingly embittered failure. "Head and Shoulders" can thus be seen as a cautionary tale written by Fitzgerald for Fitzgerald, and it carries a bivalent message. Part of the message is economic: when love leads to marriage, gainful employment becomes a necessity (no more would Fitzgerald be supported by his mother's McQuillan family fortune) and even the most gifted, intelligent, and educated husband/author may be reduced to being a performer, little better than a well-paid clown, in order to secure an income. Fitzgerald was well aware that one way of achieving money quickly through literature was to produce what he termed "trash." He felt little more than contempt for wealthy hacks like Canadian poet Robert W. Service; indeed, he worked the minor character Charley Moore into "Dalyrimple Goes Wrong" in part to be able to mention Service in the same breath as burlesque shows and billiards in the listing of this ignorant workingman's preferred diversions (160). But Fitzgerald also knew that to support a wife, and especially one with the expensive taste of Zelda, he himself might be tempted to go the way of Service—might, like the aptly named Richard Caramel of *The Beautiful and Damned,* have to resort to deliberately churning out treacly fiction for high fees.

But the other part of the message is more subtle and perhaps more frightening for Fitzgerald: it is the semiliterate Marcia who achieves the success, fame, and critical respect that Horace might reasonably have expected. Probably she had learned something from all those sets of Kipling and O. Henry in her pre-marriage apartment (84) and so, after reading Pepys' *Diary*—an activity which she likens to "digesting plate glass" (88)—she quickly writes *Sandra Pepys, Syncopated* and becomes the darling of the most powerful critics and intellectuals of the age, including France's Anton Laurier, Horace's idol, whose name she literally cannot pronounce (94). In part, of course, Fitzgerald is attacking the low literary standards of his day and the back-to-the-roots brand of literature that posited poets and fiction writers like Irvin Cobb, James Whitcomb Riley, and (slightly later) Thomas Boyd as brilliant in direct proportion to their real or feigned semiliteracy. To someone who prided himself on his intelligence and Princeton education, this trend—plus the perennial popularity of such saccharine authors as Annie Fellows Johnston and Louisa May Alcott, both of whom take a drubbing in "Bernice Bobs Her Hair"—was disgusting and frightening, and Fitzgerald would not resist the opportunity presented by "Head and Shoulders" to lampoon these authors and their adoring critics. What seems even more disturbing to him, however, is the fact that it is the wife, Marcia, who succeeds as an author. There was no denying that his own wife-to-be, Zelda, possessed some talent as a writer. Although she had only finished high school while he had almost graduated from Princeton, Zelda wrote with striking ease, originality, and insight—so much so that he used her diary and letters in his own fiction, including that odd roman à clef, *The Beautiful and Damned.*

He would not have used this material had he not recognized its literary value; he would not have signed his name to the novel had he not been sufficiently impressed by it to wish to claim it as his own; and he must have been sobered by the fact that when *The Beautiful and Damned* was published, Zelda used the most public forum possible, the *New York Tribune,* to reveal that "his" novel owed much to her: "It seems to me that on one page I recognized a portion of an old diary of mine which mysteriously disappeared shortly after my marriage, and also scraps of letters which, though considerably edited, sound to me vaguely familiar. In fact, Mr. Fitzgerald—I believe that is how he spells his name—seems to believe that plagiarism begins at home."[29] Beneath the surface joviality this is a bitter review; and what made the bitterness particularly strong was the fact that she herself, even before the marriage, was consciously considering a career as a professional writer. Having read the typescript of *This Side of Paradise,* she wrote to her fiancé, "Why can't I write?"[30] To this there had been no response save the increasing insecurity of Fitzgerald—insecurity that was hardly mitigated when Zelda began to publish her own stories under their double byline and managed to produce *Save Me the Waltz* in just a few weeks in 1932 while Fitzgerald had been struggling for years with *Tender Is the Night.* Even as he wrote "Head and Shoulders" in 1919 he evidently recognized that something like this might happen; that, like Horace—who "had meant to write a series of books" on philosophy (93)—he might stand by helplessly as his wife attained literary fame and fortune and his own career was reduced to performing for the masses. As the 180° reversal of "Head and Shoulders" suggests, the wife will rise as the husband will fall: the transference of husband/wife vitality which Fitzgerald would explore at length in *Tender Is the Night* appears to be a very real fear underlying the chatter and silliness of "Head and Shoulders," and that fear is embittered further by the fact that the wife succeeds thanks to the husband's unwitting help. It was Horace who had advised Marcia to read Pepys, and surely Fitzgerald must have sensed that by being married to a famous author (at this early stage he had a cocky faith that when *This Side of Paradise* was published "I know I'll wake some morning and find that the debutantes have made me famous overnight")[31] and by living in New York,[32] Zelda's writing ability and ambition might well blossom into a career that would challenge, if not destroy, his own. Although he apparently could not face this possibility directly, it did affect the artistry of "Head and Shoulders." He admitted to David Arnold Balch of *Movie Weekly* that he had introduced Marcia into the story "by way of a radical contrast," but "before I'd finished she almost stole the story."[33] This bewildered realization that "Head and Shoulders" had pulled itself into directions he had not intended consciously is likewise palpable in a letter to Robert Bridges: after calling the story "hands-down the best piece of light writing I've ever done," he admits that "it just naturally *would* curl itself up into a little sneer at the end" and even fears that this ostensible farce might be "a little too vinegary" for some popular magazines.[34] Here is the "little sneer":

> Horace's eyes caught a passage lower down [in the magazine clipping]; he became suddenly aghast—and read on hurriedly:
> "Marcia Tarbox's connection with the stage is not only as a spectator but as the wife of a performer. She was married last year to Horace Tarbox, who every evening delights the children at the Hippodrome with his wondrous flying-ring performance. It is said that the young couple have dubbed themselves Head and Shoulders, referring doubtless to the fact that Mrs. Tarbox supplies the literary and mental qualities, while the supple and agile shoulders of her husband contribute their share to the family fortunes.
> "Mrs. Tarbox seems to merit that much-abused title—'prodigy.' Only twenty—"
> Horace stopped reading, and with a very odd expression in his eyes gazed intently at Anton Laurier.
> "I want to advise you—" he began hoarsely.
> "What?"
> "About raps. Don't answer them! Let them alone—have a padded door." (95)

End of story. Horace has the last word, and his advice never to answer raps at the door refers directly to his answering of Marcia's rap at his door when he was a graduate student at Yale. In short, Horace advises Laurier not to marry—a rather startling way for a man about to wed to end a story. But perhaps the matter was simply too close to Fitzgerald for him to respond with conscious objectivity; he could not articulate the implications of his situation even if his character could, and it is not surprising that, years later, Fitzgerald admitted that he often read his own books for advice: "How much I know sometimes— how little at others."[35] He seems to have known, or at least sensed, quite a bit in "Head and Shoulders," and it compelled him to write a farce with a "vine-gary" undercurrent that could only be presented in an hourglass reversal. That hourglass structure, hardly just "sheer trickery—a prestidigator's 'stunt' in writ-ing,"[36] is essential to Fitzgerald's worst-case scenario featuring his own scarcely veiled fears about his marriage and career. And the story itself, far from being "meaningless in content,"[37] is one of the most meaningful and revealing stories he ever wrote—even though it is doubtful that Fitzgerald recognized the fears and problems with which it deals.

Obviously love, marriage, and career were an emotion-charged triumvirate for Fitzgerald, so in *Flappers and Philosophers* he tends to focus on a related matter from which the ugly realities and possibilities of male/female relation-ships could be excluded more readily: courtship. "The Offshore Pirate" is a veritable extravaganza of courtship, and as idyllic a fantasy as he ever wrote. And yet troubling questions about love arise so insistently that Fitzgerald can barely maintain the illusion that the story is mere entertainment, a frothy diver-sion for *Post* readers.

In "The Offshore Pirate," young Ardita Farnam,[38] on a private yacht off the Florida coast, is being urged by her well-meaning uncle to abandon all thoughts of marrying the "wicked clubman" (20) she adores and instead to marry Toby Moreland, whom she has never met. Ardita refuses what is essentially an arranged marriage, and her uncle goes ashore. Immediately the yacht is commandeered by a pirate, Curtis Carlyle, who intends to sail it with his crew of Six Black Buddies to South America. After a few days of Ardita and Carlyle dancing and high diving together, the uncle returns and reveals Curtis Carlyle to be Toby Moreland. Ardita is thrilled by the revelation, since Toby/Carlyle clearly meets her marital requirement of having "an imagination, and the courage of his convictions" (20). As the story closes they plan to wed. Or so we presume. Fitzgerald is quite careful to trace the process of their growing relationship, but not its logical conclusion, and for a very good reason: much as the relationship between Marcia and Horace works well initially precisely because they have nothing in common and can barely communicate ("Their minds moved in different spheres" [87]), the relationship between Ardita and Toby/Carlyle works precisely because it is based on a masquerade—a lie.

Fitzgerald's awareness of this essential falsehood is evident in the fact that he wrote the story tongue-in-cheek.[39] Remarkably enough, few commentators have recognized this, and hence they tend to cite it as a sterling example of Fitzgerald at his mindless worst. John A. Higgins is more diplomatic than most in dismissing it as "frivolous," while James E. Miller, Jr., argues that it "could be used to document the fact—were further documentation necessary—that Fitzgerald was investing his characters and settings with a glamour which they did not deserve. Probably the secret of the popular success of his stories is that they served as escape for all the bored five-and-ten-cent-store clerks who dreamed of being glamorous Fitzgerald flappers, lavishly courted by disguised millionaire philosophers."[40] But Fitzgerald's contemporaries recognized it as "a gem of romantic fooling,"[41] though they could see its deeper implications even less than the author himself. Much of the fooling takes the form of parodies and put-downs of popular literature, something Fitzgerald had practiced extensively while at Princeton. In part he is burlesquing the perennially popular tales of piracy, and he could have drawn the bare outlines of the plot from stories such as *Treasure Island* (1883), *Peter Pan* (1904), or even *Moran of the "Lady Letty,"* a tale of kidnapping, romance, a plucky girl, and a sinister crew published by Frank Norris is 1898.[42] Another possible source is George Washington Cable's 1881 novella *Madame Delphine*, in which the spirited heroine uses her beauty and a prayer book to turn a pirate from a life of crime, and eventually marries him.[43] But the real target of Fitzgerald's barbs would be books like *The Princess Passes,* a 1905 best-seller by C. N. and A. M. Williamson. Alice Payne Hackett notes that this was the Williamsons' "first automobile romance. . . . They specialized in the type of story in which the heroine falls in love with her chauffeur, who is actually the scion of a titled British family."[44] Such popular literature linked romance with falsehood, love with money; and "The Offshore Pirate" pokes the kind of vicious fun at these elements that can come only from a man who has had personal experience with them.

Consider the presentation of Curtis Carlyle, that dashing creation of milquetoast Toby Moreland. Supposedly he is an adventurer, a criminal with a $20,000 price on his head, who will use the yacht as a getaway boat. But he is fundamentally a poor boy, a plucky youth who parlayed his knack for playing the kazoo to go from being "a poor kid in a Tennessee town," to a ragtime violinist in Nashville, to Broadway, "with offers of engagements on all sides and more money than he had ever dreamed of" (27–28). After losing everything in stock speculations, he had turned to a life of crime and was achieving great success as an outlaw—a reverse Horatio Alger story that Fitzgerald would use to good effect in "Dalyrimple Goes Wrong." But notice Ardita's response to Carlyle's account of his relationship with Babe, one of the Six Black Buddies:

> "We used to sit together on the wharfs down on the New York water-front, he [Babe] with a bassoon and me with an oboe, and we'd blend minor keys in African harmonics a thousand years old until the rats would crawl up the posts and sit round groaning and squeaking like dogs will in front of a phonograph."
> Ardita roared.
> "How you can tell 'em!"
> Carlyle grinned.
> "I swear that's the gos—"
> "What you going to do when you get to Callao?" she interrupted. (33)

Both Ardita and Carlyle recognize that the story is a confection of "stretchers" and clichés, so much so that he has not even finished his supposedly heart-tugging life story before Ardita falls fast asleep.[45] Carlyle's hackneyed life story renders him a figure of jest far more than a figure of dashing flair and heroic proportions. This is, of course, what is to be expected of a story written tongue-in-cheek; but as Carlyle's doltish qualities begin to predominate—and in particular when he is revealed to be Col. Moreland's nephew, and not a pirate at all—the fun of the story begins to be challenged by an undercurrent as vinegary as that of "Head and Shoulders."

Much of the source of this is the presentation of Ardita. At first glance she is everything that Fitzgerald loved in the flapper. She is beautiful, "yellow-haired" (17); she is conveyed by the kind of diction usually reserved for angels (her feet are "adorned rather than clad in blue-satin slippers" [17]); she refuses to marry the young man selected for her by her mundane, hapless uncle (he has "heavy footsteps," and is "clad" in a white flannel suit [17]); and she reads *The Revolt of the Angels* by one of Fitzgerald's favorite authors, Anatole France.[46] But Fitzgerald is careful to undercut the apparent attractiveness of Ardita. Her idea of a witty comeback is "Oh, shut up!" (18); the lemons which she sucks so sensuously end up, literally, as garbage to be tossed at her uncle; she is something of a dimwit, apparently genuinely surprised that there is ship-to-shore telephone contact ("Well, I'll be darned! Gosh! Science is golden or something—isn't it?" [18]); and even *The Revolt of the Angels,* a once-controversial novel which would suggest her independence of thought and her denial of old (especially Roman Catholic) strictures, is reduced to one more missile to be thrown at her uncle during one of her temper tantrums. Her violence and rudeness suggest that she is akin to the *femme fatale* figure of much of Fitzgerald's later fiction, the kind of woman who would suck a man dry the way Ardita sucks and discards lemons; but the implied strength and independence of the true *femme fatale* is, in Ardita, essentially childishness and ignorance—qualities that make it virtually impossible for us to regard her as a sympathetic character. Even as he was writing "The Offshore Pirate" in February 1920—that is, while *This Side of Paradise,* that paean to flapperdom, was literally in press—Fitzgerald was exhibiting disillusionment and even disgust with the golden girl he is credited with creating. By early 1920, he could see the childishness and potential destructiveness of the flapper; but as even his contemporary critics recognized, he still could not quite let go of her.[47] Indeed, he had committed himself to marrying one only eight weeks after writing "The Offshore Pirate." As he explained in an interview in *Shadowland* magazine, "We find the young woman of 1920 flirting, kissing, viewing life lightly, saying damn without a blush, playing along the danger line in an immature way—a sort of mental baby vamp. . . . Personally, I prefer this sort of girl. Indeed, I married the heroine of my stories."[48] "Immature"? "Girl"? These are hardly the kinds of words one expects to find in the same breath as "married," and they may well betoken a disillusionment with Zelda even as he continued to find her attractive.

Hence the peculiar suitability of writing "The Offshore Pirate" tongue-in-cheek. Literary burlesques, by definition, embrace qualities so as to deride them; writing tongue-in-cheek enables an author to assume an approach/avoidance stance, to probe something in loving detail while simultaneously standing back to scorn it. Fitzgerald can make Carlyle as dashing and Ardita as beautiful as some part of his psyche desires, all the while backing away with a wink at the reader, letting it be inferred that he knows he's overwriting, knows that these characters cannot possibly be as attractive as he is suggesting, knows that the fun, the romance—yes, the love—is utter fakery. Hence the gilt—not golden—quality of the descriptions in "The Offshore Pirate." Consider the story's opening:

> This unlikely story begins on a sea that was a blue dream, as colorful as blue-silk stockings, and beneath a sky as blue as the irises of children's eyes. From the western half of the sky the sun was shying little golden disks at the sea—if you gazed intently enough you could see them

skip from wave tip to wave tip until they joined a broad collar of golden coin that was collecting half a mile out and would eventually be a dazzling sunset. (17)

As William Goldhurst has suggested, the "descriptive gaudiness [of] Fitzgerald's prose outshines that of the public-relations promoter, pamphleteering at the height of the Florida boom," the kind of "unbuttoned rhetoric" generated by the Florida real-estate rush of the early 1920s.[49] But even as he is doing a take-off on this kind of extravagant description, Fitzgerald, a sometime Florida vacationer, is responding to it warmly. Then again, he is going beyond mere playful burlesque to attack the sort of overwritten fluff that he himself was paid to write for the Barron Collier advertising agency. In short, he loves that sort of description—but he also scorns its fraudulence. So too with the little lake in which the yacht drops anchor:

> There was a break in the cliff entirely hidden by a curious overlapping of rock, and through this break the yacht entered and very slowly traversed a narrow channel of crystal-clear water between high gray walls. Then they were riding at anchor in a miniature world of green and gold, a gilded bay smooth as glass and set round with tiny palms, the whole resembling the mirror lakes and twig trees that children set up in sand piles . . . .
> "It's an absolutely sure-fire hiding-place!"
> "Lordy, yes! It's the sort of island you read about." (31–32)

It is indeed. This is a movie set, just perfect for two children like Ardita and Carlyle to play in. It is as unreal as the scrumptious luncheons whipped up by Carlyle's right-hand man, Babe Divine; it is as unreal as all those boring details about "coaling and provisioning" (32)—that is, the quotidian realities of the future—which will be left entirely to the resourceful Babe as they sail from Florida to Peru. But as much as Fitzgerald undercuts the fantasy of this self-admitted "unlikely" story, it obviously appeals to him. For it is fun to be kids playing—especially when it enables one to sidestep the serious issues that are attendant upon mature, adult love, issues that were creeping unpleasantly into Fitzgerald's personal life as well as into "The Offshore Pirate."

One such issue is sexuality. A major reason why the literature of piracy is so popular is that it enables the reader to fantasize about illicit sexual conduct. A Beautiful Girl, a Dashing Pirate (obviously lacking a sense of decency or he wouldn't be a pirate), together on what is essentially a floating house (complete with beds, we assume), miles away from the nearest parent or lawman . . . well, nature will probably take its inevitable course, be it a romantic interlude or perhaps a less meaningful relationship, such as rape. From the moment Carlyle boards the yacht *Narcissus*—"very young and graceful" (17), it is a personal symbol of Ardita—we keep waiting for the inevitable to happen. It doesn't. One would never guess that Ardita and Carlyle had hormones. But Fitzgerald does acknowledge the element of sexuality which their situation would be expected to generate by displacing it: he has Carlyle attended by the Six Black Buddies. Ruth Prigozy suggests that the Black Buddies constitute "a recognition, however slight, of the Harlem Renaissance," while Robert Forrey chastises Fitzgerald for presenting stereotypical blacks "who eagerly comply with all the white man's commands with a 'Yas-suh!'"[50] But to see the Six Black Buddies as a literary tribute or as "stage darkies" is to brush past their more sinister aspect: they are primitive figures whose words and actions are freighted with sexuality. That they simultaneously are associated with violence may suggest how strongly Fitzgerald felt about the potential destructiveness of human sexuality. The Black Buddies play jazz, a type of music which Fitzgerald characterized in *The Crack-Up* as full of "phallic euphemisms,"[51] and at Carlyle's command they file "noiselessly down the companionway" of the yacht, to "catch the crew and tie 'em up" (23). Sexual, sinister, and violent, they are not the chaperones that they may initially appear to be as they remain nearby while Ardita and Carlyle are left otherwise alone on a secluded beach; rather, they seem to preside over primitive impulses. It is they, after all, who play the "fantastic symphony"—"sometimes riotous and jubilant, sometimes haunting and plaintive as a death-dance from the Congo's heart"—to which Ardita and Carlyle dance, feeling as if "the shades of unnumbered generations of cannibals" were watching them (41). It may be no accident that "The Offshore Pirate" echoes another story in which a black pirate crew is associated with death and cannibalism, Melville's "Benito Cereno." Like evil Babo, Babe Divine is "a miniature mulatto of four feet nine" who "seemed to have Carlyle's implicit confidence" and thus "took full command of the situation" (23, 25). The Babo/Babe connection is further confirmed in the fact that Babe had been "a plantation hand in Bermuda, until he stuck an eight-inch stiletto in his master's back" (27). Although the revelation that Carlyle is Toby will discount this, it is still not surprising that Col. Moreland, though he knew well that his nephew and friends were staging a harmless masquerade, nevertheless had kept close to the yacht "in case you should have trouble with those six strange niggers" (45). Fitzgerald is well enough aware of what he is doing not to have Carlyle accompanied by the Six Caucasian Associates, but he is careful to back away from the implied primitivism and sexuality by presenting the story as a fantasy, an asexual fairy tale for the sexually mature.

Of course, the publishing standards of the day would not have permitted anything more racy than a kiss; but Fitzgerald's approach/avoidance treatment of sex and his very ambivalent presentation of both Carlyle and Ardita may reflect his own mixed feelings about his relationship with Zelda. There seems to be more than a little of Fitzgerald in Carlyle, the man of imagination who still laments having spent World War I behind the lines, entertaining the troops: "It was not so bad—except that when the infantry came limping back from the trenches he wanted to be one of them. The sweat and mud they wore seemed only one of those ineffable symbols of aristocracy that were forever eluding him" (29). Years later, in *The Crack-Up,* Fitzgerald was still lamenting "the overseas cap never worn overseas."[52] And there seems to be more than a little of Zelda in Ardita, the spoiled vixen who "can do any darn thing with any darn man I want to" (20), who sports a daring one-piece bathing suit "that's shocked the natives all along the Atlantic coast from Biddeford Pool to St. Augustine" (35), and who frankly covets a "big oblong watch that's platinum and has diamonds all round the edge" (40). Being with "a man of imagination" is great good fun for Ardita; she even is willing to enter into the fantasy, pleading "Lie to me by the moonlight. Do a fabulous story" (27). But where falsehood is fine during a courtship (notice how Ardita substitutes "lie" for "make love" in the moonlight), and where imagination is charming in a suitor, they are not quite enough when marriage enters the picture. It seems highly unlikely that the implied marriage of Ardita and Toby/Carlyle would ever take place were he not rich[53]—rich enough to give her the fabulous diamond bracelet of the Czar of Russia that had been promised to Ardita by her libertine lover, that equally imaginative suitor who is promptly forgotten in Palm Beach once Toby and the Czar's bauble enter the picture. Marriage requires material goods and cash, and not just imagination. Fitzgerald's wink at the reader at the story's close— "reaching up on her tiptoes she kissed him softly in the illustration" (46)—is thus not just a joke at the expense of the *Post.*[54] It is a statement that true "romance" exists only in fairy tales, that marriage has a strong economic component, and that sexuality—a touchy topic for Fitzgerald, who felt permanent guilt over his premarital experiences with Zelda—was better left sublimated. Hence perhaps the reason for the name "Carlyle." Richard Lehan argues that it reflects Toby's "romantic imagination," but perhaps Fitzgerald has in mind a sardonic passage from *Sartor Resartus:* "How beautiful to die of broken-heart, on Paper! Quite another thing in practice."[55] Through the medium of literature, Fitzgerald was able to explore (albeit largely indirectly) the discrepancy between love as depicted in popular writing and love as it exists in real life. For all its fun and exuberance, "The Offshore Pirate" is a sobering and even bitter tale which may well reflect suggestively Fitzgerald's personal situation at the time of its composition.

Both "Head and Shoulders" and "The Offshore Pirate" raise serious issues about love and marriage while denying them comically through farce and fantasy. Other stories in *Flappers and Philosophers* also raise these issues, but because the comedic or fantastic elements are downplayed or absent, they seem more controlled, more mature. These stories include "Bernice Bobs Her Hair" and "The Ice Palace." Though often dismissed as a light social comedy, "Bernice" is a painfully incisive study of the fundamental selfishness and superficiality of boy/girl relations. To be popular requires well-groomed eyebrows, straight teeth, and a willingness to let boys think that their silly opinions actually matter. It is all a tissue of lies, but it achieves the desired goal: marriage to an Ivy

Leaguer like Warren McIntyre. That Fitzgerald refuses to show Bernice at the end of the story married to Mr. Right is a reflection of her unattractive bobbed hair as well as a tribute to the kind of independent, self-assured woman Fitzgerald admired most. But it also enables him to avoid showing what would happen if a strong woman like Bernice did marry. By definition, wives are not independent: far more than husbands, they must immerse their identities in the marriage, as evidenced by the adoption of the male surname. Further, once they are safely caught, the thrill of chasing them, of luring them away from other suitors and their families, is lost—and with it goes much of the women's appeal. (No wonder Gloria begins to age with preternatural speed the moment she marries Anthony in *The Beautiful and Damned*.) Better to leave Bernice "forever panting, and forever young," to quote one of Fitzgerald's favorite poems, "Ode on a Grecian Urn" (line 27), and not to consider (even indirectly) what marriage might do to another spirited woman with Indian features, Zelda Sayre.[56]

And much as Bernice seems forever fresh, so too does Sally Carrol Happer of "The Ice Palace." What she believes to be her love for Harry Bellamy is in large measure her recognition that he can help satisfy the part of herself that has "a sort of energy," that makes her want her mind to grow, and that yearns "to live where things happen on a big scale" (50). That can only mean the North, and Harry, whom she barely knows, happens to be the most readily available Northerner. Sally Carrol's eventual rejection of both Harry and the North is based partly on her realization that (in Spenglerian terms)[57] the North represents the final stage of civilization: its technology, embodied in the statistically impressive ice palace, is attractive but deadly. The fluids that flow so freely in the South—watercolors, swimming pools, and especially tears—only freeze in the North, an emblem of the impossibility of acknowledging and acting upon one's emotions in that harsh world.[58] But that denial of emotions stems from the fact that the North is a man's world—"canine." Northern women "just fade out when you look at them. They're glorified domestics. Men are the center of every mixed group" (61). In "The Ice Palace" there are no married women depicted in the Tarleton scenes. The only wives we see are Northern, and they are conveyed consistently through images of death and grotesquerie. Sally Carrol's future sister-in-law, Myra, is "a listless lady" (55): she "seemed the essence of spiritless conventionality. Her conversation was so utterly devoid of personality that Sally Carrol, who came from a country where a certain amount of charm and assurance could be taken for granted in the women, was inclined to despise her" (61). Harry's mother seems like an egg to Sally Carrol, "an egg with a cracked, veiny voice and such an ungracious dumpiness of carriage that Sally Carrol felt that if she once fell she would surely scramble" (61–62). Though she will break off her engagement for a number of reasons, a factor unrecognized by Fitzgerald critics is that Sally Carrol has come to equate "living in the North" with "being married"—and from what she has seen, that means a living death for a woman. The final panel of the triptych of "The Ice Palace"—the depiction of Sally Carrol leaning on her windowsill in the Georgia heat, having made no apparent progress from the almost identical first panel—is thus an affirmative statement. It suggests that some women, especially those with sensitivity and courage, would be happier unwed. It is a surprisingly astute observation, especially coming from a man deeply in love with Sally Carrol's prototype, Zelda.[59] More on this later.

The women in *Flappers and Philosophers* who reject males and marriage, including Bernice and Sally Carrol, are among the most memorable characters in the collection. But the woman character who probably reveals the most about Fitzgerald's complicated feelings about love and marriage is Lois, the nineteen-year-old protagonist of one of Fitzgerald's best stories, the little-known "Benediction" (written in October 1919). Much of her impact stems from the fact that she is one of the few female protagonists in Fitzgerald's early fiction to initiate actively an illicit sexual relationship. That she has serious misgivings about this shows Fitzgerald grappling with the religious and psychological ramifications of recognizing and exploring one's adult sexuality, while trying to come to some understanding of the often complex relationship between romance and responsibility.

In "The Offshore Pirate" Fitzgerald had tried to sidestep these matters even as they forced their way into the narrative. But unlike that story, "Benediction" does not show Fitzgerald trying to deny, through farce or fantasy, the essential primitivism, power, or lawlessness of sexual urges. Thanks to a skillful melding of situation, diction, symbolism, and metaphor, Fitzgerald offers a surprisingly sensitive analysis of questions about which he seems to have been deeply concerned at the moment of its composition.

The opening of "Benediction" is one of the most effective he ever wrote:

> The Baltimore Station was hot and crowded, so Lois was forced to stand by the telegraph desk for interminable, sticky seconds while a clerk with big front teeth counted and recounted a large lady's day message, to determine whether it contained the innocuous forty-nine words or the fatal fifty-one.

As the opening continues, we see a rare instance of the young Fitzgerald presenting condensed, effective exposition through the device of a letter in lieu of a chatty explanation or lifeless summary. In addition, the act of re-reading the letter reflects Lois's thrill, nervousness, and guilt over what she is about to do:

> Lois, waiting, decided she wasn't quite sure of the address, so she took the letter out of her bag and ran over it again.
> "Darling": *it began*—"I understand and I'm happier than life ever meant me to be. If I could give you the things you've always been in tune with—but I can't, Lois; we can't marry and

we can't lose each other and let all this glorious love end in nothing.

"Until your letter came, dear, I'd been sitting here in the half dark thinking and thinking where I could go and ever forget you; abroad, perhaps, to drift through Italy or Spain and dream away the pain of having lost you where the crumbling ruins of older, mellower civilizations would mirror only the desolation of my heart—and then your letter came.

"Sweetest, bravest girl, if you'll wire me I'll meet you in Wilmington—till then I'll be here just waiting and hoping for every long dream of you to come true.

"HOWARD"

The opening continues:

She had read the letter so many times that she knew it word by word, yet it still startled her. In it she found many faint reflections of the man who wrote it—the mingled sweetness and sadness in his dark eyes, the furtive, restless excitement she felt sometimes when he talked to her, his dreamy sensuousness that lulled her mind to sleep. Lois was nineteen and very romantic and curious and courageous. (141)

Fitzgerald leads us to believe that the story we are about to read will depict the romantic meeting of Lois and Howard in Wilmington. It does not; and to judge from the other stories in *Flappers and Philosophers*, this was a very wise move. Most of the young adult males Fitzgerald depicts in these stories are far from appealing: there is poor Horace Tarbox, the naive intellectual turned circus acrobat ("Head and Shoulders"); Samuel Meredith, a foppish bully so dimwitted that it takes repeated episodes of assault and battery to knock some sense into him ("The Four Fists"); G. Reese Stoddard, "over whose bureau at home hangs a Harvard law diploma," but who inexplicably spends his time at hometown dances with sixteen-year-old Otis Ormonde and the rapidly aging Bessie Mac-Rae ("Bernice Bobs Her Hair" [116]); or Harry Bellamy, whose unconcealed pride in Northern "pep" and the linear dimensions of the ice palace place him well within the company of George Babbitt.[60] Howard probably would not have fared much better. His impulse "to drift through Italy or Spain and dream away the pain of having lost you where the crumbling ruins of older, mellower civilizations would mirror only the desolation of my heart" calls to mind the Gatsbyesque plan of Curtis Carlyle to "take ship for India. I want to be a rajah. I mean it. My idea is to go up into Afghanistan somewhere, buy up a palace and a reputation, and then after about five years appear in England with a foreign accent and a mysterious past. But India first" ("The Offshore Pirate" [33]). But as Toby/Carlyle's desperate "I mean it" suggests, he knows that all this over-blown, escapist rhetoric about exotic travel is just a joke; Howard, alas, apparently means it—either that, or he is playing upon the emotions of a naive girl. But whatever the case, by refusing to depict Howard, Fitzgerald saves "Benediction" from the element of ludicrousness which obscures the tone of even his most serious stories whenever a young adult male is introduced. Howard thus remains a deliberately obscure figure, a generic embodiment of "romantic lover." This not only helps ensure the consistently sober tone of this serious story; it also places the focus more squarely on Lois herself. Fitzgerald has very little interest in her relationship with Howard, but he has an infectious fascination with how she perceives and responds to that relationship.

This is evident in the story's opening, quoted above. It is Lois who has initiated the Wilmington tryst ("Until your letter came, dear"), and hence it is she who has to deal with the practical and frankly unromantic details of engineering a rendezvous. It is she who must endure the "sticky" Baltimore station, who must wait in line behind the dowager, who must face the slightly leering, big-toothed telegraph clerk. It is she who must compose the discreet but informative, romantic but businesslike telegram that establishes the details of the tryst:

> Arrived Baltimore today spend day with my brother meet me Wilmington three P.M. Wednesday Love
> "LOIS" (142)

Even more to the point, it is she who must literally pay for her actions. " 'Fifty-four cents,' said the clerk admiringly" in response to her telegram to Howard (142). The words in a telegram can prove either "innocuous" or "fatal" not just because of their number (forty-nine versus fifty-one) but because of the actions they inaugurate. In arranging definitely to meet Howard, Lois has in effect decided to exchange her virtue for fifty-four cents, a handful of change, and her Judas is herself. At some level she clearly has misgivings about this, her curiosity and courage notwithstanding; and Fitzgerald underscores the uncertainties underlying her apparent self-assurance by recording her response to paying for the telegram: "And never be sorry—thought Lois—and never be sorry—"(142). The repetition of "and never be sorry" suggests that she is trying to convince herself of her lack of emotional investment in what she is about to do with Howard. Further, the phrase "thought Lois" has a double edge. She is, of course, thinking rather than speaking out loud; but the reference to thought argues that she is trying to force her rational mind to act in accordance with her body. Further, the word "thought" also suggests delusion: she thought she would never be sorry—but she is already.

Hence the importance of the main story line of "Benediction." Lois does not go directly to Howard in Wilmington, but instead decides to pay a visit to her brother Kieth [*sic*], who is studying for the Jesuit priesthood in a Baltimore seminary. Although she is nineteen years old, Lois has not seen Kieth since she was five. Fourteen years is rather a long time not to see one's own brother, even if we take into account her schooling in European convents; so her remark, "How could I have gone on without practically ever having seen my only brother?" (45) thus has a false edge to it of which even Lois is aware (she spoke "quickly"). For although this would appear to be a pleasant social call, replete with meeting jovial old priests and taking long, chatty walks, it is essentially a plea for help. For all her seeming confidence and liberation, Lois is actually making a last ditch effort to be talked out of doing something she does not want to do.

Kieth would seem to be the ideal agent of this dissuasion. He is that recognized spokesman of moral order, a priest (or soon to be one); at thirty-six, he has seventeen more years of living than she upon which to draw for guidance in a crisis; and he is, after all, her own brother. But steadily in the course of "Benediction" Fitzgerald challenges and ultimately punctures each of these elements, thereby leaving the desperate Lois even more confused than she was when she arrived.

Most dramatic is Fitzgerald's exploration of Kieth's status as a priest. Since "Benediction" is essentially a rewriting of the undergraduate sketch "The Ordeal," Kieth's prototype is Thomas Delihant, the brother of Fitzgerald's favorite cousin, Cecilia, "Ceci" Taylor. While a sixteen-year-old student at The Newman School, Fitzgerald had visited Delihant at the Jesuit seminary in Woodstock, Maryland. He had been profoundly moved by the dedication and serenity of Delihant, who was about to take his final vows after the eighteen-year period of intensive study and contemplation required by the Society of Jesus. Fitzgerald never lost his admiration for Delihant, and in a 1924 magazine article he included this "obscure Jesuit priest" along with Theodore Roosevelt and Admiral Dewey in his list of personal heroes.[61] Certainly some of Delihant is apparent in Kieth, a quiet and patient man who seems very much a part of a world that involves extended services in uncomfortable chapels and the study of "thick volumes" of Thomas Aquinas, Cardinal Mercier, and Immanuel Kant (143)— precisely the kinds of material Fitzgerald himself found so intimidating in his years at Princeton. And yet there is another aspect to this preparation for the Jesuit priesthood of which Fitzgerald had been unaware when he wrote "The Ordeal" but which is at the very heart of "Benediction." It is true that the seminarians study Kant and Henry James,[62] and apparently they do pray a lot—but they also play baseball (142); they do endure a lot—but they leave the actual work of gardening to half a dozen lay brothers, "sweating lustily" (142); and far from subsisting on the stereotypical fare of bread and wine, they eat ice cream (145). There is an undeniable countermovement in "Benediction" which suggests that, far from possessing superior character and being somehow in touch with the spirit of God, these Jesuits are decidedly mundane, or what Lois (in reference to convent girls) derides as "common" (146). Revealingly, Kieth had looked to Lois's "little white soul" (155)—not to God—for guidance during his preparation for the priesthood. Further, he had received his "call" to the monastic life in a Pullman railroad car in front of twenty other passengers; and far from being an ethereal visit from a celestial agent, it was simply a pushy command from a disembodied voice: "I want you to be a priest, that's what I want" (147). No wonder Kieth is too embarrassed to talk about it. Kieth's monastic life might initially seem to be holy and cloistered, but between the selective information that filters in from the outside world (such as the shimmying craze [150]) and such pleasant diversions as baseball and ice cream, the Jesuit seminary sounds more like a lifelong summer camp for boys.[63]

And that, for Fitzgerald, was the crux of the problem. Kieth has spent the previous seventeen years in the seminary. By entering those grounds and embarking on a career in the priesthood, he effectively turned his back on his old life—and that includes his family and its very real problems. Lois was but two years old when her adult brother left her alone with their "nervous, half-invalid mother" (148); and it was she, not he, who over the years has had to deal with the woman's breakdowns and collapses. Thanks to the filtering in of information, Kieth has known all along about these matters. He frankly admits that "it's been awfully hard" for Lois, and that his little sister has been "sort of taking the place of both of us" (147). He also admits that she "oughtn't to have the weight on [her] shoulders" alone, and that he wishes he "were there to help" her (148). But these protestations and compliments are predictable and lame. The fact is that the seventeen years he has spent in the seminary have actually been seventeen years of hiding from life. It is an evasion so complete that even when he dies his troubled family cannot have his body for burial (150). There is no sense that Kieth feels the slightest real guilt over his evasion of adult responsibility: he has, after all, the most perfect excuse possible for never being around in times of crisis, plus the moral support of "a thousand others" who are avoiding life with him (150). And his hiding out in the priesthood, bad as it was when Lois was growing up, proves disastrous when she comes to him for moral guidance.

In his capacity as a priest, he cannot help her. Lois subtly tries to sound out Kieth's suitability for helping her by probing his personal past. Before receiving his call to the priesthood he was a drinker, and Lois "thrill[s] slightly" (147) at this concrete indication that he may, after all, have had enough firsthand experience of the problems of young adults to be able to advise her on the matter of romance and premarital sex. But the temporary tippling seems to have been the extent of Kieth's wild living, and with palpable misgivings she asks about the practical aspects of entering the priesthood at a young age:

"But those *boys*. Are they giving up fine chances outside—like you did?"
    He nodded.
    "Some of them."
    "But, Kieth, they don't know what they're doing. They haven't had any experience of what they're missing."

"No, I suppose not."

"It doesn't seem fair. Life has just sort of scared them at first. Do they all come in so *young?*"

"No, some of them have knocked around, led pretty wild lives—Regan, for instance."

"I should think that sort would be better," she said meditatively, "men that had *seen* life."

"No," said Kieth earnestly, "I'm not sure that knocking about gives a man the sort of experience he can communicate to others. Some of the broadest men I've known have been absolutely rigid about themselves. And reformed libertines are a notoriously intolerant class. Don't you think so, Lois?"

She nodded, still meditative, and he continued:

"It seems to me that when one weak person goes to another, it isn't help they want; it's sort of a companionship in guilt . . ." (149)

"Real help," Kieth further informs his sister,

"comes from a stronger person whom you respect. And their sympathy is all the bigger because it's impersonal."

"But people want human sympathy," objected Lois. "They want to feel the other person's been tempted."

"Lois, in their hearts they want to feel that the other person's been weak. That's what they mean by human." (149)

Kieth's conclusion—"the less human a man is, in your sense of human, the better servant he can be to humanity" (149)—is about as helpful as his "I wish I were there to help you" with their mother. Such platitudes sound fine, but they are of no practical help to poor Lois. She repeatedly mentions her would-be lover Howard indirectly ("Howa—well, another man" [153–54]) in the apparent hope that Kieth will connect him with that "gay time" he knows his sister has been having (145) and thereby direct the conversation to the Wilmington tryst; but Kieth does not—at least not openly. That he speaks of a "companionship of guilt" might suggest that he senses what is going on and is trying to steer her into the moral path; likewise his paean to her "little white soul" may be an attempt to use guilt and sentiment to dissuade her from doing anything as adult as fornication. But for all intents and purposes Kieth simply avoids the whole difficult and unpleasant matter as part of his behavioral pattern of hiding out. Lack of first-hand experience with real life crises and real human emotions have left him hamstrung in the face of Lois's crisis; and the situation is complicated further by the fact that he is her brother.

Many men have a blind spot about their sisters. They often assume a half-protective, half-bullying stance toward them (witness Fitzgerald's voluminous written instructions to his sister Annabelle on how to achieve popularity, the basis for Marjorie's lecture to Bernice in "Bernice Bobs Her Hair")[64] and may refuse to believe that their sisters (especially younger ones) have anything resembling sexual urges until the inescapable fact of pregnancy confirms otherwise. Seventeen years older than Lois, Kieth probably is incapable of perceiving her as anything more that his baby (read "prepubescent") sister. And the enormous difference in their ages further complicates matters by rendering him simultaneously her father figure—a strikingly literal manifestation of the traditional notion of priests as fathers. Even if Kieth did possess the priestly capacity and personal knowledge to serve as Lois's confessor and guide, his simultaneous status as her brother/father renders him too subjective, too close to her situation, to do so. He represents the Family as an institution for moral guidance just as surely as he represents the Church—or, more precisely, he represents the aspects of these two institutions (the subjectivity of the Family, the otherworldliness of the Church) that render them incapable of acknowledging that Lois even has a problem, let alone of helping her to deal with it. This fact is driven home with a dramatic emblem of Lois's confusion: her response to Kieth.

It is insistently sexual. Her first sight of Kieth in the seminary is presented in a passage that, taken out of context, sounds like two lovers meeting:

> He was smiling, she noticed, and he looked very big and—and reliable. She stopped and waited, knew that her heart was beating unusually fast.
> "Lois!" he cried, and in a second she was in his arms. She was suddenly trembling.
> "Lois!" he cried again, "why, this is wonderful! I can't tell you, Lois, how *much* I've looked forward to this. Why, Lois, you're beautiful!"
> Lois gasped. (144)

Not having seen him since early childhood, she reacts to him not as a brother but as an adult male. She feels "stirred by the modulations of his voice" (147) and "found herself analyzing his personality as she analyzed the personality of every man she met. She wondered if the effect of—of intimacy that he gave was bred by his constant repetition of her name. He said it as if he loved the word . . ." (146). And no wonder either that Kieth, he himself not having had contact with females for seventeen years, suddenly declares "I'm awfully in love with my little sister" (150). Be it out of fear or good judgment, Fitzgerald does not push any further the implications of Kieth's remark, and perhaps it really is nothing more than a brotherly/fatherly outburst of affection. He also does not probe the specific sources of Lois's obviously sexual response to Kieth. It may well be based upon the narcissism that underlies so many of the romances in Fitzgerald's early fiction (Lois and Kieth have eyes "of the same fiber," and he has "that odd sort of enveloping personality [Lois] had thought that she only of the family possessed" [147, 144]). It may take its origins from the simple fact that she and Kieth, by virtue of his occupation, can never have an intimate relationship—an example of the recurring pattern in Fitzgerald's fiction in which love blooms precisely because it is doomed.[65] It may also be part of the pattern of incest which recurs so often in Fitzgerald's fiction, and may well be, in very embryonic form, an early exploration of the relationship between the troubled

Nicole and her combination husband/psychiatrist/father figure, Dr. Dick Diver, in *Tender Is the Night*. To explore these elements at length would require the scope of a novel and would also blur rather than enhance an understanding of the difficulties of Lois's immediate situation. What matters is that Kieth, simultaneously the embodiment of her family and her religion, is totally ineffectual in dealing with Lois's crisis.

Probably nothing conveys Kieth's ineffectuality more vividly than the incident in the chapel. While sitting between Kieth and another seminarian during the benediction service, Lois suddenly realizes that something is horribly wrong with the candle on the altar:

> [T]he weight upon her heart suddenly diffused into cold fear. . . . It was that candle on the altar. It was all wrong—wrong. Why didn't somebody see it? There was something *in* it. There was something coming out of it, taking form and shape above it.
>
> She tried to fight down her rising panic, told herself it was the wick. If the wick wasn't straight, candles did something—but they didn't do this! With incalculable rapidity a force was gathering within her, a tremendous, assimilative force, drawing from every sense, every corner of her brain, and as it surged up inside her she felt an enormous, terrified repulsion. She drew her arms in close to her side, away from Kieth and Jarvis.
>
> Something in that candle . . . she was leaning forward—in another moment she felt she would go forward toward it—didn't any one see it? . . . anyone? . . .
>
> . . . She was calling, felt herself calling for Kieth, her lips mouthing the words that would not come:
>
> "Kieth! Oh, my God! *Kieth!*"
>
> Suddenly she became aware of a new presence, something external, in front of her, consummated and expressed in warm red tracery. Then she knew. It was the window of St. Francis Xavier. Her mind gripped at it, clung to it finally, and she felt herself calling again endlessly, impotently—Kieth—Kieth!
>
> Then out of a great stillness came a voice:
>
> *"Blessed be God."* (151–52)

Lois's response is immediate and dramatic:

> The words sang instantly in her heart; the incense lay mystically and sweetly peaceful upon the air, and *the candle on the altar went out.*
>
> "Blessed be His Holy Name."
>
> "Blessed be His Holy Name."
>
> Every thing blurred into a swinging mist. With a sound half-gasp, half-cry she rocked on her feet and reeled backward into Kieth's suddenly outstretched arms. (152)

Apparently the candle is the embodiment of evil; and since sex and evil were closely connected in Fitzgerald's mind, as much as in Amory Blaine's,[66] it would appear that the malignant candle is one of a series of supernatural incidents in Fitzgerald's fiction in which sex/evil literally becomes substantial. A comparable incident in a harlot's apartment in *This Side of Paradise* sends poor

Amory into a frenzy of terror: having hallucinations for forty-eight hours simply because a prostitute put her head on his shoulder is quite overblown, and a bemused contemporary reviewer noted dryly that "it did not sound altogether characteristic of Princeton."[67] In "Benediction" the incident is much less melodramatic (evil is seen as candlelight rather than as an odd-looking man) and hence it is less likely to be seen as comic; but it also, because it takes place during a service in a seminary chapel, has a more obviously religious dimension, albeit a perhaps unexpected one. Traditionally altar candles are very positive elements in Christian symbology; traditionally also the color red is associated with evil. Yet in "Benediction" we see a malignant altar candle challenged and conquered by a red saint. Fitzgerald clearly is trying to turn traditional symbols associated with the Church inside out and, by implication, to challenge the validity of the dictates and teachings of the Church.[68] Apparently no one else in the chapel saw what happened to the candle: be it an epiphany, a miracle, a sign from God, or whatever, a chapel-full of priests and seminarians were oblivious to it. Further, Lois had called frantically to Kieth, but he could not hear her, and hence could not help her. Being only human, all he can do is catch her after she falls, just as all his fellow seminarian Regan can do is dab her head with a wet towel (153). In short, God could protect Lois—the repeated "Blessed be His Holy Name" suggests that He put out the evil candle using St. Francis Xavier as His agent—but God's earthly intercessors, the all-too-human seminarians, offer too little help, too late.

All they can do is pray. As Lois returns to the bus station, our last view of Kieth shows him praying before the seminary's pietà:

> Later, some probationers passing noticed him kneeling before the pieta, and coming back after a time found him still there. And he was there until twilight came down and the courteous trees grew garrulous overhead and the crickets took up their burden of song in the dusky grass. (156)

Obviously Kieth prayed hard for Lois. He may even have died while praying, so careful is Fitzgerald to stress Kieth's maintaining one position over several hours; and that would help explain why in the last portion of the story Lois is unexpectedly described as wearing a veil with "big black dots" (156). But if Kieth did die praying, it was all for nought. True, Lois wires Howard to cancel their tryst, apparently still upset by the feeling of being "oddly broken and chastened" (153) by the incident in the chapel; but she just as quickly cancels the cancellation, tearing up the Dear John telegram and evidently going ahead with the initiation into sex even though, as Howard's letter makes clear, it can never lead to marriage.

Sergio Perosa completely misreads this ending, arguing that Lois was "brought to reconsider her step" and that she "reacquires a sense of traditional values"—in short, that it is a sentimental, happy ending.[69] Almost as far off the mark is Arthur Mizener. The elements of "priggish sentimentality"[70] that Mizener bemoans in "Benediction" reflect Kieth's unflattering personality—not the emotionality of Kieth's creator. John A. Higgins is likewise incorrect that "a major fault of the story" is Fitzgerald's "failure to convey clearly the reason for her decision" to go to Howard at the end.[71] Fitzgerald's whole point is that we cannot determine readily why one would willingly do something that goes against all one's better instincts. He does suggest, however, that social conditions and pressures play a large role. Lois is one of the "new" women, independent, mobile, and armed with practical knowledge of birth control (154). She thus is in an ideal position to take advantage of that perennially available temptation, sex. But that doesn't mean that she doesn't feel guilty about it. The family and the Church, those two traditional sources of guidance and dissuasion, are of no practical help to the new woman, but their former power is still evident in a pervading sense of guilt. To the lapsed-Catholic Fitzgerald, it is the Church that bears most of the responsibility for this sad legacy: by continuing to place a premium on inexperience and platitudes, the Church was by 1919 a naive anachronism, as unreal and childish in its way as the fantasy-land of "The Offshore Pirate." But however much he may have denied the Church (the summary in his *Ledger* for 1917 reads: "A year of enormous importance. Work and Zelda. Last year as a Catholic."), [72] it generated guilt in him no less than in Lois. Fitzgerald was never at ease over having slept with Zelda before their marriage, and he had the disconcerting habit of asking new acquaintances if they too had had premarital sex.[73] Likewise, although Fitzgerald actively encouraged his fiancée to have an abortion when they mistakenly believed she was pregnant, he clearly never reconciled himself to the series of abortions Zelda had when they were married.[74] Fitzgerald prided himself on being a realist, a free thinker, a man of the world; but his early Catholicism left him with a streak of guilt regarding sex that would still be evident in the *Crack-Up* essays of the mid-1930s.[75] And certainly there was nothing in his parents' strained relationship that would help him any more than there was anything in Lois's family background to help her. Thus Lois's confused feelings about love and sex seem to have much in common with Fitzgerald's own—and his, in turn, were not unusual for most men and women of his generation. Lois's uncertainties are thus those of her troubled world; and their lack of resolution, far from ruining the story, are the source of the power and poignancy of "Benediction."

Lois's situation is so difficult because she is caught between two antithetical modes of living that coexisted uneasily during the years immediately following World War I. Part of her is fiercely independent: she has no qualms about traveling alone, and even if her decision to sleep with Howard is fraught with guilt, at least the decision is hers. She is very much a woman of "now":

"everybody talks about everything now," including birth control (154). Kieth is the past, so out of touch with present realities that he literally winces at the mention of birth control. He is the double embodiment of family and Church values that are seventeen years behind the times.[76] But for all her frantic independence, Lois finds very attractive the two institutions that he represents. This is conveyed by her sexual response to her brother/father/priest, by her unconvincing tirade against the "inconvenience" of Catholicism (153), and by the "imitation of undiluted sunshine" that she pours forth when suffering from headaches, dealing with her mother's nervous collapses, or feeling "romantic and curious and courageous" (144)—the story's euphemism for agreeing to sleep with Howard. She is frightened and miserable in her independence, and clearly wishes to make meaningful contact with the two larger, older institutions that she had to reject in order to be the "new woman" of the post-World War I era. But she also is pleased and proud of her ability to take care of herself, and probably would not go back to the shelter—and strictures—of family and Church even if she could. Lois's situation thus reflects the second cluster of ideas evident in *Flappers and Philosophers:* the unresolved tensions between self and society.

After Lois, probably the most extreme case of a character torn between self and society in *Flappers and Philosophers* is Bryan Dalyrimple in "Dalyrimple Goes Wrong," written in September 1919. As the story opens, Bryan has just returned from the war in Germany:

> The generation which numbered Bryan Dalyrimple drifted out of adolescence to a mighty fanfare of trumpets. Bryan played the star in an affair which included a Lewis gun and a nine-day romp behind the retreating German lines, so luck triumphant or sentiment rampant awarded him a row of medals and on his arrival in the States he was told that he was second in importance only to General Pershing and Sergeant York. This was a lot of fun. The governor of his State, a stray congressman, and a citizens' committee gave him enormous smiles and "By God, Sirs," on the dock at Hoboken; there were newspaper reporters and photographers who said "would you mind" and "if you could just"; and back in his home town there were old ladies, the rims of whose eyes grew red as they talked to him, and girls who hadn't remembered him so well since his father's business went blah! in nineteen-twelve. (157)

Bryan thrived while part of a group, the U.S. Army. As a result of his exploits, he is honored and accepted by other groups: politicians, citizens' committees, the media, his home town. But thanks to the peculiar twist that wartime situations so often impart to reality, Bryan thrived in World War I precisely because he did not *act* as part of a group. It was his individual heroism (or foolhardiness) that enabled him to stand apart from the rest of the army, and it is for this that the groups on the home front honor him. Mixed signals are thus being sent to Bryan Dalyrimple on just the first page of "Dalyrimple Goes Wrong," and the rest of the story will trace his attempts to reconcile the antithetical pulls of self and group, to try to find some state that will enable him to draw the best from each orientation while checking the worst.

At first the pull toward society is the strongest. Bryan dismisses his war-time heroics as a "nine-day romp" and frankly enjoys being the houseguest of Mayor Hawkins, that transparent symbol of society. But society in the form of community quickly sours. Bryan suddenly realizes that he has "only fourteen dollars in the world, and that 'the name that will live forever in the annals and legends of this State' was already living there very quietly and obscurely" (157). When he hears the Mayor's upstairs-maid telling the cook that Mrs. Hawkins "had been trying for a week to hint Dalyrimple out of the house," he immediately moves out and into a local boardinghouse.

Bryan's next attempt at finding a niche in still-attractive society involves not the community but a different kind of group: the world of business. Fitzgerald frankly knew little about business until the end of his life, when he came to write *The Last Tycoon.* In *Flappers and Philosophers,* his ignorance takes the form of Samuel Meredith in "The Four Fists" being promoted for defying his boss's orders to acquire oil-rich ranchlands—lands held by a bunch of rednecks who freely admit that they have "as little chance of holding out as flies on a window-pane" (185). The fact that "The Four Fists" is essentially a moral parable wherein virtue must be rewarded does not change the fact that, from a business perspective, the story is hilarious. Likewise, in "The Cut-Glass Bowl," the complexities of the cutthroat world of the hardware wholesaler—a topic even William Dean Howells would not have tackled in anything shorter than *The Rise of Silas Lapham*—are mercifully abandoned after a few bungling paragraphs and what appears to be (but isn't) a reference to Marxian socialism.[77] But in "Dalyrimple Goes Wrong" Fitzgerald at least recognized that the world of business is essentially a closed one in which the individual rises or falls often because of politics and personal networking, nepotism and favoritism, rather than hard work and ambition. As happened in the army, Bryan hopes to be able to stand out as an individual in the business community while remaining under its protective wing. He takes a job with the Theron G. Macy Company precisely because of the prospect of working his way up to "going on the road" as a Macy representative; but even that dream of independent action, of selfhood, quickly sours. He learns first that in order to be part of the group known as the Macy Company he must face "the necessity of punching the time-clock at seven every morning" (159). Were that not bad enough, a rumpled co-worker, Charley Moore, offers further evidence of the downside of belonging to a business group. He, too, had been lured to the Macy Company with the prospect of someday going on the road, but after four years of idle promises he is a mere shell of a man, smoking endless cigarettes, reading Mutt and Jeff (165), and "listlessly struggling that losing struggle against mental, moral, and physical anaemia that takes place ceaselessly on the lower fringe of the middle classes" (160). Beyond the unintentionally comic melodrama of Moore's situation and the lumbering Dreiserian [78] description is the very real truth that absorption into the business group is, for most workers, a kind of psychic death. Indeed, in the basement of the Macy Company are the "cave-dwellers," men "who had worked there for ten or fifteen years at sixty dollars a month, rolling barrels and carrying boxes through damp, cement-walled corridors, lost in that echoing half-darkness between seven and five-thirty and, like [Dalyrimple], compelled several times a month to work until nine at night" (161). The only people able to escape this psychic death are those like Tom Everett, "Macy's weak-chinned nephew," who within three weeks had gone from packing-room to office at a fabulous salary: "So that was it! He was to sit and see man after man pushed over him: sons, cousins, sons of friends, irrespective of their capabilities, while *he* was cast for a pawn, with 'going on the road' dangled before his eyes—put off with the stock remark: 'I'll see; I'll look into it.' At forty, perhaps, he would be a bookkeeper like old Hesse, tired, listless Hesse with dull routine for his stint and a dull background of boarding-house conversation" (162).

The injustice of the world of business appalls Daylrimple, though it probably wouldn't if he were Macy's nephew; and immediately his desire to be part of this or any other group is pushed to the rear. Bryan begins to articulate the idea that all that the childhood groups of family and Church had taught him about morality was wrong:

> In my credulous years—he thought—they told me that evil was a sort of dirty hue, just as definite as a soiled collar, but it seems to me that evil is only a manner of hard luck, or heredity-and-environment, or "being found out." . . .
> . . . In fact—he concluded—it isn't worth worrying over what's evil and what isn't. Good and evil aren't any standard to me—and they can be a devil of a bad hindrance when I want something. When I want something bad enough, common sense tells me to go and take it—and not get caught. (164)

Taking what one wants in defiance of the group is a totally self-ish act, and Bryan immediately embarks on a career that not only focuses entirely on the self but that also harms the group from which he has distanced himself: a life of crime.

All it requires is a bit of imagination, a little moxie, and a piece of coat lining. Cutting jagged eye-holes in the lining and wearing it as a mask, Bryan attains immediate success by stealing a roll of bills from a pudgy man whose only sign of resistance is "an absurd little grunt" (165). Dalyrimple will attain further success as a cat burglar who works in the wealthiest neighborhoods, and derives considerable pleasure from reading exaggerated accounts of the exploits of "Burglar Bill of the Silver District" (169) in local newspapers, those voices of the groups that had praised him so warmly as a war hero before rejecting him. Dalyrimple rationalizes consciously the impulse that had led him to commit his first robbery, telling himself that his life of crime betokens unusual honesty: "Other men who broke the laws of justice and charity lied to all the world. He at any rate would not lie to himself. He was more than Byronic now: not the spiritual rebel, Don Juan; not the philosophical rebel, Faust; but a new psychological rebel of his own century—defying the sentimental a priori forms of his own mind—" (166). But the psychological rebel is not necessarily a material one: "Happiness was what he wanted—a slowly rising scale of gratifications of the normal appetites—and he had a strong conviction that the materials, if not the inspiration of happiness, could be bought with money" (166).

The contradictory logic involved in being an honest criminal, a non-group member who seeks the very things that the group recognizes as desirable, takes its toll on Dalyrimple. From the very beginning "the tremendous pressure of sentiment and tradition kept raising riot with his attitude. He felt morally lonely" (165). Like Lois in "Benediction," Dalyrimple finds that, however much one's rational mind may justify the denial of Catholicism or the pursuit of a richly rewarding career in crime, the dictates of the rejected groups retain their hold on the psyche. Even as a lone-wolf hero behind German lines Dalyrimple "had had behind him the moral support of half a billion people" (168), and the part of him that made him keep his job at Macy's while pursuing his life of crime— an element that reflects his refusal to deny totally the group as much as it does the "fear of attracting attention to his being in funds" (179)—also compels him to do what no true psychological rebel would do: he returns something he stole. Of course, when groping in the darkened house of his victim he had no idea what he was stealing; but when he finds a set of false teeth among the booty he feels a pang unbecoming a self-oriented criminal. Tormented by visions of his victim's "soft, toothless breakfast" and "weary, dispirited visits to the dentist" (169), Bryan wraps the dentures in brown paper and tosses them onto his victim's lawn under cover of darkness.

It is clear that the demands of self are not enough to maintain Bryan, and at story's end he finds himself assimilated into another group: politicians. With heavy-handed but surprisingly effective irony, Fitzgerald reveals that Bryan's employer, Theron Macy, and Alfred J. Fraser, "the biggest political influence in the city" (170), had decided that Bryan was ideal senatorial material. As Fraser perceives matters, it was with Lincolnesque spirit that Bryan had "made up [his] mind to shut up and stick to" his thankless job at Macy's (171); he also has a war record that could be resurrected readily by those infamous newspapers; but best of all he was willing to submerge himself within the group. With Fraser assured that Bryan is "'with us—that is,' and his voice hardened slightly, 'if you haven't got too many ideas yourself about how things ought to be run'"

(172), Bryan is bluntly promised a career in big-time politics: he will have the title and perks of a state senator (self), but his every move will be dictated by the political machine (group)—a handful of men who, it is suggested, probably had some "invisible realization" that Bryan was a criminal (173). A career as a puppet politician, a de facto crook with the glossy lifestyle of a hero, is the ideal compromise for a man who scorns and denies the group while being unable to reject it fully. Though "Dalyrimple Goes Wrong" offers a happy ending from Bryan's perspective, it is one of the bitterest of Fitzgerald's early efforts in short fiction.

A less dramatic but equally revealing example of a character torn between a wish to nurture the self and a longing to be part of a group is Sally Carrol Happer of "The Ice Palace." But in her case the two groups for which she feels such strong attraction and repulsion—the North/marriage and the South/spinster-hood—are actually emblems of the two aspects of her psychic self which she explores in the course of the story.

Sally Carrol is fundamentally a "romantic egotist," a character type which appears in much of Fitzgerald's early fiction. The sterling example of a Fitzgerald romantic egotist, Amory Blaine of *This Side of Paradise,* is something of a self-centered, overgrown schoolboy. His final statement—"I know myself . . . but that is all" (*TSOP*, 282)—is ironically closer to the truth than even his young creator probably realized, and it is responsible for much of the "hooting hilarity" with which Edmund Wilson, and later Fitzgerald himself, read the novel.[79] But the young Fitzgerald took quite seriously the concept of romantic egotism, and as he matured he would continue to produce characters whose *Weltanschauung* took its bearings from the self. To his credit, Fitzgerald rapidly excised those aspects of his romantic egotists that were most amenable to unintentional humor, including their passion for prolonged discussions of popular authors and the Meaning of Life that had so marred his first two novels. In their stead, he focused upon the most appealing aspects of romantic egotism, including its emphasis on the value of independent thought and action, of life experience as the source of spiritual growth, and of the need to realize one's God-given potential.

Sally Carrol's marriage to Harry Bellamy was meant to foster those elements. Life in Tarleton, Georgia, after all, nurtured only the most negative aspects of romantic egotism. Like Ulysses's crew in Tennyson's "The Lotos-Eaters," the group "Southern men" seems to have surrendered to the Southern warmth that is comforting but ultimately enervating: the swains of Tarleton "were always just about to do something" (48), yet most have been lulled into a state of almost catatonic passivity in "this languid paradise of dreamy skies and firefly evenings and noisy nigger street fairs—and especially of gracious, soft-voiced girls" (48–49). The predominant color of the Tarleton sections of the story is yellow ("the sunlight dripped over the house like golden paint over an art jar" [47]) as it is in "The Lotos-Eaters," where the yellowness of the vegetation betokens an incipient rotting. A few of the young Tarleton men do try to become active and purposeful. Clark Darrow had earned a degree from a technical college, but rather than put this training to use he "had spent the two years since he graduated from Georgia Tech in dozing round the lazy streets of his home town" (48). Even Clark's personal emblem, his "ancient Ford" (47), must be "excited into a sort of restless, resentful life" (49), and it stops with "a plaintive heaving sound, a death-rattle" (47). The living death endured by married women in the North has its counterpart in the living death of Southern men: the few who survive must first escape to the North, "to New York or Philadelphia or Pittsburgh" (48), where they can realize their selfhood in the world of business.

Sally Carrol recognizes this and reacts to it by becoming engaged to Harry Bellamy in the hope of joining the group "Northerners." True, Sally Carrol is not a Southern man, but she does have what might be termed a duality of self, an almost androgynous perception of life; and the two groups with which she must deal reflect this fundamental duality. Consider the self-analysis she presents to Clark Darrow:

> " . . . I couldn't ever marry you. You've a place in my heart no one else ever could have, but tied down here I'd get restless. I'd feel I was—wastin' myself. There's two sides to me, you see. There's the sleepy old side you love; an' there's a sort of energy—the feelin' that makes me do wild things. That's the part of me that may be useful somewhere, that'll last when I'm not beautiful any more." (50)

There are indeed "two sides" to Sally Carrol's self. The part that embodies "a sort of energy" is the part that seeks to reject the South and embrace the North. It is essentially what Sally Carrol herself will later identify as "canine," though at that stage of the story (i.e., before the incident in the ice palace) she still believes that she is entirely feline (59). This canine side of her self gives her the courage and independence to turn her back on her hometown and family, and it compels her to say "Good mawnin" (47) as a way of dissociating herself from a Southern world where (to quote Tennyson) it seemed "always afternoon" (line 4). It also wants her to be "useful" (a very positive word in Fitzgerald's moral vocabulary), and so, like those enterprising young men who manage to escape to the world of business in Pittsburgh, she gravitates toward Harry's hometown, whose lack of a name underscores its generic status as "the North."

All would be well if not for the other part of Sally Carrol's self, the "sleepy old side." It is Southern/feminine (feline), and unlike the canine side, it is evident in externals. Sally Carrol has the beauty seen in virtually all Fitzgerald's Southern women characters. The feline side of her psyche frankly recognizes her beauty (looking in the mirror, she "regarded her expression with a pleased and pleasant languor" [48]), but her canine side—"the part of me . . . that'll last when I'm not beautiful any more"—senses it is superficial and hence temporary. The feline side is also essentially childlike, an element that is especially evident in a predominantly canine setting. Harry lures her to the North with promises of "skating and skiing and tobagganing [*sic*] and sleigh-riding" (54), precisely the sorts of activities that would appeal to both her feline side (which is child-like) and the canine one (which thirsts for new experiences and knowledge). But once she arrives in the North, these activities are revealed to be just for children: "That's for kids" (55) becomes Harry's increasingly condescending response to everything she wishes to do—a reflection of his canine smugness that anything feline can be dismissed readily. What happens to Sally Carrol in the North is clearly conveyed in Mrs. Bellamy's response to her name: she calls her just "Sally," and "could not be persuaded that the double name was anything more than a tedious, ridiculous nickname" (62).[80] As Sally Carrol has come to realize away from the South, her double name represents the two sides of her psychic self: "She loved 'Sally Carrol'; she loathed 'Sally'" (62), the part of her that, as Mrs. Bellamy confirms, had not really been an issue until she was actually in the world of the canine, Harry's Northern city. In effect, Sally Carrol's trip North proves to be a test—an opportunity for her to face squarely the canine part of her self, to evaluate the feasibility of nurturing it, and espe-cially at the expense of the feline. Her experiences in the North confirm that it is not feasible. In order to maintain her psychic wholeness Sally Carrol must, as with her double name, keep the two sides of her self in tandem.

This can be done only in the South, for there are strings attached to living in the North. The most obvious is that it would require marriage to Harry, a man who exploits her feline fondness for the childlike while denigrating her canine desire for knowledge. She loses on both counts. The other problem is that, even though Sally Carrol's psychic self is androgynous, her physical self is obviously female (feline). As she comes to realize, in the North "men are the center of every mixed group" (61): it is ideal for males, offering business and technology as arenas in which they can nurture their canine selves. But for a woman—yes, even for one who has both canine and feline sides to her psyche—there are no such opportunities in the North. All she can do is marry. And, as seen earlier, marriage for women in the North involves the sacrifice of all selfhood: it is a kind of living death.

Sally Carrol's only real option is to rejoin the two groups she had tried to reject, Southerners and spinsters. As Sally Carrol had learned from painful (and almost fatal) experience in the North, she cannot nurture just the canine side, no matter where she lives. The North is a world of men and male-dominated marriage that will let no woman act on any canine urges that her psyche might generate. The situation is little better in the South, where apparently no one, male or female, nurtures the canine. But for a woman the feline part of the self at least has options in the South. While it would be crushed readily in the North (where canine males reduce their feline wives to virtual zombies), in the South it can be allowed to thrive, for the rules are different: Sally Carrol can paint paper dolls and swim all day, and her feline childishness will be seen as charming. But the conclusion of "The Ice Palace," the use of an ending that so mimics the opening, does not necessarily mean that Sally Carrol's decision to return to the South betokens lack of growth,[81] a capitulation to the feline at the expense of the canine, or a decision to hide out in the South in the way that Kieth hides out in his seminary. For she has come to realize that although the two sides of her psyche must be in tandem, they do not necessarily have to be in balance; further, for the canine side to survive at all in a woman, it must bow to the feline. Hence her return to the South, where neither element must be destroyed. True, in the South she probably never will satisfy her canine side's desire to be "useful," but her experience has shown that this never would have happened in the North, either. At least in the South she can acknowledge her canine self, freely discussing it with Clark Darrow who (unlike Harry) exhibits no condescension toward this aspect of her psyche. To return to the South is thus an act of psychic self-preservation, a means of nurturing the self within the protective confines of two receptive groups.

Sally Carrol's experiences suggest that one of those groups, Southerners, has a flexibility that is conducive to psychic health. That was Fitzgerald's apparent position at the time he wrote "The Ice Palace" in December 1919, but even as he worked on the story his increasing ambivalence toward the South was beginning to crystallize into scorn. There is a disquieting sense in "The Ice Palace" that the South can permit Sally Carrol to enjoy psychic wholeness precisely because it is so lethargic, so lazy. To nurture the canine requires action, while nurturing the feline can be quite passive; and it is infinitely easier to let Sally Carrol harbor both rather than force her to choose one at the expense of the other or (as did Harry) actively deny or exploit them. Fitzgerald's mixed affection and contempt for the South will be more palpable in his two later Tarleton stories, in which the charms of that region are increasingly seen as fraudulent.

The customary interpretation of "The Ice Palace" is that it traces not a psychic crisis, but the conflicts between Northern and Southern lifestyles and attitudes. John Kuehl, for example, writes that "the story's real conflict is cultural": "the antagonism between Sally Carrol and Harry Bellamy symbolizes a conflict between temperaments geographically determined."[82] The concept of determinism which Fitzgerald apparently derived from his reading of Dreiser, Crane, and Norris both attracted and repelled him; and this ambivalence probably had its origins in the antithetical implications that it held for his own life and work. Throughout *Flappers and Philosophers* one can see Fitzgerald alternating between a conviction that we direct our own lives, that we can in fact create imaginatively our own selves, and an equally strong contradictory conviction that outside forces—which he gropingly identified as fate, destiny, or just "life"—not only guide our lives but maliciously thwart all that we have worked for and all that we have the potential to achieve.

There are references to these outside forces in nearly every story of *Flappers and Philosophers*. In "Bernice Bobs Her Hair," for example, there is the seriocomic suggestion that Bernice's Indian blood is responsible for her atavistic behavior of "scalping" Marjorie, almost as if Bernice—despite her conscious effort to internalize the ultra-civilized models of femininity in *Little Women*— was forced by these innate primitive impulses to behave like an Indian in a crisis. In "Bernice Bobs Her Hair" the notion of outside forces is largely comic, but in "Benediction" the matter is far more serious, as they are used as a convenient excuse for succumbing to sexual urges: "It's just destiny" to sleep with Howard, thinks Lois, but she immediately qualifies it with an explanation which sounds very unlike "destiny" in its usual sense: "It's just the way things work out in this damn world." And then she qualifies it still further by suggesting that her individual will can control it: "If cowardice is all that's been holding me back there won't be any more holding back. So we'll just let things take their course, and never be sorry" (141–42). Lois's confused understanding of the relationship between "destiny" and free will is not pursued any further, but in many of the stories of *Flappers and Philosophers* these antithetical notions are of central importance. They are mentioned frequently and serve (even if sometimes unconvincingly) as the framework around which the story is constructed.

In the Dreiseresque "Dalyrimple Goes Wrong," for example, we are told that "fate had put [Bryan] in the world of Mr. Macy's fetid storerooms and corridors" (163), and up to a point it does indeed sound as if poor Bryan is doomed to spend the rest of his life little better than the "cave-dwellers" who toil in Macy's basement. But Fitzgerald is careful to emphasize that Dalyrimple, like Dreiser's Frank Cowperwood, is able to evaluate his situation and draw up a plan of individual action that will enable him to survive and thrive: "I'll go East—to a big city—meet people—bigger people—people who'll help me" (163). He does not go East; but if it is true that "bigger people" like Macy and Fraser select him for the senatorship precisely because they know he is succeeding in his self-created career as an independent criminal, then it would seem that his conscious decision to (as he puts it) "cut corners"—to sidestep the strictures and expectations of the group—has borne fruit. There is still the fact, however, that it was a local political machine, and not Bryan Dalyrimple himself, that is responsible for his career as a senator; likewise, it is the machine that will dictate all that he says and does as a politician. Obviously Fitzgerald's stance on free will versus outside forces is murky in "Dalyrimple Goes Wrong" but, ironically enough, this too may be attributable to Dreiser's influence. For all the naturalistic rhetoric about chemisms and magnetisms, Dreiser's characters do tend to act freely. By whatever means, Cowperwood does, after all, become "the titan," and the young Fitzgerald seems to have harbored a naive and almost Puritan faith that the fittest—the most intelligent, the hardest working—would indeed survive.

But when his personal situation enters the picture, that faith is often shaken, and the impact on the stories is generally unfortunate. In "Head and Shoulders," that apparent worst-case scenario about his impending marriage and future career, the many serious comments about "life" sound comic within the framework of the farcical story line. Early in "Head and Shoulders," when Marcia first arrives at the apartment of young Horace, it seems that his future life as a philosopher is unquestionable; all that remains is for him to decide which school of philosophy to concentrate upon. "He fancied he was verging more and more toward pragmatism. But at that moment, though he did not know it, he was verging with astounding rapidity toward something quite different" (73). Yes, "life" intervenes: "just as nonchalantly as though Horace Tarbox had been Mr. Beef the butcher or Mr. Hat the haberdasher, life reached in, seized him, handled him, stretched him, and unrolled him like a piece of Irish lace on a Saturday-afternoon bargain-counter" (72). It's an interesting simile even if not a particularly appropriate one, and twenty pages later Fitzgerald tries once again, this time using a metaphor that arises more readily from the story itself: "Life took hold of people and forced them into flying rings" (93). The vehemence with which he makes this point, over and over, suggests how personally concerned Fitzgerald was over the unpredictable intervention of forces that might undermine all that he had worked for, all that he hoped to accomplish—forces that might well be in motion even as he wrote "Head and Shoulders." Even at this early stage, Fitzgerald knew that he had considerable talent, and he also had a strong work ethic that made him determined to put that talent to use. He felt he had the right to succeed, and he noted in his meticulous *Ledger* all that he wrote and every dollar that he earned by his pen. But he seems also to have had a horror that it might not be enough, that despite his ability, willingness to work, and determination, other factors which he could not articulate—but which he evidently feared would have something to do with his imminent marriage and the often low standards of the literary marketplace—might intervene to ruin it all for him while catapulting someone else (perhaps even Zelda) to literary fame and fortune. Despite its comedy, "Head and Shoulders" seems in large measure a serious allegory about Fitzgerald's fear of professional failure or, what was almost as bad, professional compromise: of "Trying to choose our mediums and then taking what we get—and being glad" (93).

So concerned was Fitzgerald about the capacity of "life" or "fate" to thwart a well-meant existence that he presented "Head and Shoulders" in an hourglass framework, although the strain involved in engineering the reversal (including a multitude of clumsy foreshadowing devices) undermines its artistic integrity. A similar problem occurs in "The Cut-Glass Bowl." The story revolves around an enormous glass punch bowl that had been given to Evylyn Piper by a rejected suitor, Carleton Canby: "Evylyn, I'm going to give a present that's as hard as you are and as beautiful and as empty and as easy to see through" (97). This sounds promising with respect to future character development, but as Rose Adrienne Gallo justly observes, "the subsequent incidents of the story proper . . . provide no justification for this arbitrary and cruel assessment of Evylyn Piper."[83] The only thing that might even remotely suggest hardness or emptiness on her part is her affair, conducted five afternoons a week for half a year. But it is over by the time the story opens; furthermore, our one glimpse of the foppish lover, Freddy, leads us to suspect that the "affair" probably was as antiseptic as most of the extramarital relationships depicted by the young Fitzgerald. More cogently, the presentation of Harold Piper as a smug, distant, and demanding alcoholic renders Evylyn, if anything, a very sympathetic character whose desire for outside affection and companionship is perfectly understandable. No "coldly calculating beauty" she,[84] Evylyn comes across as a timid, long-suffering hausfrau who stands helplessly by as Freddy, trying to make a discreet final exit, bangs into the giant punch bowl ("a hollow ringing note like a gong echoed and re-echoed through the house" [99–100]); or as she frantically tries to save her little girl from blood poisoning; or as her husband, through drink and mismanagement, destroys the family business. We simply do not believe that the bowl is a projection of Evylyn's "evil" character, not only because she is obviously not evil, but also because the bowl is too insistently just a punch bowl. Unlike Henry James's golden bowl or even the pickle dish in Wharton's *Ethan Frome,* Fitzgerald's punch bowl is an ordinary serving piece that sees plenty of mundane use in a middle-class household. Evylyn and Harold even argue over whether to use it or a smaller bowl ("That one holds only about three quarts and there's nine of us" [104]) for the dinner party with the Ahearns.

But even though the bowl clearly does not work as a personal symbol of poor Evylyn, Fitzgerald pushes the unconvincing connection between her allegedly evil nature and the bowl even further by suggesting that it is somehow a malignant force in the Piper household. It is the mundane topic of Evylyn and Harold's pre-party squabble, but it also seems to preside over this open sign of their marital discord. The Pipers' daughter Julie will lacerate her hand on it and eventually, like Trina McTeague, she must have her hand amputated to arrest the blood poisoning. Their son Donald will be killed in World War I, and the letter from the War Department will be placed for safekeeping in the bowl. But all of this is too clearly forced: the bowl, after all, had not contributed to Donald's death, it had merely held a letter. And Donald's situation points to a major problem of "The Cut-Glass Bowl": the presentation of the children. We barely see them in the story. Since Julie hadn't been mentioned in the story before the laceration, we initially mistake her for the Pipers' "first maid" ("Hilda, the second maid" [108], reports the child's accident to Evylyn). Likewise, son Donald jumps from being a "little boy" (101) to a fourteen-year-old away at school (102) to a soldier whose "division had been abroad for three months" (111) to a corpse (112) without our ever seeing him. Julie and Donald are total innocents who are introduced into the story to be mutilated and killed because their mother supposedly is not nice, and somehow their misfortunes are connected to an evil punch bowl. This is all rather difficult for a reader to comprehend, and matters are hardly clarified when Fitzgerald explains that poor Donald had been only "a marker in the insidious contest that had gone on in sudden surges and long, listless interludes between Evylyn and this cold, malignant thing of beauty" (113). What contest? And how can there be a contest if the bowl is a projection of Evylyn's supposed evil?

The answer comes down to the question of free will versus fate. Evylyn had tried consciously to be a good wife after the Freddy Gedney affair, taking an active interest in Harold's hardware business and patiently trying to curb his drinking. Evylyn also had tried to be a good mother: Fitzgerald reports that she "had attempted vainly to keep [Donald] near her as she had tried to teach Julie to lean less on her" (111) by encouraging the girl to live with her disability. (She even has the pockets removed from Julie's dresses so that she will not be able to conceal the artificial hand [111].) But Evylyn's efforts to be good, to do well, did not matter; for the suddenly vocal punch bowl gleefully reveals the truth:

> "You see, I am fate," it shouted, "and stronger than your puny plans; and I am how-things-turn-out and I am different from your little dreams, and I am the flight of time and the end of beauty and unfulfilled desire; all the accidents and imperceptions and the little minutes that shape the crucial hours are mine. I am the exception that proves no rules, the limits of your control, the condiment in the dish of life." (114)

This announcement is totally unexpected. It pulls the story in a direction for which we have not been prepared; and it is yet another dramatic instance of the bowl being forced to carry a symbolic dimension which it cannot sustain. Indeed, it is so inappropriate as an emblem of fate that Fitzgerald must turn it literally upside-down to convey its cosmic implications: "The bowl seemed suddenly to turn itself over and then to distend and swell until it became a great canopy that glittered and trembled over the room, over the house . . . until the whole panorama of the world became changed and distorted under the twinkling heaven of the bowl" (113–114, ellipsis added).[85] The element of supernaturalism which works so well in "Benediction" seems ridiculous in this story, as a punch bowl turns into some sort of sneering cosmic jellyfish. Finally Evylyn does what she should have done years earlier: she tries to remove it from the Piper home. But as part of the litany of Piper family disasters, she trips on the house's stone steps as she attempts to carry it outside:

> [S]he slipped and, losing balance, toppled forward with a despairing cry, her arms still around the bowl . . . down . . .
>
> Over the way lights went on; far down the block the crash was heard, and pedestrians rushed up wonderingly; up-stairs a tired man awoke from the edge of sleep and a little girl whimpered in a haunted doze. And all over the moonlit sidewalk around the still, black form, hundreds of prisms and cubes and splinters of glass reflected the light in little gleams of blue, and black edged with yellow, and yellow, and crimson edged with black. (115)

The shattering of the bowl coincides with the physical collapse (or death) of Evylyn; but if the bowl were truly an emblem of fate, it does not seem that it could be destroyed so completely, so easily. Sergio Perosa is probably correct that, in his unconvincing presentation of the bowl as a symbol of fate, Fitzgerald was following the example of Hawthorne, but with more enthusiasm than understanding.[86] Yet the very fact that Fitzgerald was looking to Hawthorne argues that he recognized in him the same terrified awareness that outside forces—what Fitzgerald and the talking bowl summarized as "the flight of time and the end of beauty and unfulfilled desire"—could destroy the life of a well-meaning individual and the lives of innocent people around him just as surely as the guilt-ridden weight of the past could ruin several generations of Pyncheons. The seemingly gratuitous instances of violence and disaster which so pervade "The Cut-Glass Bowl" and most of the other stories of *Flappers and Philosophers* suggest how much Fitzgerald felt that "self and destiny are . . . inseparable,"[87] how frightened he was that "life" or "fate" could step in to destroy those who, according to his strong moral sense, had done nothing to deserve it. Whether or not we agree that the presentation of Evylyn reflects Fitzgerald's insight into the "inner and outer destructiveness" of Zelda,[88] the fact remains that Fitzgerald in "The Cut-Glass Bowl" reveals his very personal fear of "life." This fear would war against his spiritual approach to love, his resilient faith in a moral universe and the power of the individual, for the rest of his days.

For all its surface froth and comedy, *Flappers and Philosophers* is a serious and even disturbing book, and its flaws seem to be those of a troubled man as much as of a fledgling writer. But it also has much to commend it, including the finely wrought "Benediction" and "The Ice Palace," two stories in which Fitzgerald's personal misgivings and his limited but growing fictional craftsmanship were happily in accord. Louis Untermeyer's dismissal of *Flappers and Philosophers* as "nothing better than a gifted twenty-five-year-old author's hackwork,"[89] unfortunately the position of most critics, is thus hasty and unfair. More accurate is Robert Sklar's appreciative response to Fitzgerald's early fiction:

> The wide gap between the strongest and the weakest of these stories was created in part by the turmoil in Fitzgerald's mind over conflicting intellectual and professional commitments. But it also represents the fertility of his imagination, his willingness to take risks, and most important, his capacity to question and criticize within his art his own newly developed points of view.[90]

All one can add is that his *personal* misgivings and commitments seem to have contributed further to that turmoil. *Flappers and Philosophers* is an essential book for an understanding of the young Fitzgerald's mind and art.

2

Tales of the Jazz Age

When in January 1922 Fitzgerald began planning what was to become *Tales of the Jazz Age*, there was simply not enough new short fiction of sufficient quality to justify a second collection of stories. That creative explosion of May 1919 to February 1920 which had resulted in all eight tales of *Flappers and Philosophers* had not been duplicated in the months that followed, but Fitzgerald had hardly been idle, as other literary genres and projects commanded his attention. As of early January 1920 he was already asserting a preference for novels over short fiction, the reflection, perhaps, of the late-nineteenth- and early-twentieth-century attitude that the novel was an inherently more respectable fictional form than the short story; and thus much of his creative energy in the early 1920s was channeled into what he hoped would be a novel worthy of succeeding the immensely popular *This Side of Paradise*. But *The Beautiful and Damned* was long in coming. A series of false starts (variously known as "The Demon Lover," "The Drunkard's Holiday," "Darling Heart") were a drain on his creative, emotional, and financial resources, and when his second novel finally was published in early March 1922, having taken far longer to produce than he had ever anticipated, it did not achieve the enormous popular, critical, and financial success that both he and Max Perkins had anticipated. Even more disappointing was a second creative project, a satirical play entitled *The Vegetable; or, From President to Postman*. Fitzgerald's letters throughout its creation attest to his confidence that it was brilliant writing ("It is, I think, the best American comedy to date & undoubtedly the best thing I have ever written") and the permanent solution to all his financial difficulties ("I'll be rich forever"),[1] so he had no reservations about dedicating himself wholeheartedly to the project beginning early in 1922. Not until its dismal reception in Atlantic City in November 1923 did he realize he had devoted nearly two years to a play that would never make it to Broadway. Between the considerable difficulties and disappointments involved in *The Beautiful and Damned* and *The Vegetable*, Fitzgerald had had little time or interest to spare for short stories since early 1920. For long stretches he produced few if any stories ("The Curious Case of Benjamin Button," for example, was the only one he wrote during the entire first half of 1922), and they seem to have had value for him primarily in relation to his other projects. He claimed that he wrote " 'O Russet Witch!' " only because he needed a break from the stresses generated by *The Beautiful and Damned (TJA,* ix), and even "May Day," one of a handful of stories from the first half of 1920, reflects his desire to salvage something from one or several false starts on his second novel while bringing him some badly needed funds ($200 from the *Smart Set*).[2]

But despite the dearth of new material, there is nothing in Fitzgerald's private correspondence to suggest that he had any misgivings about preparing a second collection of short stories for publication in the Fall of 1922. After all, he still had some good stories remaining from 1920 that had not been included in *Flappers and Philosophers*, such as "The Jelly-Bean" (written in May 1920) and "May Day" (written March 1920)—a novella which, at over sixty pages, would occupy a substantial portion of the three-hundred-page second collection. Further, during the burst of creativity that had produced *Flappers and Philosophers* he had written two playlets, "Porcelain and Pink" and "Mr. Icky," both of which had been warmly received when they appeared in *The Smart Set*. He also had available "The Lees of Happiness," written quickly in July 1920 for the *Chicago Tribune*; " 'O Russet Witch!,' " a fantasy composed in November 1920; "The Camel's Back," written in less than twenty-four hours and good enough to earn him $500 from the *Saturday Evening Post*; and one long fantasy, "The Diamond as Big as the Ritz," to which he had devoted three weeks of intensive effort in October 1921. But there was still not enough material to fill a $1.75 book, so after rejecting the few other magazine stories that had not yet been collected ("The Popular Girl," "Two for a Cent," "Myra Meets His Family," "The Smilers"), Fitzgerald resurrected two apprentice pieces: the burlesque "Jemina" (written in October 1916) and "Tarquin of Cheapside" (written in February 1917), both of which had appeared in the *Nassau Literary Magazine* at Princeton. With characteristic ebullience, this rising young author with budding reputation to consider saw nothing dubious in including a novella, two plays, a handful of tales left over from the *Flappers and Philosophers* period, and a couple of meager undergraduate sketches in what was ostensibly a fresh collection of short stories. Even Max Perkins (who had wisely vetoed the inclusion of several poems in *Flappers and Philosophers*) had only one reservation about Fitzgerald's choice of material: he felt that the reading public might object to the depiction of Shakespeare as a rapist in "Tarquin of Cheapside."[3] But Fitzgerald prevailed, and so confident did he feel about the new collection that he took even more pleasure and care than usual in the production of the volume, devoting considerable attention to its title and dust jacket, the arrangement of the stories into sections, and the composition of a preface for each story.

The various proposed titles of the collection illustrate Fitzgerald's attitude toward these stories and what he hoped to accomplish with them. The original title Fitzgerald suggested in January 1922 was *Sideshow* or *A Sideshow*.[4] Although Fitzgerald did not explain the rationale behind this title, it is not difficult to determine its appeal for him. It suggests, first of all, entertainment; and however seriously Fitzgerald took his career as a writer, he never quite surrendered his early conviction that part of his purpose was to entertain the public, be it through magazine stories, plays, or motion pictures—a medium that attracted him from the very beginning of his career. And he felt he had a strong sense of the audience he sought to entertain. In a letter to Perkins written in May 1922, Fitzgerald asserted confidently that this new collection would "be bought by *my own personal public*, that is by the countless flappers and college kids who think I am a sort of oracle,"[5] and in the infamous Table of Contents of *Tales of the Jazz Age* Fitzgerald declared, "I tender these tales of the Jazz Age into the hands of those who read as they run and run as they read" (*TJA*, xi). As Robert Sklar points out, Fitzgerald's understanding of his "personal public" had "unpleasant implications" for his career, since it suggests that he was writing for an indiscriminating audience with no interest in art or intellect.[6] In the early 1920s, however, this seems not to have been a concern for Fitzgerald.

Sideshow also suggested something even more fundamental about Fitzgerald's attitude toward his work in short fiction. By definition, a sideshow occurs on the periphery of the main event—and at this stage of his career Fitzgerald was already beginning to perceive himself as a novelist who incidentally wrote short fiction as a kind of lucrative hobby. In early January 1920 he told Max Perkins that he wanted to begin his second novel, "but I don't want to get broke in the middle & start in and have to write short stories again—because I don't enjoy it & just do it for money." Just one month later he announced his plan "to do 3 stories a month, one for *Smart Set*, one for Scribners, and one for the *Post*" to support himself as he worked on his "fall novel" during the early months of his imminent marriage.[7] This attitude that short stories were somehow ancillary to the novels would, if anything, only intensify during the 1930s when he came to depend upon them as his major source of income.

Sideshow has another dimension which is evident from Fitzgerald's story "The Camel's Back." The circus party which Perry Parkhurst attends in a camel costume features an elaborate sideshow that includes bearded ladies and tattooed men (45). The word thus suggests a great *variety* of attractions, and Fitzgerald seems to have been especially pleased by the capacity of story collections to showcase his wide range of talents, including the ability to work in different genres and fictional modes. In *Tales of the Jazz Age* there are fantasies ("Diamond," "The Curious Case of Benjamin Button," " 'O Russet Witch!' "); a farce, "The Camel's Back"; and the domestic melodrama, "The Lees of Happiness." There is a technically innovative novella ("May Day"), a sexually suggestive vaudeville playlet ("Porcelain and Pink"), a burlesque of popular fiction

("Jemina") which sounds oddly like Kurt Vonnegut's prose, and a play ("Mr. Icky") which anticipates the theater of the absurd, and in particular Ionesco, though it was intended as a farce.[8] The title *Sideshow* would have suggested this versatility, but it also had other, more unfortunate connotations—cheap sensationalism, fraudulence, even freakishness—which effectively undercut its suitability.

The next possible title was *In One Reel*, which Perkins apparently liked, and Robert A. Martin is correct in seeing a correlation between the one-reel motion picture and the short story.[9] But there is more to *In One Reel* than just an imaginative acknowledgment of the mutual brevity of short movies and short stories. As Fitzgerald wrote to his agent Harold Ober in late June 1922, "None of the 11 stories or playlets in [the collection] have been sold to the movies and I'm hoping that some of them may yet bid for it when its in book form." Fitzgerald had great faith that, for example, "Diamond" was ideal movie material,[10] and what more transparent way to convey this to producers than to identify *Tales of the Jazz Age* as a collection of potential one-reelers? The ploy did not work, however. Only "The Camel's Back" was bought by Hollywood, and by the time it was released by Warner Brothers in 1924 as *Conductor 1492* it had been reduced to a fleeting scene in a film that otherwise had nothing to do with Fitzgerald's story.[11]

By May 1922 a weary Fitzgerald was declaring "I hate titles like *Sideshow* and *In One Reel* & *Happy End*[.] They have begun to sound like viels [veils] and apologies for bringing out collections at all,"[12] and in their stead he offered three possibilities. One was *"The Diamond as Big as the Ritz" and Other Stories*. Though not particularly catchy, it does suggest the pride that Fitzgerald took in "Diamond," a pride that was not qualified by the difficulties he had encountered in marketing what is now regarded as one of his finest achievements in short fiction. (Cut from 20,000 to 15,000 words, it was eventually sold to *The Smart Set* for just $270.) In a pique of frustration he half-jokingly suggested that the collection be called *Nine Humans and Fourteen Dummies*, though he admitted that in order to use such a title "I'd have to figure out how many humans & how many dummies there are in the collection." Sklar is probably correct that Fitzgerald was assuming, "off the cuff, that there were more dummies than humans in the stories,"[13] an assumption which may indicate serious disenchantment with the volume even as he prepared it for publication. By June he was admitting that "Mr. Icky" "does not seem very good to me" despite Edmund Wilson's effusive praise,[14] but it was not feasible to abandon the project even if his improved critical sense indicated that some of the works were not worthy of inclusion in the collection. What he needed was a title that would signify that Fitzgerald was bidding farewell to materials that even he realized he was outgrowing rapidly, while simultaneously playing upon the interests of his "own personal public." His choice was *Tales of the Jazz Age*. Fitzgerald fought for this admittedly "passé" title, arguing that "it is better to have a title & a title-connection that is a has-been than one that is a never-will-be." Further, no one knew better than this former advertising copywriter that "The splash of the flapper movement was too big to have quite died down—the outer rings are still moving."[15] All those affluent "flappers and college kids" would thus find the title *Tales of the Jazz Age* comfortingly familiar, and in fact it proved to be a big selling point.

This dual motivation, the desire to disassociate himself from dated material while cashing in on its continuing popularity, is evident in other aspects of the volume. The stories of *Tales of the Jazz Age*, unlike those of *Flappers and Philosophers*, are divided into labeled sections. As of early February 1922 Fitzgerald was considering calling these sections "Fantasies," "Comedies," and "And So Forth,"[16] but by the time *Tales of the Jazz Age* went to press he had decided to utilize labels which more obviously cut across generic lines. "And So Forth" was replaced with "Unclassified Masterpieces." The new label involves a self-denigrating humor which seems appropriate for such sorry efforts as "Mr. Icky" and "Jemina." Rejecting the old section called "Comedies," Fitzgerald retained "Fantasies" and included within it "Diamond," "The Curious Case of Benjamin Button," "Tarquin of Cheapside," and " 'O Russet Witch!' " But from the very beginning Fitzgerald insisted on including a section called "My Last Flappers," a label which used "last" not in the sense of "most recent" (cf. Browning, "My Last Duchess") but in the sense of "final." For Fitzgerald was by now aware of the need to grow beyond such immensely popular but fundamentally ridiculous stories as "The Camel's Back" and "Porcelain and Pink," flapper tales which he already was identifying as works in his "first manner." The blurb which Fitzgerald proposed for *Tales of the Jazz Age* suggests this conscious impulse to reject flapperdom: "Satyre upon a Saxaphone by the most brilliant of the younger novelists. He sets down 'My Last Flappers' and then proceeds in section two to fresher and more fantastic fields."[17] It was apparently fantasy (with serious undertones) that he saw as the new phase of his career, for he identifies "Diamond," "Curious Case," and " 'O Russet Witch!' " as stories written in "my 'second manner' " (*TJA*, viii). (His inclusion of "Tarquin of Cheapside" in this section of *Tales of the Jazz Age* thus suggests that he saw it not simply as padding for a too-short collection of stories but as an early example of his work in the "second manner.") Fitzgerald would consciously try to exclude flappers from this new phase ("And the flapper idea— God knows I am indebted to it but I agree with you that it is time to let it go"),[18] so by placing "My Last Flappers" *first* in the collection and then following it with the "Fantasies" section, Fitzgerald could convey semiotically this shift in orientation from frivolous flappers to serious fantasies. And other aspects of *Tales of the Jazz Age* also suggest this shift. The dedication of the book ("Quite Inappropriately, To My Mother") and the use of a cover illustration by John

Held, Jr., further signified a simultaneous acknowledgment and rejection of the past, for Fitzgerald had little to do with either parent once he reached adulthood, and he recognized in Held a pictorial satirist of the Jazz Age.

Matters were not, of course, as tidy as all this would suggest. Fitzgerald inexplicably included two of his most mature stories, "May Day" and "The Jelly-Bean," in the "My Last Flappers" section. In addition, the third section, "Unclassified Masterpieces," looks all the more like shameless padding in light of its placement after the second section, those four fantasies in the "second manner." And there seems to be no rationale behind including "The Lees of Happiness," a surprisingly effective piece of domestic melodrama, in the same section as the silly "Jemina" and "Mr. Icky." But overall it is obvious what Fitzgerald was attempting to do with the sections: to assure himself of sales (hence the buzz-word "flappers") while sending out the strongest possible signals that he did not wish to be identified any further with the materials that had initially established his reputation in the literary marketplace.

And sales were admittedly quite important to him. It was with the conscious intention of generating interest in *Tales of the Jazz Age* that he developed what is arguably the most controversial feature of the collection, the prefaces to the stories which he included in the Table of Contents. He stated frankly to Max Perkins that "I'm sure in any case the stories will be reviewed a great deal, largely because of the *Table of Contents*,"[19] and he was quite correct. Virtually every contemporary reviewer mentioned the prefaces, and many discussed them as much as the stories in their reviews. But the prefaces also served other purposes, of which Fitzgerald seems not to have been always aware. For one thing, they were a rather childish way of drawing attention to what he felt were his brilliance and adroitness. "The Camel's Back," we are told, "cost me the least travail and perhaps gave me the most amusement. As to the labor involved, it was written during one day in the City of New Orleans, with the express purpose of buying a platinum and diamond wrist watch which cost six hundred dollars. I began it at seven in the morning and finished it at two o'clock the same night" (vii).[20] As Edna St. Vincent Millay noted dryly about this feat, "Fitz affects all the attributes he believes a genius should have."[21] Further, some of the prefaces seem to be attempts to draw fire away from his less rewarding efforts by pointing out their weaknesses even before the critics. Of "The Lees of Happiness" he reveals that "it came to me in an irresistible form, crying to be written. It will be accused perhaps of being a mere piece of sentimentality, but, as I saw it, it was a great deal more. If, therefore, it lacks the ring of sincerity, or even of tragedy, the fault rests not with the theme but with my handling of it" (x). He likewise identified "May Day" as a "somewhat unpleasant tale" and declared that it was not as strong technically as he had hoped: "Each of the three events made a great impression upon me. In life they were unrelated, except by the general hysteria of that spring which inaugurated the Age of Jazz, but in my story I have tried, unsuccessfully I fear, to weave them into a pattern" (viii).

But the strategy of using the prefaces to this self-protective end backfired on him. Even those favorable reviewers who found the prefaces intriguing and entertaining nevertheless bemoaned the poor handling of the material in "The Lees of Happiness" and the failure to reconcile the three plot lines in "May Day," while the prefaces proved to be ammunition in the hands of less enthusiastic commentators. The reviewer for the *Minneapolis Journal* (whom one might have expected to be favorably inclined toward St. Paul's most famous son) remarked bitterly: "In commenting on 'Jemina' (a booze extravaganza), [Fitzgerald] tells us that he has 'laughed over it a great deal, especially when I first wrote it, but I can laugh no longer.' Presumably, he has developed somewhat. Has it occurred to him that the reader may also have been doing something in the developing line?"[22] Another 1922 reviewer wrote, "F. Scott Fitzgerald undoubtedly thinks the brightest thing about his new collection of not-so-new short stories is the table of contents, in which he comments in a contemptuous fashion on his literary offspring. And truly, if an author has no love for his work, what can he expect of a reviewer!"[23] Far from deflecting criticism, the prefaces generally invited it, and modern critics continue to look to these public statements as indicators of Fitzgerald's personal or artistic shortcomings. André LeVot asserts that in *Tales of the Jazz Age* Fitzgerald "had stopped worrying about quality; it was sales that concerned him now. But he was airily good-humored about it. Each of the titles in the tables of contents was [followed] by a winning little commentary, which seemed to warn his readers that this stuff may not be great literature, but it was entertaining."[24] Less indulgent than LeVot, James E. Miller, Jr. sees Fitzgerald's preface to "Mr. Icky" as exhibiting his "frivolous, perhaps even irresponsible, attitude toward his work," while "it is impossible not to become irritated at [the] flagrant and even defiant waste of talent" expressed by the preface to "The Camel's Back." Miller is especially dismayed that the prefaces reveal "the defects in his stories which he recognized in the writing but simply did not bother to correct."[25]

In large measure Miller is justified in chastising him, for Fitzgerald was aware of the various weaknesses in *Tales of the Jazz Age,* weaknesses that apparently became clear as he revised them for the collection; and the same confessional impulse responsible for *The Crack-Up* evidently made him wish to acknowledge these shortcomings. And yet at the same time it seems clear that part of his denunciation of his own work was essentially a pose. Sklar argues that Fitzgerald was assuming a "role of self-denigration not unfamiliar to Mark Twain" when he declared that he preferred "The Offshore Pirate" to "The Diamond as Big as the Ritz," precisely as "Twain might have said he preferred *The Prince and the Pauper* to *Huckleberry Finn.*"[26] It was the same self-deprecating pose that led Fitzgerald in the summer of 1922 to begin using personalized stationery with letterhead reading F. SCOTT FITZGERALD / HACK WRITER AND PLAGIARIST. Though there was a part of him that feared the prospect of his turning into a hack and another part of him that acknowledged he owed some of his success to Zelda, these two labels are accurate only up to a certain point; beyond that point they are jokes, and one of the most challenging aspects of studying Fitzgerald at any given moment in his career is to determine where that point lies. It shifted almost constantly, depending upon the critical and popular response to his books, the state of his marriage, and the stage of his alcoholism; it was responsible for the often dramatic retrospective shifts in his attitude toward individual works; and it accounts for the odd mixture of self-congratulation and self-denigration that striates not only the prefaces of *Tales of the Jazz Age* but his essays and personal letters as well.

But however the critics may have responded to those prefaces, the fact remains that *Tales of the Jazz Age* did sell well, at least initially. In July 1922 he wrote to Max Perkins that "with the title, the jacket + the table of contents the *Jazz Age* will get a lot of publicity and may sell ten or fifteen thousand copies." By late fall 1922, Fitzgerald reported to Harold Ober that it had sold "almost 18,000 copies—pretty good for short stories," but the flush times were short-lived. Though *Tales of the Jazz Age* earned Fitzgerald over $3,000 in 1922, in 1923 that figure had plummeted to $270.43, according to his *Ledger*. As of 1931, *Tales of the Jazz Age* had earned him just $3,416—even less than *Flappers and Philosophers*.[27] *Tales of the Jazz Age* was, in fine, approximately as successful as his first collection had been, and the critical response to the second volume was not substantially different from that accorded the first, even if we take into account the interest generated by the prefaces. As with *Flappers and Philosophers*, those critics who loved *Tales of the Jazz Age* usually did so for doubtful reasons: "To review a book by Mr. Scott Fitzgerald is always a pleasure. . . . There is so much to be said about Fitzgerald—his method is always interesting and original, and there are many interesting stories told about his life, his wife and his work."[28] Predictably, most saw it as entertaining and, in particular, amusing. "Natural gayety straight from a bubbling heart is one of the many gifts which his fairy godmother must have dropped into his inkwell," gushed the reviewer for the *Rochester* [New York] *Democrat and Chronicle*, while John Gunther praised "Porcelain and Pink" for being a "little gem" and "Mr. Icky" for "shin[ing] out very successfully,"[29] But much of the hilarity was ill-placed. One reviewer found "The Curious Case of Benjamin Button" to be "vastly amusing"; he even "laughed out loud" when he read it[30]—a rather odd response to the story of a man who, born at the age of seventy, grows increasingly younger and ultimately dies in his crib. This is not the stuff of comedy. To generate unintended laughter must be sobering for any author, so Fitzgerald must have derived some comfort from the almost universal admiration for one farce, "The Camel's Back." Typical appraisals were "tremendously amusing" and "the cleverest tale of the collection,"[31] and virtually every favorable reviewer singled it out for high praise. But even Fitzgerald termed it "cheap,"[32] and frankly admitted in its preface that "I like it least of all the stories in this volume" (vii). Most sobering of all, however, must have been the response to one of the strongest efforts in *Tales of the Jazz Age*, "The Diamond as Big as the Ritz." Although some reviewers saw it as imaginative and amusing, most responded negatively. One critic dismissed it as "a schoolboy composition"; another insisted "it is not so much fantasy, as labeled, as phantasmagoria—it misses fire"; and Stephen Vincent Benét stated, "It is good, in spots, but not in enough spots. Nor is it fantastic enough. It just doesn't come off. A fantasy is rather like an alligator pear—if it isn't superb it is wretched."[33] So excoriating were the reactions to "Diamond" that one feels only relief that Fitzgerald did not use it as the title of the collection as he had briefly wished.

The praise lavished upon "The Camel's Back" and the scorn garnered by "Diamond" did not bode well for Fitzgerald's "second manner." But this must have paled beside the surprisingly large number of reviews which effectively performed autopsies on a career which, to some, had ended already:

> Those who have been wishing the best for Mr. Fitzgerald's career are likely to resent his very evident intention to make financial hay while the popular sun is shining. There is not a well conceived story in this volume; not one that has any depth; and throughout the collection silliness is mistaken for comedy. . . .
>   . . . many who have looked forward to Mr. Fitzgerald's future with a great hope are likely to wonder if, after all, he is himself only a symptom of the "Jazz Age." Verily, he seems to be having his reward; and it is a pity.[34]

John Gunther searched frantically for the silver lining, but his appraisal of *Tales of the Jazz Age* is typical of the 1922 reviews: "Some of the stories in the book are good stories, true enough, but a collection containing only a few mere good stories is hardly enough from a man with the promise of Fitzgerald. And some of the stuff in the volume is absolute rot."[35]

The hostile reviewers found a wide range of shortcomings to attack. The unusual variety in subject matter and style of which Fitzgerald had been so proud ("I don't suppose such an assorted bill-of fare . . . has ever been served up in one book before in the history of publishing"),[36] and which several favorable reviewers admired, seemed only to antagonize other commentators, who saw it as symptomatic of crude padding, poor taste, and/or lack of judgment. One generally enthusiastic reviewer remarked that the variety of material produces "on the reader an impression of odds and ends that is unfortunate. The book is more like a magazine than a collection of stories by one man, arranged by an editor to suit all tastes and meant to be thrown away after reading."[37] Margaret Culkin Banning spoke for many in asserting that "at the risk of making the volume too short to be sold at one-seventy-five he might have left out the bathroom stupidity"—that is, the playlet "Porcelain and Pink," which the favorable reviewers had especially enjoyed. Continued Miss Banning,

> This group of republished stories, for which the author seems to have scraped the bottom of the filing case in which he keeps his work, will probably accomplish those things for which its publication is intended. It will make a little more money for author and publisher and keep the name of Scott Fitzgerald before the public. The stories will not enhance Fitzgerald's reputation nor create any furor because they are in the main his "old stuff" and partly because they vary so greatly in quality that even the author's attempt to classify them does no more than give him an excuse for some smart phrases.[38]

Other reviewers were especially dismayed by the references to drinking: "If one could hold a burning match to the mouths of most of Mr. Fitzgerald's characters, they would burn with a pale blue flame. Nearly all of them are soaked, soused, pickled, pifflicated, lit up, thoroughly stewed hooch fiends."[39] John Farrar of the *New York Herald* admitted that after reading the first three stories in *Tales of the Jazz Age*, he felt "like an 'Old Soak' and not a particularly happy soak, either": "There is so much to admire in the writing of F. Scott Fitzgerald that those of us who admire him most are now hoping that he will grow up properly."[40] The wish that he would "grow up properly," plus the repeated references (in even the most favorable reviews) to Fitzgerald's "promise" as a writer, were being directed, let us remember, to a twenty-six-year-old professional author who already had produced two novels and two collections of short fiction and who was hard at work on a play that he believed would be a milestone in American drama.

On balance, there was much for Fitzgerald to consider in the contemporary critical response to *Tales of the Jazz Age*. The favorable reviewers often were enthusiastic for all the wrong reasons, or singled out for high praise precisely those stories which Fitzgerald himself had come to recognize as weak. And the hostile reviewers were often quite astute: the weaker pieces do come across less as samples of Fitzgerald's versatility than as leftovers used to fill out an undersized collection; the farcical tales really are often sophomoric and crude, and not worthy of inclusion in the same volume as "May Day" and "Diamond"; and the drinking does seem to receive unwarranted attention in the volume—an impression created, however, largely by the placement of the most offensive stories in the first section of the book, "My Last Flappers." Ironically, what was meant to be Fitzgerald's farewell to flapperdom (a world characterized by irresponsible drinking) created a negative and decidedly skewed first impression of *Tales of the Jazz Age*, which in fact barely mentions liquor—or flappers—after the opening section. (The notable exception is "Jemina," a farce about moonshining.) The response to *Tales of the Jazz Age* was, in fact, not qualitatively different from that accorded *Flappers and Philosophers*. Essentially recycling old material in an attractive package, it does not, as Fitzgerald fondly hoped, show him making great strides or abandoning shopworn material in favor of the fresh and new. As his contemporary Stephen Vincent Benét observed, *Tales of the Jazz Age* "leaves him in every sense exactly where he was before": the book "is competent enough, but it doesn't mean anything. It shows neither that Mr. Fitzgerald is a flash in the pan nor that he is a constellation. It shows nothing."[41] Though Fitzgerald made no public response to the critical reaction to *Tales of the Jazz Age*, it evidently was becoming clear to him that writing for his "own personal public" could not continue indefinitely. Creatively and financially, *Tales of the Jazz Age* was transparently no improvement over *Flappers and Philosophers;* and, to his credit, Fitzgerald seems to have taken stock of the situation in the months following its publication in the fall of 1922. It would be four more years of writing, reading, and reflection before he produced his third story collection, *All the Sad Young Men* (1926)—a slimmer, tighter, and more mature volume, and a worthy companion to his masterpiece, *The Great Gatsby.*

As noted, *Tales of the Jazz Age* largely contains old material. The only pieces to be produced after the publication of *Flappers and Philosophers* in August 1920 were "The Curious Case of Benjamin Button," "The Diamond as Big as the Ritz," and "'O Russet Witch!'"—just three stories out of the eleven in the collection. Consequently the personal preoccupations that underlie *Flappers and Philosophers* are precisely those that underlie *Tales of the Jazz Age*: his fledgling career and his marriage to a woman who, for better or worse, was a major factor in that career. All of the topics that were examined in the discussion of *Flappers and Philosophers*—love, sex, and marriage, self versus society, and free will versus fate—are likewise prominent in *Tales of the Jazz Age*, and their presence in this collection will be readily apparent from the analysis of the second cluster of topics: (1) dreams and disillusionment, (2) the historical sense, and (3) home. Ultimately they are the concerns and strategies of a troubled man, one too intelligent and perceptive to deny his problems and fears completely, but one still too romantic at this early stage to face them squarely.

Probably the most dramatic manifestation of Fitzgerald's troubled existence in the early 1920s is his fictional preoccupation with dreams and disillusionment. At first glance, one might not think that Fitzgerald had anything to feel disillusioned about during this key period of his life. His first novel, *This Side of Paradise,* had been accepted by Scribners in September 1919 and had created a sensation when it was published in late March 1920. His short stories, whether new or revisions of old ones, were being accepted by the top magazines at prices that seemed to increase exponentially, while Hollywood was interested in securing the movie rights to them for extraordinary fees. And he had won the Golden Girl, with the wedding taking place in April 1920. But there was plenty to put

a damper on all these personal and professional triumphs. For one thing, he had
very nearly not published *This Side of Paradise*. Scribners had rejected "The
Romantic Egotist," and the revision of this manuscript into *This Side of Paradise*
had involved several painful months of hard work and separation from Zelda.
In retrospect he would term this period "a long summer of despair," and as if
to intensify it he had taken a job as a laborer with a St. Paul railroad gang (his
first and only encounter with the middle class) while waiting to hear Scribners'
verdict on the revised manuscript.[42] To outsiders looking retrospectively at these
few months of toil and uncertainty, Fitzgerald's anguish over this, his starving-
artist-in-the-garret period, seems ludicrous. But one must remember that, like
the young Dickens pasting labels on jars for four months in a London ware-
house, Fitzgerald had no way of *knowing* that he would soon emerge as a major
author; and thus the period of uncertainty in St. Paul would always loom larger
and more painful than it actually was. Fitzgerald certainly had hopes, and an
almost superstitious conviction that he was meant to succeed as an author ("Do
you realize that Shaw is 61, Wells 51, Chesterton 41, [Shane] Leslie 31 and I
21?"),[43] but there were no guarantees that outside agents—fate, life, the need
to earn a living, the fickle editorial board at Scribners—would not ruin all.
Further, the uncertainties and misgivings attendant upon the creation of *This
Side of Paradise* came shortly after a series of major disappointments: that
abortive career as a New York advertising copywriter, a glorious stint in war-
torn Europe prevented by a (to him) ill-timed armistice, the inability to make
the Princeton football squad, and the failure to graduate from college. His great
dreams of success on the battlefield and gridiron, and his bitterness and shock
over their failure to materialize, were matters that would haunt him literally for
the rest of his days. As late as 1934 he was still trying to lull himself to sleep
with visions of himself single-handedly leading Princeton to football victory
over Yale, or commanding an army division in the defense of Minnesota during
a Japanese invasion.[44] Though Glenway Wescott is astounded that in the mid-
1930s Fitzgerald would "still think seriously of so much fiddledeedee of boyhood," the fact remains that to Fitzgerald himself these things were not "fiddledeedee" but the first real shocks in the life of a highly sensitive and imaginative
man. Nothing would be more appropriate than for his personal and professional
disillusionments later in life to be (in Wescott's words) "couched in alumnal
imagery."[45]

But even when *This Side of Paradise* was finally accepted by Scribners, it
proved to be a mixed blessing. It not only failed to negate his earlier disappointments but even set Fitzgerald up for some new ones, as it created an
unrealistic professional self-confidence coupled with the pressure to continue
producing fiction that would satisfy not only himself but the American reading
public. According to his letters to Max Perkins, Fitzgerald had already begun
work on a second novel when Scribners accepted *This Side of Paradise* for

publication. As of 18 September 1919 he had already devoted a month to "a very ambitious novel called 'The Demon Lover' which will probably take a year."[46] But he apparently abandoned it quickly, and by January 1920 he had also abandoned two other projects, "The Drunkard's Holiday" and "The Diary of a Literary Failure," titles that perhaps reflect the state of mind of a young author whose self-generated desire to write was now compounded by the realization that his publisher and reading public were expecting him to follow up *This Side of Paradise* almost immediately with a second novel of comparable quality. He likewise abandoned the novel "Darling Heart," reportedly because of a sudden popular reaction against novels of seduction, and his realization that he had made yet another false start on his second novel left him visibly shaken: "I certainly touched the depths of depression tonight" he wrote Max Perkins in early February 1920. Two months of labor had come to nought; but, always the economical author, Fitzgerald decided "to break up the start of my novel & sell it as three little character stories to *Smart Set*" for $40 each[47]—slim consolation to a man who simply could not get started on a new novel. Not until August 1920 was he on track, explaining to Charles Scribner that "The Flight of the Rocket" focused on "the life of one Anthony Patch between his 25th and 33d years,"[48] and in the meantime he had been frustrated and even frantic in his struggle to create *The Beautiful and Damned*.

As he tried to find his footing with the second novel, there was consolation in the success he was enjoying as a writer of short stories. But this often incredible success made his occasional failures all the more disillusioning. That he could produce "The Camel's Back" literally overnight, sell it for $500 to the most popular magazine of the day (the *Post*), then sell it to Hollywood, and then see it chosen for inclusion in that year's *O. Henry Prize Stories* was certainly encouraging. But Fitzgerald was admittedly stunned to find that his best short fiction was often extremely difficult to place: "I am rather discouraged that a cheap story like *The Popular Girl* written in one week while the baby was being born brings $1500.00 + a genuinely imaginative thing into which I put three weeks real enthusiasm like *The Diamond in the Sky* [the original title] brings not a thing."[49] Shortened considerably, "Diamond" eventually was sold to *The Smart Set* for half the fee commanded by "The Camel's Back." By the early 1920s Fitzgerald already was painfully aware that quality and effort guaranteed nothing in the literary marketplace.

His personal life held similar rude awakenings. As we have seen, even as he rushed into marriage with Zelda on the strength of his early success as a writer, he was unable to forgive her for doing "the sensible thing," for breaking off their engagement when his self-confidence had been at its lowest. An incongruous combination of hard-nosed practicality and frivolous childishness, Zelda was already emerging as something less than Fitzgerald's dream girl. But he married her anyway on Easter Saturday 1920, at the dawn of a decade whose dreams and disillusionments seemed to mirror, even magnify, Fitzgerald's own. Though he is usually posited as the Chronicler of the Jazz Age, it would be more accurate to say that he is the chronicler of that era's dreams and disappointments. He seemed to experience them more intensely, and report them more honestly, than any other individual of his time.

This is particularly evident in "May Day." Fitzgerald's novella has been lauded, and justly so, as a vivid rendering of the social, economic, and political forces that had emerged and begun to clash immediately after World War I. Between the demobilized lower-class soldiers and waiters, the middle-class shopgirls, and the upper-class collegiate types and debutantes, Fitzgerald has provided a cross section of American society in 1919 as well as an incisive study of the enormous disparity in economic and political realities of the different classes of society. As the representatives of these groups meet and separate through a series of coincidences at Childs' Fifty-Ninth Street, Delmonico's and the office of the *New York Trumpet,* Fitzgerald sets up a tightly organized story which belies the apparent chaos it conveys, while the rhythm of the alternating story lines simulates a heartbeat.[50] For this is a living society, and despite its fragmentary and impersonal appearance, the individuals it embraces have very real and often painful stories to tell.

Fitzgerald has chosen to focus on one of these individuals, Gordon Sterrett. As most commentators on "May Day" point out, Gordon is a rendering of Fitzgerald himself—or, more accurately, an imaginative projection of what could have happened to him the previous spring. Though the story was finished at Princeton a few weeks before his wedding in 1920, it reflects his state of mind in the spring of 1919 when, like Gordon, Fitzgerald was "rejected in love, failed in his art, and estranged from his wealthy former classmates."[51] The story is not, however, autobiographical in the usual sense. Gordon, unlike Fitzgerald, has been overseas during the war, and so the reuniting with Edith Bradin comes after a prolonged and ugly period in which any Rupert Brooke pabulum about glorious deaths on Flanders fields had been essentially obliterated by millions of flu deaths and such ignoble realities as mustard gas and army tanks. Fitzgerald himself had never been overseas, much to his dismay; but like Gordon he too had had some harsh experiences, which to a man of his temperament rivaled Belleau Wood: the twin battles to establish himself as a writer and to win Zelda. In the spring of 1919 these two battles still had not ended, and Fitzgerald was frankly no longer confident that he would prevail. The worst that could happen was that he would fail on both counts, and "May Day," not unlike "Head and Shoulders," presents a potentially cathartic worst-case scenario of what might have happened had his dreams not begun to come true in the ensuing year. It also shows, albeit melodramatically, how he might have responded to that disillusionment: with self-destruction.

Gordon's professional failures are rendered with a poignancy (and self-pity) that can come only from one who has been in a similar situation. Gordon is an artist; and in his various fictional representations of himself Fitzgerald does tend to utilize artists or writers of some sort. (Similarly, Zelda depicts her husband as painter David Knight in *Save Me the Waltz*.) Gordon believes he has talent ("I've got talent, Phil; I can draw" [66]), but he simply cannot break into the world of magazine illustrating, that golden world offering "piles of money" (66). At the time of the May Day riots of 1919, Fitzgerald too was trying to break into the lucrative magazine market, but his stories (usually slightly refurbished undergraduate sketches) were being accepted only by low-paying publications like *The Smart Set*, and it was not until Scribners accepted *This Side of Paradise* that fall that he would begin to place his work in the *Post*. Further, he was at that time already floundering in his attempts to begin his second novel. Much as Gordon's surname, Sterrett, betokens sterility,[52] Fitzgerald, during that grim spring of 1919, was finding himself in an artistic dry spell and deeply frustrated as a result.

What exacerbates Gordon's situation is his poverty, though one should not make the same mistake that Gordon does in assuming that this is his primary problem. When Gordon roams through Phillip Dean's glitzy hotel room, bemoaning his frayed shirt cuffs and lamenting the dearth of funds that prevents him from obtaining formal art training and the proper supplies, he is not a literal rendering of Fitzgerald (as Turnbull points out, Fitzgerald "never descended" to the level of "a dissipated wreck sponging off friends").[53] Instead he is a rather melodramatically rendered victim of the very real matter that was presenting problems for Fitzgerald in the spring of 1919 but which, unlike being too poor for art school or drawing supplies, was impossible to represent tangibly: a kind of free-floating sense of disillusionment.

It is often difficult to pinpoint the sources of disillusionment, and when one does manage to articulate an apparent cause—such as realizing with a chill that your entire future is at the mercy of the Scribners editorial board—it can sound rather ridiculous, especially to those who have never been in a comparable situation. In depicting Gordon, therefore, Fitzgerald has wisely decided not to explore the specific causes of his despair and decline. Most critics, unfortunately, see this as a major flaw in the story. Charles R. Anderson maintains that Gordon's "deterioration is too rapid and his exit too melodramatic to be convincing." Richard Lehan similarly maintains that Gordon's relationship with Jewel, his motives for marrying her, and his ultimate suicide are "vague and unconvincing." Likewise, James W. Tuttleton argues that "Jewel Hudson may be over-rouged and pulpy of lip, but marriage to her seems hardly a cause for suicide."[54] But the seeming unreasonableness of Gordon's distress and death—that is, our lack of concrete knowledge regarding his motivations—is quite desirable from an artistic standpoint. Fitzgerald has opted to depict, not the process of decline, but the end of it—the final level. To examine the process of decline at length would have required the scope of a novel; but more importantly, to trace the specific sources of his decline might have made Gordon seem ridiculous. (Were the horrors of World War I responsible? Or had he, too, been bumped from his college football team? Or did he have a manuscript that had been rejected by Scribners?) By showing Gordon at the final stage of his decline, Fitzgerald lets his readers plug in their own ideas of disillusioning experiences, while at the same time placing the focus squarely on the feeling of disillusionment itself—a feeling that, whatever its causes, can be spiritually crippling.

It is too easy, of course, to mistake the symptoms for the disillusionment itself, and in fact most Fitzgerald critics do just that. Two elements that recur time and again in Fitzgerald's fiction, love and money, had little intrinsic value for him. True, they were emblems of success, but they attained that status, that value, precisely because of their theoretical capacity to protect the self against disillusionment, to turn dreams into realities. But the fact that they were so difficult to obtain—and, once obtained, to keep—simultaneously rendered love and money the most commonplace *agents* of disillusionment. The irony was not lost on Fitzgerald. He would grapple with this situation repeatedly in his fiction, but perhaps most dramatically in "May Day."

There is no question that Gordon is having problems with the ladies. An avowed heterosexual,[55] Gordon has been in love with Edith Bradin for years, and though Fitzgerald tells us little about their relationship beyond the fact that they dated while Gordon was at Yale, it is clear that they had felt strongly about each other. The subsequent cooling of their relationship seems to have been initiated by Gordon. Never having had any sort of showdown with upper-class Edith, Gordon has become involved with lower-class Jewel—a scaling-down of romantic expectations which reflects his own sense of being no longer worthy of Edith. Edith, however, still clings to the collegiate dream image of pre-disillusionment Gordon. "I'm made for love" she thinks as the dance at Delmonico's begins, and having rejected her date for accidentally mussing her hair, she finds herself conjuring up "another dance and another man, a man for whom her feelings had been little more than a sad-eyed, adolescent mooniness. Edith Bradin was falling in love with her *recollection* of Gordon Sterrett" (84–86, emphasis added). Fitzgerald makes it clear that what Edith had felt for Gordon was not mature love, but an infatuation with a dream. Her continued affection for him reflects a selective memory, an idea, rather than the reality, and she is jolted visibly when she sees the actual Gordon at the dance: "She had seen Gordon—Gordon very white and listless, leaning against the side of a doorway, smoking and looking into the ballroom. Edith could see that his face was thin and wan—that the hand he raised to his lips with a cigarette was trembling" (89). The closer she comes to him, the more disillusioning he is. His eyes are "blood-streaked and rolling uncontrollably" (90), he whines that he has become "a damn beggar, a leech on my friends" (92), and he admits that he's "very gradually going loony" (92): "As he talked she saw that he had changed utterly. He wasn't at all light and gay and careless—a great lethargy and discouragement had come over him" (92). No wonder talking to him generates only "an unutterable horror" (90), and she withdraws her hand when he tries to touch it. But unlike Gordon, the resilient Edith recovers from her disillusioning encounter with her former lover and immediately begins planning her next affair: "—Love is fragile—she was thinking—but perhaps the pieces are saved, the things that hovered on lips, that might have been said. The new love words, the tendernesses learned, are treasured up for the next lover" (93).

The case of Jewel Hudson is more problematical. Refusing to depict her as a girl of the streets with a heart of gold, Fitzgerald has her threaten to blackmail Gordon over their intimacies; but he also depicts her as apparently genuinely concerned over Gordon's well-being. Learning he has been ill, she announces, "I don't care about the money that bad. I didn't start bothering you about it at all until you began neglecting me," and she goes on to say, "I wanted to see *you,* Gordon, but you seem to prefer your somebody else" (102). She seems like an essentially decent woman—yet Gordon will commit suicide when he realizes that he is "irrevocably married" to her (125). The problem, then, is not Jewel, but what marriage to her represents: it confirms that he can no longer maintain the dream of a relationship, now or ever, with the girl who symbolizes his pre-disillusionment life, Edith Bradin.

A relationship with a woman can, then, confirm either the attainment of a dream or its irrevocable loss. But matters become complicated when the woman herself becomes the dream, the goal, the illusion. In "'O Russet Witch!'" Merlin Grainger adores Caroline for his entire adult life. She represents (in Fitzgerald's own words) "that inhibited attraction that all men show to a 'wild + beautiful woman.'"[56] In "The Diamond as Big as the Ritz," John T. Unger falls hard for Kismine Washington, "a girl who seemed to him the incarnation of physical perfection" (161). In "The Jelly-Bean," Jim Powell is hopelessly smitten by Nancy Lamar, while in "The Camel's Back" Perry Parkhurst invests all his emotions in Betty Medill, the pride of Toledo. But these women prove to be unworthy dreams. The "russet witch" Caroline turns out to be a dancer and corespondent in a messy divorce case who deteriorates into a bossy old woman. Lovely Kismine Washington is sufficiently dull-witted to be thrilled at the prospect of orphanhood ("Free and poor! What fun!" [181]), and her "diamonds" turn out to be rhinestones. Nancy Lamar runs off with an heir to a razorblade fortune, leaving Jim Powell as much of a jelly-bean as ever. The only time women prove to be suitable repositories of dreams is in farces: exhibitionist Betty Medill is ideally suited to drunkard Perry Parkhurst, and their marriage suggests that, as long as one does not mistake "Mirth and Folly" (52) for mature love, the illusion of romance will continue unabated.

The problem is that women are only human, and not the Golden Girls or sexually alluring witches for which men too often mistake them. As Michael Paul Gruber observes, "one might dream, and even strive toward fruition, but finally such visions are too like the desirable Edith Bradin: 'if you touched her she'd smear.'"[57] Idealized to a level which they cannot possibly maintain, women ironically become the agents of disillusionment. So, too, with money. In "May Day," Gordon honestly believes that $300, borrowed from Philip Dean to purchase supplies and buy off Jewel, will somehow solve all his problems. Of course it would only forestall the inevitable; and however much one may scorn Philip for refusing to part with his allowance ("it'd put a crimp in me for a month" [73]), the fact remains that he is realistic enough to perceive that Gordon is only deluding himself by thinking that he will quickly sell some illustrations and be able to pay him back. But in fondly assuming that money is a worthy goal, a kind of golden key to unlock all doors, Gordon is simply behaving in typical American fashion. The most direct statement of this in the Fitzgerald short-story canon is probably "The Diamond as Big as the Ritz." As a kind of plantation-owner-cum-miner-cum-entrepreneur in that ultimate land of pioneering opportunity, the Far West, Braddock Washington (with the help of a "moving-picture fella" [171]) has created a kind of personal Disneyland that to middle- and lower-class Americans would be a kind of heaven on earth, much as the serenely ordinary town of Hades on that river of Middle America, the Mississippi, is perceived as hell.[58] For two generations the wealth discovered by Fitz-Norman Washington, Braddock's father, has been concealed thanks to bribery, gigantic magnets, and the rerouting of a river, and the family has managed to maintain the illusion of security and happiness: the golf course is "all a green, you see—no fairway, no rough, no hazards" (164), and the brick path near the chateau leads "in no particular direction" (160). But the money only fitfully creates an illusion of serenity, for the Washingtons must resort to unnatural means (including murder) to preserve their fortune. By the time the airplanes have bombed the compound and the elder Washingtons have literally blown themselves up in the diamond mountain, Fitzgerald's point is clear: when one has invested all one's dreams in money, the loss of it—or even the prospect of its loss—can logically lead to only one thing: suicide.

The immediate cause of the Washington family's disaster was the aerial attack on the compound or, more precisely, the American government, and the people it represents, who themselves wish to acquire that wealth. Often in Fitzgerald's early short fiction the disillusionment that results from investing one's dreams in romance or money is brought about, or at least accelerated, by outside factors. One such factor is Fitzgerald's perennial fear, the intervention of "fate," of events that one cannot foresee or control. This is particularly evident in one of his least-known collected stories, "The Lees of Happiness." Jeffrey Curtain and Roxanne Milbank have invested all their emotions in their love for each other, and their marriage seems destined to be one of the happiest in the Fitzgerald canon. But fate intervenes. When a "blood clot the size of a marble" breaks in Jeffrey's brain (284), leaving him paralyzed for eleven years before killing him, the Curtains' world effectively collapses. The once-pampered Roxanne must learn how to cook and administer medicine in her doomed effort to maintain some semblance of a marriage and stave off Jeffrey's inevitable demise, and the Curtains' friend Harry Cromwell, transparently speaking for Fitzgerald, wonders why there had to be such cruel disillusionment in the Curtains' marriage and his own:

> What had he and Roxanne done that life should deal these crashing blows to them? Upstairs there was taking place a living inquest on the soul of his friend; he was sitting here in a quiet room listening to the plaint of a wasp, just as when he was a boy he had been compelled by a strict aunt to sit hour-long on a chair and atone for some misbehavior. But who had put him here? What ferocious aunt had leaned out of the sky to make him atone for—what? (290)

There is no answer, and Fitzgerald offers none, any more than he can offer a means of ignoring what, for him, was arguably the most terrifying (because inevitable) source of disillusionment of all: the passage of time.

There is some justice to critics' often bemused discussions of Fitzgerald's preoccupation with growing old; even his daughter, Scottie, "always wondered why a well-organized group of his readers didn't have my father tarred and feathered for his blatant impertinence" in depicting people in early middle age as if they had one foot in the grave.[59] All those nineteen-year-old hags and poor Gloria Patch becoming hysterical at the sight of crow's-feet are in fact reflections of Fitzgerald's personal dread of aging: "God! How I miss my youth" the twenty-one-year-old Fitzgerald had written to Edmund Wilson in January 1918,[60] and he was being quite serious. But the problem seemed to be less the horror of getting older per se than the peculiar relationship between time and disillusionment. As one aged one lost the dreams of youth: disillusionment, in other words, was the inevitable consequence of time passing. But the passage of time also cost one the willingness—indeed, even the ability—to maintain what few dreams remained, let alone to create new ones. This complex relationship between time and disillusionment is evident in virtually every story in *Tales of the Jazz Age,* but strikingly so in "'O Russet Witch!'"

As the story opens, Merlin Grainger is "a thin young man of twenty-five, with dark hair and no mustache or beard or anything like that" (235)—that is, he does not have the facial hair which is the traditional emblem of a male's maturity. Rather contentedly mired in a nine to five-thirty job in a New York bookstore, the Moonlight Quill, Merlin has created for himself a safe, predictable daily routine consisting of work, eating a deli supper off the bureau in his tiny flat, and watching from afar the young woman in a neighboring apartment building, whom he calls Caroline. Initially, Merlin's myopic vision of Caroline enables him to enter into a self-protective, vicariously satisfying relationship with this woman he has seen but presumably will never meet. He relishes watching her smoke cigarettes on her chaise lounge (cf. Rev. Hartman watching Kate Swift in the "Strength of God" segment of *Winesburg, Ohio*), he likes seeing her dress in front of her mirror, and he even "enjoyed" watching her entertain her army of gentlemen callers (236). It is clear to the reader that this young man facing a drab life in a Gotham bookstore invests whatever imagination and romantic dreams he possesses in these non-interactions with his alluring neighbor, but, typical of the early Fitzgerald, he intrudes into the story to deny that this is what is happening: "Now, Merlin's whole life was not 'bound up with this romance he had constructed'; it was not 'the happiest hour of his day'" (237)—but such protests are unconvincing. In frantically insisting that "'O Russet Witch!'" is different from the conventional sentimental love fantasies of his day, Fitzgerald unwittingly reveals how responsive he is to the idea of the Dream Girl, and in fact the bulk of the story confirms that Caroline certainly was, for Merlin, intimately bound up with dreams he found difficult to acknowledge or articulate.

This becomes apparent in the visit Caroline makes to the Moonlight Quill. Leland S. Person, Jr. argues that the bookshop sounds like a Poe dream chamber,[61] but in fact the description Fitzgerald provides makes it sound like something more suggestive. With its stock of books "that had passed the literary censors with little to spare," its "red and orange posters of breathless exotic intent," its smell of musk, and its "great squat lamp of crimson satin" (234), the Moonlight Quill could readily be mistaken for a house of ill repute. Even the name of the shop, suggestive of darkness and the phallus, argues that Merlin is spending his life surrounded by a world of sexuality, of potential new experiences, but that he cannot, or will not, respond to it. The nearest he comes to acknowledging the possibility of a more exciting existence is to play Peeping Tom with Caroline, but when she unexpectedly arrives at the Moonlight Quill, her status as the symbol of his dormant erotic side—or, more importantly for Fitzgerald, of a larger, more imaginative life beyond his workaday world—becomes clear. Her first act is to pick up a volume of poems and, "with an easy gesture, [she] tossed it upward toward the ceiling, where it disappeared in the crimson lamp and lodged there. . . . This pleased her—she broke into young, contagious laughter, in which Merlin found himself presently joining" (238). Soon both Caroline and Merlin are flinging books into the lamp, and within minutes they enter into "a perfect orgy of energy," throwing books "in all directions, until sometimes three or four were in the air at once, smashing against shelves, cracking the glass of pictures on the walls, falling in bruised and torn heaps on the floor" (241). For the first time in his life, Merlin risks the literal destruction of his safe world, but immediately he reacts against the implications of what he has done. He cleans up the disordered shop, and impulsively asks a co-worker, Olive Masters, to dinner. As her name suggests, drab Olive is a peacemaker: she serves as a force for ordinariness, a check on whatever Merlin's dreams, symbolized by his awakening sexuality, might lead him to do. He rushes into a relationship with Olive and eventually marries her, knowing that he has the capacity to "master" those aspects of his psyche that Caroline has activated.[62] But the moment he decides to pursue this safe, domestic course, Merlin begins to age visibly. Within the year, at age 26, he "had let his exterior take on the semblance of a deserted garden." He unquestioningly wears the red skull cap tendered by his employer "as a symbol of decay." And abandoning his youthful compulsion for order, like a distracted old man he throws his socks willy-nilly "into the shirt drawer, the underwear drawer, and even into no drawer at all" (244–45). Though it may seem ludicrous for twenty-six-year-old Merlin to seem so senile, Fitzgerald is using premature aging to make a point: without dreams, our lives may as well be over. But the desire to dream, to respond imaginatively to the world, is difficult to eradicate readily: it will reassert itself when we least expect or wish it to do so. This is apparent in the engagement scene in a local restaurant. Merlin proposes marriage to Olive (an "almost involuntary step" for him [245]), and she accepts. The dreams they formulate as an engaged couple are emphatically ordinary and hence attainable:

> There would be a cottage in a suburb, a cottage painted blue, just one class below the sort of cottages that are of white stucco with a green roof. In the grass around the cottage would be rusty trowels and a broken green bench and a baby-carriage with a wicker body that sagged to the left. And around the grass and the baby-carriage and the cottage itself, around his whole world would be the arms of Olive, a little stouter, the arms of her neo-Olivian period, when, as she walked, her cheeks would tremble up and down ever so slightly from too much face-massaging. (247–48)

But as soon as these mundane dreams are formulated, Caroline arrives at the restaurant and begins dancing on the tables. Realizing that Caroline represents the possibility of an existence far richer than that offered by marriage and suburbia, Merlin initially finds himself responding to her (he literally cannot hear Olive speaking to him), but then forces himself to deny what she represents by suddenly insisting that Olive marry him in just two months, thereby ensuring her imminent assistance in keeping him in a world of attainable dreams: "Helplessly, listlessly, and then with what amounted to downright unwillingness, Merlin rose [and] followed Olive dumbly" (251) out of the restaurant and into marriage—with the wedding moved up by yet another month when Olive, sensing Caroline's attraction for her fiancé ("I despise that girl. I can't *bear* to look at her" [251]), decides they must wed as quickly as possible.

Their plan seems to work. Within three years Merlin has achieved most of his middle-class goals, what with his raise in salary, the part ownership in the bookshop, and the birth of their son, Arthur. Everything does seem to confirm that a life of modest dreams is the best, and even the failure to realize the dream of the cottage (they compensate for it with a month in a New Jersey boarding-house each summer [255]) does not challenge his apparent contentedness. But then, at age thirty-five, Merlin sees Caroline once again, causing a riot and traffic jam on Easter Sunday as "men of all ages who could not possibly have known Caroline" (258) fight to be near her. The implications are disturbing for Merlin, and Olive is stunned that Caroline has re-emerged to remind Merlin of the richer life he has tried to deny through the confines of marriage. Olive literally drags her husband and son away from this psychic threat, and for the next thirty years Caroline poses no apparent problems for the little family. During this period, the process of aging, which has been so dramatic when Merlin was twenty-six, seems even more accelerated, as the limited scope afforded by the short story makes his descent into old age appear to be almost instantaneous:

> At forty, then, Merlin was no different from himself at thirty-five; a larger paunch, a gray twinkling near his ears, a more certain lack of vivacity in his walk. His forty-five differed from his forty by a like margin, unless one mention a slight deafness in his left ear. But at fifty-five the process had become a chemical change of immense rapidity. Yearly he was more and more an "old man" to his family—senile almost, so far as his wife was concerned. . . .
> . . . At sixty-five he distinctly doddered. He had assumed the melancholy habits of the aged so often portrayed by the second old man in standard Victorian comedies. He consumed vast warehouses of time searching for mislaid spectacles. He "nagged" his wife and was nagged in turn. He told the same jokes three or four times a year at the family table, and gave his son weird, impossible directions as to his conduct in life. Mentally and materially he was so entirely different from the Merlin Grainger of twenty-five that it seemed incongruous that he should bear the same name. (261)

The Merlin of sixty-five is, of course, the one who has devoted his adult life to sidestepping the kinds of dreams that the twenty-five-year-old Merlin might well have nurtured; but regardless of his ancient exterior and limited life, part of Merlin never forgot what he might have had with the guidance of Caroline. This is especially evident in their final encounter at the Moonlight Quill.

When we last see Caroline in the story, she is a querulous dowager who manhandles her hapless chauffeur and foppish grandson. To the reader, she has essentially become what she is: a demanding old lady. But to Merlin she is still his "russet witch" who, he continues to believe, had tried to lead him to a richer life. At the moment of his engagement, Merlin recalls, Caroline had been "making an attempt at me" by dancing on the table: "Olive's arms were closing about me and you warned me to be free and keep my measure of youth and irresponsibility" (269). Likewise, he tells Caroline that the Easter riot had been a personal performance with a message just for him: "Also I have not forgotten what you did to me when I was thirty-five. You shook me with that traffic tie-up. It was a magnificent effort. The beauty and power you radiated! You became personified even to my wife, and she feared you. For weeks I wanted to slip out of the house at dark and forget the stuffiness of life with music and cocktails and a girl to make me young" (269). But he didn't; and the problem was that, at thirty-five, Merlin "no longer knew how" (269) to pursue what Caroline embodied, and the matter has only worsened over the ensuing thirty-five years. And yet it is clear that, at some level, he had clung to the possibility of dreaming for three decades after the Easter riot. Consequently Merlin essentially ceases to function when he learns from a bookstore employee that Caroline, far from being a witch with special messages for him, was simply a gold-digging dancer who had caused a riot one Easter when she appeared publicly during a sensational divorce trial in which she was the Other Woman. Merlin's shock at learning the truth about Caroline is palpable:

> Merlin sat very quiet, his brain suddenly fatigued and stilled. He was an old man now indeed, so old that it was impossible for him to dream of ever having been young, so old that the glamour was gone out of the world, passing not into the faces of children and into the persistent comforts of warmth and life, but passing out of the range of sight and feeling. He was never to smile again or to sit in a long reverie when spring evenings wafted the cries of children in at his window until gradually they became the friends of his boyhood out there, urging him to come and play before the last dark came down. He was too old now even for memories. (272)

As far as Merlin is concerned, his life has been a waste:

> He knew now that he had always been a fool.
> "O Russet Witch!"
> But it was too late. He had angered Providence by resisting too many temptations. There was nothing left but heaven, where he would meet only those who, like him, had wasted earth. (272)

And so the story ends. Arguably the ending is the weakest part of "'O Russet Witch!'" because its meaning does not seem to square with all the implications of the story. In particular, it appears to compromise the sympathetic portrait of Merlin that Fitzgerald has sought to create. In order to drive home his point that Merlin (like so many other male characters created by Fitzgerald) had foolishly tied his dreams to a flesh-and-blood (and hence fallible) woman, Fitzgerald must reveal that Caroline was actually a self-serving strumpet whose sexual adventures rendered her "the most notorious character in New York" (271) for a decade. But in revealing the truth about her, in proving that she is not a witch but only seemed so to one man and his sexually insecure wife, Fitzgerald has made Merlin seem like a dolt or, in his own words, "a fool." How then did he anger Providence? By refusing to act on the impulses generated by an amoral danseuse? By so conducting his life that he goes to heaven rather than to the hell full of those who *had* given in to temptation? If Fitzgerald had maintained the fantasy to the end, had "Caroline" truly been a never-aging witch with the message that "all is a dare" (hence her actual name, "Alicia Dare"),[63] Fitzgerald might have presented more effectively his argument that we need to pursue dreams that are beyond the mundane; that we should be more willing to indulge our desire to range beyond the straight and narrow (a desire reflected in the acknowledgment of our sexuality); and that time, that waits for no man, imparts an urgency to the situation, since its passage will reduce or destroy what dreams we do have while robbing us of the capacity to generate new ones. At the same time, by revealing the truth about Caroline and reducing Merlin to what Olive terms a "death's-head" (272), Fitzgerald is able to argue that we *need* dreams, even false or admittedly unattainable ones. Merlin's collapse, his sense that he "had wasted earth," thus has less to do with the revelation of Caroline's true self than with his realization that he had done none of the things that she (worthy or not) could have inspired in him. His response to Caroline, his imaginative transmutation of her into a witch with personal messages for him, suggests that he truly did have the capacity to pursue great dreams. Thus the revelation of her true identity leaves the responsibility for his failure to pursue them entirely with him: however much he may have been disillusioned by Caroline, he was more disillusioned with himself. No wonder Merlin, at age sixty-five, can only wait for death.

"'O Russet Witch!'" demonstrates clearly the difficulties posed for Fitzgerald in his pursuit of the "second manner." Writing the story as a fantasy certainly makes it entertaining and enables it to convey the wonder of dreams. But in order to suggest that each of us contains the capacity for both the magical (hence "Merlin") and the mundane (hence "Grainger," literally "farmer")—and that it is our individual responsibility to nurture the former rather than submit to the latter—Fitzgerald has to undercut the fantasy of the story, literally to deny that the story is anything but real. As John A. Higgins observes, "the fundamental weakness of the story is inherent in the irony of its dream-and-disillusion theme. The story must pretend to be what it is not, a fantasy, for that is how Merlin sees it; consequently the bizarre events that would be acceptable in fantasy become unbelievable."[64] Potentially one of Fitzgerald's most powerful stories, "'O Russet Witch!'" loses much of its impact in the reader's uncertainty as to how to respond to its final pages. Not surprisingly, Fitzgerald would soon begin to abandon stories in his "second manner" in favor of realism.

At this early stage of his career, however, Fitzgerald still saw fantasy as an ideal vehicle by which to probe the hard fact of disillusionment. Whether the problem was the investment of one's dreams in the wrong things (love, money), the intervention of fate or the passing of time, or the self-generated inertia that finds it easier to deny dreams than to pursue them, the fact remained that disillusionment is endemic in human life. And Fitzgerald recognized fully that disillusionment could be not simply emotionally painful, but physically destructive. The characters in his early fiction thus formulate a series of strategies, some evasive and some constructive, for dealing with disillusionment.

One such evasive strategy is drinking. When the budding attorney Perry Parkhurst of "The Camel's Back" realizes that Betty Medill will not marry him and help him create a comfortable life in Toledo, he considers any number of actions or, more precisely, non-actions: "He would never go to any more parties. Classical phrases played in his mind—that side of his life was closed, closed. Now when a man says 'closed, closed' like that, you can be pretty sure that some woman has double-closed him, so to speak. Perry was also thinking that other classical thought, about how cowardly suicide is. A noble thought that one—warm and inspiring" (31). But within the hour he has found a less drastic means of dealing with his disillusionment, and that is by getting drunk; and it is in that state that Perry shows up at the wrong party, disguised as a camel. Since the story is a farce, Fitzgerald is able to create a happy ending in which the disillusioned Perry regains his dream: the "mock" wedding of the camel and Betty turns out to be real (the black waiter who married them as a joke at the party is revealed to be the pastor of the Firs' Cullud Baptis' Church [56], while the "marriage license" proves to be genuine). But this happy inversion of disillusionment did not happen in real life, so perhaps the essential falsity of the resolution of "The Camel's Back" explains why Fitzgerald liked it the least of the stories in *Tales of the Jazz Age*.

In "May Day," Gus Rose and Carrol Key likewise turn to drink as, "wanting fearfully to be noticed," they find themselves wandering through a city that is "thoroughly fed up with soldiers unless they were nicely massed into pretty formations and uncomfortable under the weight of a pack and rifle" (71). Though the rhetoric of war had posited them as "pure and brave, sound of tooth and pink of cheek" (62), the reality of these men—"ugly, ill-nourished, devoid of all except the very lowest form of intelligence" (74)—proves disillusioning to the city. By the same token, the city's rejection of the soldiers is disillusioning to them and quickly drives them to drink. Their drunkenness will, of course, be an immediate factor in the death of Key, who falls head first out of an open window in the office of the *New York Trumpet*. Remarkably often death, either accidental or suicidal, is the direct result of disillusionment in Fitzgerald's early

short fiction. Braddock Washington hopes to invert his disillusionment by brib-
ing God into arranging that "matters . . . be as they were yesterday at this hour
and . . . so remain" (185). But when God refuses to manipulate time in this
fashion, Washington literally blows himself up inside his diamond mountain.
Less dramatically, Merlin Grainger of " 'O Russet Witch!' " waits passively for
his death to release him from his disillusionment, while stroke victim Jeffrey
Curtain, his career and marriage in irrecoverable fragments, dies after eleven
years in "The Lees of Happiness." The only story in *Tales of the Jazz Age* in
which death does not seem to be the negative capstone of disillusionment is
another fantasy, "The Curious Case of Benjamin Button," but that is only
because time does not move in a normal fashion in this story.

At the time of his birth, baby Benjamin Button is seventy years old. His
young father is understandably shocked to see his newborn "partially crammed
into one of the cribs" in the hospital nursery: "His sparse hair was almost white,
and from his chin dripped a long smoke-colored beard, which waved absurdly
back and forth, fanned by the breeze coming in at the window" (195). Benjamin's father does not adjust well, and from the moment he first sees his
seventy-year-old baby, he is a study in disillusionment. As the member of a
wealthy, socially prominent Baltimore family, Roger Button finds it impossible
to "ignore the fact that his son was a poor excuse for a first family baby" (200)
and the intended partner and heir of his hardware business. Mr. Button therefore
deals with his disillusionment in the most primitive way possible: denial. After
denying that the septuagenarian in the crib is his child ("You lie! You're an
impostor!" [196]) and wishing that the baby had been born black instead of
elderly,[65] Mr. Button races to the nearest clothing store in the fond belief that a
juvenile outfit can disguise the reality. Decked out in "dotted socks, pink pants,
and a belted blouse with a wide white collar" (200), Benjamin still looks like
what he is, an old man. "The remaining brush of scraggly hair, the watery eyes,
the ancient teeth, seemed oddly out of tone with the gayety of the costume"
(200), and even the determined "clipping and dyeing of his eyebrows" cannot
disguise the fact the "the eyes underneath were faded and watery and tired"
(201). Mr. Button's strategy of denial nonetheless continues unabated. "To
perfect the illusion which he was creating—for himself at least" (201), Mr.
Button buys a pink toy duck for his cigar-smoking baby, as well as the obligatory rattle: he "insisted in no uncertain terms that [Benjamin] should 'play with
it,' whereupon the old man took it with a weary expression and could be heard
jingling it obediently at intervals throughout the day" (201). Benjamin spends
"stiff jointed" afternoons "trying to work up an interest in tops and marbles"
with neighborhood children (202), and makes it a point to break something
every day because such naughtiness was "expected of him" (202).

So successful is Mr. Button's strategy of denial that his disillusionment
gradually fades. Twelve years after Benjamin's birth, his parents "no longer felt

that he was different from any other child" (203), thanks in large measure to Mr. Button's "silent agreement with himself to believe in his son's normality" (204). Indeed, the components of the denial continue to be modified as the situation changes, with Mr. Button going from "he's not my son" to "he's perfectly normal" to "he's my brother"—the illusion that both he and Benjamin create as the father continually ages and the "baby" grows continually younger until finally they appear to be the same age. But the semblance of brotherhood can exist for only a short time; and as Benjamin's encroaching youth pulls him steadily out of step with the rest of the normally aging world, he finds that it becomes as harsh as it was when he was born. His once-lovely wife becomes shrewish, accusing Benjamin of deliberately growing younger so as to antagonize her (214), while his son Roscoe tries to force him to wear eyeglasses, glue on imitation whiskers, and call him "uncle" instead of "son" (218). Despite these disappointments, however, Benjamin does not succumb to permanent disillusionment, but that is only because of his unique situation. As Benjamin grows increasingly infantile, Fitzgerald uses strikingly Joycean prose to convey the fading of his mind and memory:[66] "There were no troublesome memories in his childish sleep; no token came to him of his brave days at college, of the glittering years when he flustered the hearts of many girls. There were only the white, safe walls of his crib and Nana and a man who came to see him sometimes, and a great big orange ball that Nana pointed at just before his twilight bed hour and called 'sun'" (223). As for the events of his long life, "all these had faded like unsubstantial dreams from his mind as though they had never been" (223). Though he dies at the end of the story, Benjamin Button is arguably the happiest character in the Fitzgerald canon. At the age of seventy (i.e., at his birth) he had experienced nothing and thus was not tormented by the disillusionment of most elderly people, while at the time of his death seventy years later, he simply cannot remember the few unhappy events of his life. And without memory, there is no sense of disillusionment.[67]

But the other Fitzgerald characters do not have the option of avoiding disillusionment by growing younger. For those who do not resort to drink, suicide, or denial, there do, however, remain several other strategies. One is to cling frantically to the past—not to deny the disillusioning events, but to focus just behind them, on what used to be. This is the strategy adopted by Roxanne Milbank in "The Lees of Happiness." Not unlike the situation in Bret Harte's short story "Miggles," Roxanne is an attractive former actress who devotes eleven years to the loving care of her young husband Jeffrey, who has been debilitated by a stroke:

> Had it not been for her unceasing care the last spark would have gone long before. Every morning she shaved and bathed him, shifted him with her own hands from bed to chair and back to bed. She was in his room constantly, bearing medicine, straightening a pillow, talking

to him almost as one talks to a nearly human dog, without hope of response or appreciation, but with the dim persuasion of habit, a prayer when faith has gone.

Not a few people, one celebrated nerve specialist among them, gave her a plain impression that it was futile to exercise so much care, that if Jeffrey had been conscious he would have wished to die, that if his spirit were hovering in some wider air it would agree to no such sacrifice from her, it would fret only for the prison of its body to give it full release.

"But you see," she replied, shaking her head gently, "when I married Jeffrey it was—until I ceased to love him"

"But," was protested, in effect, "you can't love that."

"I can love what it once was. What else is there for me to do?" (295–96)

Nothing, Fitzgerald would say. By the end of the story Roxanne at age thirty-six is a tad thick-waisted, but hardly the crone that most Fitzgerald women of early middle age seem to be. Her remarkable youth despite years of stress and drudgery may be attributed to this decision to orient herself toward the past. Immediately after Jeffrey's death, "she went back in spirit to that wonderful year" when they were first married, to "that intense, passionate absorption and companionship" (297). She denies herself even the possibility of future happiness with now-divorced Harry Cromwell, who had visited her faithfully throughout Jeffrey's illness:

> They lingered for a moment just below the sloop, watching a moon that seemed full of snow float out of the distance where the lake lay. Summer was gone and now Indian summer. The grass was cold and there was no mist and no dew. After he left she would go in and light the gas and close the shutters, and he would go down the path and on to the village. To these two life had come quickly and gone, leaving not bitterness, but pity; not disillusion, but only pain. There was already enough moonlight when they shook hands for each to see the gathered kindness in the other's eyes. (301)

Not disillusion, Fitzgerald stresses, but this is possible for Roxanne only by compartmentalizing the eleven years of Jeffrey's illness and by behaving as if the first, happy year of their marriage had never ended. Though she is realistic enough to ask Harry for investment advice and to understand the need to turn her home into a boardinghouse, she is spiritually unrealistic, maintaining the fiction that she is still married to a young, healthy Jeffrey. But if this strategy for dealing with disillusionment is not as extreme as, say, Mr. Button's forcing his seventy-year-old son to play with a rattle, it still is not quite healthy. At only thirty-six, Roxanne has already decided to make do with "the lees of happiness" for the rest of her life, not even being willing to risk another marriage for the sake of the baby she would love to have (299).

But however much his characters formulated strategies for dealing with (or evading) disillusionment, Fitzgerald was beginning at this early stage to work toward the attitude that disillusionment is not only inevitable, but often constructive—a "shabby gift," according to John T. Unger (191), but a gift nonetheless. It can, for example, lead to greater maturity and a more accurate understanding of reality. As Roxanne Curtain learns to bake biscuits and balance the checkbook, her "nature . . . suddenly deepened" (285), and she seems far more human at the end of the story than when she was a photograph on the theatrical page or a new bride living in a series of chic hotels. Likewise, Kismine Washington never sounds more sensitive and mature than when she suddenly notices the stars at the end of "Diamond": "I always thought of them as great big diamonds that belonged to some one. Now they frighten me. They make me feel that it was all a dream, all my youth" (191), in much the same way that the disillusioned Gatsby "looked up at an unfamiliar sky through frightening leaves and shivered as he found what a grotesque thing a rose is" (chap. 8). And the process of growth through disillusionment works for the reader as well. Once one realizes with a jolt that the rapist of "Tarquin of Cheapside" is William Shakespeare, one can never again think of the Bard in totally exalted terms. By descending from his pedestal, he seems somehow more human, more accessible; and if anything, this makes us appreciate his achievement all the more.

The realization that one could grow from disillusionment was probably vital for a man who was himself already having more than his share of personal and professional disappointments, but Fitzgerald's sense that one must endure disillusionment, must accept it somehow and hopefully learn from it, would not become a strong element in his short fiction for several more years. True, the drinking on the part of his later characters does increase (the reflection, perhaps, of Fitzgerald's personal situation), but so too does the degree of calm acceptance in the face of disillusionment. And early and late, Fitzgerald would never deny the *need* for dreams and illusions, no matter how painful the disillusionment itself might be. Dreams were necessary, for example, for the nurturing of the spirit. The twelve men of Fish in "Diamond," we are told, suffer precisely because they had lost "the vital quality of illusion which would make them wonder or speculate." Had they possessed this quality, "a religion might have grown up" around the mysterious figures alighting periodically from the Transcontinental Express. But if all they have left is a "dim, anaemic wonder" (145), the fact remains that the capacity for wonder is still extant—much as it is still within the jolly diners at Childs' restaurant who are so visibly moved by the resplendent "magical, breathless dawn" over Columbus Circle (116).[68] Of course, Fitzgerald's personal sense of commitment "to the possibilities of romantic wonder offered by his time and place and social class"[69] is responsible for some of the apparent infelicities of his early writings. Most obvious is a wide streak of sentimentality that many modern readers find intolerable. He lampoons sentimental fiction in his stories: Jasmine Washington's favorite books, for example, "had to do with poor girls who kept house for widowed fathers" (170), while she desperately wished to serve as a "canteen expert" in

World War I (170). Indeed, Tom d'Invilliers had attacked the current state of American literature in *This Side of Paradise* by arguing that "our specialty is stories about little girls who break their spines and get adopted by grouchy old men because they smile so much. You'd think we were a race of cheerful cripples" (book 2, chap. 2)—and yet Fitzgerald created a similarly mawkish story in "The Lees of Happiness." His fondness for sentimentality even affects Fitzgerald's work at the level of style, although his overwriting can sometimes be defended. Brian Way, for instance, attacks as "romantic gush"[70] the following passage from "May Day": "They went into the Biltmore—a Biltmore alive with girls—mostly from the West and South, the stellar debutantes of many cities gathered for the dance of a famous fraternity of a famous university" (73). "Romantic gush" it certainly is—and as such it effectively conveys the romantic wonder generated (justly or otherwise) by the lifestyle of the youthful upper class, while also serving as the counterpoint to a disillusioned outsider's response to this vision: "But to Gordon they were faces in a dream" (73). The very text thus helps to convey Fitzgerald's complex attitudes toward dreams and disillusionment, entities which at this stage of his career and personal life were not yet fully understood by the young Fitzgerald and hence often resulted in sentimental excesses.

The mature yoking of both wonder and disillusionment, the need to nurture the one while not denying the other, is precisely what Fitzgerald had in mind when he wrote in *The Crack-Up* that "the test of a first-rate intelligence is the ability to hold two opposed ideas in the mind at the same time, and still retain the ability to function." Most commentators seem not to have noticed the rest of Fitzgerald's statement: "One should, for example, be able to see that things are hopeless [i.e., be disillusioned] and yet be determined to make them otherwise [maintain the dream]."[71] This psychically healthy balance was expressed in 1936, but in the early 1920s Fitzgerald was already attempting to work his way toward this frame of mind by trying to see the world from the broadest possible view: that is, from the historical perspective.

Fitzgerald had always been fascinated by history. He had a lifelong antiquarian's habit of compiling endless lists of key historical dates and of European rulers, and he especially enjoyed reading about life during the Napoleonic Era, the Elizabethan Age, and the medieval period. But his sense of history was also acutely personal. His childhood was enriched by his father's accounts of the Civil War, and Fitzgerald's earliest efforts as a writer reflect his own imaginative response to this period of American history. (That he evinced little interest in U.S. history before the mid-nineteenth century may reflect his unwillingness to acknowledge his maternal bloodline. The "black Irish" McQuillans had come to America during the potato famine, and gave him what he himself termed an "inferiority complex.")[72] As he matured, Fitzgerald's understanding of history would go beyond the antiquarian to something deeper, broader, and hence more meaningful. This process was already underway by the time he wrote *Tales of the Jazz Age*. Thanks to Shane Leslie, Fitzgerald was beginning to formulate "two different, but not contradictory, historical perspectives on his own experience; on the one hand the war marked a definite and conclusive break with Victorian civilization, on the other it was simply a phase, though a major one, of world-historical movements centuries old and with centuries yet to run."[73] By the mid-1920s, Fitzgerald's exposure to the theories of Oswald Spengler was confirming his own conviction that an informed historical perspective could help one make sense of the disordered era in which he himself lived—an era which, as Fitzgerald was keenly aware, seemed uncannily to parallel and reflect his own experiences. Virtually all of the stories in *Tales of the Jazz Age* are carefully grounded in a particular time and place, as Fitzgerald acknowledges that what happens to people on a personal level is inextricably bound up with when and where they are living—that is, their historical niche.

The story that illustrates most dramatically the interconnectedness of the personal and the historical is of course "May Day." Fitzgerald approaches the spring of 1919 with an objectivity bordering on aloofness—a startling achievement considering that he was recording that era from the retrospective vantage point of not quite one year. The opening of the story is justly famous: *Zelda*

> There had been a war fought and won and the great city of the conquering people was crossed with triumphal arches and vivid with thrown flowers of white, red, and rose. All through the long spring days the returning soldiers marched up the chief highway behind the strump of drums and the joyous, resonant wind of the brasses, while merchants and clerks left their bickerings and figurings and, crowding to the windows, turned their white-bunched faces gravely upon the passing battalions.
>
> Never had there been such splendor in the great city, for the victorious war had brought plenty in its train, and the merchants had flocked thither from the South and West with their households to taste of all the luscious feasts and witness the lavish entertainments prepared— and to buy for their women furs against the next winter and bags of golden mesh and varicolored slippers of silk and silver and rose satin and cloth of gold. (61)

The opening is redolent of the historical vagueness peculiar to fairy tales ("Once upon a time . . ."), though there is some justice in the critical commonplace that the detached tone and stilted rhetoric are quasi-biblical.[74] Whatever the case, Fitzgerald initially is careful not to give the reader any cues as to when and where the story takes place. (He even substitutes "white, red, and rose" for the customary "red, white, and blue" to avoid any suggestion of America.) In removing these cues, Fitzgerald forces the reader to see the events of 1919 as nothing special—as simply one of any number of phases in history in which the world seemed plunged into unprecedented, and apparently irremediable, chaos. The same effect is achieved with the story's title. As Robert Emmet Long points out, "May Day" suggests "both the rite of spring renewal celebrated in the dance around the maypole in earlier day England" as well as "the Marxist revolution."[75] Though Long sees these echoes as ironic, as underscoring the very lack of renewal and rebirth, it would appear that Fitzgerald is actually positing the events of 1919 within the framework of the saturnalia, an ancient event in which people throughout the world have participated for thousands of years. Though some individuals have been injured or killed by such saturnaliae (hence the third meaning of the title, a distress signal), the vast majority survive unscathed, and time goes marching on. However grim the world may have seemed in May 1919, by the time Fitzgerald finished the story in March 1920 it had not only recovered but was launched well into the Jazz Age: "The uncertainties of 1919 were over . . . America was going on the greatest, gaudiest spree in history."[76]

But at the time there had been much disillusionment: the soldiers, no longer perceived as heroes, were once again "driftwood" moving inexorably to their deaths (74); Edith Bradin found her old beau Gordon Sterrett a drunken, penniless wreck; and Henry Bradin was injured by the very men he had sought to help with his socialist newspaper. But as early as the spring of 1920 it had become clear that the seeming crises of 1919 had had no adverse effect on the world, and this is reflected in what happens to these characters. For the duration of their lives, the soldiers not killed in the May Day riots would remain within the protective confines of one institution or another ("army, business, or poorhouse" [76]); Edith would simply be moving on to the next lover; and Henry (or someone like him) would begin again "to pour the latest cures for incurable evils into the columns of a radical weekly newspaper" (86)—for after all, "incurable evils" have always existed and probably always will.[77] Individual instances of personal disillusionment are thus short-lived and, from the broad historical perspective, of slight import. Gordon's suicide at the end of the story is consequently a waste from the personal perspective and a meaningless act from the historical one. Had he waited longer, even a year, Gordon's situation would probably have so changed that he might have come to see his early death for what it was: a permanent personal solution to a temporary historical situation.

As "May Day" suggests, Fitzgerald's approach to his own era was less as a mindless recorder of fads than as an historian or cultural anthropologist, examining his own society at a particular historical moment. Many of the seemingly irrelevant passages in his early fiction reflect this impulse to capture all of society by studying its artifacts, language, and shifting sense of identity. In "The Camel's Back," for example, though Fitzgerald records the farcical adventures of the drunk Perry Parkhurst, he is quite careful to place the story in a particular place (Toledo) at a particular time (Christmas 1919)—that is, literally a few weeks before he wrote the story. Not unlike William Dean Howells in *A Hazard of New Fortunes,* Fitzgerald is an astute observer of the shifts in social class and the influx of immigrants that coexisted with, and indeed made possible, the rather frivolous lifestyles of certain strata of American society. Native-born, upper-crust Perry Parkhurst is able to attend the fanciest parties in Toledo thanks, in part, to a service offered by Mrs. Nolak: she is the owner of the costume shop that rents Parkhurst the camel suit. "Mrs. Nolak was short and ineffectual looking, and on the cessation of the world war had belonged for a while to one of the new nationalities. Owing to unsettled European conditions she had never since been quite sure what she was" (33). Perry Parkhurst's hosts likewise owe their standing in Toledo to socioeconomic realities of their particular historical moment:

> The Howard Tates are, as every one who lives in Toledo knows, the most formidable people in town. Mrs. Howard Tate was a Chicago Todd before she became a Toledo Tate, and the family generally affect that conscious simplicity which has begun to be the earmark of American aristocracy. The Tates have reached the stage where they talk about pigs and farms and look at you icy-eyed if you are not amused. They have begun to prefer retainers rather than friends as dinner guests, spend a lot of money in a quiet way, and, having lost all sense of competition, are in [the] process of growing quite dull. (41)

There would be no camel costume for Parkhurst, and no party for him to attend so as to dazzle Betty Medill, if not for Mrs. Nolak and the Howard Tates. Hence we cannot understand Parkhurst's situation outside of his historical milieu—although admittedly there is so little to understand about him that much of Fitzgerald's point is lost, while the flippancy with which Fitzgerald treats this aspect of the story obscures the serious thought behind it.

More effective in its use of the historical milieu is "The Lees of Happiness," written a few months later. Fitzgerald seems to suggest that we cannot comprehend the Curtains fully—or the magnitude of Roxanne's sacrifice—unless we understand their historical background. Those chroniclers of the historical moment, newspapers and magazines, reveal that Jeffrey's writing career had coexisted with that of other turn-of-the-century luminaries:

> If you should look through the files of old magazines for the first years of the present century you would find, sandwiched in between the stories of Richard Harding Davis and Frank Norris and others long since dead, the work of one Jeffrey Curtain: a novel or two, and perhaps three or four dozen short stories. You could, if you were interested, follow them along until, say, 1908, when they suddenly disappeared. (275)

Though Fitzgerald never states whether Jeffrey in fact wrote adventure stories or naturalistic fiction, the historical perspective suggests that Jeffrey had been of the caliber and popularity of Davis and Norris—a situation which adds poignancy to his tragedy as he, too, prematurely joins the ranks of writers "long since dead." Likewise, his wife, a popular actress of "the days of 'Florodora' and of sextets, of pinched-in waists and blown-out sleeves, of almost bustles and absolute ballet skirts" (276), will end up, six months after Jeffrey's death, "in a black dress which took away the faintest suggestion of plumpness from her figure" (297). Her personal change from the chic attire of her youth to the black dress she affects at age thirty-six suggests less Fitzgerald's interest in the quaint vicissitudes of the garment industry than the fact that this widow, once the fashionable trend-setter for other women, has effectively tried to cut herself off from history in the face of her tragedy. Far from living in history and even helping to direct it with her fashion example, Roxanne tries to step out of history by wearing the most timeless garment possible: a mourning dress. It is an act that parallels her decision not to dwell on the previous eleven years but to place her marriage in a timeless limbo in which she focuses on their happy first year together and ignores all else.

Roxanne's attempt to step out of history is atypical for Fitzgerald's early short fiction. Evidently he saw such an attempt as ultimately counterproductive, for Roxanne's desire to "freeze" her marriage at the perfect historical moment, although understandable, effectively precludes the possibility of any future happiness or growth. It is a strategy that Fitzgerald himself personally rejected, opting instead to pursue his dreams of literary achievement, fame, and fortune, and scaling them down only when Zelda's illness and the fluctuations of the literary marketplace during the Depression necessitated such change. Much more commonplace in Fitzgerald's early short fiction is the situation in which he depicts individual characters or families whose very lives embody the historical eras in which they live, in much the same way that he, born in 1896, was destined to come of age during World War I, enjoy glamour and success in the 1920s, suffer personal and financial setbacks in the 1930s, and begin a comeback at the dawn of World War II.

The most dramatic example of an individual Fitzgerald character whose life encapsulates his era is Benjamin Button. As John Gery explains in the only critical essay devoted to this story, "During the Golden Age of capitalism, [Benjamin Button] turns the family hardware concern into a thriving business, receives a medal for heroism at San Juan Hill in 1898, perfects all the fashionable dance steps at the turn of the century, and scores seven touchdowns and fourteen field goals against Yale as he stars for the 1910 Harvard football team. . . . In short, [Benjamin] depicts *ideally* the appropriate age for an American male to be, as the author imagines him, between 1860 and 1930."[78] Since Benjamin had been born at age seventy in 1860 and had steadily grown younger until his death in his crib, it would appear that Fitzgerald has indeed so arranged matters that Benjamin dies in 1930—rather surprising for a story written eight years before that, in 1922, and quite atypical of an author whose fondness for fantasy did not extend to futuristic tales. It would be characteristic of the early Fitzgerald to intend to bring Benjamins' story up to 1920, in much the way that "The Lees of Happiness" ends in the present (i.e., eleven and a half years after

Jeffrey's stories ceased to be published in 1908). The confusing suggestion of 1930 is hardly clarified by the opening of "The Curious Case of Benjamin Button":

> As long ago as 1860 it was the proper thing to be born at home. At present, so I am told, the high gods of medicine have decreed that the first cries of the young shall be uttered upon the anesthetic air of a hospital, preferably a fashionable one. So young Mr. and Mrs. Roger Button were fifty years ahead of style when they decided, one day in the summer of 1860, that their first baby should be born in a hospital. Whether this anachronism had any bearing upon the astonishing history I am about to set down will never be known. (192)

If the Buttons were "fifty years ahead of style" in 1860, then the "present" is 1910, and neither 1920 nor 1930. Perhaps this mangling of time cues à la "A Rose for Emily" is simply a reflection of Fitzgerald's well-documented incompetence in arithmetic, but two things do seem clear: he had to have Benjamin be visibly old at birth, and that argued for a least age seventy; and he wanted to have his story begin at a particular time and place in history, 1860 Baltimore. For the Buttons' dismay over the birth of their seventy-year-old baby reflects their sense of their position in the Old South: "The Roger Buttons held an enviable position, both social and financial, in ante-bellum Baltimore. They were related to the This Family and the That Family, which, as every Southerner knew, entitled them to membership in that enormous peerage which largely populated the Confederacy" (192). Whereas their newborn would hardly be welcome in any family at any time, it was especially untenable given the Buttons' prominence in the South during "that picturesque period" (193). In light of this, Fitzgerald is able to make a statement about the inconsistencies and cruelties of society at that time, for as the new father imagines walking home with Benjamin past the slave market, Mr. Button for "a dark instant . . . wished passionately that his son was black" (197). As William Faulkner would begin to document just a few years later, there was a well-established place in the Old South for babies of mixed blood; as such, they were "acceptable," even when born into a family as prominent as the Buttons. But the purest Caucasian baby was unacceptable if there were anything out of the (upper-class, white) norm about him. By being born seventy years old, Benjamin is definitely outside the norm; and Gery may be correct that, if in fact the story ends in 1930, Fitzgerald is "suggesting perhaps, in keeping with the earlier phases of [Benjamin's] adaptability, that a model for the American of the Twenties is found in the carefree and careless lifestyle of the child."[79] America in the post-World War I period was certainly far less rigid than ante-bellum Baltimore, but the faint mockery so evident in some of his renderings of contemporary American life would argue that Fitzgerald saw this new flexibility, however refreshing and potentially humane, as nonetheless symptomatic of a general breakdown in standards and morals, as characteristic of "a world in which no moral decisions can be made because there are no values in terms of which they may be measured."[80] And if indeed Benjamin's situation was meant to reflect the infantile carelessness and amorality of the 1920s, then Fitzgerald's foresight when he wrote the story in 1922 was astounding: much as Benjamin would die in 1930, the Jazz Age "leaped to a spectacular death in October, 1929."[81]

The confusion of dates notwithstanding, it is apparent that Fitzgerald perceives Benjamin as the beneficiary of a particular historical moment in the United States: though he had been an unacceptable member of Baltimore society in 1860, he became acceptable, even prominent, thanks to the Gilded Age. "In the fifteen years between Benjamin Button's marriage in 1880 and his father's retirement in 1895, the family fortune was doubled. . . . Needless to say, Baltimore eventually received the couple [Benjamin and his wife, Hildegarde] to its bosom." Indeed, even Benjamin's father-in-law became reconciled to him when he financed the publication of the old man's "'History of the Civil War' in twenty volumes, which had been refused by nine prominent publishers" (211–12). A particular historical period of accelerated economic growth thus made possible the money that guaranteed social prominence, even for an individual of unprecedented freakishness like Benjamin Button. No wonder the socially insecure Fitzgerald so valued money.

The complex relationships between history, money, and social status, plus the capacity of these elements to evade, deny, or (ironically) cause disillusionment, is apparent in Fitzgerald's best-known rendering of a family whose story parallels and encapsulates the American experience: the Washingtons of "The Diamond as Big as the Ritz." As Brian Way points out, their story is the story of the American West: Fitz-Norman Washington's discovery of a diamond mountain in an unexplored section of Montana is hardly more fantastic than some of the actual rags-to-riches episodes of lawless adventure and enterprise during the Westward movement. Further, as a miner, Fitz-Norman literally and symbolically conveys the "economic activity of the Gilded Age: ruthlessly and often wastefully exploitative, [mining] is the ultimate expression of personal greed and of indifference to the idea of civilization."[82] Certainly Fitz-Norman does seem to embody what Way terms "the exploitative phase of American capitalism": his given name calls to mind the Norman conquerors who used barbarity to take and keep what they wanted, while imposing "a system of steep class differences" on Britain.[83] More cogently, since Fitz-Norman Washington had been "a twenty-five-year-old Colonel with a played-out plantation" at the end of the Civil War (155), he apparently was born circa 1840—that is, at the same time as a host of other exploiters of American resources, including James J. Hill (born 1838), Andrew Carnegie (1835), and John D. Rockefeller (1839). Fitz-Norman's career after discovering the diamond is not fundamentally different from theirs:

From 1870 until his death in 1900, the history of Fitz-Norman Washington was a long epic in gold. There were side issues, of course—he evaded the surveys, he married a Virginia lady, by whom he had a single son, and he was compelled, due to a series of unfortunate complications, to murder his brother, whose unfortunate habit of drinking himself into an indiscreet stupor had several times endangered their safety. But very few other murders stained these happy years of progress and expansion. (158)

At the time of Fitz-Norman's death, the Washington family fortune is in the hands of his son, the symbol of the phase of economic consolidation that follows exploitation. Though essentially a caretaker of the family's wealth, he is not qualitatively different from his father, as is signified by his name, Braddock Tarleton Washington. Both General Edward Braddock (1695–1755) and Sir Banastre Tarleton (1754–1833) have gone down in history as unsavory characters, with Tarleton remembered for the barbarism of his military campaigns in the South and Braddock for his "obstinacy and arrogance" during the French and Indian War. Even the surname Washington takes on a negative cast, as one recalls that the first president was in fact "a Southern, slave-owning plantation owner" and thus "at least implicated in proprietary interests."[84] And the fact that the good name of Washington has come to be associated with the callous and arrogant Braddock underscores Fitzgerald's keen sense of the irony underlying the historical perspective. Much as George Washington's proprietary impulses have been conveniently forgotten by history, so too Braddock Washington's realization of the American Dream, his acquisition of literally immeasurable wealth, has turned from something admirable into something reprehensible: "By his own super-American success, Braddock Washington has paradoxically turned himself into an enemy of America."[85] That he bribed the American government, killed American pilots, and even rerouted an American river does not change the fact that Braddock Washington was simply doing what he felt he had to do to protect the American Dream, including the economic interests of "all the property-holders in the world" (159). No wonder Fitzgerald seems to feel a grudging admiration for this monster.[86] If the attainment of the American Dream was proving to be disillusioning for Fitzgerald and for those of his generation, that still did not negate its attractiveness, its capacity to symbolize achievement.

The cultivation of a broad sense of history had the potential to serve as a source of stability during times of personal and national chaos, but it also, as in the case of the Washingtons, had the capacity to illustrate how badly admirable dreams could deteriorate, could even become inverted, with the passage of time. History was, then, of mixed effectiveness in helping one to understand America in the twentieth century, so Fitzgerald turned instinctively to another element which, if it did not always help us to understand our world, theoretically enabled us to tolerate it: a sense of home. Home in this context is used to mean any number of matters, including one's hometown (or regional or national origins), one's house of birth or childhood, or one's household in adulthood. In its many forms, the idea of home appealed strongly to Fitzgerald, early and late; but even in his earliest fictional efforts he recognized (as he did with the historical perspective) that there was a downside to the concept of home. Though ostensibly a source of security and stability, an anchorage from which one could launch ambitious dreams and to which one could return should they fail, the home could also be a source of anger, frustration, and lifelong psychic damage.

F. Scott Fitzgerald literally had no home. When in St. Paul, young Fitzgerald, his sister, and his parents lived in a succession of increasingly humble rented homes, usually moving each year. Indeed, though Fitzgerald was born at 481 Laurel Avenue, it is another house, at 599 Summit Avenue, that has been designated a National Historic Landmark, since he happened to be living there at the time he completed *This Side of Paradise*. Though these houses had always been within the limits of St. Paul, the city itself had not been a source of stability to the young Fitzgerald, for in fact he spent little of his childhood there. Though born in St. Paul (1896), at age one-and-a-half he moved with his family to Buffalo (1898) and then to Syracuse (1901) before moving back to Buffalo (1903) and eventually back to St. Paul (1908), a city that he rejected for both its cold weather (which he found intolerable) and its provinciality. No wonder he listed Buffalo as his own place of birth on daughter Scottie's birth certificate.[87] His schooling and young manhood also took him away from Minnesota. He prepped at the Newman School in Hackensack, New Jersey, and then attended Princeton for several years, followed by army stints in Kansas, Long Island, Kentucky, and Alabama, where he met Zelda. After the wedding, they immediately moved into New York's Biltmore Hotel, and from there to the Commodore; soon they rented a house in Westport, Connecticut, but restlessly took a motor trip to Alabama in the summer of 1920. (Their somewhat embellished adventures are recorded in a series of essays entitled "The Cruise of the Rolling Junk.") They then made the first of several trips to Europe with the unfulfilled intention of settling there, staying for various periods in Italy, England, and France. The record of their homes throughout their married life is exhausting: a series of rented houses (at the White Bear Yacht Club in Minnesota; "Ellerslie," an estate in Delaware; "La Paix," another estate in Maryland); rented villas and apartments in France; and a succession of different asylums in Europe and the United States for Zelda. Even when he returned to Hollywood in 1937 (after two earlier stays in early 1927 and late 1931), Fitzgerald lived in a series of apartments and died in yet another, the one rented by Sheilah Graham. The pattern of homelessness that characterized his life was well established by the time he wrote his first two collections of short fiction; and, not surprisingly, Fitzgerald seems to have had little understanding of what a home and family are really like. He apparently was not close to his parents or his sister at any point in his life,[88] and Zelda's family life was likewise far from ideal. Too much younger than her siblings to form close bonds with them, Zelda was alternately spoiled by her mother (who suckled her until the age of four) and bullied by her father, a workaholic judge who insisted on renting his homes to avoid the indebtedness of a mortgage and who is rumored to have once chased Zelda around the table, knife in hand, during a family dinner.[89] As happens so often with individuals who themselves have had little exposure to a normal, secure home life and a positive family circle, Fitzgerald placed great emphasis on the importance of home. But because he had had no first-hand experience of it, that emphasis assumed two antithetical forms: (1) homes are presented in sentimental, even melodramatic terms, or (2) they are posited as sources of relentless misery.

The sentimental approach is particularly evident in "The Lees of Happiness," written in July 1920, just a few months after his Easter wedding. As Kenneth Eble suggests, the Curtains are much like the Fitzgeralds.[90] The newlywed husband, Jeffrey, is a magazine writer and the author of "a novel or two" (275); his wife, Roxanne, is a fashionably attired media darling; and their early married life, not unlike the Fitzgeralds', is spent living in a series of glamorous hotels from "California, to Alaska, to Florida, to Mexico" (277). But the three-months-married Fitzgerald, already rather gushy in his presentation of the newlywed Curtains ("She loved the swift tones of his voice and his frantic, unfounded jealousy. He loved her dark radiance, the white irises of her eyes, the warm, lustrous enthusiasm of her smile" [227]), can only imagine what a marriage would be like after the first year—and his imagination at this early stage was inclined toward the sickly sentimental. The Curtains "tired of hotels" (277), unlike the Fitzgeralds, and thus settled down in suburbia: "They bought an old house and twenty acres near the town of Marlowe, half an hour from Chicago" and dreamed of making home improvements that would reflect their happy marriage and Jeffrey's burgeoning career—a nursery, a sleeping porch, and a "writing-room" for Jeffrey to be constructed out of the garage (277–78). Fitzgerald even introduces a foil couple, Harry and Kitty Cromwell, whose miserable existence in a dirty pink Chicago apartment underscores how utterly peachy is the marriage of the Curtains. One can well imagine that Fitzgerald himself hoped that his own married life with Zelda, a twelve-week-old relationship that already was making it almost impossible for him to write, would somehow resolve itself into a quiet, productive existence in a suburb of Middle America. But Fitzgerald must also have seen that such domestic bliss was a pipedream. He hated the prosaic Midwest, and by temperament he was attracted to large cities rather than suburbs. What we have in "The Lees of Happiness" thus seems to be a kind of fantasy marriage turned inside out: it reflects the bliss that he wanted to achieve in his own marriage while simultaneously arguing its impossibility.

Consider the presentation of Roxanne. With Jeffrey felled by a stroke, poor Roxanne changes from a flighty "little girl" (280) into Wonderwife. For example, she learns to cook. She had tried early in the marriage to bake biscuits ("I think every woman should know how to make biscuits. It sounds so utterly disarming" [278]), but the results had been so disastrous that Jeffrey had literally nailed the biscuits one by one on the wall of his library.[91] Yet adversity brings out the domestic best in her. Forced to dismiss the servants to conserve funds, Roxanne does indeed learn to prepare edible food, just as she learns to handle money and negotiate with Jeffrey's publishers. Why, she even teaches herself to ice skate so as to get to the drugstore for Jeffrey's medicine during those nasty Midwestern winters (294). Unfortunately it all sounds ridiculous, and one can readily forgive Edmund Wilson for originally believing that "The Lees of Happiness" was a parody.[92] But Fitzgerald is quite serious in his presentation of Roxanne as Wonderwife, and that includes her absolute fidelity to Jeffrey. Though an attractive and admired young woman, Roxanne dutifully fends off all suitors. And after Jeffrey's death, she resolves to live a nun-like existence, rejecting even Harry, whom Jeffrey himself had known was a Real Nice Guy. Roxanne is thus an inadvertently comic, sentimentalized rendering of a wife who literally wants to shake Kitty Cromwell (who, like Zelda and Gloria Patch, lets laundry pile up around the house) for complaining about wifely duties (288). But in creating the Wonderwife Roxanne, the newly married Fitzgerald may in part have been driving home the point that Zelda was not like Roxanne—and probably never could be.

Cooking was hardly of interest to Zelda. One of the charms of living at 38 West 59th Street, New York, in the fall of 1920 was that the Fitzgeralds could send out for their meals at the nearby Plaza Hotel, and years later, when they were living at Ellerslie in Delaware, there literally was not sufficient food available even to make a sandwich.[93] Similarly, the free-spending Zelda never comprehended money, and even late in life maintained a childlike belief that there would always be plenty; indeed, the business end of writing, even when it involved her work alone, she left entirely to her husband. And far from being eternally faithful to Fitzgerald, Zelda flirted openly with her husband's friends soon after their wedding.[94] No one knew better than Fitzgerald that Zelda was a non-domesticated flapper when he married her, but the comically overblown depiction of Roxanne Curtain may suggest that, only three months after the wedding, he was already fantasizing about the kind of devoted, domestic wife he wished he had.

His disillusionment with his married home life would also help explain the immediate source of the Curtains' tragedy. As so often happens in Fitzgerald's early fiction, the imaginative projection of himself, the writer-husband, falls from grace. But instead of simply being reduced to a circus acrobat à la Horace Tarbox, Jeffrey Curtain is felled by a massive stroke, reduced to a vegetative existence for eleven years, and then killed off. At first glance it appears that this is yet another reflection of Fitzgerald's fear that fate/destiny/life might cut short his career as a writer, but the situation is more complex than this. For Jeffrey's work as a writer was essentially entertainment: "Here were no master-pieces—here were passably amusing stories, a bit out of date now, but doubtless the sort that would then have whiled away a dreary half hour in a dental office. The man who did them was of good intelligence, talented, glib, probably young. In the samples of his work you found there would have been nothing to stir you to more than a faint interest in the whims of life—no deep interior laughs, no sense of futility or hint of tragedy" (275). Fitzgerald's contempt for Jeffrey is palpable, and the implication is that the world of literature has suffered no great loss in Jeffrey's untimely demise. Fitzgerald did not need hostile critics to perform autopsies on his career, for it would appear that in "The Lees of Happiness" he was taking stock of his own achievement as of mid-1920 and realizing that he too had yet to produce anything of permanent literary value, that if he became incapacitated or died within the first year of marriage he would have as little to show for his efforts as Jeffrey. Hence Fitzgerald's decision to reduce Jeffrey to a comatose state for eleven years rather than kill him off immediately. To spend more than a decade as a vegetable would be, to a writer, no worse than spending that time producing worthless fiction. Jeffrey's coma may thus be seen as an emblem of non-productivity as well as a kind of punishment for his previous mediocrity as a writer. But at the same time it cannot be overlooked that Jeffrey's coma coincides almost exactly with his marriage. However much Fitzgerald may be transforming Roxanne into Wonderwife, there still seems to be an implied connection between being married and turning into a vegetative non-writer, a connection not fully obscured by the deflection of our attention away from the obvious problem (marriage) and onto a more neutral agent (a faulty blood vessel).

The implication that marriage itself is destructive—that a marriage can be "happy" if one spouse (read "the husband") happens to be comatose or dead—is a chilling statement coming from a newlywed; and in fact most of the marriages and households Fitzgerald depicts in his early fiction are quite unappealing. And not surprisingly, most parent/child relationships Fitzgerald depicts are very negative. In "'O Russet Witch!'" Merlin Grainger essentially forced himself to marry Olive Masters in an attempt to deny the power of dreams and sexuality embodied in Caroline. That her initial arrival at the Moonlight Quill occurs on a dark, stormy day "threatening rain and the end of the world" (237) argues that what she represents is potentially destructive, but Merlin's drab courtship and marriage with Olive hardly seems like a pleasant alternative. Their apartment is as limited as Merlin's life as a husband, and it is not surprising that his son Arthur, whose twentieth-century career selling bonds is a far cry from the career of his namesake, treats his father with scorn: "'Let him sit quiet,' growled

Arthur. 'If you encourage him he'll tell us a story we've heard a hundred times before'" (272). Even "The Diamond as Big as the Ritz," though usually examined as a tale of the American Dream, is a story about households. We barely see one of the few happy families in the Fitzgerald canon, the Ungers of Hades; instead, the focus is squarely on the Washingtons. Their diamond mountain is the House of Washington much as the House of Usher reflects the family which lives within it, an identification that is insistently negative. The very hospitality of the Washingtons is insidious: the chair in which John sits seems "to engulf and overpower him" (151–52), the black servants who undress and bathe him seem to be disconcertingly forward (an impression confirmed by their later role as executioners), and even the diamond room that John visits ("it dazzled the eyes with a whiteness that could be compared only with itself" [151]) seems about as homey as the glittering prison of the lightbulb-lined room of Ralph Ellison's *Invisible Man*. The Washington children have little interaction with their parents (Mrs. Washington literally ignores her daughters [170]), and in retrospect it is not surprising that Percy had muttered a "taciturn 'We're home'" (150) when he had first arrived there with John.

Other stories in *Tales of the Jazz Age* likewise reflect this sense of homes as either non-existent or miserable. In "May Day," George Key has no interest in his brother Carrol and literally does not realize he has been serving overseas (80); even the whiskey he supplies him, far from being a welcome-home gift, must be purchased (81). In a more extreme case, in "Jemina" the heroine's family and home are sources of her destruction. The feud between the Tantrum and the Doldrum families has been going on for generations. Jemina herself is thus in no way responsible for it, but because she is a Tantrum she is killed, while her home, far from protecting her, serves as a trap in which she burns to death. Even the household in the playlet "Mr. Icky" is a source of unhappiness and death. Mr. Icky's typist daughter Ulsa leaves him to marry wealthy Londoner Rodney Divine, while his son Charles, a rope on his shoulder and an anchor around his neck, goes to sea declaring, "I can't stay here and rot with you. I want to live my life" (307). As Mr. Icky's "several dozen" other children abandon him, he is left alone on stage to die, gradually being buried under thousands of gray and white moths (310). Whether from ungrateful offspring, cruel fathers, or nagging, dull wives, virtually all of the households and families in Fitzgerald's early fiction are unhappy. No wonder the houses themselves do not fare well. The Washingtons' home is blown up, while the Curtains' house, that emblem of their life together, deteriorates visibly: "After a while the coat of clean white paint on the Jeffrey Curtain house made a definite compromise with the suns of many Julys and showed its good faith by turning gray. It scaled—huge peelings of very brittle old paint leaned over backward like aged men practising grotesque gymnastics and finally dropped to a moldy death in the overgrown grass beneath. The paint of the front pillars became streaky; the white ball was knocked off the left-hand door-post; the green blinds darkened, then lost all pretense of color" (293–94).

As sources of comfort, serenity, and psychological security, homes and family circles thus have little to offer Fitzgerald's earliest fictional characters. And because they fall so short of what one wishes they might be, they often ironically are sources of disillusionment, not unlike history itself, often failing its potential to comfort. One story in *Tales of the Jazz Age* which illustrates how dreams and disillusionment, the historical sense, and home interact is "The Jelly-Bean." Written in May 1920, it is one of Fitzgerald's so-called Tarleton stories. In fact, it uses some of the same characters as "The Ice Palace," but despite some similarities, the two stories are qualitatively different. In particular Fitzgerald keeps "The Jelly-Bean" firmly within the South, not just geographically but historically, for it records what happens when the "New South" clashes with the Old South of romance.

Jim Powell, the story's titular hero, is in fact an antihero who embodies what was left of the archetypal southern gentleman by 1920. He was born "in a white house" with "pillars in front and a great amount of lattice-work in the rear that made a cheerful criss-cross background for a flowery sun-drenched lawn" (4). The brief description of the symbolic home connotes purity, strength, abundance, fecundity, brightness—qualities evidently associated with the now-powerless Powell family in the past, but which have no relationship to the shiftless Jim. The deterioration of the Powell family and home had been going on for years: "Originally the dwellers in the white house had owned the ground next door and next door to that and next door to that, ... " but by the era of Jim's father (killed ignominiously in a brawl) the proud homestead had shrunk to the single lot, and Jim himself had known it only as a boardinghouse in which he was raised by a "tight-lipped lady from Macon," Aunt Mamie (4). By the time the story opens, the shrinking process has run its course. The symbolic family home has been sold; the money acquired from the sale is rapidly dwindling as it pays for Aunt Mamie's residence in an insane asylum; and Jim's current "home" is a bleak little room over Tilly's garage, a room for which he does not pay. The fall of the House of Powell is virtually complete.

The decline of his family is reflected not only in the systematic reduction of Jim's home, but also in his physical appearance and daily activities. Jim looks emaciated, sickly: he is "long and thin and bent at the waist from stooping over pool-tables" (3), and his blue eyes are "faded" like (significantly) "very good old cloth long exposed to the sun" (5). The old family which once was itself "very good" now consists of a crazy old lady and the town loafer; like the cloth, the Powells have had their day in the sun. Jim's lack of physical strength and color is reflected in his drab, unsubstantial lifestyle. As the unsympathetic first-person narrator explains, a "jelly-bean" is "one who spends his life conjugating the verb to idle in the first person singular—I am idling, I have idled, I will idle" (3–4). His only real occupation and source of income is gambling, shooting craps—a reliance upon luck which is a far cry from the Protestant work ethic that made possible the establishment of the great plantation-based families, like the Powells, of the Old South.

The passion for gambling is something Jim shares with Nancy Lamar, a woman who, in her way, is as much a jelly-bean as Jim. Her primary source of income is her father, the local doctor; she spends most of her time riding about in roadsters and gambling; and consequently she would seem to be ideally suited to the equally shiftless Jim, with whom she enters into a kind of bizarre courtship.

The courtship is short-lived (less than twenty-four hours), and it is handled with an irony that verges on open mockery. It begins, unromantically enough, at Soda Sam's, where Jim says hello to Nancy, a woman he has not seen for fifteen years. Destined to see her again that night at a country club dance, Jim, who may or may not be aware of her reputation as a gambler, begins to sing to himself:

> Her Jelly Roll can twist your soul,
> Her eyes are big and brown,
> She's the Queen of the Queens of the Jelly-beans—
> My Jeanne of Jelly-bean Town. (7)

It is clear from the stanza that Jim sings earlier in the tale that "Jeanne, the Jelly-bean Queen" is a crapshooter: "She loves her dice and treats 'em nice" (6), and, as such, the stanzas have personal implications for Nancy. Since she is associated with royalty (she moves through Tarleton in a kind of royal progress, "taking an orange as tithe from a worshipful fruit-dealer" [12]), Nancy is literally Tarleton's "Jelly-bean Queen"—that is, she is both fundamentally lazy and a gambler. Further, Jim perceives her in sexual terms: "Jelly Roll" is slang for female genitalia, and it does indeed "twist" Jim's "soul" as he realizes she will probably marry Ogden Merritt, the safety-razor heir whom Jim reduces to his fashionable white trousers (11). The undercurrent of sexuality in the relationship between Jim and Nancy becomes blatant in the scene at the country club dance wherein Jim attempts to help her remove gum from her shoe by using gasoline drained from parked cars:

> He turned the spout; a dripping began.
> "More!"
> He turned it on fuller. The dripping became a flow and formed an oily pool that glistened brightly, reflecting a dozen tremulous moons on its quivering bosom.
> "Ah," she sighed contentedly, "let it all out. The only thing to do is to wade in it."
> In desperation he turned on the tap full and the pool suddenly widened sending tiny rivers and trickles in all directions.

"That's fine. That's something like."
Raising her skirts she stepped gracefully in.
"I know this'll take it off," she murmured.
Jim smiled.
"There's lots more cars." (14)

In true knightly fashion, Jim is aiding a damsel in distress—the kind of behavior one would expect of a gentleman of the Old South, which was weaned on the novels of Sir Walter Scott.[95] The same courtly behavior is seen in Jim's rescue of Nancy at the postdance crap game wherein he gallantly inquires, "May I—can't you let me roll 'em for you?" (20) After the passionate scene in the parking lot and the chivalrous rescue at the craps table, Nancy is sufficiently grateful to Jim to announce what is, in effect, their engagement: "Ladies and gentlemen, Nancy Lamar, famous dark-haired beauty often featured in the *Herald* as one th' most popular members of the younger set as other girls are often featured in this particular case. Wish to announce—wish to announce, anyway, Gentlemen—" (21). Nancy could not be more explicit ("—I *love* him" [21]); and in keeping with the expectations of a love story, an aubade scene follows: as a rooster crows, Jim and Nancy kiss, and she departs.

Thanks to Nancy, Jim is inspired with a dream: he will abandon his jelly-bean ways and consciously discontinue being "weak and wobbly like" (24). His dreams of personal and financial improvement hinge on what's left of the family home: "Been thinkin' of goin' up on the farm, and takin' a little that work off Uncle Dun. Reckin I been bummin' too long." After Aunt Mamie dies, he will take what little family money is left, invest it in the old homestead, and "make somethin' out of it. All my people originally came from that part up there. Had a big place." Meanwhile, he realizes that he can and must cease to be the jelly-bean of Tarleton immediately: "So I'm through. I'm goin' to-day. And when I come back to this town it's going to be like a gentleman" (24). But Jim's dream, his attempt to enter into the historical moment of the New South rather than cling pathetically to the remnants of the Old, is shattered in an instant: he learns that Nancy, the Golden Girl, has eloped with Ogden Merritt.

Jim's dream-inspiring courtship of Nancy Lamar had meant nothing to her. The scene in the moonlit country club parking lot may sound romantic out of context, but it was intended not to foster love but to scrape gum off her shoe. The damsel in distress is no damsel (Nancy has "scars all over her reputation" [11]), and Jim's "rescue" of Nancy at the crap game is actually his attempt to avert her possible arrest on a bad-check charge. Likewise, the "engagement announcement" is the joke of a drunk, and the aubade scene (coming after a night of draining gas tanks instead of making love) ends with her riding off into the sunrise with another man. Their courtship was thus a mockery, as once again a male character has foolishly invested all his emotions and dreams in an unworthy woman. And what makes the situation even more pathetic is that Nancy took advantage of his Old Southern remnants of courtliness to get him to help her. She resurrects Old Southern qualities which, within the context of the New South, make him a patsy, a pathetic victim of anyone who can even seem to reflect the romantic era in which the Powell family had flourished. Unable to return to the Old South, all Jim has left are some meaningless courtly impulses that make him seem almost effeminate. Even his body language at the dance is that of a wallflower, a role traditionally assumed by women ("Jim, unmolested, . . . was to view the spectacle from a secluded settee in the corner where Clark [Darrow, the young man who invited him to the dance] would join him whenever he wasn't dancing" [9]). But Jim does not have the capacity to join in the current historical moment, the New South, in which tough-talking, dark-eyed women like Nancy seem far more aggressive and masculine than most men, especially those whose identities are tied to the Old South. No wonder Nancy marries a manufacturer of razor blades, devices traditionally utilized for symbolic emasculation, and no wonder either that her last name is Lamar, a *corruption* of "l'amour." Totally disillusioned, Jim performs his one aggressive act in the story: his fingers slightly dent Clark's car from pressing on it (25). As his dreams die, Jim feels "something was going on inside him, some inexplicable but almost chemical change" (26), and he lapses back into the life of a jelly bean, his home a room over Tilly's garage. It is not, as Piper suggests, that Jim embodies "the best and worst qualities of the Old South"[96] but that the best qualities of the Old South leave him vulnerable, and hence readily disillusioned, in the New. Caught between two historical moments, Jim cannot maintain his dreams any more than he can maintain what little is left of the family home.

"The Jelly-Bean" is a good story, well-crafted, thoughtful, and perceptive. So too are "The Diamond as Big as the Ritz" and "May Day." But the eight other stories in *Tales of the Jazz Age* are either uneven (e.g., "The Lees of Happiness," "'O Russet Witch!'"), too sophomoric to be included in any worthwhile collection, or not short stories at all. With his next collection, *All the Sad Young Men,* Fitzgerald would finally be hitting his stride as a major American writer of short fiction.

3

All the Sad Young Men

The F. Scott Fitzgerald who published *All the Sad Young Men* on 26 February 1926 was strikingly different from the one who had published *Tales of the Jazz Age* in the fall of 1922. Though the pace of Fitzgerald's life had always seemed more accelerated than most, including instantaneous fame with his first novel in 1920, the three-and-a-half years between the appearances of his second and third collections of stories featured a crowding of events and a litany of crises that were unusual even for him. Having devoted many months of intensive work and worry to it in 1922–23, it was clear by late 1923 that his play *The Vegetable* was a resounding failure. Worse, it had intensified his financial difficulties. Frantic over the loss of the funds he had invested in the play and the debts he had incurred to Scribners during the months of its preparation, Fitzgerald immediately repaired to the garage over his rented house in Great Neck, Long Island, and, subsisting on endless pots of coffee, managed to produce in rapid succession at least ten short stories, including one, "The Baby Party," that was written literally overnight.[1] True to form, when the immediate financial crisis seemed well in hand, the three peripatetic Fitzgeralds left for Europe in mid-April 1924, where they would remain, moving from villa to apartment to hotel, until December 1926. In part due to the repeated moves, the extended stay in Europe did not bring Fitzgerald the peace that he desperately needed at this stage of his life and career. Though he was able to work on *The Great Gatsby,* he also had to deal with the first major rift in his already foundering marriage, Zelda's involvement with French aviator Edouard Jozan in the summer of 1924. The actual seriousness of the Jozan affair need not concern us here, and in fact the relationship probably was not even consummated.[2] What matters is that Fitzgerald himself, never entirely secure in his own sexuality, was badly shaken by it. Further, in retrospect it was the first concrete indication that Zelda's increasingly troubled state could not be dismissed simply as the residue of a spoiled childhood or the restlessness of a bored housewife; there was something radically amiss not only in the Fitzgeralds' marriage, but in Zelda herself. Once the Fitzgeralds returned to the United States, Zelda would take up the study of ballet; but what she perceived as an outlet for her creativity and unusual level of energy, and what her husband hoped would keep her occupied harmlessly while he pursued his career, would turn into an obsession destined to contribute to Zelda's first nervous breakdown in April 1930. Her mental illness would be the central issue in Fitzgerald's life in the 1930s, and its impact upon his work and outlook is everywhere evident in his final collection of stories, *Taps at Reveille* (1935). In the early and mid-1920s, however, Zelda's emotional impairment was obscured by a series of physical ailments which may well have been psychosomatic in origin, and it is indicative of the conditions under which Fitzgerald wrote and revised the stories of *All the Sad Young Men* that Zelda's appendectomy in the summer of 1926 made her seem well "for the first time in a year and a half."[3] Considering that these stories were written by a frankly autobiographical author trying to deal with his wife's infidelity and ill health, apparently chronic debt, and the creative blow of the failure of *The Vegetable,* one can only stand amazed at the lack of bitterness in *All the Sad Young Men.*

And yet, that lack points to an increasingly important factor in the evolution of Fitzgerald's mind and art. Though often inclined toward melodramatic pessimism, especially when in his cups, Fitzgerald by temperament was quite sanguine; and if in his youth this quality sometimes led to an ingenuous cockiness, by the mid-1920s he was able to draw upon it so as to formulate a strategy for survival: he quickly came to perceive the crises which befell him after the fall of 1923 as conducive to personal and professional growth. In August 1924 he wrote to Ludlow Fowler that "I feel old too, this summer—I have ever since the failure of my play a year ago,"[4] and though this sense of aging reflects Fitzgerald's acute disappointment and chronic distress, it reflects more importantly a growing feeling of maturity—an important change of attitude in a man who once vowed to commit suicide rather than face middle age.[5] Consider the letter he wrote to Maxwell Perkins in the same month he wrote Fowler: "Its been a fair summer. I've been unhappy but my work hasn't suffered from it. I am grown at last."[6] His primary work during those months was, of course, *Gatsby,* an artistic breakthrough which clearly coincided with Fitzgerald's emotional breakthrough—his recognition, nurtured by personal and professional crises, that maturity can be a positive entity, that it is qualitatively different from simple aging, and that it is conducive, indeed vital, to one's growth and development as a writer. And his work as an author was clearly essential to Fitzgerald: his letter to Perkins stresses his relief at being able to function as a creative writer despite his unhappiness, and by this stage he was beginning to recognize that his work was in fact a refuge from a troubled personal life, something he could control and in which he could immerse himself, be it in a Long Island garage or a French villa, when his private life was most intolerable. But far more importantly, it was a means of truly coming to grips with that life. No longer content simply to exploit the bare facts of his existence (as he had done in *This*

Side of Paradise and *The Beautiful and Damned*) or to deny their implications by reducing them to farce (witness 1919's "Head and Shoulders"), Fitzgerald by early 1924 seems to have been using his writing to try to understand his increasingly troubled life, and in particular his marriage: where Zelda would have her psychiatrists, Fitzgerald would have his writing as the medium through which to face a barrage of increasingly challenging personal and professional crises. Of course, he had always valued his work as a source of income and fame and would certainly continue to do so; but in his new-found maturity Fitzgerald was acquiring a kind of reverence for his stories—or, at least, for the ones that he regarded as worthy of preservation. For it was during this juncture that he began to compartmentalize his writings, to dismiss some as "junk" or "trash," and to see others as the work of "a pure artist."[7] The latter stories were the ones he chose to preserve in the two last authorized collections, with the others either "stripped and junked," with usable passages worked into other stories, or left to be forgotten in the magazines in which they first appeared, or—what is perhaps the most painful thing for a writer to accept—never published at all. Some, indeed, have not been published to this day.

It was this more mature, more discriminating Fitzgerald who selected, revised, and arranged the nine stories of *All the Sad Young Men,* and he approached his task with the confidence (not cockiness) and the care (not fussiness) that were so palpably lacking in *Tales of the Jazz Age.* As we have seen, Fitzgerald had approached that second collection with the gusto of a showman confident of dazzling his "own personal public" while wowing the toughest critics in America. The endless title changes and frankly imprudent selection of material suggest more enthusiasm than good judgment, but a cooler head had prevailed with *All the Sad Young Men.* It was, after all, the companion volume to *Gatsby,* the masterpiece in which Fitzgerald never lost faith despite its disappointing sales; and John Peale Bishop's post-*Gatsby* exhortation—"For God's sake take your new place seriously"[8]—seems to have been in perfect keeping with Fitzgerald's increasing sense of vocation in the mid-1920s.

That mature attitude is evident in the very selection of stories for his third collection. After the fiasco of *The Vegetable,* Fitzgerald had produced at least ten stories, and there were over a dozen more tales written after 1920 which had not yet been reprinted in collections. But he selected just nine for *All the Sad Young Men,* making it not only a physically slimmer volume than *Tales of the Jazz Age,* but one that is not so visibly padded: there are no playlets in the third collection, and no apprentice fiction. There seems to have been little question as to which stories to include, with "Absolution" being substituted for "Dice, Brass Knuckles, & Guitar" quite early in the prepublication stage, in the summer of 1925.[9] Further, no one story seems to have been intended to carry the volume. "The Rich Boy," though long enough to necessitate the postponement of the volume's publication,[10] is not much shorter than the novella "May Day," but Fitzgerald seems not to have been relying on this one story to take up the bulk of the collection. Similarly, there are no apologetic prefaces in the austere table of contents, and no effort has been made to arrange the stories in meaningful units, as was the intention in *Tales of the Jazz Age*. Even the title was clear from the outset, with only "Dear Money" considered momentarily as a possible alternative.[11] The only visible fretting over the collection, aside from Fitzgerald's customary meticulous revision of the magazine versions of the story texts, involved the author's photograph on the dust jacket (which Fitzgerald bemoaned as a "leering, puffy distortion")[12] and the volume's blurb. Fitzgerald had always been acutely sensitive about jacket blurbs, perceiving them early on as a means of self-promotion and a potentially lucrative mode of rekindling interest in his earlier books. But by the mid-1920s he had come to realize that they could be counterproductive in their insistence upon earlier achievements. When he prepared *The Great Gatsby* for publication, Fitzgerald actually insisted that he wanted no blurb at all, maintaining that "I'm tired of being the author of *This Side of Paradise* and I want to start over."[13] His changing stance regarding blurbs was likewise evident in his handling of *All the Sad Young Men*. In June 1925 Fitzgerald composed what he identified as "suggested line for jacket":

> Show transition from his early exuberant stories of youth which created a new type of American girl and the later and more serious mood which produced *The Great Gatsby* and marked him as one of the half dozen masters of English prose now writing in America. . . . What other writer has shown such unexpected developments, such versatility, changes of pace.[14]

The transition in his professional career that he had tried so unsuccessfully to convey in the "My Last Flappers" segment of *Tales of the Jazz Age* would, he hoped, be more obvious if identified in the blurb itself—that is, he would use the blurb to key the reader to ongoing trends rather than to cash in on past ones. But within six months Fitzgerald's growing artistic confidence led him to reconsider his position. In December he proposed the following to Max Perkins:

> I suggest somthing *very* simple like this for the announcement of the short stories. In my opinion the blurb has had its day.
>
> Scott Fitzgerald's new book
> All the Sad Young Men
> (containing THE RICH BOY)
> CHAS. SCRIBNERS[15]

The boyish need to call attention to his past fame, to point to the bulk and variety of his work as if they were proof of his productivity and talent, was falling away rapidly, and Fitzgerald was exceptionally well pleased with his third collection of short fiction. As early as March 1925 he was declaring to Perkins, "It ought to be awfully good and there will be no junk in it"; in May he termed it "an excellent collection."[16] He was correct, and the situation of *All the Sad Young Men* offers a good example of why critics should not always accept automatically Fitzgerald's estimates of his own work as the bases of their evaluations—and especially so when his estimates were made while in particular frames of mind. Looking back at the frantic winter of 1923–24, Fitzgerald wrote to Edmund Wilson, "I really worked hard as hell last winter—but it was all trash and it nearly broke my heart as well as my iron constitution."[17] Fitzgerald tended to write to "Bunny" Wilson when he was most depressed (or drunk) or most ebullient, and his letters to him are full of the kind of histrionic poses that creep so readily into letters to old friends. Such is the case with this letter, and one must not take literally the implication that every one of the stories written during this period, including "Hot and Cold Blood," "Gretchen's Forty Winks," and "The Baby Party," were just "trash" to their author. Indeed, in a less-known letter, Fitzgerald termed "The Baby Party" a "fine story,"[18] and the unjust critical neglect of this little gem can be explained only by critics taking too literally Fitzgerald's implied denigration of it. He was pleased with the story and the collection in general, and Perkins was likewise enthusiastic.

But it was characteristic of Fitzgerald's new attitude that he recognized that the unquestionable quality of the collection was no guarantee of either popular success or critical acclaim. Notably absent from his letters are smug predictions that it would make him rich for life—*The Vegetable* had cured him of that inclination—and his statements about the potential success of *All the Sad Young Men* were strikingly guarded. In October 1925 he remarked that the stories "probably won't sell 5,000" copies; by December the disappointing sales of *Gatsby* were such that Fitzgerald wrote to Perkins, "I hope the short stories sell seven or eight thousand or so"; and less than a week before its publication, he prayed that the volume would sell 10,000 copies so that he would be out of debt to Scribners for the first time since 1922.[19] Much to his pleasant surprise, *All the Sad Young Men* sold 16,170 copies in 1926, bringing him $3,894.[20] But more importantly, it was warmly received by the critics.

True, some critics made predictable jabs at the collection, citing most of the stories as "regulation magazine trade goods, capably executed, smoothly written, revealing a stroke here and there above prevalent mediocrity, but on the whole mere standardized products."[21] Such was the price Fitzgerald paid for having a career as a magazine writer, as critics seemed not to realize that the original texts had been revised heavily for publication in the collection. Other reviewers, knowing only too well the details of the Fitzgeralds' well-publicized extravagant lifestyle, argued that "one naturally feels, behind most of the writing in this book, the pressure of living conditions rather than the demand of the spirit."[22] But these negative responses were actually quite atypical. Most critics lauded *All the Sad Young Men* and were delighted—even relieved—that it seemed to fulfill the promise of *Gatsby* and boded well for Fitzgerald's future as a writer. The critic for the *New York World* spoke for many in declaring that, with these nine stories, "Mr. Fitzgerald has graduated from the jazz age"[23]—the very thing, of course, that he had been attempting to do in *Tales of the Jazz Age* several years earlier. Malcolm Cowley likewise recognized that the characters depicted in *All the Sad Young Men* were not the flappers and sheiks from whom Fitzgerald had been trying to disassociate himself since 1920. Most of the stories, observed Cowley, "describe the later adventures of characters like those he introduced in his earlier volumes. With the coming of years his flappers have learned to accept responsibility, and there are tiny wrinkles round their rosebud mouths. His jazz-age heroes, having succeeded in business, reflect upon their careers sorrowfully."[24] Cowley might have added that Fitzgerald's new orientation carefully omits the juvenile angst of "Bernice Bobs Her Hair," the glitzy fantasy of "The Diamond as Big as the Ritz," the farce of "The Offshore Pirate," and—at least one critic's comments notwithstanding[25]—the drunkenness of "The Camel's Back." As befits an author who was himself married, a father, and an established professional, Fitzgerald focuses for the most part on middle-class couples facing very real problems—not only those that are timeless and universal, but also those that had been generated by the loss of old values and the shifting of social roles during the Jazz Age. Fitzgerald was indeed "growing up, and letting his stories mark that growth. And that is as it should be."[26]

One consequence of that growing up, it would appear, is the onset of what Fitzgerald himself identifies as sadness. Most of Fitzgerald's contemporaries, taking their cue from the collection's title, cite a pervading melancholy in *All the Sad Young Men*. A few, especially those whose understanding of Fitzgerald owed far more to preconceived and outdated notions of his work than to the nine stories themselves, found this subdued note to be forced, even ludicrous:

> So long as Mr. Fitzgerald's young men make love and money with such confident facility, the wistful mantle which he throws over their shoulders somehow does not fit. There isn't room enough in all the high-powered roadsters nor upon all the polished dance floors for the requisite melancholy, and the author's endeavors to reconcile his people and their emotions serve but to make both appear artificial. By the time they are thirty, these young men are saturated with a weariness which Sherwood Anderson reserves for the middle forties.[27]

But most regarded the "wistful mantle" as quite fitting, and Cowley spoke for many of Fitzgerald's contemporaries in seeing the subdued quality as a new element in his fiction. It wasn't. There was sadness galore in "The Cut-Glass Bowl," "Benediction," "May Day," "The Curious Case of Benjamin Button," "The Jelly-Bean," and "The Lees of Happiness," but the initial unfortunate public perception of Fitzgerald as the chronicler of the more vapid aspects of flapperdom had tended to overshadow the serious stories which Fitzgerald had been writing literally from the outset of his career. But Cowley was correct in another regard: *All the Sad Young Men* was the first collection in which Fitzgerald's most sober efforts were not surrounded by farces like "The Offshore Pirate," "The Camel's Back," and "Jemina." The process of careful "winnowing"[28] which led Fitzgerald to select these nine stories out of some two dozen available to him involved a conscious effort on his part to present himself as a mature, serious writer of mature, serious fiction. Even the ostensible comedies of *All the Sad Young Men,* such as "Rags Martin-Jones and the Pr–nce of W–les," "The Baby Party," and "Gretchen's Forty Winks," are fundamentally tragicomic tales with far more depth than might be apparent from a cursory reading. The title *All the Sad Young Men* was clearly formulated with an eye to reader response, designed to guide the reader to look beyond, say, a toddler's party to broader, more serious—yes, even "sad"—questions of mortality and generativity.

Even so, "sad" was perhaps an unfortunate choice of word, since, as shall be seen, there are few genuinely sad young men in these stories. True, there appear to be an inordinate number of references to insanity and nervous breakdowns, but these tend to be fears rather than realities, and most of the young men in the collection fare rather well in their personal and professional lives—much better, in fact, than do Horace Tarbox, Gordon Sterrett, Benjamin Button, Merlin Grainger, Jim Powell, Jeffrey Curtain, or John T. Unger. The apparent overall improvement in the lot of Fitzgerald's male characters—and, quite strikingly, the concomitant worsening of the situation of the female characters—seems to reflect a pervasive process of deglorification, a more realistic understanding of the very elements—love, sex, and marriage; the self versus society; free will versus fate—which had so intimidated the earlier male characters as well as, one suspects, Fitzgerald himself. Having been jolted out of their youthful, romanticized notions about women, selfhood, and destiny, Fitzgerald's young men may well be what he himself vaguely terms "sad." But it is clear from studying the stories themselves that what they actually feel is something quite different. These are men who believe that they can exert some degree of control over their lives. For the most part, these are men at peace.

At first it may seem unreasonable to speak in terms of men in control, of men at peace in Fitzgerald's fiction, and especially so in regard to a volume with a title like *All the Sad Young Men.* After all, this is the collection most noted for the forlorn Anson Hunter, trying to sail away from his loveless life after the death in childbirth of Paula Legendre, and for Dexter Green, in tears in his Manhattan office after learning that Judy Jones is now a faded hausfrau. But although "The Rich Boy" and "Winter Dreams" are by far the best-known stories in *All the Sad Young Men,* they are but two of the nine tales, and unfortunately they provide a very skewed impression of what the rest of the collection is like. For the most part, *All the Sad Young Men* probes not men disappointed in love, like Anson and Dexter, but men coming to grips with marriage—not marriage as Fitzgerald learned of it from his reading of naturalistic fiction (see the Pipers in "The Cut-Glass Bowl") or imagined it during the last days of a troubled courtship (the Tarboxes in "Head and Shoulders"), but as he himself had experienced it. Published when the Fitzgeralds had been married nearly six years, *All the Sad Young Men* shows a man rethinking his earlier, almost ingenuous attitudes toward love, sex, and marriage while formulating strategies for dealing with his immediate situation and the years to come. And however unsuccessful Fitzgerald himself may have been in implementing those strategies, the male characters in the collection fare notably well. Where husbands are concerned, art had a distinct edge over life.

Certainly marriage to Zelda had palled rather quickly during those six years. It is true that the Fitzgeralds felt, and would always feel, that they were genuinely in love; but enough had happened to them in that short time to make Scott realize that marriage, especially to someone of Zelda's temperament, was far more a brutal testing of love than a perpetual indulgence of it. This is not to say that the affianced Fitzgerald had had no inkling of what was in store for him. Near the end of his life he wrote to his daughter Scottie:

> When I was your age I lived with a great dream. . . . Then the dream divided one day when I decided to marry your mother after all, even though I knew she was spoiled and meant no good to me. I was sorry immediately I had married her but, being patient in those days, made the best of it and got to love her in another way.[29]

As Milton Stern points out, this retrospective appraisal is not entirely fair, inasmuch as Fitzgerald himself entered into the excesses of the era at least as much as Zelda.[30] Further, the self-defensiveness of the letter is quite characteristic of Fitzgerald's personal writings after the diagnosis of his wife's mental illness in the early 1930s. But the fact remains that Fitzgerald did sense that Zelda would be a less than ideal wife even before he married her, and the ensuing years only confirmed the justice of his misgivings. It may well be that this confirmation, plus some fanciful ways of responding to it, underlie two little-known stories of *All the Sad Young Men*, "Gretchen's Forty Winks" and "The Adjuster."

As Scott Donaldson notes in *Fool for Love*, "the worst disillusionment of all awaited Fitzgerald's fictional *alter egos* who actually win the girl and then discover . . . that they have married creatures of exquisite irresponsibility and selfishness. For Fitzgerald as for Emily Dickinson, 'It was the Distance— / Was Savory—.'"[31] Exquisitely irresponsible and selfish Gretchen Halsey surely is, and increasingly so as "Gretchen's Forty Winks" progresses. But of primary interest is not Gretchen's rather tame and predictable straying from the norms of wifely conduct. Rather, it is the way in which Fitzgerald modernizes and ultimately inverts what one might term a fairy-tale norm of marriage. In many fairy tales, a handsome prince is forced to marry an old hag who, as it turns out, is actually a beautiful young princess. Marriage breaks the curse, and they live happily ever after. But in "Gretchen's Forty Winks," as in so many stories of *All the Sad Young Men,* a man discovers to his dismay that his princess is (in Donaldson's apt phrasing) a "creature" harboring qualities that can upset or even harm a husband: marriage curses a man, as it were. If their stories went no further, these would indeed be sad young men. But Fitzgerald adds a further twist to the inverted fairy tale: he gives the husband the capacity not simply to cope with the situation, but to gain the upper hand. In "Gretchen's Forty Winks," the husband's power is established through one of the most venerable devices in the fairy tale tradition: a potion.

The opening of "Gretchen's Forty Winks" gives no indication that this is the course the story will take. Fitzgerald's avoidance of the intrusive essayistic opening—a technique that causes such difficulties in "The Jelly-Bean" and "The Four Fists"—suggests a degree of confidence that the story can speak for itself. But more importantly, it suggests that Fitzgerald is sufficiently sensitive to reader response to be willing to establish—and then undercut—reader expectations. The story opens with Roger Halsey, an advertising executive, contemplating a snow sky from the porch of his suburban cottage. There is nothing particularly original about the opening, as the coming darkness and imminent winter do indeed portend a crisis in the Halseys' marriage. But what is striking is Fitzgerald's ability to draw the reader's attention away from the transparent symbolism to what is the true central concern of the story: the ways in which a man's career can alienate a weak wife, jeopardize his marriage—or lead to his total control over both. The story opens: "Snow before night, sure. Autumn was over. This, of course, raised the coal question and the Christmas question; but Roger Halsey, standing on his own front porch, assured the dead suburban sky that he hadn't time for worrying about the weather" (239). "The coal question and the Christmas question" are elements that initially suggest that Halsey's primary concern, his raison d'être, is to provide well for his family. That impression seems confirmed moments later when his wife Gretchen, "her voice...full of laughter," calls him to "come see baby" upstairs (239). The first page of the story thus offers an idyllic suburban scene, what with the concerned daddy, the adoring mommy, "the recurrent sound of small, venturing feet" upstairs, and the "red silk lamp" in the cozy living room (239). But the image of the romantic family circle is shattered immediately: Roger curses at being asked to see his own baby (240). This coarse note is quite unexpected, and the shock of it is enhanced by the layout of the text, which places "he swore softly" as a one-sentence paragraph at the top of the second page of the story: it is not what the reader expects to find upon turning the page. With the cursing of Roger, other elements in the story's opening—his nervous smoking, his "bulging portfolio" (239)—suddenly make sense: Roger's life revolves around his career, and apparently the providing of coal and Christmas presents for his wife and child are not the primary motives behind his obsession with his job. As with most workaholics, Roger's is a marriage in trouble.

Fitzgerald is quick to point the finger of blame at the wife. The seeming Madonna of the first page of the story turns out to be a "bright-colored, Titian-haired girl, vivid as a French rag doll" (240), and just about as sensitive. She is so unsympathetic to her husband, so out of touch with his dreams and emotional state, that she seems deliberately to antagonize him as he tries to explain the urgency of devoting the next six weeks to landing the Big Account. Batting her fawn eyes, smoking cigarettes, and interrupting him repeatedly, Gretchen has no interest in seeing her husband achieve success in his business. Even her ostensible reason for getting him to cut back on his work, the fear of his having a nervous breakdown, is shown to be fundamentally false, as she announces that—like a bored child waiting for Christmas—she would rather sleep than watch him work intensively for forty days: "It seems such a long time—when everybody else is always having fun. If I could only sleep for forty days" (248). When Roger does land the Garrod Shoe account after nearly driving himself to collapse, all his rag doll of a wife can say is, "Can I get a new dress?" (264). One might expect that the exhausted Roger would grow angry at this childishness, but in fact he seems not troubled in the least. Part of the reason is, as Donaldson points out, that Fitzgerald had not yet entirely lost his admiration for attractive flappers,[32] and in fact Roger was "still actively sensitive" to the beauty of Gretchen (240). But more importantly, in making a brilliant showing in his career, Roger has simultaneously defeated a rival for his wife's affections, the dashing George Tompkins.

Gretchen is visibly smitten by Tompkins, an interior decorator who invites the Halseys to dinner at his home, full of such macho gewgaws as ship models and Colonial whiskey bottles (244). "I love this house" (244) coos Gretchen, as in fact she adores the attentive Tompkins, whose personal life is a 1920s model of orderliness that would do Ben Franklin—or George Babbitt—proud:

> "Well, in the morning I get up and go through a series of exercises. I've got one room fitted up as a little gymnasium, and I punch the bag and do shadow-boxing and weight-pulling for an hour. Then after a cold bath—There's a thing now! Do you take a daily cold bath?"
>
> "No," admitted Roger, "I take a hot bath in the evening three or four times a week."
>
> A horrified silence fell. Tompkins and Gretchen exchanged a glance as if something obscene had been said.
>
> "What's the matter?" broke out Roger, glancing from one to the other in some irritation. "You know I don't take a bath every day—I haven't got the time."
>
> Tompkins gave a prolonged sigh.

"After my bath," he continued, drawing a merciful veil of silence over the matter, "I have breakfast and drive to my office in New York, where I work until four. Then I lay off, and if it's summer I hurry out here for nine holes of golf, or if it's winter I play squash for an hour at my club. Then a good snappy game of bridge until dinner. Dinner is liable to have something to do with business, but in a pleasant way. . . . Or maybe I sit down with a good book of poetry and spend the evening alone. At any rate, I do something every night to get me out of myself." (245–46)

Apparently one way that Tompkins "gets out of himself" is to chase Gretchen, and as a new woman of the post-World War I era she is quite blunt about their cozy but as yet unconsummated liaison, blithely reporting to her husband their happy hours of horseback riding and skiing. But when Gretchen puts a picture of Tompkins "in an expensive frame" on the Halseys' bedroom wall (249–50), it has become clear that she is increasingly receptive to the idea of her escort becoming her lover, of his literally assuming her husband's sexual role. Certainly the Halseys' conjugal relations have not been good: "At twelve there was always an argument as to whether he would come to bed. He would agree to come after he had cleared up everything; but as he was invariably sidetracked by half a dozen new ideas, he usually found Gretchen sound asleep when he tiptoed up-stairs" (249). Tompkins is increasingly willing to fill this conjugal void, and a sexual tug-of-war rapidly ensues between the two men, with Gretchen as the prize.

About all Roger can fight back with is career success, but that can be attained only through the intensive work that alienates the restless and sexually deprived Gretchen. But knowing that it is his only hope, Roger deliberately risks intensifying the vicious cycle, embarking upon a daily schedule that is even more work-oriented, more unlike that of Tompkins, than ever before:

From eight until 5.30 he was in his office. Then a half-hour on the commuting train, where he scrawled notes on the backs of envelopes under the dull yellow light. By 7.30 his crayons, shears, and sheets of white cardboard were spread over the living-room table, and he labored there with much grunting and sighing until midnight.

After the customary midnight argument with Gretchen, Roger would return to his labors:

Sometimes it was three o'clock before Roger squashed his last cigarette into the overloaded ashtray, and he would undress in the darkness, disembodied with fatigue, but with a sense of triumph that he had lasted out another day. (249)

Predictably, this more complete immersion in his work drives his wife to her most explicit act of sexual retaliation yet: she has a date with Tompkins in the Halseys' home. As Gretchen and Tompkins enjoy their tête-à-tête in the living room, Roger repairs, appropriately enough, to their bedroom, where he tries to

immerse himself in the advertising accounts that, if successful, would win his
wife back from the sexual rival:

> When Roger had spread out his materials on the bed up-stairs he found that he could still
> hear the rumble and murmur of their voices through the thin floor. He began wondering what
> they found to talk about. As he plunged deeper into his work his mind had a tendency to revert
> sharply to his question, and several times he arose and paced nervously up and down the room.
>
> The bed was ill adapted to his work. Several times the paper slipped from the board on which
> it rested, and the pencil punched through. Everything was wrong to-night. Letters and figures
> blurred before his eyes, and as an accompaniment to the beating of his temples came those
> persistent murmuring voices.
>
> At ten he realized that he had done nothing for more than an hour, and with a sudden
> exclamation he gathered together his papers, replaced them in his portfolio, and went down-
> stairs. They were sitting together on the sofa when he came in.
>
> "Oh, hello!" cried Gretchen, rather unnecessarily, he thought. "We were just discussing
> you."
>
> "Thank you," he answered ironically. "What particular part of my anatomy was under the
> scalpel?" (252–53)

As his papers slip and the pencils punch through, it is obvious that Roger's
career literally is not compatible with beds, with marriage. "Gretchen's Forty
Winks" thus may illustrate what apparently had become a serious problem in the
Fitzgeralds' marriage: when he was working intensively, Scott evidently lost
much of his interest in sex.[33] To get it back, he had to stop working; but if he
stopped working for long, his income would cease—as would much of the ardor
of a wife who counted on him for an exciting, fashionable, and frankly expensive lifestyle, and who herself occasionally had extramarital liaisons that would
have made even a more secure husband feel castrated ("What particular part of
my anatomy was under the scalpel?"). The intimate relationship between love,
sex, marriage, money, and career—an often vicious cycle evident throughout
All the Sad Young Men, including such stories as "Rags Martin-Jones," "The
Sensible Thing," and "Winter Dreams"—may explain why Fitzgerald had
briefly considered calling the volume "Dear Money."

But perhaps because this story of a workaholic, sexually inactive husband
and a restless, antagonistic Southern wife was so close to Fitzgerald's personal
situation, he resolves the marital crisis in "Gretchen's Forty Winks" in a manner
that may initially seem comic and evasive, but that in fact is both sobering and
provocative. Needing one more day of intensive effort to land the Garrod account, and realizing that Gretchen is planning to elope momentarily with his
more attentive rival, Roger slips Gretchen a potion that puts her into a sound
sleep for one day. Predictably, Roger does win the Garrod Shoes account. It
brings him an income of $40,000 a year, cash still being the concrete indication
of success for a Fitzgerald hero. And he saves his marriage in the process. The

newly awakened Gretchen is once again the adoring wife, while the rival Tompkins has suffered a nervous breakdown from adhering too strictly to his regimen of work and play in ostensibly perfect balance. Even Tompkins' picture on the Halseys' bedroom wall becomes appropriately askew. And Roger further confirms his dominant role in the now "happy" marriage by taking total control over his wife's mind as well as her body. Armed with the date on that morning's newspaper, he torments her with the realization that she cannot account for one day in her life. But more cogently, he steals all her shoes—the focus of the Garrod account and, hence, the emblem of Roger's husbandly efforts. Without her shoes, Gretchen thinks she has lost her mind—unlike the powerful Fitzgerald vamps, the Fitzgerald wives are stymied readily—and she promptly goes where all good wives go: to bed. If the "Gaslight" treatment of Gretchen seems needlessly cruel, one must consider its symbolic ramifications: it confirms the completeness with which a husband, successful in his own career, can control the wife who depends on him for her financial and emotional well-being. She may thwart him momentarily, but as long as his career succeeds he will gain the upper hand.

At first blush, the sleeping potion resolution seems facile, and feminist readers may well take offense at it. Further, it seems to evade a series of fundamental questions generated by the story, including the reasonableness of two grown men becoming intense rivals over someone as childish as Gretchen; or the possibility that Roger was fighting far more for his self-esteem, his male pride, than for his wife and marriage; or that Gretchen may well have been wanting to be forced into a role of submission—it was she, after all, who had earlier expressed a desire to sleep for forty days rather than face the unpleasantries of reality. Granted, the limited canvas of the short story effectively precludes the possibility of treating these complex issues at any length, and in fact it would not be until *Tender Is the Night* that Fitzgerald could explore a situation in which a self-absorbed wife and a dedicated husband—one whose vocation should theoretically endear the wife to him and nurture their relationship—are unwilling or unable to continue living together. As the case of *Tender Is the Night* suggests, there cannot be a mutually acceptable resolution when a marriage involves two confused people whose actions are increasingly at cross purposes and who do not even fully understand their own motives. Fitzgerald seems to have been aware of this as early as January 1924, when he was at work on "Gretchen's Forty Winks," but it evidently was a reality that he could not yet acknowledge openly—perhaps not even to himself. Thus the ending of the story, although usually regarded as farcical, is actually fantastic in the most serious sense of the term: it offers an expeditious conclusion to a difficult situation, while at the same time maintaining the integrity of the very sober subtext. Hence the perennial attractiveness of fantasy for Fitzgerald, and his deliberate effort to write stories in his second manner: "unreal" elements woven into a "real" story often can enhance the serious, sometimes semiconscious issues at its core.[34]

Properly speaking, "Gretchen's Forty Winks" is not a story in Fitzgerald's second manner, but the sleeping potion does suggest his wistful desire for a solution to what had already become a crisis in his personal and professional life: the behavior of Zelda. Like Roger Halsey, Fitzgerald must have longed occasionally to incapacitate his wife, who seemed to make a deliberate effort to prevent him from working in peace. This pattern first became evident immediately after the Fitzgeralds' wedding. Writes Matthew Bruccoli:

> During the spring of 1920, Fitzgerald tried to be a writer in the confusion of hotel rooms. Zelda was not interested in housekeeping. She was bored when he was writing and would go off by herself to seek amusement; then Fitzgerald couldn't write because he was worried about what she was doing. Nonetheless, he admired her escapades and reported them with pride. Zelda's attentions to Fitzgerald's friends sometimes upset him. She would neck with party acquaintances. Once she tried to sleep with [John Peale] Bishop, although her intentions were not sexual; another time she wanted Townsend Martin to bathe her. The pattern of quarrels and reconciliations established during their courtship continued.[35]

Small wonder that Fitzgerald had such a struggle even to begin *The Beautiful and Damned*. And though he was not always a reliable reporter of the Fitzgeralds' relationship, Ernest Hemingway sensed the chilling implications of Zelda's distinctive smile: "She smiled happily with her eyes and her mouth too . . . I learned to know that smile very well. It meant she knew Scott would not be able to write."[36] Too much in love with her to wish to divorce or hurt her, and too self-destructive to wish to change permanently her compulsion to thwart his writing, Fitzgerald must nonetheless have harbored an occasional urge to incapacitate her temporarily—to keep her quiet so that he could work in peace and, perhaps, to have her awaken as a more tractable wife. And ultimately the sleeping potion used by his fictional alter ego, a device from one of the most venerable forms of Western literature, points to a similarly dated attitude toward marriage: for all his ostensible liberation and fondness for flappers, Fitzgerald was Victorian enough to believe that husbands are supposed to be in charge of their marriages—that as long as they fulfill their role of breadwinner they should be able to count on their wives to be supportive, passive, and maternal. Career success thus allowed the husband to fulfill his end of the Victorian marriage bargain and, at least theoretically, to be in firm control of a serene family unit.

If it didn't work out quite that way in the case of the Fitzgeralds, the paradigm seems nonetheless to have had considerable appeal to him, and time and again in *All the Sad Young Men* the husbands do ultimately gain the upper hand—sometimes through absolutely no effort on their part. Consider "The

Adjuster," in which time and social pressures are emphatically on the side of the male. As the story opens in 1920, Luella Hemple is a society wife, chafing at marriage. "Even my baby [Chuck] bores me," she sighs to a friend over tea at the Ritz. "That sounds unnatural, Ede, but it's true. He doesn't *begin* to fill my life" (162). Neither, apparently, does her husband Charles, who's "lukewarm about the theatre, hates the opera, hates dancing, hates cocktail parties" (164). This dullard even lacks interest in the time-killing soirée Luella has planned for that evening, "an interesting engagement, a supper after the theatre to meet some Russians, singers or dancers or something" (165). But Charles's problem is one that faces many of Fitzgerald's sad young men: he works too hard, trying desperately to earn enough money to please an attractive young wife who chooses not to be pleased. Already trying frantically to satisfy his wife with material goods (they even own their own glitzy Broadway apartment), poor Charles might well be excused for lacking enthusiasm for those Russian "singers or dancers or something," and it comes as no surprise when this hapless husband, his hair already "iron-gray" though he is still in his mid-thirties (167), suffers a total collapse that very night.

Though the opening of the story is dramatized, the collapse itself is simply reported—a device that keeps the focus firmly on Luella. We are told in a vague way that "twenty years of almost uninterrupted toil upon his shoulders" had taken their toll on Charles, but Fitzgerald is careful to emphasize that it was "recent pressure at home"—read "Luella"—that actually triggered the disaster:

> His attitude toward his wife was the weak point in what had otherwise been a strong-minded and well-organized career—he was aware of her intense selfishness, but it is one of the many flaws in the scheme of human relationships that selfishness in women has an irresistible appeal to many men. Luella's selfishness existed side by side with a childish beauty, and, in consequence, Charles Hemple had begun to take the blame upon himself for situations which she had obviously brought about. It was an unhealthy attitude, and his mind had sickened, at length, with his attempts to put himself in the wrong. (174–75)

Substitute "Scott" for "Charles," and "Zelda" for "Luella," and it seems possible that in "The Adjuster" Fitzgerald is offering a remarkably astute appraisal of the psychological components of his relationship with his own wife—including the implied admission that he himself was at least partly to blame for their troubles. But true to form, Fitzgerald places most of the responsibility on the wife, Luella, whose selfish and undutiful behavior could drive a well-meaning husband to a nervous breakdown in, appropriately enough, that traditional domain of a good wife, the kitchen. The Hemples' maid reports that when Charles's mind broke, he went into the kitchen and began throwing all the food out of the ice box (174), an action that makes symbolic sense in light of Luella's other unnatural confession at the Ritz earlier that day:

"I'm a vile housekeeper, and I have no intention of turning into a good one. I hate to order groceries, and I hate to go into the kitchen and poke around to see if the ice-box is clean, and I hate to pretend to the servants that I'm interested in their work, when really I never learned to cook, and consequently a kitchen is about as interesting to me as a—as a boiler-room. It's simply a machine that I don't understand. It's easy to say, 'Go to cooking school,' the way people do in books—but, Ede, in real life does anybody ever change into a model *Hausfrau*— unless they have to?" (163)

There's nothing quite like her husband's nervous breakdown to show a woman the error of her unwifely ways, but Luella initially resists the prospect of caring indefinitely for the sick Charles—especially since that very day she had planned to abandon him, poor baby Chuck, and their apartment full of antiques purchased so as to make their European honeymoon worthwhile (166). But Luella cannot resist her wifely/motherly roles for long, since in anticipation of his imminent collapse Charles had brought home with him the mysterious Dr. Moon.

Dr. Moon is one of the most intriguing characters Fitzgerald ever created, though he seems not to have been presented with optimum effectiveness. With his "round, pale, slightly lined face" (168) he does indeed resemble the moon, and one can understand readily why his "tired placidity" and "heavy, leisurely voice" would irritate rather than soothe Luella, whose pre-disaster restlessness changes into shrill hysteria as she tries to handle a catatonic husband, a feverish baby, and the mutiny of a series of servants who are understandably reluctant to work for a bullying woman who is literally overwhelmed by all those "doors and ovens" (181) on her stove. The "servant problem" adds an unfortunate note to the story—few readers can empathize with a wealthy woman visibly distraught by having to deal with an army of doctors, housekeepers, and baby nurses—but it is no worse, in its way, than the presence of Dr. Moon, who illustrates the problem inherent in stories of Fitzgerald's second manner. A fantasy element in an otherwise realistic story, Dr. Moon drifts in and out of the apartment at will (couldn't the Hemples afford a lock on the door?) spouting vague platitudes like, "Your husband needs you" (184). As the story progresses, Dr. Moon turns into a kind of psychotherapist, leading Luella to consider, and eventually to articulate, sundry grown-up ideas about responsibility:

"I congratulate you on the way you've taken hold of things."
"But I haven't taken hold of things at all," she said coldly. "I do what I have to—"
"That's just it."
Her impatience mounted rapidly.
"I do what I have to, and nothing more," she continued; "and with no particular good-will."
Suddenly she opened up to him again, as she had the night of the catastrophe—realizing that she was putting herself on a footing of intimacy with him, yet unable to restrain her words.
"The house isn't going," she broke out bitterly. "I had to discharge the servants, and now

I've got a woman in by the day. And the baby has a cold, and I've found out that his nurse doesn't know her business, and everything's just as messy and terrible as it can be!"

"Would you mind telling me how you found out the nurse didn't know her business?"

"You find out various unpleasant things when you're forced to stay around the house."

He nodded, his weary face turning here and there about the room. (177)

But Luella's unwifely impulses are so deeply ingrained that it still takes her a while to understand and accept all that Dr. Moon is helping her to see. Shortly after their conversation, things get noticeably worse for Luella: baby Chuck dies, the nurse faints, the cook quits, and poor Luella is left alone in the kitchen, trying to figure out how to prepare ("to boil or stew or something") the carrots needed by her invalid husband (181). Since things couldn't get much worse, Luella decides once again to run away from her marriage; but she is stopped by the increasingly direct and aggressive Dr. Moon, who announces that she has "only begun" her wifely duties. He orders her to take her husband out for a drive, and suddenly she "knew that she would obey. With the conviction that her spirit was broken at last, she took up her suitcase and walked back through the hall" (188). Once Luella admits that she is chastened, matters improve dramatically: Charles recovers, two charming children are born, and Luella—"a little stouter," with "a mature kindness about her face at twenty-eight" (192)—is contented at last: "if the world seemed less gay and happy to her than it had before, she experienced a certain peace, sometimes, that she had never known" (189).

Fitzgerald would have us believe that all that this miraculous transformation from flapper-wife to Earth Mother required was time. At the end of the story, Luella finally asks Dr. Moon who he is:

"Who am I?—" His worn suit paused in the doorway. His round, pale face seemed to dissolve into two faces, a dozen faces, a score, each one different yet the same—sad, happy, tragic, indifferent, resigned—until threescore Doctor Moons were ranged like an infinite series of reflections, like months stretching into the vista of the past.

"Who am I?" he repeated; "I am five years." (192)

But this identity is ultimately unconvincing. It is abundantly clear from the story itself that it was not time itself (Luella has been married for three years when the story opens) but the fact that she had to deal with a series of crises, including the death of a child and the practical necessity of running a household, that fostered maturity and contentment. Those elements emerged in a direct cause-and-effect relationship with Luella's willingness to submit to her duties as wife and mother. The passage of time itself seems somehow ancillary, though Fitzgerald's insistence upon its importance leads to one of the most memorable passages in the story. Explains Dr. Moon,

"We make an agreement with children that they can sit in the audience without helping to make the play," he said, "but if they still sit in the audience after they're grown, somebody's got to work double time for them, so that they can enjoy the light and glitter of the world."

When Luella resists the implications of this metaphor, Dr. Moon explains her new, special role:

"It's your turn to be the centre, to give others what was given to you for so long. You've got to give security to young people and peace to your husband, and a sort of charity to the old. You've got to let the people who work for you depend on you. You've got to cover up a few more troubles than you show, and be a little more patient than the average person, and do a little more instead of a little less than your share. The light and glitter of the world is in your hands." (190)

Though a sense of the justice of this metaphor comes usually with the passage of time, this is not necessarily the case. Hardworking young Charles Hemple had known it, and even Luella's friend Ede felt only "impatience and distaste" (166) at Luella's chronic complaining over tea. And Fitzgerald has clouded the issue even further by suggesting that Luella's inability to function as a wife is due not to her lack of maturity, but to the socioeconomic conditions of the historical period in which she lives:

If she had been a pioneer wife, she would probably have fought the fight side by side with her husband. But here in New York there wasn't any fight. They weren't struggling together to obtain a far-off peace and leisure—she had more of either than she could use. Luella, like several thousand other young wives in New York, honestly wanted something to do. If she had had a little more money and a little less love, she could have gone in for horses or for vagarious amour. Of if they had a little less money, her surplus energy would have been absorbed by hope and even by effort. But the Charles Hemples were in between. They were of that enormous American class who wander over Europe every summer, sneering rather pathetically and wistfully at the customs and traditions and pastimes of other countries, because they have no customs or traditions or pastimes of their own. (164–65)

If in fact this is true (and it certainly seems challenged by the comparative maturity of Charles and Ede), then it is hardly the sort of thing that can be rectified with the passing of five years. What Fitzgerald seems to be arguing quite directly in "The Adjuster" is that the old-fashioned values of marriage had more to offer than the new freedoms of the Jazz Age. As Christiane Johnson points out, at the time he was working on "The Adjuster," Fitzgerald was writing essays which lamented the breakdown of the American family, including "What Kinds of Husbands Do 'Jimmies' Make?," "Wait Till You Have Children of Your Own!," and "What Became of Our Flappers and Sheiks?"[37] But the primary focus of his criticism was women: as the flappers of 1920 became the wives and mothers of 1925, Fitzgerald expressed public concern over what he perceived as their neglect of their obligations. Indeed, it was her failure to fulfill what Fitzgerald termed her wifely and motherly "duties" that he would cite, several years later, as the first indication of Zelda's mental illness, and her Swiss psychiatrist, Dr. Oscar Forel, would pursue a program of "'re-education' of Zelda in terms of her role as wife to Scott" as his cure for her schizophrenia.[38] Certainly by the mid-1930s it would become clear that mere time, far from improving matters, could actually exacerbate them; but in the mid-1920s Fitzgerald apparently still clung to a naive hope that chronological age was directly related to maturity level. If he held on long enough, in other words, perhaps Zelda—and with her, the Fitzgeralds' marriage—would settle into a Victorian norm. That Zelda was temperamentally ill-suited to such a role seems not to have been worthy of consideration.

The rather simplistic insistence upon time as a marital cure-all and the often unconvincing presentation of Dr. Moon should not obscure the fact that "The Adjuster" is a complex story which reveals much about Fitzgerald's interest in the emotional and social components of marriage. Part of its complexity is due to the fact that it offers serious consideration of children. True, the death of baby Chuck is perhaps too transparently a punishment for Luella's unmotherly feelings, just as the subsequent birth of two children is designed to more than compensate for his death when Luella finally submits to her wifely role. Even so, the inclusion of juvenile characters does suggest a major shift in Fitzgerald's perspective. In *Flappers and Philosophers*, marriage was presented in terms of husbands and wives; in *All the Sad Young Men*, marriage has been expanded to include small children, and with that expansion comes a greater subtlety in Fitzgerald's depiction of husband/wife dynamics. At the same time, the children suggest a more mature breadth of vision, one that is sensitive to what Erik Erikson in the 1950s would identify as the psychosocial stages of human development.

Consider "The Baby Party." Few modern scholars have commented upon it, apparently taking at face value the appraisals of Fitzgerald's contemporaries that "it simply is the account of how a tussle between a couple of infants embroiled the fathers in a bitter battle of fists" and that a story this slight is "hardly worth cutting down good trees to reprint."[39] But Sanford Pinsker is much closer to the mark, observing astutely that it is "a death-haunted story," one that reflects Fitzgerald's own "pathos and guilt" regarding his daughter Scottie[40] and, more broadly, his growing awareness that our children are a means of making a permanent mark on the world. Whatever immortality we possess comes through the next generation.

Hence Fitzgerald's decision to give the same name, "Edith," to both the little girl and her mother in "The Baby Party," while still differentiating between the two by calling the child "Ede" and the adult "grown-up Edith" (e.g., 92).

Of course, in part Fitzgerald is setting up the story's comic role reversal: "grown-up Edith," her husband, and Mr. and Mrs. Markey will act more childishly than their children, who dance so soberly to phonograph records at little Billy Markey's party (94). But Fitzgerald is also underscoring the concept that identity continues through successive generations: little Ede embodies some of grown-up Edith in much the same way that little Scottie Fitzgerald embodied part of her father Scott. To a certain extent, this parent/child relationship reflects Fitzgerald's growing understanding of a child's capacity to bring forth the best in a parent—a notion that would not be probed fully until "Babylon Revisited" in late 1930. But even at the time he was writing "The Baby Party" in February 1924, Fitzgerald had so broadened his perception of marriage that he could accept it rather abstractly as an instrument of procreation—and not just as what he termed a practical outcome of "the mating instinct."[41] Feeling like two "small children in a great unexplored barn"[42] might have been fine for a young couple in 1920, but by 1924 Fitzgerald clearly felt that people who reached adulthood in the Jazz Age had a serious responsibility to grow up, to nurture and protect the next generation which they themselves had produced—and which was their only hedge against oblivion. That Fitzgerald managed to present this argument in "The Baby Party" without resorting to the pedantic tone of, say, "The Four Fists," or the preachy aggressiveness of a Dr. Moon, is a testimony to the sureness of touch that was becoming increasingly evident in his work in the mid-1920s.

That sureness is seen particularly in Fitzgerald's presentation of little Ede. He refrains from the impulse toward sentimentality that so often intrudes into his work when he feels strongly about an issue, presenting her not as an angel but as a normal little girl. Her father, John Andros, though not "bored" with her as Luella Hemple was with little Chuck, nonetheless has a similar appreciation of the fact that flesh-and-blood toddlers can get on a parent's nerves:

> It was little Ede as a definite piece of youth that chiefly interested him. He liked to take her on his lap and examine minutely her fragrant, downy scalp and her eyes with their irises of morning blue. Having paid this homage John was content that the nurse should take her away. After ten minutes the very vitality of the child irritated him; he was inclined to lose his temper when things were broken, and one Sunday afternoon when she had disrupted a bridge game by permanently hiding up the ace of spades, he had made a scene that had reduced his wife to tears. (91–92)

Andros even acknowledges a degree of resentment toward the child: "She had interrupted his rather intense love-affair with his wife, and she was the reason for their living in a suburban town, where they paid for country air with endless servant troubles and the weary merry-go-round of the commuting train" (91). The relationship between Andros and baby Ede is in fact so unsentimental, even guarded, that one does not expect it to serve as the focal point of the story. This initial impression seems confirmed when "grown-up Edith," so amused at the prospect of taking her daughter to a baby party next door while her husband is at work, seems at first to emerge as the story's main character.

Unlike Luella Hemple, Edith Andros appears to relish the roles of wife and mother. She "calculates shrewdly" that the child's new pink dress "would stand out more sensationally against vestments already rumpled," and so plans to arrive at 5:00, half an hour after the party is scheduled to begin (93–94). But this strategy points to an element that Fitzgerald saw as undesirable in parent/ child relationships, and especially on the part of the mother: narcissism. Much as Luella Hemple could respond to little Chuck only when she saw herself in him ("His face was the same shape as hers; she was thrilled sometimes, and formed new resolves about life when his heart beat against her own" [170]), grown-up Edith sees little Ede primarily as a projection of herself—a lateral projection rather than a transgenerational one—who can be used in an elaborate game of one-upmanship with the other young mothers in the neighborhood:

> "Little Ede looks perfectly darling," said Mrs. Markey, smiling and moistening her lips in a way that Edith found particularly repulsive. "So *grown-up*—I can't *believe* it!"
> Edith wondered if "little Ede" referred to the fact that Billy Markey, though several months younger, weighed almost five pounds more. Accepting a cup of tea she took a seat with two other ladies on a divan and launched into the real business of the afternoon, which of course lay in relating the recent accomplishments and insouciances of her child. (95)

The narcissistic nature of the relationship between little Ede and her mother becomes especially apparent when the child, acting on the feelings of superiority and aggressiveness that her mother carefully conceals behind a smiling facade, pushes little Billy Markey to the bare floor in an attempt to confiscate his teddy bear:

> "Why Ede," [Edith] whispered perfunctorily, "you bad girl!"
> Ede put back her little head suddenly and laughed. It was a loud laugh, a triumphant laugh with victory in it and challenge and contempt. Unfortunately it was also an infectious laugh. Before her mother realized the delicacy of the situation, she too had laughed, an audible, distinct laugh not unlike the baby's, and partaking of the same overtones. (98)

The only false note in the story comes when Edith, whose astuteness does not extend beyond regarding Mrs. Markey as "snippy and common" (94), ostensibly recognizes the broader implication of the laughter she shares with her daughter:

> Pressing her handkerchief to her mouth she giggled irrepressibly. It was more than nervousness—she felt that in a peculiar way she was laughing with her child—they were laughing together.
> It was in a way a defiance—those two against the world. (99)

That is the kind of sentiment one would expect from John Andros, who arrives at the party shortly thereafter. Not having witnessed the incident, he responds only to the fact that his wife and child (whom the Markeys term a "brat" [100]) are feeling threatened; similarly, Joe Markey responds to the injury to his fallen son and the insult to his wife. There ensues a literal fistfight between the two fathers, which seems startlingly primal against the backdrop of a toddler's party:

> Edith, still weeping, had started for home. After following her with his eyes until she reached her own walk, John turned back toward the lighted doorway where Markey was slowly coming down the slippery steps. He took off his overcoat and hat, tossed them off the path onto the snow. Then sliding a little on the iced walk, he took a step forward.
>
> At the first blow, they both slipped and fell heavily to the sidewalk, half rising then, and again pulling each other to the ground. They found a better foothold in the thin snow to the side of the walk and rushed at each other, both swinging wildly and pressing out the snow into a pasty mud underfoot.
>
> The street was deserted, and except for their short tired gasps and the padded sound as one or the other slipped down into the slushy mud, they fought in silence, clearly defined to each other by the full moonlight as well as by the amber glow that shone out of the open door. Several times they both slipped down together, and then for a while the conflict threshed about wildly on the lawn.
>
> For ten, fifteen, twenty minutes they fought there senselessly in the moonlight. They had both taken off coats and vests at some silently agreed upon interval and now their shirts dripped from their backs in wet pulpy shreds. Both were torn and bleeding and so exhausted that they could stand only when by their position they mutually supported each other—the impact, the mere effort of a blow, would send them both to their hands and knees. (103–4)

The incident at the party was actually quite insignificant; indeed, little Billy was so unhurt that "he immediately stopped crying and pulled himself upright" the moment his mother placed him on the sofa in order to scream at Mrs. Andros unencumbered (102). But insignificant or not, it was sufficient to resurrect primal instincts of defense and so trigger a brutal fight: these two men, who have absolutely no quarrel with one another, are actually trying to draw blood, to inflict pain, and in fact Markey's face will end up looking like a piece of roast beef (107). Beneath the business suits and vests beat the hearts of two archetypal males (the name "Andros" of course means "male") defending their brood and their descendants, and the primal impulses underlying their actions are so deeply ingrained that each automatically honors the "silently agreed upon interval" for removing their coats and vests—not unlike two animals in the wild abruptly ceasing a battle for supremacy until an outside threat to the herd has been quelled. It is remarkable that Fitzgerald manages to depict the primitive basis of the violence of these two civilized men without resorting to the atavistic rhetoric which so mars similar passages in the works of the literary naturalists whom Fitzgerald so frankly admired. Not quite able to articulate the primitive impulses behind their battle, which they gropingly call "this thing" (104), they cease their efforts when they hear a stranger come near: "When they heard [his] footsteps they stopped fighting, stopped moving, stopped breathing, lay huddled together like two boys playing Indian until the footsteps had passed" (104). This metaphor contributes to the adult/child role reversal around which "The Baby Party" is structured, but the seemingly comic reversal should not obscure the fact that Fitzgerald is making some serious observations: that modern man sometimes is motivated by primitive impulses; that to act on those impulses may make one look—and feel—quite ridiculous; and that many of them stem from the desire to protect one's tribe, and in particular one's progeny. By the time the end of the primitive Andros/Markey battle is signalled by the civilized rumbling of the 7:00 commuter train (105), it has become clear that the story is less about a baby party than about a parent's willingness to act on the abstract concept presented at the very opening of the story:

> When John Andros felt old he found solace in the thought of life continuing through his child. The dark trumpets of oblivion were less loud at the patter of his child's feet or at the sound of his child's voice babbling non sequiturs to him over the telephone. The latter incident occurred every afternoon at three when his wife called the office from the country, and he came to look forward to it as one of the vivid minutes of his day.
>
> He was not physically old, but his life had been a series of struggles up a series of rugged hills, and here at thirty-eight having won his battles against ill-health and poverty he cherished less than the usual number of illusions. (91)

Far more than Edith, whose perspective does not extend beyond her social standing in the neighborhood, John Andros realizes that he literally lives through his child, that being who is able "permanently" to conceal the ace of spades (92)—the card of death. And though he behaves in a primitive fashion, Andros has a modern psychological understanding of generativity, what psychologist Erik Erikson would identify thirty-five years later as the impulse to organize and direct one's life so as to nurture and protect one's progeny.[43] His wife, Edith, however, has apparently not yet reached this most mature psychosocial stage. Whereas Andros and Markey shake hands warmly at the end of the front-yard battle and go to their respective homes, their wives continue to sizzle. When the Markeys show up at the Androses' home later that evening, Mrs. Markey is "mighty mad" and Edith has to be forced by her husband to go apologize to her (107). Andros's own more mature understanding of the situation makes him wish only to drop the matter, preferring to devote his time to his real concern, his child:

> John Andros waited until she had closed the door behind her; then he reached over into the bed, and picking up his daughter, blankets and all, sat down in the rocking-chair holding her tightly in his arms. She moved a little, and he held his breath, but she was sleeping soundly, and in a moment she was resting quietly in the hollow of his elbow. Slowly he bent his head until his cheek was against her bright hair. "Dear little girl, dear little girl."
>
> John Andros knew at length what it was he fought for so savagely that evening. He had it

now, he possessed it forever, and for some time he sat there rocking very slowly to and fro in the darkness. (108)

And so the story ends. This is not yet another example of what John A. Higgins terms Fitzgerald's perennial "ending trouble: he trips into sentimentality in the final scene by the bed of the 'dear little girl.'"[44] Nor does it simply show Fitzgerald "play[ing] with the precipitous theme of *vanitas*."[45] Rather, it confirms that "The Baby Party" expresses what a sensitive contemporary reviewer termed "the ache of immortality."[46] Far from being a domestic comedy about a silly argument,[47] "The Baby Party" is a sober study of what one will endure to ensure the continuation of life.

John Andros emerges as cool-headed and perceptive, the hardworking breadwinner who endures long commutes and the stresses of the modern business world so that his flighty wife can stay home and plot new ways to outdistance the neighbors. This flagrant marital cardstacking on Fitzgerald's part points to the prevailing pattern in *All the Sad Young Men:* consistently more mature, more perceptive, and stronger than their wives, the husbands invariably emerge as the more powerful member of the relationship. This is true even in "Hot and Cold Blood," which initially depicts a marriage in which the wife seems to harbor all the personal strength and reasonableness. "Hot and Cold Blood" is a slight parable, in which the wife Jaqueline [*sic*], dismayed that her husband readily lends money to old friends and gives up his seat on trolley cars to "enormous" fifty-year-old matrons with "puffy, disagreeable eyes" (198), belittles him for being "a professional nice fellow" (199). Under this pressure from his wife, Jim Mather declines to lend money to Mr. Lacy, an old man who had been a dear friend of his late father, and later refuses to relinquish his seat on an overcrowded streetcar to a weary female standee. In good O. Henry fashion, the woman collapses, and is revealed to be Jaqueline herself. At the end of the story, Mather has decided to make that loan to poor Mr. Lacy, and his now chastened wife, recovering at home, presumably has learned her lesson: husbands know best. True, Fitzgerald does seem to ride roughshod over generativity, since by not giving up his seat to the pregnant Jaqueline, her husband has unwittingly jeopardized his progeny; but because there is no actual baby in the story, "Hot and Cold Blood" readily becomes a parable depicting the struggle between kindly husbandly impulses and selfish wifely ones. The male of course prevails.

The comparative ineffectuality of the wives in *All the Sad Young Men* points to a fundamental shift in the outlook of the older Fitzgerald: he no longer sees women as *femmes fatales,* as vamps whose beauty and energy give them power over men. Even the would-be vamps in the volume's courtship stories are strikingly malleable. Rags Martin-Jones, for example, initially appears to be a classic *femme fatale,* and is usually identified as such by Fitzgerald critics.[48]

Indeed, her arrival in the port of New York at the opening of "Rags Martin-Jones and the Pr–nce of W–les" is heralded by mass destruction:

> Tap! Her one hundred and five pounds reached the pier and it seemed to sway and bend from the shock of her beauty. A few porters fainted. A large, sentimental shark which had followed the ship across made a despairing leap to see her once more, and then dove, broken-hearted, back into the deep sea. Rags Martin-Jones had come home. (135)

As the snoopopathic tone of the passage suggests, Fitzgerald is here resurrecting an extravagant style of writing which he had affected as an undergraduate.[49] But to judge from this and other stories in *All the Sad Young Men,* by 1923 Fitzgerald apparently was no longer bewitched by the idea of beautiful, rich young women; and because of this process of deglorification, he was able to use more effectively the style of writing he had learned from Canadian humorist Stephen Leacock, eschewing silliness as an end in itself, and simply reporting facts ("a few porters fainted") which five years earlier he would have expanded hyperbolically to the detriment of the story. So unintimidated is Fitzgerald by the dazzling Rags that he has her affect, of all things, a monocle, which keeps popping out of her eye of "clear childish blue" (135)—so much for sophistication—and has her do what no true Fitzgeraldian *femme fatale* would ever do: be subdued by a man. All it requires to woo and win this childish creature is a mysteriously heated Manhattan rooftop restaurant, an elevator boy posing as the Prince of Wales, a fake arrest warrant for murder, and a little well-choreographed gunplay—in short, a bit of imagination and a great deal of money. Far from resenting or resisting this manipulation and foolery, Rags is thrilled: "Was the whole thing just *mine*?" she demanded. "Was it a perfectly useless, gorgeous thing, just for me?" (158). Yes indeedy, and so she gladly trots off to City Hall to marry her well-heeled Prospero, John Chestnut.

Even would-be vamps with a bit more substance than Rags have little real control over men. In "The Rich Boy," Dolly Karger would appear to be a match for Anson Hunter, and there is some justice in Peter Wolfe's observation that these two characters are essentially mirrors of one another.[50] But by the time Dolly is left staring at the ceiling of a Port Washington bedroom, abandoned but not seduced, it is clear that once again a male has prevailed. Even Judy Jones, who so frequently is cited as a sterling example of the Fitzgeraldian *femme fatale,* is presented with such qualifications that she hardly warrants that label. Judy so dominates "Winter Dreams" that Milton Hindus has suggested that a more apt title for the story might be "The Rich Girl."[51] Certainly she does seem to occupy an inordinate amount of space in the story and, more importantly, in Dexter Green's imagination. But one must remember that from an early age Dexter "wanted not association with glittering things and glittering people—he wanted the glittering things themselves" (63). In other words, he does not want the glittering Judy herself, and this makes his attitude qualitatively different from that of, say, Amory Blaine toward Rosalind Connage, or even of Jay Gatsby toward Daisy Fay. This reduction in the status of the *femme fatale* is signified by her name. "Judy Jones," however much it may owe to the alliterative precedent of "Ginevra" King, is, as Edith Andros would say, a decidedly common name for a fundamentally common woman.[52] The closest she comes to being "fatale" is to swing a golf club at her nanny, a prosaic debunking of the whole idea of the beautiful but deadly woman, and even that is ineffectual, thanks to the nanny's well-placed arm (61). Even her spiteful breaking of Dexter's engagement to another woman seems tepid, so dull is Irene Scheerer and so unconcerned seems Dexter about the whole matter. Dexter's interest in Judy in fact has so little to do with her as an individual that he feels no apparent misgivings at moving away from her to New York for seven years. Indeed, the farther away from her he is the clearer his sense of the glittering things can be; and when at the end of the story he cries, it is because the confirmation of her fundamental commonness in a dreary marriage to a drunkard tarnishes the glittering "things" with which Dexter had for years unjustly associated her. Just twenty-seven years old at the end of the story, Mrs. Lud Simms[53] is a faded frump who stays home with her children all day and endures marriage to yet another dominant male who "treats her like the devil"—mistreatment that she apparently enjoys ("When he's particularly outrageous she forgives him") (88).

The case of Judy Jones, that would-be maneater turned masochist, illustrates most dramatically what became of the *femmes fatales,* the amoral flappers of the early Fitzgerald. First they were reduced to ineffectual flirts, with commonplace, juvenile names like Judy and Rags and Dolly—no Eleanor Savages here. And then they were reduced even further—through marriage. Forced into roles they do not want (Luella Hemple), physically overwhelmed (Jaqueline Mather), deluded into thinking they are insane (Gretchen Halsey), prematurely aged (Judy Jones), and dominated readily by both males and societal expectations that are male-supported (everybody), the women characters in *All the Sad Young Men* seem not "sad" but empty. There is no female character in the entire collection with the strength and color of Sally Carrol Happer; none with the imagination and gusto of Marcia Tarbox; none with the sexual urgency and courage, however misplaced, of Kieth's sister Lois. Indeed, of all the stories in *All the Sad Young Men,* only "The Adjuster" is told from a woman's point of view; but Luella is so unappealing that this narrative stance only intensifies the reader's reaction against her.

All this is not to say that the more mature Fitzgerald's understanding of love, sex, and marriage was fundamentally misogynistic. What it does suggest is that his youthful fascination with tough-minded, attractive young women—a fascination so powerful that he himself willingly married a woman he realized would create problems for him—had given way to a more realistic appraisal of the limitations of women. In turn, that appraisal had led to a surprisingly conservative attitude toward the marital roles of men and women—an attitude conveyed with almost allegorical simplicity as a series of kind but strong husbands prevail over selfish, flighty wives. That Fitzgerald did not necessarily see these roles operative in his own marriage is perhaps evident from the fairy tale resolution of "Gretchen's Forty Winks" and the transparent didacticism of "The Adjuster." Whatever the case, however retrogressive this rather melodramatic conservatism regarding love, sex, and marriage may strike some readers, it does seem to point to an important breakthrough in Fitzgerald's world view: his greater appreciation of selfhood, and especially of the male self.

The stories of *All the Sad Young Men* would suggest that Fitzgerald had come to see selfhood as intimately related to marriage. Further, the relationship is qualitatively different for men and women: time and again in these stories, a male's sense of selfhood is expanded, enriched, and nourished by marriage, while a female's is qualified, diminished, even desiccated. As she submits to her wifely role (a "self" imposed by society), Luella Hemple seems less narcissistic and childish, but she also seems more drab and intellectually limited. The spunky Rags Martin-Jones, her "bee-*oo*-tiful love" having been purchased by a wealthy suitor (160), has no apparent qualms about surrendering her silver fox furs, monocle, purple lap-dogs, and personal fortune of $75,000,000 in order to become just another old Chestnut. Even Gretchen Halsey loses much of her spirit and attractiveness as her husband leads her to believe she is going insane. A woman's selfhood, however limited it might have been in the first place, is effectively lost once she enters into marriage and merges her identity with that of her husband. In contrast, the man's selfhood really blossoms within the context of a "happy" marriage. John Chestnut had groveled when he thought that he would lose Rags Martin-Jones (136–37), but the moment they become engaged he is a new man, coolly manipulating a hapless European nation's rate of exchange and heading off a second world war from his Manhattan skyscraper, the adoring Rags at his side (158–59). And Roger Halsey's fabulous success as a businessman and artist coincides exactly with his newly established power over his chastened wife's body and mind. But the capacity of marriage to nurture a male's sense of selfhood is but one facet of the more mature Fitzgerald's increasing understanding of the complexities of self. In many ways, *All the Sad Young Men* is a book of the self, probing the components and sources of selfhood while raising profound questions about the degree to which an individual should, or even can, strive to create a new self.

One of the most dramatic illustrations of this is "Absolution," a story which shows the genesis of a sense of self in a young boy and, conversely, what happens when one's sense of self has been repressed over a long period or channelled into inappropriate outlets. At eleven years of age, Rudolph Miller is a boy already chafing at the restrictions placed upon him by a non-nurturing family, an austere Roman Catholicism, and the physical isolation of life in the Dakota wheat country. He does, however, possess a vivid imagination, one that enables him to escape these limits and, at least momentarily, to entertain notions of a finer, freer life, a more attractive, confident self. That imagination leads him to create Blatchford Sarnemington, whose insistently Anglo-Saxon name calls to mind another Midwesterner of German ancestry who sought to recreate himself, Jimmy Gatz.[54] But because the norm of Rudolph's life is so restricted, the free spirit Blatchford is identified as something almost evil. It is Blatchford who is allegedly responsible for Rudolph's sinning in the confessional—he lies by claiming that he never lies (116)—and Blatchford whom Rudolph conjures by repeating the wonderful name as he walks home. But the lie itself is an attempt on Rudolph's part "to make things finer in the confessional, brightening up the dinginess of his admissions by saying a thing radiant and proud" (131), and this suggests that what is really "evil" about Blatchford is his capacity to raise Rudolph to a higher, even celestial level of selfhood—to be not a terrified little boy in a Dakota confessional, but a special individual capable of entertaining God. Rudolph longs for a sense of selfhood far finer than the one offered him in his little Swede town; and it is this longing to which those around him respond.

Rudolph's personal life revolves around two father figures: his biological father, freight agent Carl Miller, and his parish priest. Carl Miller is a study in repression as unsparing as anything in Sherwood Anderson.[55] He "had floated with the second wave of German and Irish stock to the Minnesota-Dakota country" at a time when, "theoretically, great opportunities lay ahead of a young man of energy." But Miller's immense success never materialized. "Somewhat gross, . . . suspicious, unrestful, and continually dismayed" (118), Miller has seen die whatever youthful dreams of selfhood he may have once held. His son senses this. When the unshriven Rudolph tries to drink water so as to have an excuse for not taking Holy Communion, he is caught by his enraged father and fears, not so much the beating his father will administer, but "the savage ferocity, outlet of the ineffectual man, which would lie behind it" (122). But Carl Miller is not simply venting his frustrations on the hapless Rudolph. He is, rather, trying to instill in his son a reverence for one of the few sources of selfhood left to those living in that small Dakota town: the Church.

Fitzgerald is explicit that Miller's "two bonds with the colorful life" were "his mystical worship of the Empire Builder, James J. Hill," in whose "gigantic shadow" he was growing old, and the Roman Catholic Church: "For twenty years he had lived alone with Hill's name and God" (118). His marriage—that source of selfhood for so many other Fitzgerald husbands—is hollow, with his miserable wife sleeping in a separate bedroom (119), and his dead-end job as a freight agent is as close as Miller's sense of self will ever approximate Hill's. Consequently Miller's life, what he has left of his sense of self, is derived from the Church. Indeed, whereas he beats his son at home, in church he allows himself to acknowledge that he "was proud of Rudolph in his heart," and he feels "truly as well as formally sorry" for punishing his son (125). This troubled man seems at peace only in church, and so in his unarticulated love and concern for little Rudolph he wishes—indeed, demands by physical force—that the boy, too, look to the Church for a sense of selfhood.

But the Church, however viable it may be as a source of self for an otherwise miserable freight agent, is hardly ideal for everyone. Fitzgerald conveys this through the ironic case of the parish priest, Rudolph's other father figure. As the similarity in the boy's and the priest's given names suggests, Adolphus "sees mirrored in Rudolph his own frustrated longing for a fuller, more aesthetically satisfying and adventurous life": an "incurable romantic,"[56] Adolphus yearns for a selfhood comparable to that budding in his youthful counterpart, Rudolph—a selfhood he had apparently sought to realize in the priesthood. But far from finding the Church a source of growth, of self-realization, the priest has literally lost all sense of self in his priestly status. He goes mechanically through his clerical duties, hoping that somehow God "would help him to act correctly" (111) and bitterly spouting theological axioms that he can no longer believe and that no little boy could comprehend: "Apostasy implies an absolute damnation only on the supposition of a previous perfect faith. Does that fix it?" (129). So lost and confused is the priest that Fitzgerald gives him the surname Schwartz. It is a Jewish-sounding name (in fact, the protagonist of Fitzgerald's story "The Hotel Child," Fifi Schwartz, is identified as Jewish); as such, it seems incongruous for a Catholic priest—and thus is ironically appropriate for one undergoing a vocation-related crisis of selfhood. But what is perhaps more revealing is that "schwartz" literally means "dark."

The darkness refers to the literal and symbolic situation in which the priest finds himself. He spends his time in the confinement and blackness of the confessional, "that large coffin set on end" (113),[57] or in his office, that gloomy "haunted" room (110) with a dark walnut desk where little Rudolph goes to ask for help and guidance. Darkness is associated with his priestly duties, much as the darkness of his vestments marks him, ironically, as one so special that God has chosen him to devote his life to the highest calling known to man. But Father Schwartz seems also to be in a hell of his own making for, like a more extreme version of Kieth in "Benediction," he seems to be hiding out in the darkness of the Church, living in a constant terror of "the hot madness of four o'clock" (109). Fitzgerald has chosen to present that hot madness in fundamentally sexual terms, with Father Schwartz acutely aware of the "Swede girls" who walk past his office window every day at 4:00, girls whose "legs were shaped under starchless gingham" and who at night would lie with "the tall young men from the farms" (109, 132). Father Schwartz is so obsessed with these girls that when Rudolph confesses he has "committed a terrible sin," the priest automatically projects his own obsession onto the little boy: "A sin against purity?" (110). Obviously not; the worst this eleven-year-old has done is to listen to a girl and "a fella" saying "immodest things" in the loft of a local barn (115). But Father Schwartz is correct in recognizing instinctively that little Rudolph's curiosity about sex is indicative of a broader pattern of interest in life itself.[58] It is something that Father Schwartz, in entering the priesthood, had attempted to deny, but even as he hides in his dark office the Swede girls—that is, warmth, light, laughter—are just outside his window, a constant reminder of the price he has paid in denying his natural selfhood for the selfhood of a priest. He sees in Rudolph a boy who, like himself, had wanted to please God, Rudolph by claiming he never lies, Adolphus by entering the Church; so Father Schwartz tries to steer him clear of the mistake he made by encouraging him to nurture his budding selfhood, to embrace rather than reject life:

> "Did you ever see an amusement park?"
>
> "No, Father."
>
> "Well, go and see an amusement park." The priest waved his hand vaguely. "It's a thing like a fair, only much more glittering. Go to one at night and stand a little way off from it in a dark place—under dark trees. You'll see a bug wheel made of lights turning in the air, and a long slide shooting boats down into the water. A band playing somewhere, and a smell of peanuts—and everything will twinkle. But it won't remind you of anything, you see. It will all just hang out there in the night like a colored balloon—like a big yellow lantern on a pole." (130)

The priest certainly knows that life can be threatening ("But don't get up close," he warned Rudolph, "because if you do you'll only feel the heat and the sweat and the life" [130]), and in fact that may be why he was attracted to the restrictive role of a priest in the first place; but nevertheless he urges Rudolph to accept life rather than reject it, to nurture the self through experience rather than confine it.

One might expect Rudolph to be confused by the mixed signals he receives from his two father figures. The drab Carl Miller, knowing only too well the disappointments of daily life, pushes him to the Church for a sense of self, while the priest—who by the end of the story is so unbalanced that his rosary beads seem to crawl about his desk like snakes (127)—pushes the boy away from the Church, toward life. But the imaginative Rudolph manages to combine these antithetical orientations into a kind of coda with which he can live and that will enable him to acknowledge and nurture the self while not denying God. As E. R. Hagemann has argued, the fragment of Psalm 90 which heads section five of the story suggests that Rudolph, having weighed the attractions and limitations of both life and Church, comes to see the spiritual and practical value of the implication of that psalm: God is his protector and shelter.[59] The deliberate avoidance of life does not hold all the answers (witness the mad priest), and there is no question that life is not always benign (witness the brutal father); but Rudolph has come to realize that he has a kind of personal relationship with God that will permit him—indeed, that encourages him—to immerse himself in life in his quest for selfhood. Further, that quest has the capacity to range well beyond God, limited only by Rudolph's imagination:

> [H]e felt that his own inner convictions were confirmed. There was something ineffably gorgeous somewhere that had nothing to do with God. He no longer thought that God was angry at him about the original lie, because He must have understood that Rudolph had done it to make things finer in the confessional, brightening up the dinginess of his admissions by saying a thing radiant and proud. At the moment when he had affirmed immaculate honor a silver pennon had flapped out into the breeze somewhere and there had been the crunch of leather and the shine of silver spurs and a troop of horsemen waiting for dawn on a low green hill. (131)

Taking his cue from the mad priest, Rudolph feels it is his privilege—indeed, his God-approved responsibility—to pursue this gorgeous thing.

Despite the acute frustration of Carl Miller and the insanity of the priest, "Absolution" is fundamentally a positive story. It posits the imagination as not simply desirable, but as absolutely essential for the development of self; and it suggests further that Rudolph, learning from the examples of his elders, will somehow achieve a healthy sense of selfhood through the embracing of life. Far from being evil, Blatchford Sarnemington is the embodiment of a self realizing its romantic possibilities. This concept is, of course, fairly abstract, and the presentation of the material is correspondingly what many commentators persist in deeming " 'arty' and confused."[60] One can, like E. R. Hagemann, readily point out Fitzgerald's bungled Latin, imprecise descriptions (just what does he mean by Rudolph's "staccato eyes, lit with gleaming points of cobalt light"? [110]), or, most damning of all, that "blue sirocco trembl[ing] over the wheat" (132)? Hagemann did not need to consult government experts to confirm that there can be no such thing: "U.S. government meteorologists have categorically told me that sirocco, of the family of winds known as foehn (from the German), can never be used accurately in this country."[61] (Hagemann would probably call in the Audubon Society to chastise Poe for creating a talking raven.) Such gleeful and irresponsible attacks on Fitzgerald's "inaccuracies" overlook the need for a poetic style in "Absolution" to convey the poetic understanding of self which is at the heart of the story—witness the exquisite discursive prose in *Gatsby*, the novel which ultimately evolved from "Absolution" and conveys the same fundamental idea. But though Fitzgerald had immense faith in the capacity of the imagination to enhance, even create, an exciting new self, he apparently recognized that this rarely happened. Most people too readily confused the enhancement of self with something far more prosaic: the enhancement of socio-economic standing.

In probing this confusion, Fitzgerald was conveying dramatically a phenomenon that had been increasingly evident to social historians for at least a century. As Milton Stern explains, the American Dream from the outset had been "a dream of self rather than community": the true measure of value had always been "the liberated individual." But early on, an essential problem arose: the liberation became associated with financial success, and the individual's worth came to be equated with his wealth. "Like Emerson and Thoreau, Fitzgerald knew that in America there had been an enormous displacement of the possibilities of self by the possibilities of wealth,"[62] and it is this awareness, far more than a childish obsession with the rich, that compels him time and again to depict wealthy people who are miserable due to problems of selfhood. One such problem is the repression of true self in the pursuit of a seemingly more attractive one, that of a wealthy sophisticate. Consider the case of Dexter Green. The image of this self-made millionaire crying uncontrollably in his Manhattan skyscraper because Judy Jones had faded "just like *that*" (89) strikes some readers as ludicrous, but in fact it is far more tragic. An insistently ordinary woman, by virtue of her family's wealth, had led an otherwise intelligent, capable young man to pursue a particular image of selfhood, to assume that "glittering things" must be acquired to realize that false self, and to devote literally years pursuing the wrong path to the wrong goal. Part of that foolish pursuit involved passing up the state university for an Eastern (presumably Ivy League) college; using the connections made there, Dexter opened up a string of laundries, and quickly became one of the wealthiest young men in his part of the country (72–73). But what he had not recognized was that in pursuing his goal of wealth, he had been pursuing a self that had nothing to do with Dexter Green. Those around him certainly sensed this: for all his prosperity, Dexter would always remain fundamentally at the level of a caddy,[63] washing the socks of wealthy country club members and occasionally being permitted to play golf with them—but only as a guest, and never as an equal. And what is worse, in pursuing the phantom self he had failed to nurture his true self: his expensive education had essentially been a business move, not an attempt to broaden himself spiritually and intellectually. His hysteria at the end of "Winter Dreams" suggests that he is belatedly undergoing an epiphany, realizing with a jolt not simply that the glittering things had become tarnished, but that his true self-hood—what he vaguely terms "that thing"[64]—had become lost in their pursuit.

But what if an individual's true self really is that of a wealthy sophisticate? Would he not be infinitely happier than Dexter, exploring the endless possibilities for the development of self through the education, travel, and leisurely reflection that are afforded by great wealth? Not necessarily; in fact, that individual might be worse off than his poor counterpart, as is seen in the case of Anson Hunter.

That "The Rich Boy" is a story not about the rich as such but rather about the complex relationship between selfhood and wealth, and the potential destructiveness of that relationship, is signified at the outset:

> Begin with an individual, and before you know it you find that you have created a type; begin with a type, and you find that you have created—nothing. That is because we are all queer fish, queerer behind our faces and voices than we want any one to know or than we know ourselves. (1)

On the basis of this, the self would appear to be all-important; but immediately that impression is undercut, as self is seen as defined by socioeconomic realities:

> Let me tell you about the very rich. They are different from you and me. They possess and enjoy early, and it does something to them, makes them soft where we are hard, and cynical where we are trustful, in a way that, unless you were born rich, it is very difficult to understand. (1–2)

The narrator's earlier protest ("There are no types, no plurals" [1]) notwithstanding, there does appear to be a type, "the very rich," and they are qualitatively different from "you and me."[65] The entire story is thus intended to illustrate the ways in which those differences, while making Anson feel superior, actually render him a "boy" for his entire life. His sense of self, drawn from his wealthy background, had crystallized when "he reached the age of reason—is it seven?—at the beginning of the century" (2), and the crystallization is so complete that Anson's sense of self cannot adjust to accommodate a variety of changes occurring around him and in the country at large. The crystallized self compels him childishly to let the "psychological moment" (12) slip past, to refuse to express his love for Paula Legendre, since to do so would involve compromising momentarily the feeling of superiority which is at the heart of that self: why should he admit that he loves her, "when he might hold her so, biding his own time, for another year—forever?" (18). But the notion that he could postpone change indefinitely points to a more fundamental problem: if a man's sense of self is crystallized in childhood, and if it is defined by his belonging to "the very rich," what happens when that social class grows increasingly meaningless in the face of socioeconomic change? The Hunters had "old money"; that is, they were one of the New York families that had been "rich before 1880" (20). But the $15,000,000 from the turn of the century which was to be divided among Anson and his five siblings (2) was paltry compared to the $75,000,000 inherited by Rags Martin-Jones in 1923. What Brian Way identifies as the Whartonesque quality of "The Rich Boy" is thus very apt,[66] for this story, like *The Age of Innocence,* examines the impact of accelerated socioeconomic change on old New York families that had believed themselves permanently secure in their financial and social superiority. But Fitzgerald's interest in the selfhood derived from old money is more complex than this might suggest. Quite unexpectedly, Anson's siblings have no interest in retaining the Connecticut estate where he had spent childhood summers basking in "the half-grudging American deference" paid him by the villagers (3), and he is especially dismayed when his youngest sisters begin to "speak rather respectfully of families that hadn't 'existed' twenty years ago" (42). Even more cogently, Anson's parents, though they lived through "the snobbish and formalized vulgarity of the Gilded Age," had themselves enjoyed "a happy and successful marriage" (3, 33). Mere social class alone, therefore, does not explain why Anson would not marry a woman he loved, any more than it explains how he does not share his siblings' flexibility in the face of socioeconomic change.[67] The opening of the story notwithstanding, it is not that "the very rich" are different from "you and me," but that counterproductive qualities which are associated with the very rich (most noticeably a sense of superiority) can do immense damage in those *individual* cases wherein the self crystallizes at a very young age.

In Fitzgerald's estimation, the most damning aspect of that sense of superiority is that it precludes the desire to dream and strive: "Most of our lives end as a compromise—it was as a compromise that his life began" (5). Like the Charles Hemples in "The Adjuster," Anson had no need to struggle "to obtain a far-off peace and leisure" (164), and without some kind of struggle a mature self—even a false self such as that pursued by Dexter Green—could not emerge. By the mid-1920s, Fitzgerald seems to have recognized that a vital aspect of that struggle was work. The stories written during this period suggest that Fitzgerald was beginning to differentiate carefully between jobs and careers that primarily earned money (Dexter and his laundries; Carl Miller and his job as a freight agent) and those that kept one's time occupied in a socially acceptable fashion (Anson and his Wall Street investment firm); between those which denied the true self (Father Schwartz and the priesthood) and those in which the self could be nurtured. A particularly striking example of this last type is the case of Roger Halsey in "Gretchen's Forty Winks."

As has been seen, Roger defeats his rival George Tompkins and regains control over his wife by landing the Garrod Shoes account after forty days of intensive effort on his advertising projects. Fitzgerald is explicit that one reason Gretchen became involved with Tompkins in the first place was Roger's neglect of her. Tompkins even accuses Roger openly of being selfish: "You only consider yourself in the matter. Don't you think Gretchen has any rights?" (253), and there is the distinct possibility that initially Gretchen's interest in George was due in large measure to her desire to make Roger jealous and so to win him back. But though Tompkins quickly becomes a serious rival for Gretchen's affections, it takes a while for Gretchen to comprehend that she has a rival of her own for Roger's affections: his work. To Roger Halsey, work has become an end in itself: it is the great passion of his life—so great that he not only doesn't mind, but actually seems to encourage his wife's interest in another man. Gretchen's relationship with Tompkins is perfectly acceptable—but only as long as it doesn't interfere with his work. When that interference is inevitable, he takes swift action. At the time Gretchen announces that she is running off with Tompkins—the sort of announcement that is made by desperate women who want to be stopped—Roger is but one day short of his self-imposed work deadline. It is thus the optimum moment for Gretchen to articulate, through her announcement and her actions, that she knows only too well that his work has displaced her as the love of his life: "I hate you," she said slowly. "And I'd like to take all the work you've done and tear it up and throw it in the fire" (256). This direct attack on Roger's work impels him to give her a sleeping potion— symbolically speaking, to kill her—so that he can devote a few more precious hours to the mistress who has given him his greatest pleasure, his work. He had no hesitation in laboring until 3:00 A.M., night after night, in order to feel that exquisite "sense of triumph that he had lasted out another day" (249). And he knows his work is beautiful: "Money alone couldn't buy such work; more than he realized himself, it had been a labor of love" (250). The endless cigarettes, the bulging blood veins, the caffeine jitters, even the very real risk of a nervous breakdown could not change the fact that his "labor of love" gave Roger everything he valued in his life. Significantly, he has no illusions about the advertising business, even calling it "useless" (253)—but "Gretchen's Forty Winks" nevertheless does begin to explore the work/selfhood paradigm that is central to the late stories of *Taps at Reveille*.

This idea had, of course, been gropingly expressed in the early stories of *Flappers and Philosophers*. When Horace Tarbox is prevented by outside circumstances from pursuing his intended work (namely, writing books on philosophy), he loses his true self (scholar) and is forced to accept an inappropriate and hence unsatisfactory one (circus acrobat). It was not until the mid-1920s, in the stories of *All the Sad Young Men*, that Fitzgerald began to explore more openly the intimate relationship between work and self, and without resorting to this sort of farce; but even so, his handling of this issue is still rather clumsy—not so much because of a lack of technical skills as because of a kind of tunnel vision on the part of Fitzgerald himself. Consider again the case of "Gretchen's Forty Winks." Though he deliberately drives himself to the brink of a nervous breakdown, Roger seems not to recognize that there is something not quite healthy, psychologically speaking, about his obsession with his work. Drugging his wife may have stopped her from interfering with his unreasonable self-imposed work deadline, and it may have prevented her from articulating any further the harsh truth that he loved his work more than he loved her; but this is hardly a long-term solution to a serious problem. Further, Roger seems not to entertain the possibility that he was actually using his work to avoid intimacy with his wife: his lack of ardor may thus have been a cause of his devotion to his work rather than simply the result of it. Finally, Roger seems not to have recognized that what he perceives as viable goals in his quest for self-realization—business success, creative achievement as a graphic designer, dominance in his marriage—may not have been as worthy as they might appear. And if Roger does not understand these matters, it is probably because Fitzgerald did not, either. He seems literally to reward Roger Halsey with financial success and personal power for engaging in precisely the kinds of behavior—keeping impossible hours, smoking and drinking to excess, alienating his wife—of which Fitzgerald himself was increasingly guilty as of the mid-1920s. This rewarding of Roger may help explain why Fitzgerald seemed to act in increasingly self-abusive ways throughout his adult life, and especially so after *The Great Gatsby;* it was almost as if he came to harbor a superstitious belief that there was a direct relationship between the level of his self-directed abuse and the level of his success as an author. But if indeed Roger Halsey is a fictional projection of one aspect of his creator's psyche, Fitzgerald seems to have brushed past the implications of the paramount difference between Roger's success and his own: Roger's marathon of work and self-destructive behavior had ended after forty days. Once he landed the Garrod Shoes account, Roger's continued success in advertising was guaranteed for an indefinite period of time. His efforts had been a short-term investment for long-term dividends. But F. Scott Fitzgerald was not so fortunate. He literally had to keep working and producing fiction, not only to support his extravagant family circle, but to ensure the continuation of his professional reputation. There was no respite for Fitzgerald after forty days: his personal marathon was doomed to continue literally for the rest of his life.

Probably too close to his material to face the implications for himself, Fitzgerald in "Gretchen's Forty Winks" nonetheless seems to be expressing a growing conviction that whatever sense of self one acquires is intimately related to one's commitment to work. Reflecting on his achievement of the mid-1920s, Fitzgerald shortly before his death regretted that he had not acted more vigorously on that realization:

> What little I've accomplished has been by the most laborious and uphill work, and I wish now I'd *never* relaxed or looked back—but said at the end of *The Great Gatsby:* "I've found my line—from now on this comes first. This is my immediate duty—without this I am nothing."[68]

Though he still had a long way to go, Fitzgerald had made considerable progress since "Dalyrimple Goes Wrong" (1919), in which his understanding of self was expressed clumsily through Bryan Dalyrimple's repeated efforts to interact with a series of discrete groups: the army, Macy's department store, the local political machine. He likewise was no longer seeing selfhood in black-and-white terms, like the intriguing but ultimately simplistic concept of feline and canine selves in "The Ice Palace" (1919). Virtually every story in *All the Sad Young Men* examines selfhood, and especially male selfhood, in terms of the complexities of marriage, social class, and work; but more importantly, Fitzgerald implies that no one factor necessarily foredooms a person to have a particular kind of self. Even Anson Hunter's arrested sense of self could not have been due solely to his social class, as his siblings' comparable open-mindedness makes clear. The sense of peace which seems to pervade *All the Sad Young Men* is due in large measure to Fitzgerald's more mature awareness that, much as we have the need and responsibility to nurture our sense of self, we have the need and the capacity to direct and control our lives. Free will is a viable, if not always omnipotent, entity in *All the Sad Young Men.*

Compared to *Flappers and Philosophers, All the Sad Young Men* is strikingly free of the first volume's quasi-naturalistic rhetoric about "fate," "destiny," "outside forces," and "life." True, Fitzgerald does once use "life" as he did in *Flappers and Philosophers,* to mean relationships with women:

> I found that despite the trusting mothers, his attitude toward girls was not indiscriminately protective. It was up to the girl—if she showed an inclination toward looseness, she must take care of herself, even with him.
> "Life," he would explain sometimes, "has made a cynic of me."
> By life he meant Paula. (21)

This is not the vague, fearful understanding of "life" conveyed in, say, "Head and Shoulders," but a very specific and hence comprehensible entity. Similarly, it is not "necessity" but "some vague necessity for verisimilitude," later attributed to "the honesty of his imagination," that leads Rudolph Miller of "Absolution" to leave a wet glass by the kitchen sink as physical evidence of his attempt to avoid Holy Communion (121). There is likewise an implied reference to "forces" in "Hot and Cold Blood," as the pregnant Jaqueline "brood[s] . . . on the shape into which her life was now being arbitrarily forced." But because she obviously had personal input into the course her life was taking, and because pregnancy was hardly unique to her, Jaqueline's brooding is said to be "without fear or depression" (200). Fitzgerald even introduces playfully the idea of fate, which had so intimidated his characters in *Flappers and Philosophers.* It amazes Luella Hemple sometimes "that the specially created apartment and the specially created limousine were hers, just as indisputably as the mortgaged suburban bungalow out of *The Ladies' Home Journal* and the last year's car that fate might have given her instead" (167). As fate is reduced to a whimsical force that can bring tacky old flivvers to stylish housewives, it is obvious that abstract forces have lost most of their capacity to terrorize his characters. However, this does not mean that the characters in *All the Sad Young Men* are Nietzschean masters of their own destinies. Rather, Fitzgerald is careful to suggest that, although free will is a strong component in the lives of his characters (and especially the males), they nevertheless can be inclined to feel or behave in particular ways as the result of outside factors.

One such factor is the actions of others. Though Jim Mather of "Hot and Cold Blood" initially refuses to lend money to old Mr. Lacy under pressure from his wife, he quickly modifies his position and makes the loan. His change of heart is due in part to his temperament (he was "essentially and enormously romantic" [205]) and in part to the incident on the crowded streetcar, a near tragedy which illustrates the importance of kindly acts. But even more important was Jim Mather's guilty awareness that Mr. Lacy, many years before, had lent money to his father:

> "Once upon a time almost forty years ago your father came to me and asked me for a thousand dollars. I was a few years older than he was, and though I knew him only slightly, I had a high opinion of him. That was a lot of money in those days, and he had no security—he had nothing but a plan in his head—but I liked the way he had of looking out of his eyes— you'll pardon me if I say you look not unlike him—so I gave it to him without security."
>
> Mr. Lacy paused.
>
> "Without security," he repeated. "I could afford it then. I didn't lose by it. He paid it back with interest at six per cent before the year was up." (208)

As a result of Lacy's loan in the dim past—"Once upon a time"—Jim's family's hardware business had come into being: "Once," thought Mather, "he helped my father. Perhaps, if he hadn't, my own life would have been different than it has been" (212). One man's act forty years earlier had affected the quality and direction of several other lives, much as Mather's sudden decision to lend money to the old man after all will presumably affect the lives of both Lacy and his daughter. Fitzgerald is careful to qualify matters with a "perhaps," but it is nevertheless evident that he recognized how a discrete act in the past could actually reverse the conduct of even a businessman striving consciously to be callous.

Jim Mather is quite aware of his guilt feelings and their source. But more subtle in *All the Sad Young Men* is the situation in which psychological factors unconsciously affect a character's values, feelings, and behavior. This is especially evident in "Winter Dreams." Fitzgerald is quite explicit that Dexter Green "was unconsciously dictated to by his winter dreams" (62). They even "persuaded" him to bypass the state university in favor of "an older and more famous university in the East": "Often he reached out for the best without knowing why he wanted it—and sometimes he ran up against the mysterious denials and prohibitions in which life indulges" (63). Once again these actions and feelings owe much to an individual, Judy Jones, whose "casual whim" to invite Dexter to dinner "gave a new direction to his life" (70). Though he acted with apparent freedom in his choice of school, his creation of a laundry empire, and his eventual success on Wall Street, Dexter had been manipulated to a startling degree by psychological factors of which he had been unaware. His tearful epiphany at the end of the story thus reflects the shock of his sudden discovery that he owed his drive, his ambition, and ultimately his business success—the components of what was identified above as his false self—to psychological urges over which he had had no control. Now consciously aware of his manipulation, he cries "for himself" (90).

A third outside factor capable of qualifying one's free will in *All the Sad Young Men* is marriage, but it is striking that marriage performs this function only in regard to women characters. Consider once again "The Adjuster." At the beginning of the story, Luella Hemple is admittedly self-centered, even declaring to her friend Ede, "I'd rather that [husband Charles] be unhappy than me" (164). But under pressure from a series of marriage-related crises, Luella finds herself being literally forced into the more selfless roles of wife and mother. The agent of that forcing is Dr. Moon, who insists that he himself does not act freely as he compels her to articulate the silly complaints underlying her restlessness:

> "Don't be afraid, Mrs. Hemple," said Doctor Moon suddenly. "This was forced upon me. I do not act as a free agent—"
> "I'm not afraid of you," she interrupted. But she knew that she was lying. She was afraid of him, if only for his dull insensitiveness to her distaste.
> "Tell me about your trouble," he said very naturally, as though she were not a free agent either. He wasn't even looking at her, and except that they were alone in the room, he scarcely seemed to be addressing her at all.
> The words that were in Luella's mind, her will, on her lips, were: "I'll do no such thing." What she actually said amazed her. It came out of her spontaneously, with apparently no co-operation of her own.
> "Didn't you see [Charles] rubbing his face at dinner?" she said despairingly. "Are you blind? He's become so irritating to me that I think I'll go mad."
> "I see." Doctor Moon's round face nodded. (172–73)

Having no control over her words is the first step in the breaking of her will. Dr. Moon next predicts that she will do something contrary to her conscious intention. Vowing that "in five minutes I'm going out of this house and begin to be alive" (173), she is stunned by Dr. Moon's response:

"You're not going out," he said after a moment; "I'm quite sure you're not going out."
Luella laughed.
"I *am* going out."
He disregarded this. (174)

And in fact she never leaves the house, as moments later her husband suffers a
nervous collapse that will endure for several years. In the course of taking care
of him, Luella's free will crumbles even further: "as the days passed, she found
herself doing many things that had been repugnant to her before. She stayed at
home with Charles; and when he grew better, she went out with him sometimes
to dinner, or the theatre, but only when he expressed a wish. She visited the
kitchen every day, and kept an unwilling eye on the house, at first with a horror
that it would go wrong again, then from habit" (189). As the word "habit"
suggests, Luella's free will is replaced with automatic behavior that is perfectly
suitable for good wives, and perfectly contrary to everything Luella thought,
felt, or did at the opening of the story. Indeed, in the final scene of "The
Adjuster," the recovered Charles returns home from work and is greeted "as
usual" by his adoring wife (192). As Christiane Johnson points out, it is never
clear "whether behavior modification is the cause or the effect of growing up,
whether growing up is achieved through, or results in, changed habits."[69] Whatever the case, Luella's free will is challenged and ultimately obliterated by
marriage.

Even where marriage itself is not at issue, it is still the man who, thanks
in large measure to his own free will, gains control in the relationship with the
woman and ultimately over his life. This is evident in " 'The Sensible Thing,' "
a story which Fitzgerald freely admitted was based upon his courtship of
Zelda.[70] What he does not acknowledge so readily is that his fictional alter ego,
George O'Kelly, enjoys a degree of free will that Fitzgerald himself had not
possessed during his own courtship and engagement of 1919–20.

O'Kelly is smitten by Jonquil Cary, the belle of a small town, while on an
engineering project in Tennessee. He unfortunately does not have the funds to
convince her to marry him, so he accepts a job as a forty-dollar-a-week insurance clerk in New York. Predictably, his strategy does not work: he is miserable
being so far from Jonquil, his minor post in the insurance world clearly will not
lead to immediate and lucrative advancement, and he is being perpetually tormented by Jonquil who, like Zelda, writes letters to him describing her dates
with other men. She even uses Zelda's pet word, "nervous," to describe her
restlessness over having no prospect of imminent marriage to O'Kelly. Typical
of the stories in *All the Sad Young Men*, O'Kelly comes across as hardworking
and sincere, while Jonquil seems flighty and insensitive: in fact, Fitzgerald
states categorically that it was Jonquil herself who "had made this mess" (219).
Though it seems that Jonquil is emerging as yet another *femme fatale* with

O'Kelly as yet another hapless male victim, Fitzgerald is careful to break and invert the pattern, as he does so often in *All the Sad Young Men:* George O'Kelly will emerge the victor. After Jonquil does "the sensible thing" by rejecting his last desperate plea for marriage, O'Kelly takes a drastic step: he accepts a job as third assistant engineer on an expedition to Peru. It had "not seemed an extraordinary opportunity" at the time; indeed, apparently he had initially agreed to go to South America simply to get as far away as possible from the scene of his broken heart. But with most of the crew dying from yellow fever, O'Kelly is faced with "his chance, a chance for anybody but a fool, a marvellous chance—" (237). Whereas in the earlier Fitzgerald "chance" would have suggested the whim of malevolent outside forces, in the context of " 'The Sensible Thing' " it means a golden opportunity. The plucky and resourceful O'Kelly puts to excellent use his honors degree in engineering from the Massachusetts Institute of Technology, and proves to be an immense success on the Peruvian expedition. In just ten months, O'Kelly "had made an admittedly remarkable showing for a young engineer": "In this short time he had risen from poverty into a position of unlimited opportunity" (230). Catapulting a poor but talented young man into great success and seeing its effect on his love life is, of course, a typical Fitzgerald plot device. But where " 'The Sensible Thing' " varies from the formula is that the hero doesn't get the golden girl—and frankly doesn't care. Contrary to most interpretations of the story, there is nothing at the end to suggest that O'Kelly and Jonquil will wed. She is in fact quite blunt that she no longer loves him—such is the power of time, even ten months, to erode a woman's love—and states flatly that she will never marry (234, 235). But instead of being crushed by her lack of interest in him, O'Kelly rises to the occasion:

> Well, let it pass, he thought; April is over, April is over. There are all kinds of love in the world, but never the same love twice. (238)

And so the story ends, with O'Kelly in total control of his emotional situation. Ten months earlier, her rejection had been devastating: "He broke into a long monologue of self-pity, and ceased only when he saw that he was making himself despicable in her sight. He threatened to leave when he had no intention of leaving, and refused to go when she told him that, after all, it was best that he should" (227). But though he still finds her attractive after his sojourn in Peru, O'Kelly is no longer bewitched by her, will no longer permit his emotional state to be manipulated by her whims. O'Kelly has consciously formulated a strategy that spares him Jonquil's ability to inflict pain upon him: he acknowledges that time changes all things, including love. That self-protective strategy permits any man to walk away from any woman; and if to rationalize the integrity of his own free will seems a bit naive (in effect O'Kelly can say that he doesn't want to marry Jonquil any more, since their love has changed), it at least enables him to tolerate more readily whatever disappointments in love he will encounter in his life.

George O'Kelly's attitude had not been held by the young Fitzgerald in his troubled premarital relationship with Zelda. Emotionally he had been at her mercy, caught in the throes of despair as she wrote to him of her "nervousness" and the details of her dates with other men. For all intents and purposes, it had been as if he had lost his free will in his pursuit of Zelda; and from the vantage point of November 1923, when he was re-examining that courtship in the creation of " 'The Sensible Thing,' " he could see how needless, even how tragic that loss had been, as it led him into a marriage with a woman who "meant no good" to him. Thus though " 'The Sensible Thing' " records many of the details of the Scott/Zelda courtship, it is more accurately seen as an imaginative re-creation of that courtship—one with, in retrospect, a "happy" ending: no marriage, and the man's free will intact.

In reality, of course, Fitzgerald was committed to Zelda for life. But as he found himself dealing with her insecurities and limitations, qualities that had become glaringly apparent during their three years of marriage, Fitzgerald clearly needed by the mid-1920s an explanation for how love in marriage could differ so dramatically from love in courtship, for how he could have so surrendered his free will in pursuing this difficult woman; in short, he needed a strategy for dealing with love as he was experiencing it with Zelda. George O'Kelly provides that strategy: if love is never the same way twice, then a man can be excused for being obsessed with his fiancée, can be excused for coming to love his wife—as Fitzgerald admitted in the letter quoted earlier—"in another way." This new-found flexibility would enable Fitzgerald to enjoy a modicum of peace in the face of Zelda's mental illness, the professional threats she posed to him, and the frequent enforced separations that would batter their marriage literally until the day Fitzgerald died in 1940.

Like so many male characters in *All the Sad Young Men,* George O'Kelly has evolved a kind of resiliency in dealing with life, and especially with love. His "April is over" lament is, ultimately, not really "sad." It is simply an acceptance of the fact that, over time, one's youthful, romantic notions of love must be changed, adjusted downward, as it were, to levels that are more in keeping with reality—and that are more likely to spare the individual any disappointment. But adjustment does not necessarily imply total abandonment. The men of *All the Sad Young Men* still seek to love and marry, still seek to develop their sense of self. But because they have strong self images and faith in the efficacy of their free will, because they are now mature enough to comprehend that things will not always work out in accordance with their dreams, and because they are more emotionally flexible, they can more readily accept what life has to offer them—and especially so since women no longer seem to be the powerful, bewitching creatures of the early Fitzgerald. Thus these young men are not, as Maxwell Geismar would have it, "studies in masculine defeat."[71] Fundamentally they are men at peace. As the title of the collection suggests, Fitzgerald's primary concern by the mid-1920s was men, and in particular men as survivors. It is a concern that would be even more evident in his fourth and final authorized collection of short stories, *Taps at Reveille*.

4

Taps at Reveille

Far more than with the creation of any of the three previous authorized collections, *Taps at Reveille* (1935) generated the most anguish for Fitzgerald. From the selection and arrangement of stories, to book production, to marketing, to critical reception, *Taps* seemed to offer nothing but problems and, ultimately, disappointment to a man whose professional confidence had once been unbounded. It was, consequently, a peculiarly fitting companion volume to *Tender Is the Night*, a novel that had taken nine painful years to create, and the imaginative structure of which he quickly came to regret. The difficulties attendant upon the creation of both books mirrored, and indeed were largely the result of, a series of crises in Fitzgerald's personal life. The visibly declining state of Zelda's mental health after the publication of *All the Sad Young Men* would culminate in the first of a series of severe breakdowns in April 1930—a situation which uncannily paralleled the difficulties on the world and national scene during those years. Considering the conditions under which he was living and working after 1926, one can only be astounded that Fitzgerald continued to function at all as a writer, let alone that he managed to produce a collection of stories as uniformly impressive as *Taps at Reveille*.

A necessarily brief overview of the Fitzgeralds' lives up to the publication of *Taps at Reveille* in March 1935 gives some idea of the challenges faced by Scott after his career peaked in the mid-1920s. After *All the Sad Young Men* appeared in February 1926, the Fitzgeralds moved to the Riviera, where they lived in a succession of villas until December of that year. In January 1927 they moved to Hollywood, where Fitzgerald worked on an unproduced film (*Lipstick*) for United Artists and became involved, evidently platonically, with starlet Lois Moran. Taunted by Fitzgerald's unconcealed admiration for the ambition and self-discipline of Miss Moran, the twenty-seven-year-old Zelda began frantically to study ballet in the hopes of pursuing a belated professional career as a prima ballerina. Her first lessons were with Catherine Littlefield in Philadelphia, to which she commuted from the Fitzgeralds' rented estate, Ellerslie, near Wilmington, Delaware—a home selected precisely because of its remoteness from the distracting allures of New York City. Returning to France in April 1928, Zelda in the mid-summer began even more intensive dance training with Mme. Lubov Egorova, formerly of Diaghilev's Ballet Russe. She attended lessons faithfully and spent hours every day in frantic practice at home, but her apparent dedication was not yet recognized as bordering on the pathological.

The Fitzgeralds returned to Ellerslie in September 1928, where they remained for six months, Zelda all the while continuing her ballet training. In March 1929 they returned to Europe, wandering from Italy, to France, and even to North Africa. This overseas junket did not produce the kind of serenity and objectivity that had enabled Fitzgerald to complete *Gatsby* in France and Italy in 1924. During an October 1929 drive to Paris, Zelda grabbed the steering wheel and attempted to drive the car off a cliff, maintaining that it was acting of its own will. Shortly thereafter she claimed that the flowers in a Parisian flower market were talking to her. The February 1930 vacation in Algeria, ironically intended to calm Zelda, proved disastrous as she chafed at the ballet lessons she was missing. Within two months of the trip to North Africa, the situation had reached a crisis. Late for a ballet lesson in April, Zelda had frantically changed into her tutu while en route to Mme. Egorova's studio in a Paris taxi. Her escort, C. O. Kalman, an old friend from St. Paul, was unable to reason with her, and she ran from the cab down the streets of Paris when it was momentarily detained at a crossing. Shortly after this incident, in late April 1930, Zelda had her first breakdown and was admitted to the Malmaison Clinic near Paris while in a state of hysteria. Reportedly she paced the room, repeating:

> "It's dreadful, it's horrible, what's to become of me, I must work and I won't be able to, I should die, but I must work. I'll never be cured. Let me leave, I must go to see 'Madame' [Egorova], she has given me the greatest possible joy; it's like the rays of the sun shining on a piece of crystal, to a symphony of perfumes, the most perfect harmonies of the greatest musicians."[1]

Against her doctor's recommendation, Zelda was released in early May 1930, but in less than a month (22 May) she was in the Valmont Clinic in Switzerland. Within two weeks (5 June), she was moved to Les Rives de Prangins Clinic on Lake Geneva and placed under the care of Dr. Oscar Forel. Her husband lived in Switzerland to be near her, while little Scottie remained in Paris with a governess. This arrangement would continue until September 1931, with Fitzgerald leaving Europe only once, to attend the funeral of his father in late January 1931.

Between September 1931 and September 1932 the Fitzgeralds lived in Montgomery, Alabama, with Scott spending a few months alone in Hollywood late in 1931 to work on the film *Red-Headed Woman* for Metro-Goldwyn-Mayer. While he was away, Zelda's father died in Montgomery (17 November

1931), and though at the time she seemed to have handled the crisis rather well, she suffered another breakdown later that winter, in February 1932. Zelda was placed in the Phipps Psychiatric Clinic of the Johns Hopkins University hospital, and to be near her Scott rented "La Paix"—"La Paix (My God!)"²—a fifteen-room house on the Bayard Turnbull estate at Towson, near Baltimore, Maryland. Though discharged from Phipps in late June 1932, Zelda was not fully recovered and in fact would never be completely well again. Her third breakdown occurred in January 1934, and from that point on Zelda's life was spent primarily in a series of institutions: the Sheppard-Pratt Hospital near Baltimore, the Craig House in Beacon, New York, and Highland Hospital in Asheville, North Carolina, where she would burn to death in a fire in a locked ward in March 1948.

These are hardly the kinds of conditions under which any writer can work readily, but other aspects of Zelda's situation made Fitzgerald's personal and professional existence even more troubled. For one thing, it placed an enormous financial burden on him alone. Though she had written essays and short stories (sometimes published under Scott's by-line) in an attempt to pay the $300 a month that Mme. Egorova charged for her lessons, Zelda, after the breakdowns began, was able to contribute very little to her own maintenance. The gross receipts for the paintings she sold at a New York exhibit in the spring of 1934 were just $328.75, while the novel she published in October 1932, *Save Me the Waltz,* earned $120.73.³ Her expenses were staggering, however. Refusing to place Zelda in any but the finest private psychiatric hospitals, Fitzgerald was faced with bills which in some cases were high even by today's standards: a single consultation with Dr. Paul Eugen Bleuler in November 1930 cost $500; the minimum fee for the Craig House was $175 a week; the bill for Zelda's stay at Prangins came to $13,000.⁴ The only way Fitzgerald could meet his family's high and continuous expenses was to write short stories, which by 1929 were commanding his all-time high fee of $4,000 each from the *Saturday Evening Post.* (Matthew Bruccoli estimates that this fee was roughly equivalent to $20,000 in 1981.)⁵ Though Fitzgerald had always been remarkably productive as a writer of short fiction and had managed before Zelda's first collapse to finance extensive foreign travel and the leasing of villas and estates, Zelda's medical bills and the need to maintain multiple households beginning in 1930 put a serious, permanent drain on even Fitzgerald's resources.

Further, Zelda's mental difficulties created a problem for her husband in a less obvious but perhaps more serious way: in order to concentrate more fully on the high-paying short fiction, Fitzgerald had to delay work indefinitely on the novel that was to become *Tender Is the Night.* For a writer who took particular pride in his achievement as a novelist, and especially for one who had set almost impossibly high standards for himself with the creation of *The Great Gatsby,* Fitzgerald had been distraught over his lack of progress with his fourth novel even before Zelda's first breakdown. From February 1926 to June 1927 he had written literally no short fiction, concentrating instead on trying to find his footing with a novel he variously called *The Boy Who Killed His Mother, Our Type,* and *The World's Fair.*[6] As he failed to wrestle the various manuscript versions into shape, Fitzgerald set himself a series of optimistic deadlines and reported his "progress," far more imagined than real, to friends and editors. "My novel to be finished July 1st," he wrote to Ernest Hemingway in April 1927. "No work this summer but lots this fall. Hope to finish the novel by 1st December," he blithely reported to him in November.[7] Early in July 1928 Fitzgerald wrote Max Perkins that he was "on the absolute wagon and working on the novel, the whole novel, and nothing but the novel. I'm coming back [from Europe] in August with it or on it," but more than a year later he was still "working hard"—"Prospects bright."[8] By May 1930 he was frankly making excuses for the delay of his long-awaited novel: "I wrote young & I wrote a lot & the pot takes longer to fill up now." But, he continued, "the novel, my novel, is a different matter than if I'd hurriedly finished it up a year and a half ago. . . . I think time seems to go by quicker there in America but time put in is time eventually taken out—and whatever this thing of mine is its certainly not a mediocrity."[9] Part of what made "this thing" so "different" was that the events of the preceding days and weeks had enabled him to visualize a workable focus for his novel: the impact of a woman's mental illness on her talented husband. But it was a focus that created its own difficulties. In the four painful years that followed, Fitzgerald was forced to face not only Zelda's schizophrenia, but his own possible role in exacerbating her illness through drinking and irregular living—a role which he denied with telltale vehemence.[10] Every personal situation had always been potential fictional material for Fitzgerald, but the immediacy of Zelda's crisis and his own implication in it led him to study and analyze their relationship, to immerse himself in the world of psychiatric medicine, even to study Freud and Jung with renewed intensity. Ultimately, Zelda's mental illness, which initially had seriously impeded any progress on Fitzgerald's difficult fourth novel, gave it a focus and a poignancy that enabled him to conceptualize and finally complete a novel which rivals *Gatsby* as Fitzgerald's finest achievement in long fiction.

But before this transmutation could occur, Zelda's mental difficulties only increased her husband's frustration over his inability to write his fourth novel. For one thing, whereas he was destined to struggle over *Tender Is the Night* for nearly a decade, Zelda managed to produce a novel of her own in a matter of weeks. Completed at the Phipps Clinic in March 1932, *Save Me the Waltz* was good enough to be published by Scribners in early October; and though it did not earn much in royalties, it did garner some appreciative reviews. Fitzgerald's dismay over his wife's self-discipline and productivity was palpable in his letters to Max Perkins, whom he urged not to praise Zelda's achievement too much—

for therapeutic reasons, of course: "I'm not certain enough of Zelda's present stability of character to expose her to any superlatives."[11] Zelda was astute enough to downplay her achievement by suggesting that she had written the novel to pass the time at Phipps, but the fact remained that while Fitzgerald struggled with *Tender Is the Night,* his schizophrenic wife, who suffered periodically from bouts of head-to-toe eczema and "awful sleep-killing asthma attacks" (which Scott attributed to moose hair),[12] had sufficient ambition and self-discipline to produce a publishable novel, in addition to several marketable stories and paintings. Worse still, the early drafts of *Save Me the Waltz* utilized material that Fitzgerald was already incorporating into the newly focused *Tender Is the Night.* Zelda's statement that *"I was . . . afraid we might have touched the same material"* was, to Fitzgerald, tantamount to an admission that she was consciously plagiarizing, stealing material to which he felt entitled as a professional author. After all, "my writing [is] more important than hers by a large margin because of the years of preparation for it, and the professional experience, and because my writing [keeps] the mare going, while Zelda's belongs to the luxury trade."[13] Perhaps so, but as Zelda observed bluntly, the story of her mental illness was her story in the profoundest sense. Her revisions of her novel were, therefore, to be purely aesthetic; all else had cost her *"a pretty emotional penny* to amass"[14] and would not be deleted at her husband's whim. He had of course been drawing upon his wife's personal experiences in his writing since the dawn of his career, but this was their first direct confrontation over what Zelda was at last challenging as her husband's exploitation of her private miseries. The ill feelings it generated on both sides caused a serious emotional rift in a marriage that had always combined genuine love, mutual self-advancement, and keen competition.

Much as Zelda's increasingly serious psychiatric difficulties after the mid-1920s had first impeded and then accelerated the creation of *Tender Is the Night,* so too they had affected Fitzgerald's short fiction. Zelda's illness had, if anything, stimulated his production of short stories,[15] not simply out of the need to acquire ready cash to pay her medical bills and to support himself and Scottie, but also out of the impulse to use this medium to explore the emotional and spiritual underpinnings of his troubled marriage and career. Not since *Flappers and Philosophers* had Fitzgerald written stories so blatantly autobiographical, in sentiment if not in fact. "Babylon Revisited" (written in December 1930) was so transparently a statement of Fitzgerald's guilt, remorse, and desire to create a new home for himself and his daughter that he actually sent the manuscript's carbon copy to his sister-in-law Rosalind Sayre Smith, the prototype for the judgmental Marion Peters.[16] "The Last of the Belles" (November 1928) is his farewell to the Southern-belle-cum-flapper with whom he had fallen in love so many years earlier. "Two Wrongs" (October-November 1929) melodramatically shows his fictional counterpart, Bill McChesney, selflessly exiling himself to Denver so that his talented Southern wife can pursue a belated career as a ballerina. Even the Basil stories, so frequently and erroneously dismissed as an exercise in escapist nostalgia, show Fitzgerald re-examining actual events in his youth in an attempt to understand his adult life. The impulse to use the writing of short fiction as self-therapy, an impulse so apparent in the stories of *All the Sad Young Men,* was, if anything, even more pronounced in *Taps at Reveille.*

But self-therapy is not evident in all the stories produced after *Gatsby,* and the often miserable conditions under which they were written were not necessarily conducive to uniform excellence. Fitzgerald published approximately fifty stories between 1926 and 1934. As is to be expected with such a large body of work, some of these stories are regrettable, obviously produced in haste for ready money (e.g., "A Change of Class," written in July 1931). A few, such as those of the "Philippe" series, are ambitious but seriously flawed—in this case, by putting slang-filled 1934 American dialogue into the mouths of ninth-century Frenchmen.[17] But it is still striking that of those fifty stories, Fitzgerald felt that eighteen were worthy of inclusion in *Taps at Reveille.* And worthiness had become a critical matter for him: the seriousness with which Fitzgerald had always approached his collections of short stories was particularly intense with *Taps at Reveille.* Financially, emotionally, and professionally, Fitzgerald had a lot riding on *Taps at Reveille,* and no one knew it better than he.

One indication of the trepidation with which he approached this companion volume to *Tender Is the Night* is that Fitzgerald wavered on preparing a collection along the same lines as *Flappers and Philosophers, Tales of the Jazz Age,* and *All the Sad Young Men.* In a letter to Max Perkins (15 May 1934), Fitzgerald outlined what he termed four "plans" for the follow-up volume to *Tender Is the Night.*[18] Plan One was to publish "a big omnibus including both new stories and the pick of the other three collections," a scheme which suggests an unwillingness to gamble (and perhaps lose) on a volume of entirely new material. Plan Two would be to publish the Basil and Josephine stories in a collection totalling 120,000 words. Fitzgerald was an astute enough observer of the literary marketplace to recognize the potential value of this plan, for Booth Tarkington's "Penrod" stories had been immensely popular. But though Fitzgerald terms this scheme "the best commercial bet," he also felt that it was *"the most dangerous artistically,"* for "the people who buy my books might think I was stringing them by selling them watered goods under a false name." Though Perkins urged him to pursue Plan Two despite these misgivings, Fitzgerald quickly abandoned the idea, declaring to his agent Harold Ober that if he ever did publish these stories as a book, "I might as well get tickets for Hollywood immediately."[19] Plan Three, the one eventually adopted, was to publish a collection of new short stories. Of those that had been published in magazines but were not yet collected in book form, Fitzgerald felt that he had approximately twenty-nine stories good enough for a collection. Plan Four was to publish a volume of "personal stuff"—

articles, reviews, and "random pieces," including "My Lost City," "Princeton," "How to Live on $36,000 a Year," and "The Cruise of the Rolling Junk," the account of the Fitzgeralds' automobile trip from Connecticut to Alabama in 1920 that had appeared in *Motor* magazine. Fitzgerald's impulse was characteristically sound, for many of these personal pieces would eventually be published in *The Crack-Up*, edited by Edmund Wilson in 1945, and *Afternoon of an Author*, edited by Arthur Mizener in 1957. But the same passion for orderliness that led him to insist upon uniform bindings for his books, and that seems so incongruous within the context of Fitzgerald's singularly disordered life, eventually won out: as with the previous three story volumes, the fourth was to contain only recent, uncollected magazine pieces.

The decision to go with Plan Three proved to be the least difficult aspect of the creation of *Taps at Reveille*. The very quantity of stories from which he had to make a selection in itself posed a problem, but several factors further complicated what was already a difficult task. One was the desire to showcase a variety of material. This impulse had of course proved to be a liability with *Tales of the Jazz Age*, which too many critics regarded as a heavily padded potpourri; so the resurrection of variety as an asset in 1934 would at first glance appear to be ill-considered and, in light of Fitzgerald's status as a professional author, quite needless. But Perkins felt strongly that a variety of material would "show more sides" of Fitzgerald than did *Tender Is the Night:* it would demonstrate "that you understand more different sorts of people than are in that,"[20] an important consideration in light of the unreasonable critical attacks on *Tender Is the Night* for being a paean to the wealthy in the midst of the Depression. Further, Fitzgerald was making a great effort at this juncture to change his public image as a writer, primarily out of financial and artistic necessity. By the 1930s Fitzgerald was widely perceived as a *"Post* writer"—not a bad thing in the 1920s, when the *Saturday Evening Post* enjoyed a wide circulation and paid high fees, but a mixed blessing during the Depression when advertisements (and hence story fees) fell off, while the demand for lengthy material continued. Fitzgerald was attempting to expand his market and increase his artistic options, including the option of writing brief, experimental pieces. The rather late decision (December 1934) to include "The Fiend" and "The Night of Chancellorsville" in *Taps at Reveille* in lieu of "Her Last Case" reflects this. These brief stories, his first pieces in *Esquire* magazine, "would give people less chance to say [that the stories in *Taps at Reveille*] are all standardized *Saturday Evening Post* stories, because, whatever can be said about them, they are not that."[21]

But the factor that most seriously complicated the selection of stories for *Taps* was something that Fitzgerald had somehow not foreseen. Phrases, metaphors, lengthy descriptions, even plot elements had been lifted wholesale from many of his stories and incorporated into *Tender Is the Night*. This was a keenly sensitive issue for Fitzgerald. Evidently part of the problem was a fear that to borrow from one's own material "as if [one's] imagination were starving"[22] was symptomatic of a writer's loss of creative power—a prospect that haunted Fitzgerald increasingly as he approached middle age. But the recycling of material also was a point of honor with him. The same public which he felt expected and deserved more than a book of Basil and Josephine stories also had a right to expect fresh material for its money, so he set to work searching the stories for echoes of the novel. Not surprisingly, Fitzgerald initially handled the situation by refusing to consider for inclusion in *Taps at Reveille* those stories which too obviously had been "stripped" extensively for *Tender Is the Night,* including such excellent pieces as "One Trip Abroad," "The Swimmers," and "Jacob's Ladder." As he wrote actress Lois Moran a few days before the volume's publication, he had especially wanted to include "Jacob's Ladder," which Miss Moran had inspired, "but I found that I had so thoroughly disemboweled it of its best descriptions for 'Tender is the Night' that it would be offering an empty shell."[23] Far more problematical, ironically, were those stories which had been stripped less extensively. Fitzgerald searched frantically for those passages that had found their way into *Tender Is the Night,* but a decade of false starts and manuscript changes made this task all but impossible: "there were so many revisions of 'Tender' that I don't know what I left in it and what I didn't leave in it finally."[24] Perkins frankly did not see this as a problem. He cited Hemingway as an example of a writer who repeated brief passages in different works, but Fitzgerald was not convinced: "The fact that Ernest has let himself repeat here and there a phrase would be no possible justification for my doing the same. Each of us has his virtues and one of mine happens to be a great sense of exactitude about my work."[25] That sense of exactitude made the process of revising the stories even more prolonged and painful than had been the case with the previous three collections, but the exhausted Fitzgerald resisted Perkins' urgent advisory that *Taps at Reveille* be published as soon as possible after *Tender Is the Night.* Wrote Fitzgerald, "I am not in the proper condition either physically or financially to put over the kind of rush job that this would be," and in fact it would be nine more months before *Taps at Reveille* finally appeared.[26] By that time, what little interest had been generated by *Tender Is the Night* was forgotten, and consequently the sales of both the novel and the collection failed to enjoy mutual enhancement. Worse, Fitzgerald never did catch all the elements that had found their way from the stories into *Tender Is the Night.* In a disclaimer at the foot of the first page of "A Short Trip Home" Fitzgerald admits that "in a moment of hasty misjudgment" a paragraph from the story was incorporated into "a novel of mine": "I have ventured none the less to leave it here, even at the risk of seeming to serve warmed-over fare" (323).[27]

Compared to the selection of stories for the volume and the deletion of material used in *Tender Is the Night,* the effort involved in arranging the chosen stories within *Taps at Reveille* was minimal. But it is nonetheless important to note that, far more than the previous three story collections, Fitzgerald was insistent that the stories of *Taps at Reveille* be arranged in a meaningful order, that the volume as a whole have what he termed "some real inner unity."[28] Consequently, early in the process of book production he asked that "The Night of Chancellorsville" be placed between "Two Wrongs" and the subsequently deleted "Jacob's Ladder."[29] Further, Maxwell Geismar is surely correct that "the point of the volume" is reflected in the Basil and Josephine stories which open it and in "Babylon Revisited" which closes it[30]—that is, the stories are so arranged as to offer a kind of overview of Fitzgerald's life from his boyhood in the Midwest to his personal and professional crash in Europe in 1930. That the five Basil and three Josephine stories were included less as a concession to Max Perkins' love of the series or as a marketing ploy than as part of an intricate pattern seems confirmed by the fact that Fitzgerald did not include all of the available Josephine stories. By ending the Josephine sequence with "A Woman With a Past," Fitzgerald withheld what Constance Drake terms the "Posty" fifth and final tale in the series, "Emotional Bankruptcy"[31]—and in doing so he let virtually every other story in the collection explore the phenomenon which is seen in its earliest stages in the first three Josephine stories. That is, emotional bankruptcy becomes a volume-wide concern rather than one peculiar to a particular adolescent female, and a "real inner unity" is indeed imparted to *Taps at Reveille* as a result.

Though Fitzgerald was clearly concerned about story arrangement, he experienced more distress and uncertainty regarding even the most mundane aspects of book production. He was shocked by the jacket illustration which, in Dickensian fashion, was intended to depict all the major characters: "it's rather discouraging to spend many hours trying to make the creatures in a book charming and then have someone who can't draw as well as Scottie cover five square inches with daubs that make them look like morons."[32] He prepared a Foreword to the collection, but by Christmas 1934 had convinced himself that it was a mistake, so "snappy-snooty" in tone that it would jeopardize the reception of the collection.[33] Perkins obligingly deleted the Foreword, and it is now lost. Not surprisingly, the selection of a title for the collection, that perennial source of anxiety for Fitzgerald, posed particular problems. In June 1934, he sent a list of projected titles to Max Perkins, including "Basil, Josephine and Others," "Many Blues," and "A Dance Card." (Fitzgerald frankly acknowledged that "I don't seem very fertile . . . at present" on the matter of titles.) Other possibilities on the list were "When Grandma Was a Boy," either a throwback to the sophomoric humor of the early Fitzgerald, or a revealing nod to the sometimes aberrant sexuality of his late works; and "Last Year's Steps," "The Salad Days," and "Just Play One More"—titles whose sentimental insistence on the past were actually quite inappropriate for the stories in *Taps at Reveille*.[34] Perkins preferred "Basil, Josephine and Others," but a few days later suggested "Babylon Revisited: Stories by Scott Fitzgerald."[35] Even Zelda in a lucid moment jokingly suggested that the volume be called "Eighty Thousand Dollars," since that was Fitzgerald's magazine income from the stories it contains.[36] It is not clear how the title *Taps at Reveille* came to be a possibility, although one may surmise that at some level Fitzgerald was responding to *First and Last,* the title of Gilbert Seldes' posthumous edition of the writings of Fitzgerald's old friend Ring Lardner.[37] Whatever the case, the notion of playing taps at reveille is characteristic of Fitzgerald in its ironic juxtaposition of opposites resulting in an emphasis on the negative (cf. the title of his 1935 story, "The Intimate Strangers"). Further, Richard L. Schoenwald points out that the merging of dawn (reveille) and dusk (taps) perfectly conveys Fitzgerald's sense that "the clocks have gone wrong"[38]—and few things convey disorder more eloquently than the inversion of that most relentlessly orderly entity, the passage of time. Even so, Fitzgerald had serious doubts about the title *Taps at Reveille* as the date of the volume's publication drew near. A desperate February 1935 wire to Perkins reads "TITLE SEEMS INCREASINGLY MEANINGLESS . . . OLD TITLE INVITES DISASTER WOMEN COULDNT PRONOUNCE AND WOULD FIND NO INTEREST." The wire offers a series of shamelessly romantic alternatives ("Last Night's Moon," "In the Last Quarter of the Moon," "Golden Spoons," "Moonlight in My Eyes") which would have been totally inappropriate for the collection. The ever-patient Max Perkins assured Fitzgerald that "reveille" was known "to every man who was ever in the national guard, the army, military school, boys' camp or girls' camp," and even if it were an intimidating word to some readers, "'Taps' is not."[39] *Taps at Reveille* it remained.

The collection was published on 20 March 1935 in a modest run of 5,100 copies. It sold less than 3,000 copies, but the title was hardly to blame. A major factor was the Depression, which had been hurting the book trade, a "luxury" industry, for over five years. Fitzgerald's boast to Hemingway in May 1934 that *Tender Is the Night* was the fifth bestseller in the country was qualified by the fact that sales had not broken 12,000.[40] Given the response to *Tender Is the Night,* Fitzgerald feared the worst for *Taps at Reveille,* and his unprecedented fretting over story selection and arrangement, book production, and titles at least partly reflects his impulse to prepare a volume so attractive that one could justify purchasing it in the midst of the Depression. Indeed, the very decision to market such a large book—at 407 pages, it is by far the longest of the four authorized collections—seems partly the result of Fitzgerald's newly articulated consciousness of the psychology of book buying. A decade earlier, Perkins had tentatively suggested that the poor sales of *Gatsby* were due to its brevity,[41] and this possibility loomed even larger in the mid-1930s. Indeed, Fitzgerald explained bluntly to Bennett Cerf in 1936 why he wanted to include the bulky *Tender Is the Night* in the "Modern Library" series:

> I have an idea that even among your clientele the actual bulk of a book, the weight of it in the hand, has something to do with buyer psychology. That is, that you would do better with, say, Willa Cather's *My Antonia* than you would with *Lost Lady*. All the first Modern Library books were small. Your tendency toward the giant size shows that you [are] alive to this psychological trait in the potential buyer.[42]

Eighteen stories for $2.50 apparently struck Fitzgerald as a good bargain even in 1935, but the buying public apparently did not agree. *Taps at Reveille* was never reprinted.

The other factor in the collection's poor sales was less obviously related to economics. The critical response to the collection ranged from lukewarm to excoriating. Declared Arthur Coleman in the *Dallas Morning News*, "One does not have to recall the Gatsby cameo to realize, reading these stories, that herein is recorded the petrifaction of a talent that in 1925 looked like one of the best in American literature." Critics had eulogized Fitzgerald's career in the past, but rarely so categorically as this: "I am sorry this book was published. I would rather remember Fitzgerald by Gatsby and 'Tender Is the Night' and a few of the really glittering stories he has done. For this is entirely too conclusive a group of documents for even the stoutest faith to stand against."[43] T. S. Matthews in the *New Republic* offered the Jekyll-Hyde approach to Fitzgerald which has remained something of an unfortunate critical commonplace:

> Scott Fitzgerald is supposed to be a case of split personality: Fitzgerald A is the serious writer; Fitzgerald B brings home the necessary bacon. And "Taps at Reveille," a collection of avowed pot-boilers, was written with his fingers crossed by Fitzgerald B. There seems to be a feeling abroad that it would be kinder not to take any critical notice of the goings-on of Fitzgerald B, since his better half is such a superior person and might be embarrassed. Mr. Fitzgerald himself, however, obviously doesn't feel that way about it, for he signs his moniker to all and sundry, and even collects the offerings of his lower nature in a book.[44]

But there frankly seems little justice in the remarks of Coleman, Matthews, and a host of other caustic reviewers. The modern critical estimation of *Taps at Reveille*—based, admittedly, largely on its three best-known stories, "Babylon Revisited," "Crazy Sunday," and "The Last of the Belles"—is that it is an excellent book. Kenneth Eble feels that *Taps at Reveille* is "the richest" of the four authorized collections; K. G. W. Cross finds it Fitzgerald's "most rewarding" story volume; Maxwell Geismar terms it "in some respects [his] most interesting collection of tales"; and Malcolm Cowley states bluntly that *Taps at Reveille* is "by far his best collection."[45] Were one to read all eighteen of the stories, and in the order in which Fitzgerald arranged them, one would tend to agree. Its three best-known stories are almost universally regarded as among the finest achievements in American short fiction. Further, the Basil stories, even if read superficially as charming accounts of actual incidents in Fitzgerald's childhood and young manhood, are consistently well-crafted, consistently moving. But even the most neglected or denigrated stories—including "Majesty," "One Interne," "A Short Trip Home," and "Family in the Wind"—are far more poignant, far more artistically wrought, than a cursory reading might suggest. For as Fitzgerald during the post-*Gatsby* period searched for new fictional ways to explore and convey the personal and professional crises which at times seemed so relentless and overwhelming, there was, as evidenced by the solid stories he chose so carefully for his fourth collection, a concomitant refinement of his literary artistry. With their generally uncluttered styles, simplified plots, restrained dialogue, subtle metaphors, and gentle humor, these stories show not the petrifaction of a talent, but its final blooming.

No small factor in that blooming is Fitzgerald's mature understanding, tempered in tragedy and disappointment, of dreams and disillusionment, of home, and of the historical sense. Not the lugubrious tome that its title might suggest, *Taps at Reveille* shows Fitzgerald objectively re-examining his early life, evaluating his current situation, and, rather unexpectedly, attempting to develop a personal vision broad enough to accommodate the crises of the post-*Gatsby* years and, ultimately, positive enough to give him the strength and hope to look beyond them. Much as Charlie Wales of "Babylon Revisited" had "larger plans" (386) that enabled him to tolerate the torments and uncertainties of the present by focusing on the dream of a future home with his Honoria, so too did F. Scott Fitzgerald.

In retrospect, Fitzgerald's treatment of dreams and disillusionment in his second volume, *Tales of the Jazz Age,* had been simplistic, almost fatuous. For a young man whose own personal life and writing career were almost preternaturally successful, Fitzgerald's understanding of "dreams" in the early 1920s tended not to range much beyond Golden Girls and cash, with "disillusionment" the result of the loss or denial of such. Even stories which dealt subtly with the possible failure of his writing career tended to posit the sources of that failure melodramatically as both tangible and beyond the victim's control, such as suffering a massive stroke or simply growing old. But the Fitzgerald of the late 1920s and early 1930s had come to realize that the most worthwhile dreams were far more abstract, more fragile: mental and physical health, domestic tranquility, and a firm sense of vocation, even if it did not lead to "success" in the Jazz Age understanding of the word. And his new attitude toward disillusionment was, if anything, even more subtle, as the late Fitzgerald came to see it not as a chance thing to be feared, but as a probable eventuality. And yet, far from railing against the seeming injustice of that eventuality, he seemed actually to embrace disillusionment as a natural, even necessary component of growth and maturity which, perceived rightly, could enable one to deal with the subsequent tragedies and challenges one was destined to face.

This is not to say that the late Fitzgerald had abandoned his early position that a major source of disillusionment was the pursuit of unworthy dreams. Money certainly remained an unworthy dream; but the obviousness of this fact to the mature Fitzgerald is reflected in its lack of importance in *Taps at Reveille*. In only one story, "Babylon Revisited," is money a major source of disillusionment; but because this is essentially a post-disillusionment story (Charlie Wales had lost his fortune long before the story opens), it offers an examination of Charlie's emotional regrouping, his new world vision in which one needs enough money to maintain a small apartment in Prague and a governess [i.e., a mother] for one's child, but not so much that one has the leisure to ride tricycles around Montmartre—an appropriately infantile image of the pre-Crash, "dissipating" Good-Time-Charlie Wales.[46] As was evident in regard to love in *All the Sad Young Men*, Fitzgerald does not deny the practical importance of money in *Taps at Reveille*, but he does recognize the need to scale it down, to put into more limited perspective its importance in one's life. Indeed, the psychological damage that can be generated by money-based disillusionment is evident in the characterization of the grasping and judgmental Marion Peters. Garbed in a dress faintly suggesting mourning (393), Marion seems motivated less by love for her dead sister than by jealousy over Charlie's former wealth (the Peterses had not shared in the pre-Crash bonanza) and for his present financial security in Prague. Also insidiously affected by money is her husband: "humiliated by his own failure to make money,"[47] Lincoln submits to his vindicative wife, standing by impotently as she effectively allies herself with Lorraine and Duncan to ensure Charlie's continued anguish.[48] In a perfect illustration of the late Fitzgerald's sensitivity to the nuances of irony, the ostensibly moralistic and selflessly maternal Marion is herself amoral and vindictive, and hence an unsympathetic character; but her inability to comprehend that money is an unworthy dream leaves her doomed to perpetual disillusionment, and hence a quasi-sympathetic character. Much as the mature Fitzgerald seems to have resented Zelda as a professional threat and a financial burden while never wavering in his love for her, so too his late characters evince a complexity that helps explain the variety of critical responses this story has engendered, including the perennial controversy over whether Charlie Wales is a self-deceiving fraud or a saint. The point of the story, ultimately, is that he is neither, and both—in a word, human. By the same token, Joel Coles of "Crazy Sunday" is both a hard-working, well-meaning writer and a two-faced scoundrel who assures Miles Calman that his wife is safe with him ("You can trust me absolutely" [214]) and then tries to seduce her shortly thereafter. The emotional complexities of the late Fitzgerald's private life, including the antithetical impulses to condemn and exonerate himself for Zelda's mental illness, enabled him to grasp functional ambiguity as a fact of human existence and to exploit it as a rich fictional device. There is a pervading sense of tolerance about the stories of the late Fitzgerald which may be attributed to his hard-won understanding of human frailty, including his own.

This is not to say, however, that the late Fitzgerald had turned into Pollyanna. He can be strikingly judgmental, as evidenced by his new appreciation of satire. Consider his late treatment of that other unworthy dream, the Golden Girl. The ultimate example in *Taps at Reveille* is Ailie Calhoun of "The Last of the Belles," like Zelda the cynosure of all enlisted men and officers in the camps surrounding her hometown in the South of World War I. Fitzgerald's initial presentation of Ailie makes her seem so bewitching that most readers seem not to recognize the falling away of her mask, the revelation of the chill-minded flapper under the alluring Southern belle. But as Scott Donaldson points out, Ailie is "all artifice (Fitzgerald knew what he was doing with Ailie's 'adroitness sugar-coated' and her 'soft, wheedling notes' ")[49] and by relentlessly including every popular notion regarding Southern belles (e.g., the pose of sexual innocence in her adjustment of Andy's phallic collar pin: "Your guns are all crooked" [256]), Fitzgerald gradually instills in his reader the realization that the presentation of Ailie is satiric. Thanks to the objectivity of the first-person retrospective narration—a device Fitzgerald would not have considered using in the first of the Tarleton stories, "The Ice Palace" (1919)—Fitzgerald suggests that the true Ailie is the one we last see, "rambl[ing] on in the half-laughing, half-desperate banter of the newer South" (271). She had never been worth the trouble of the narrator or of any other man, including Lt. Horace Canby, who killed himself after being rejected by a woman who essentially was simply a good imitation of a kind of figment of the Southern imagination. That the narrator is not incapacitated by the disillusioning vision of the true Ailie is a tribute to his capacity to see her in proper perspective as a part of his personal past which, like the rusty tomato cans, is necessarily and mercifully behind him.

But even as he downplayed and frankly satirized the dubious allure of money and Golden Girls, the late Fitzgerald addressed more subtle, more insidious unworthy dreams. One such dream is to become like someone else, an element he explores with gentle humor in the Basil series. In "The Scandal Detectives," fourteen-year-old Basil consciously apes the pint-sized Lothario of St. Paul, Hubert Blair, whose gift for pratfalls—"He cocked one foot behind the other and pretended to lean an elbow against a tree, missed the tree on purpose and gracefully saved himself from falling" (11)—is the envy of the neighborhood. In a story set a year later, "The Captured Shadow," Basil so admires Andy Lockheart, "a living symbol of the splendid, glamorous world of Yale" (86), that for a year he mimics Lockheart's walk and tries, unsuccessfully, to play the piano by ear, as Andy does. Still later, in "The Perfect Life," the prep school gridiron hero Basil, at the urging of Princetonian John Granby, dreams of living a "perfect life" characterized by devotion to schoolwork, regular letters home to Mom, no smoking, and no sexual dalliance, including the dreaded kissing. Of course, Hubert's talent for pratfalls is silly; Andy's gait is superficial and his musical ability is innate; and poor John Granby is so out of touch with reality that he can't even get to the station in time to catch his bus. The maturing Basil eventually abandons all these ill-placed dreams, but Fitzgerald's point is still clear: throughout life we are tempted to follow the examples of others, to try to create our dreams out of their gifts and obsessions.

Though young Basil was able to emerge unscathed from the pursuit of a succession of unworthy dreams, other characters in *Taps at Reveille* are not so fortunate. One almost disastrous case involves Bill Tulliver of "One Interne." As "the fifth in an unbroken series of Dr. William Tullivers who had practised with distinction" in Baltimore (350), Bill has entered the medical profession almost by default. True, there is no doubt that he has an aptitude for medicine, and Fitzgerald surely does not suggest that to pursue a career as a physician is not worthwhile. But it does seem clear that Bill's decision to become a doctor was as much a matter of family tradition, of a dream imposed from without, as it was self-generated. Bill will in fact undergo a serious identity crisis as he begins his internship at Johns Hopkins, culminating in a near-fatal illness. And though by the end of the story Bill has been restored to physical health and emotional equanimity, it is nonetheless clear that "One Interne" is fundamentally a parable arguing that outsiders, including one's own family and community, can impose dreams which lead to disastrous consequences.

In addition to familial and community expectations, a major source of questionable dreams in the stories of the late Fitzgerald is the popular imagination, especially as nurtured by literature and the theater. Once again the experiences of young Basil serve as a benign and gently comic parallel to those of the older characters. For example, inspired by two "crook comedies" he had seen in New York and also by his reading of Arsène Lupin, Basil dreams of pursuing a career as a "gentleman burglar," a "romantic phenomenon lately imported from Europe and much admired in the first bored decades of the century" ("The Scandal Detectives," 3). But Basil's emulation of criminals does not last long. In "The Scandal Detectives" he abandons his plan to kidnap Hubert Blair, tie him up, and stuff him in a garbage can, not only because of a logistical glitch (co-conspirator Riply Buckner cannot manage the rope) but more importantly because he felt "morally alone" when faced with the reality of abducting Hubert (24). However attractive literature made the dream of a life of crime, it was incompatible with Basil's personality and moral code, and so he could not act on it. How appropriate, then, that Basil channels this still-alluring dream of becoming a criminal into the safe medium of art, writing a play about a gentleman burglar, "the Shadow," rather than attempting to be one in real life. Indeed, he does not even perform the lead role, allowing two other young actors to portray the character he himself created.

But where young Basil quickly establishes the impossibility of acting out the dreams he has acquired from the popular imagination and thus experiences minimal disillusionment, other characters in the stories of *Taps at Reveille* are not always so fortunate. Josephine Perry, a shopworn seventeen-year-old in "A Woman With a Past," fails to attract a man she truly loves, basically because all she knows of romance, and of herself, is derived from popular music. In "First Blood" she is depicted writing a love letter like a child, quoting passages from popular songs "as if they expressed the writer's state of mind more fully than the verbal struggles of her own" (146). Ruth Prigozy is doubtless correct that Fitzgerald was keenly aware of the extent to which popular music "was a source of romantic illusion and pseudo-feeling, as well as a deterrent to profound and mature emotions."[50] Even someone older and better educated than Josephine, Yale football star Ted Fay, has difficulty differentiating between romantic dreams and reality. In "The Freshest Boy" Basil overhears him trying to convince his actress-girlfriend to run away with him, despite her commitment to a director:

> "Tell him the truth—that you love me. Ask him to let you off."
> "This isn't musical comedy, Ted." (49)

Even Basil, who derived all his knowledge of prep schools from popular literature and who slips easily in and out of fantasies about crime and football at will, never has to be reminded that real life is not a musical comedy. And even where the specific sources are not so readily ascertained, it is clear that the popular imagination is responsible for dubious dreams that lead to disillusionment, and occasionally death. Popular notions of the romance of war lead Ailie Calhoun of "The Last of the Belles" to be smitten by Earl Schoen, whose background as a boorish streetcar conductor is well-concealed behind a dashing uniform. And aviator Horace Canby wears spurs "with which he presumably urged on his aeroplane" (256), the reflection of the early Fitzgerald's naive conviction that "aviation sounds like the romantic side of war . . . like cavalry used to be, you know" (*This Side of Paradise,* 150).[51] Disillusionment is inevitable. Ailie is in a state of "stupefaction" at the post-war sight of Earl in mufti: "His hat was green, with a radical feather; his suit was slashed and braided in a grotesque fashion that national advertising and the movies have put an end to" (268). (Apparently popular culture isn't all bad, especially where clothing is concerned.) And Horace Canby, who in the popular literature of the Civil War would have responded to Ailie's rejection by leading a charge, kills himself by deliberately crashing his plane. "I never believe much in happiness," wrote Fitzgerald to his daughter in 1933. "I never believe in misery either. Those are things you see on the stage or the screen or the printed page[;] they never really happen to you in life."[52] Wishful thinking perhaps on his part, but the fact remains that Fitzgerald was acutely sensitive to the capacity of the popular imagination to dictate our thoughts, values, actions—the very quality and direction of our lives.

What further complicates the issue of dreams and disillusionment in the late Fitzgerald is his mature understanding that even admirable, self-generated dreams can lead to disillusionment. Characteristically, he first probes this matter in the series of stories devoted to Basil Duke Lee. As Rochelle S. Elstein points out, these stories collectively constitute a kind of *Bildungsroman,* with Basil progressing clearly (if sometimes painfully) toward self-understanding. Early in "He Thinks He's Wonderful," for example, we learn that Basil's "fantastic ambition was continually leading him to expect too much" (53). "He wanted to be a great writer, a great athlete, popular, romantic, brilliant, and always happy" continues the earlier magazine text of the story, though in the slightly revised version used in *Taps at Reveille* Fitzgerald deleted "a great writer" and "romantic"[53]—perhaps because they too obviously identified the young Basil with the young Fitzgerald. Whatever the case, it is clear that the series shows a good boy, moral and above all imaginative, coming to grips with a world that does not always cherish such qualities. This is perhaps most obvious in "The Captured Shadow." Basil works hard on his little play (also named *The Captured Shadow*), even experiencing the writer's compulsion to commit to paper the entire scenes that exist in his head, though to work all night might well lead to madness (83). His playmates are dazzled by his achievement; even the exquisite Evelyn Beebe is momentarily distracted from Andy Lockheart when she learns that Basil himself wrote the entire play. Basil clings to his dream of theatrical success, patiently casting the parts, salving the fragile egos of his actors, enduring the presence of the flighty Miss Halliburton as nominal "director," and averting disaster by dropping the curtain and apologizing to the audience when Mayall De Bec inadvertently begins performing Act III in the middle of Act II. Basil's dream is unquestionably achieved: the play is a resounding success, he gains city-wide fame as a fifteen-year-old playwright, and the proceeds are donated to a worthy cause, the local Baby Welfare League. But Basil is disillusioned to the point of utter despair. Part of the problem is, once again, purely moral. In order to ensure that the play's leading lady, Evelyn Beebe, does not leave town with her family until the performance is over, Basil arranges for her little brother Ham to contract mumps from another child. Basil is "fully aware that it was the worst thing he had ever done in his life" (95), and the enormity of his malicious actions hangs like a pall over the success of his play. After the performance, despite the laughter, the congratulations, and the interviews, Basil is miserable. His alarmed mother tries to reason with him:

> "You shouldn't feel sad. Why, people told me after the play—"
> "Oh, that's all over. Don't talk about that—don't ever talk to me about that any more."
> "Then what are you sad about?"

"Oh, about a little boy."
"What little boy?"
"Oh, little Ham—you wouldn't understand." (102–3)

Actually she does understand, in spirit if not in detail. When at the end of the story she prays, "God, help him! help him, . . . because he needs help that I can't give him any more" (103), she is acknowledging that Basil is now old enough to respond to the cruel fact of adult life that success is no guarantee of happiness—and, ironically, especially so for an intelligent, sensitive boy like Basil. He cannot quite accept the fact that evil means (infecting Ham Beebe) can lead to noble ends (a generous donation to the Baby Welfare League, plus public recognition of his hard work as a writer). The incompatibility of questionable conduct and artistic achievement was a truth becoming increasingly evident to Fitzgerald as he wrote the Basil stories in the late 1920s. Leslie A. Fiedler may be correct in surmising that Fitzgerald had deliberately cultivated self-destructive behavior, and especially drinking, in the belief that it was conducive to his own great dream of success as a productive and critically acclaimed author.[54] One of the most revealing statements Fitzgerald ever made appears in the draft of a 1932 letter to the institutionalized Zelda: "Is there not an idea in your head sometimes that you must live close to the borders of mental trouble in order to create at your best?"[55] Young Basil's schoolboy fear that he would go insane if he stayed awake all night to write his play actually hit close to home with Scott Fitzgerald, for both he and Zelda had been living near those "borders" for years. But though they had in fact created a great deal in a variety of media, it was increasingly evident by the late 1920s that the ends could not possibly justify the means. Thus Basil's negative response to the success of his play ("he felt a great vacancy come into his heart. It was over, it was done and gone—all that work, and interest and absorption. It was a hollowness like fear" [102]) is not simply the postpartum depression familiar to any writer who has just completed a substantial project. It seems far more an emblem of Fitzgerald's response to his own career, and especially the lives that had been compromised and sacrificed to make it possible. The price had been high indeed.

The simple fact that the realization of worthy dreams can lead to disillusionment, even physical pain, helps explain Fitzgerald's impulse to write two series, the Basil Duke Lee and the Josephine Perry stories. Each series probes a particular scenario of success and disillusionment; each utilizes a protagonist who has emotional connections to Fitzgerald himself. That the young Fitzgerald was the prototype for Basil is a critical commonplace, as a series of scholars have traced the verifiable connections between people and events in the stories and those in real life.[56] Less obvious is the fact that Basil responds as Fitzgerald did to events around him only up to an optimal point; beyond that point, teen-aged Basil seems far more mature than his middle-aged creator. For example, despite his negative response to his play's success, Basil does not wallow in his despair for long, nor does he simply abandon his dreams of prep school, Yale, and a career as a writer. He recognizes and accepts the fact that disillusionment is an inevitable part of life—something that Fitzgerald himself would not acknowledge outside a fictional context until 1936: "This is what I think now: that the natural state of the sentient adult is a qualified unhappiness."[57] "Qualified" is the operative word; unhappiness is unavoidable, but life goes on. Since young Basil rather quickly becomes attuned to this, it seems most reasonable to maintain not that he is a photographic autobiographical portrait of the young Fitzgerald, but that he is a portrait of what Fitzgerald *wished* he had been—accepting, stable, functional.

Conversely, Josephine Perry seems to be a double portrait limning partly what Fitzgerald had been, but primarily what he could see himself becoming: an emotional bankrupt. True, Josephine's immediate prototype was Ginevra King Mitchell Pirie, the great love of Fitzgerald's youth; even she frankly admitted to Arthur Mizener that Miss Perry and Mrs. Pirie were remarkably similar.[58] But far less obvious is the possibility that another, more emotion-centered prototype for Josephine may have been Fitzgerald himself. That he presents her "career" in terms of love rather than writing should not obscure the fact that Josephine, like Basil, pursues a series of dreams, some of which are successfully achieved. There the similarity ends, however, and nothing could be less accurate than the relentless critical assumption that Josephine is "a female Basil Duke Lee."[59] The two characters are completely different in their temperaments and their responses to life crises. Josephine's definition of success is to achieve the dream of love, especially as it is defined by the popular imagination. "First Blood," the first of the three Josephine stories in *Taps at Reveille,* shows her infatuation with the Poesque Travis de Coppet, he of the "very dark" eyes, blazing white teeth, and obligatory blue cape (135), as well as with Anthony Harker, whose primary charms seem to be that he is an older man (twenty-two to Josephine's sixteen [140]) and already involved with Josephine's own sister, Constance. In the second story, "A Nice Quiet Place," the willful Josephine, exiled to dreary Island Farms for the summer vacation, seems actually to conjure up the dashing Sonny Dorrance—"model legs," riding crop, "blond Viking head," and all (160)—while writing a letter that is a tissue of lies about her successful summer romances. Even Sonny's eventual revelation that he is married to a mulatto (yet another lie of love) is not enough to dampen her passion. It is only the truth, the disillusioning fact that he is unmarried and deliberately avoiding her, that sends her into the arms of yet another inappropriate male, Malcolm Libby, moments before he marries Constance. Not surprisingly, the Josephine of "A Woman With a Past" is self-admittedly disillusioned; indeed, Fitzgerald is explicit that her failure to grow excited over a visit to New Haven, that hotbed of eligible Yale men, leaves her "wonder[ing] at the extent of her own disillusionment" (178). However, she gives love one last chance by attempting to lure the charming Mr. Dudley Knowleton away from her school-mate Adele Craw, "a pretty girl with clear honorable eyes and piano legs" (178). Josephine fails utterly to attract Knowleton, evidently the one man of her multitude of conquests that she truly cares for; and the major problem is her "past"—one from which she had apparently learned nothing about love. Though Fitzgerald included neither of the remaining Josephine stories in *Taps at Reveille*, the title of the fifth and final story of the series, "Emotional Bankruptcy" (1931), suggests that "First Blood," "A Nice Quiet Place," and "A Woman With a Past" illustrate the initial and intermediate stages of a spiritual deterioration with which Fitzgerald himself—and not the more resilient Basil—was all too familiar. The Basil stories thus offer collectively a scenario of what Fitzgerald should have done, how he should have learned to accept and grow from whatever disillusionments—whatever their sources—he experienced in his career and personal life from the very outset. And the Josephine series conversely offers a chilling scenario of what did happen to Fitzgerald, including what Bruccoli identifies as "self-destructive" behavior.[60] Working so close to himself spiritually that he had to present his fictional counterpart as a female,[61] Fitzgerald ultimately could not bear to continue tracing the sorry career of Josephine, and he would write no more stories about her after "Emotional Bankruptcy." But in a way Josephine's tale of woe did not end there. Much as Basil's happier story is essentially continued in *This Side of Paradise*,[62] Josephine's is continued in *The Crack-Up*.

The creation of a series of stories that probe antipodal modes of responding to disillusionment was an imaginative and highly effective way of examining the crises Fitzgerald was facing in the late 1920s and early 1930s. Earlier in his career he had possessed neither the objectivity nor the artistry to attempt such a feat; but far more importantly, in the early 1920s he had not been able to face squarely the fact that disillusionment was not simply inevitable, but actually necessary for spiritual growth. He had begun to rationalize the desirability of disillusionment early in his career, as evidenced by such stories as "The Lees of Happiness" and "The Four Fists"; but he seems not to have felt it in his heart until the crises of the late 1920s. Once his heart caught up with his mind, Fitzgerald was able to produce a series of convincing, poignant, and artistically satisfying parables delineating how maturity and contentment can be born of disaster and disappointment. They predominate in *Taps at Reveille*, and they include some of his best efforts in short fiction.

Consider once again the case of Bill Tulliver of "One Interne" (written in August 1932). He is a fifth-generation Baltimore physician with a genuine aptitude for medicine—or, more precisely, for a particular aspect of medicine. Unquestionably he has a good technical knowledge of pathology, having helped his friend and foil George Schoatze get through difficult courses in clinical medicine and a particularly difficult textbook on toxicology (367). He also was undeniably correct in his diagnosis of a patient, Mr. Doremus. But Bill has so misdirected this talent that his dreams and self-image are unworthy of a man of medicine. Bill's great professional ambition is not to care for the ill but to upstage his mentor, the venerable diagnostician Dr. Norton: "His whole life was pointed toward the day when his own guess would be right and Doctor Norton's would be wrong" (350). He composes verses about himself to be used in the annual "roast" of Johns Hopkins' most respected physicians. He competes for Thea Singleton less out of love, one suspects, than out of a desire to prove himself a better man than her beau, the brilliant surgeon Howard Durfee. In brief, Bill Tulliver has arrived at an intense "pitch of egotism" (350) that is totally inappropriate for one entering that most ideally selfless of professions, the practice of medicine; and this egotism is especially inappropriate in that it is unjustified. True, he diagnoses correctly Mr. Doremus's illness, but only after nervously making such a needlessly large number of blood tests that the patient almost requires a transfusion (361). Even worse, some of his diagnoses are the result of pure luck. "He had made a few nice guesses and Doctor Norton had given him full credit" (361), while the mysterious Van Schaik case is determined to be a hangover only when a lowly student nurse tells him about the liquor bottles in the patient's suitcase (356–57). And unable to admit his incompetence, he hides behind excuses: "'Kind of puzzling case in here—contradictory symptoms,' he lied" (356). Fundamentally an egocentric fraud, Bill will experience his true "interneship" through his subjection to a series of publicly disillusioning experiences that are essential for his emergence as a doctor in the most admirable sense of the word. Some of these experiences are engineered by the wise Dr. Norton, who deliberately gives Bill and George Schoatze complex cases that are difficult to diagnose. "'Humbling us a little,' said Bill rather resentfully" (357) in response to one of these; but the situation is more involved than this, as is signified by Fitzgerald's subtle handling of the characterization of Thea Singleton. She proves to be considerably more than a belated Golden Girl, much as "One Interne" is considerably more than a hospital-based soap opera. Thea is first seen literally catching a falling man at a bus-stop, and thereafter her primary function in the story is to oversee both the "fall" and the rebirth of young Dr. Tulliver. After witnessing the bus-stop incident, Bill next sees Thea in the shadow of the famed statue of Christ which "gesture[s] in marble pity over the entrance hall" of the hospital at Johns Hopkins University (353). She is a "real" girl, real enough for Bill to date, and at first glance Bill's response to seeing her near the Christ sounds like a melodramatic depiction of hormones gone wild: "Suddenly Bill was in a condition of shock, his tranquility was rent asunder, he could not have given a rational account as to why he was where he was" (353). But in fact this is symptomatic of not a sexual but a spiritual crisis. "[S]tricken, haywire, scattered and dissolved" by his first direct exposure to Thea (353), the more Bill gets to know her, the more spiritually unsettled he becomes. Still striving to be a self-assured prig, some of Bill's cockiness is shaken when Thea reminds him that he is merely an interne, and not yet a full-fledged doctor (363). Far more dramatic is his reaction to Thea's explanation that she is not truly in love with the surgeon she dates, Dr. Durfee. Rather, her one great love had been the famous Dr. John Gresham, who "had died by inches from radium poisoning, got by his own experiments" (363). The notion of dying selflessly in the name of medicine is shocking to the still egocentric Bill, who shortly after hearing Gresham's story suddenly develops a physical illness which corresponds to his spiritual one: Bill has an attack of "volvulus," a disorder in which "a loop of the intestine gets twisted on itself" (370)—a graphic emblem of self-involvement. Tellingly, Bill literally cannot diagnose his own condition. That is left to his more humane foil, the patient and gentle George Schoatze; and with Schoatze's correct diagnosis Bill is subjected to the ultimate "humbling," an operation performed by his rival Dr. Durfee. Appropriately enough, the anesthesiologist is none other than Thea Singleton. By helping him literally to lose all consciousness of himself, Thea facilitates Bill's emergence from his physical crisis as a spiritual whole. Equally appropriate, she almost mystically disappears from the story once Bill's physical/spiritual crisis is over. After the operation is deemed successful, Thea "leaned over him and kissed his hungry lips good-by; and faded back into her own mystery, into those woods where she hunted, with an old suffering and with a memory he could not share" (372). But "what was valuable" in that mystery "she had distilled; she knew how to pass it along" to Bill, so that he emerges from his operation no longer simply an imitation of a "white apostle" (354), but a physician in the purest sense: not a cold clinician, but a selfless humanitarian.

A rare example of a late story in Fitzgerald's "second manner," "One Interne" is a surprisingly effective parable of the humanizing of a physician. The sole lapse in its uniform artistry is the omniscient narrator's blunt explanation of Thea's symbolic role in Bill's spiritual awakening: "The truth of his situation was that his initial idealism which had been centred in Doctor Norton had transferred itself to Thea. Instead of a God, it was now a Goddess who symbolized for him the glory and the devotion of his profession" (361). One would think that by naming her "Thea" (literally, "Goddess") Fitzgerald had sufficiently underscored her well-handled function in the story, but perhaps this rare lapse in artistic judgment, this needless doubt that the text could speak for itself, may point to the story's emotional genesis in Fitzgerald's own life. Like Dick Diver, yet another doctor with a Johns Hopkins connection, Bill would appear to be a fictional projection of his creator. Fitzgerald, too, early in his career had immense talent, ambition, and cocky self-confidence; but it was not until he had ceased to be wrapped up in himself, not until he had been forced to deal with his wife's mental illness and the immediate necessity of raising

Scottie alone that he began to mature fully as a man and an artist. Perhaps the Fitzgeralds' manifold tragedies were indeed blessings in disguise.

That Bill Tulliver must suffer acute personal and professional disillusionment before he can become a true doctor, must in effect lose himself to find himself, is a strikingly Catholic notion which may remind some readers of the fiction of Flannery O'Connor. Though they are never subjected to the kinds of violence and bereavement suffered by Joy-Hulga, Mrs. May, or Julian Chestny, and though they do not receive God's grace as explicitly as do Miss O'Connor's characters, many of Fitzgerald's characters in *Taps at Reveille* do experience symbolic deaths—and, more importantly, symbolic rebirths. Whereas the characters of the early Fitzgerald resorted to suicide (Braddock Washington of "The Diamond as Big as the Ritz"), a frantic clinging to a happier past (Roxanne Curtain of "The Lees of Happiness"), or alcoholism to assuage their disillusionment, the characters of the late Fitzgerald tend to accept the situation (albeit sometimes less than graciously) and then move on to hopefully better lives.

A striking illustration of a character undergoing a disillusioning situation and consciously moving on to a better life is Dr. Forrest Janney of "Family in the Wind" (written in April 1932). Inexplicably ignored by Fitzgerald scholars, this little gem set in rural Alabama is at first glance a total departure for Fitzgerald, but upon closer examination it would appear to be a vivid and imaginative rendering of the shock, the fear, and above all the disillusionment engendered by Zelda's mental breakdowns. More importantly, it seems to show Fitzgerald formulating a strategy for emerging from that disillusionment and forging a dream of a new life centered around Scottie and work.

Dr. Janney had by his own initiative left his lower-class family and trained to become an excellent surgeon in much the same way that Fitzgerald himself had pursued a career in literature without the blessings of his family. (They preferred that he become a businessman; his mother literally destroyed his earliest writings.)[63] Despite this worthy dream and unquestionable talent, Dr. Janney commits "professional suicide" (303): acute alcoholism, coupled with bitterness over his nephew Pinky's abuse of a young woman he himself had loved from afar, makes him unwilling and unable to continue practicing medicine. When the story opens, he is living alone, quietly managing a modest drugstore in his little Southern hometown, and effectively estranged from his family. Then tragedy strikes: two tornadoes rip through the area. Dr. Janney unexpectedly rises to the occasion, helping direct the relief effort, distributing drugs and supplies from his little pharmacy, and, as the ultimate sign of his regeneration, even agreeing to remove a bullet from Pinky's brain, an operation which, before the tornado, he had refused to perform. As the story closes, Dr. Janney has clearly derived hope and renewed vigor from the tragedy around him. No longer spiritually paralyzed by disillusionment, he buys a one-way ticket to a new life in Montgomery. There he will raise a surrogate daughter (orphaned in the storm), and hopefully return to the practice of medicine: "I'll maybe try it" (321). Not the sentimental fluff which this brief synopsis might suggest, "Family in the Wind" is a curious blend of humor and anger, with a grittiness and restraint that can come only from a writer who has survived a few tornadoes of his own.

And that is the point, ultimately. True, there were freak tornadoes in Alabama in March 1932, when Fitzgerald was living in Montgomery,[64] but as usual the bare facts do not explain this story. What matters is Fitzgerald's ability to take these facts, respond to their symbolic potential, and construct a story around them that has meaning and relevance for his personal situation. Consider what we know of tornadoes: they seem to come out of nowhere; they are immensely destructive; and their movements are frustratingly capricious.[65] The first tornado in "Family in the Wind" catches the townspeople totally off guard. It destroys cars, homes, and that ultimate symbol of conjugal bliss and family security, bedding: "Sometimes the trail [of the tornado] could be traced by cotton fields, apparently in full bloom, but this cotton came from the insides of hundreds of quilts and mattresses redistributed in the fields by the storm" (313). And while it kills some people and flattens some houses, it completely spares others.

Fitzgerald seems to have perceived this situation as eerily paralleling the impact of Zelda's April 1930 breakdown on himself and his household. It, too, had seemed to come out of nowhere. As Fitzgerald gropingly described Zelda's collapse to her sister Rosalind in 1930, "this mess . . . arrived like a thunder-clap,"[66] though of course an objective outside observer could have detected signs of it as early as 1927, when Zelda began her ballet training. Further, it obliterated what little serenity the three Fitzgeralds had enjoyed, scattering them into different homes, even into different countries, and leaving Scott himself in desperate emotional and financial straits. And Zelda's mental collapse seemed, at least initially, to be totally capricious and unfair. Though the Sayre family had a long history of mental illness, Scott could not seem to comprehend how or why this tragedy had struck his own family circle, any more than one could fathom why Zelda's sister Rosalind was perfectly normal while their brother Anthony suffered a breakdown and committed suicide.[67] Fitzgerald was, however, somewhat better able to handle Zelda's second breakdown in February 1932, which he characterized not as a thunderclap but as a "storm"—"and I'm afraid Scotty and I will weather it better than [Zelda]."[68] The two tornadoes depicted in the story—the first a complete surprise, and the second ("popularly thought to be the first one come back" [319]) far less destructive because "everyone had developed some scheme of self-protection" (319)—are thus perfect emblems of Zelda's two mental breakdowns in 1930 and 1932, with the story itself depicting Fitzgerald's imaginative response to them.[69]

Inasmuch as "Family in the Wind" is a parable, it is a moot point whether

Fitzgerald actually managed to salvage a decent life from the wreckage of his personal life and household. What does matter is that he used the medium of fiction to work through a strategy of both attitude and action that would enable him to survive. Like Dr. Janney, Fitzgerald immersed himself in his work. *Tender Is the Night,* which had for so many years proved impossible to write, suddenly came together in the early 1930s under the impact of Zelda's collapse. It was not simply a matter of borrowing details from Zelda's medical history and treatment for the creation of Nicole Diver, but apparently also a situation in which Fitzgerald used the writing of literature as a way of working through his own feelings about his personal life and, concomitantly, of confirming that he could impose a modicum of order and control on "this mess." Further, Zelda's breakdown had stimulated the increased production of short fiction, with many of these stories among his best. Like Dr. Janney, then, Fitzgerald found his profession a spiritual refuge, a source of stability in troubled times: "Something purely professional . . . had been set in motion inside him" (313), and it offered him far more than just a livelihood. Even alcoholism, which for a while had seriously compromised his ability to create, could be accommodated within this renewed sense of vocation. As Julie Irwin suggests, by having Dr. Janney be an admitted drunkard, Fitzgerald demonstrated that he viewed his own alcoholism in 1932 "as almost hopeless, but not quite completely so": like Dr. Janney, Fitzgerald could "still perform if necessary."[70] But what is especially striking is that Dr. Janney signifies his personal and professional rebirth after the tragedy and disillusionment by consciously setting out to create a new home for himself and an orphaned little girl in Montgomery. By the early 1930s Fitzgerald had come to a new appreciation of the concept of home, even if he himself could not quite act on it: Scottie rarely lived with her father after Zelda's collapse, and Fitzgerald himself bought not one but a series of one-way tickets (to Asheville, to Baltimore, to Hollywood). Even so, the impulse to create a home is an element of hope and positivism that permeates *Taps at Reveille.* Far more than in his earlier collections, virtually every story in this book probes the idea of home to some degree. And while it is a tribute to Fitzgerald's maturity, judgment, and artistry that this emotion-charged concept never does pull any story into the dregs of sentimentality, it is likewise a tribute to his acceptance of reality that he does not deny the darker aspects of home.

As was evident in the early stories of *Tales of the Jazz Age,* from the very beginning of his career Fitzgerald was fascinated by the concept of home, but his understanding of it—and hence his artistic treatment of it—was characteristically simplistic. He had been inclined to present homes either sentimentally as havens of loving, devoted couples living in suburban bungalows ("The Lees of Happiness"), or scathingly as sources of intense anger, frustration, and lifelong psychic damage ("'O Russet Witch!'"). By the time he prepared the stories of

Taps at Reveille, Fitzgerald was mature enough to understand that light and dark elements could actually coexist in the "normal" home: after all, having a schizophrenic wife like Zelda in the house did not prevent Scottie from being popular, intelligent, loving, and mentally stable. Fitzgerald knew, however, that instability in Scottie was a very real possibility, if not from genes then from poor parental example; and thus he consciously went to great lengths to minimize her interactions with Zelda after the breakdowns began, just as he tried to hide his own alcoholism from her for as long as possible. Further, the voluminous letters which Fitzgerald sent to Scottie beginning in the early 1930s exhibit the curious mixture of effusive love and almost bullying peremptoriness that one might expect from a man who fears his beloved daughter might follow in her parents' questionable footsteps. But above all, Fitzgerald made it a point to place Scottie in sheltering, often restrictive environments, usually either strict boarding schools or the home of his happily married literary agent, Harold Ober; for if a home with Zelda and Scott could be a liability for a young girl, a home with attentive, firm adults could be instrumental in insuring lifelong stability—even if, indeed especially if, they were not related to her by either blood or marriage. After all, no matter how severe the crises in his own household, never did Fitzgerald consider sending Scottie to live with her grandparents or aunts and uncles.[71]

For by the early 1930s, Fitzgerald knew too well that a home full of blood relatives did not guarantee anything, and that in fact the much-revered "nuclear family" could be quite destructive. Parents in the late Fitzgerald are often posited as domestic fifth columns, ostensibly offering nurturance and security, but in fact frequently having insidious negative effects on hapless offspring. Other parents in the late stories of *Taps at Reveille* are well-meaning but frankly ineffectual, even bumbling—and damaging to their children for that very reason. One may recall that parents are virtually nonexistent in the very early stories of *Flappers and Philosophers,* as the focus is squarely on unmarried young people or newlyweds. There likewise are few parents depicted in *Tales of the Jazz Age,* where aside from an imaginative response to Zelda's pregnancy ("The Curious Case of Benjamin Button"), Fitzgerald once again concentrates on what he knew best at the time, young couples. Children begin to enter the picture in *All the Sad Young Men,* though only in "The Baby Party" are they anything more than ciphers to be disposed of in accordance with the demands of the plot. The parents themselves and their relations within the context of marriage are the primary concern in *All the Sad Young Men.* But in *Taps at Reveille* Fitzgerald is deeply concerned with the complexities of parent/child dynamics, not only due to the sudden necessity to serve as both parents to Scottie, but probably also due to the failing health of his own mother (she would die in Washington, D.C., in 1936) and the death of his father (in late January 1931). Scott's relations with Edward and Mollie McQuillan Fitzgerald had never been particularly sound, and his attitude toward them had always involved a desire to be accepted and loved by them, coupled with embarrassment and dismay over their lifestyles and values. His father's career difficulties, both as owner of the American Rattan and Willow Works and as salesman for Procter & Gamble, were sources of financial insecurity for the Fitzgerald household and of emotional distress and humiliation to young Scott. The family could not have survived without the McQuillan fortune, as the boy knew well. Emotionally he rejected Edward Fitzgerald, and thus it was his mother who seems to have been the most important influence on his life. Perhaps to compensate for the two daughters who died in an epidemic shortly before the birth of Scott, Mollie Fitzgerald lavished attention on her handsome, intelligent little boy, sending him to the best schools and arranging for the dancing lessons that would expose him to the children of the most prominent families of St. Paul. But Mollie, an unattractive woman who had married late and was known around town for seeming "witchlike,"[72] was blamed, rightly or not, for the lion's share of Fitzgerald's adult problems. "Why shouldn't I go crazy?" wrote Fitzgerald to Max Perkins in 1926. "My father is a moron and my mother is a neurotic, half insane with pathological nervous worry." All questions of intelligence aside (between them they haven't "the brains of Calvin Coolidge"),[73] this letter gives some sense of the extent to which Fitzgerald perceived his own parents in decidedly non-sentimental terms, a perception which began increasingly to affect his fiction as the behavior of his own child's mother grew progressively worse. If he had not thought much about his own upbringing before, the deterioration of Zelda's sanity prevented him from repressing his feelings any longer, and in particular his feelings about the role of mothers in family circles. Fitzgerald was increasingly vocal to the effect that, as in his own case, "American children belong to their mother's families,"[74] and the stories of *Taps at Reveille*—especially those devoted to Basil Duke Lee—argue that this can be a serious problem. As Kenneth Eble points out, Basil's father is already dead as the series opens,[75] a situation that puts emphasis squarely on the relationship between Basil and his mother and perhaps reflects Fitzgerald's adult recognition that it was Mollie, thanks to her money and personal aggressiveness, who set the emotional tenor in his own childhood home. Poor Basil Duke Lee finds his mother to be something of a liability, as her letter to Dr. Bacon, the headmaster of St. Regis, makes public the humiliating fact that he is "one of the poorest boys in a rich boys' school" ("The Freshest Boy," 32). What seems even worse, however, is that Mrs. Lee's upbringing of Basil has left him socially inept and, hence, spiritually and socially isolated. Repeatedly Fitzgerald emphasizes that Basil is hopelessly "fresh," a word for which there seems to be no exact modern equivalent, but which in general suggests that poor Basil doesn't know when to keep his mouth shut. Whether boasting to Minnie Bibble's father about his academic prowess ("He Thinks He's Wonderful") or giving unwanted advice to Jobena Dorsey ("The Perfect Life"), Basil has no comprehension of how he sounds and looks to others. The problem is emphatically a matter of upbringing. Time and again we are told that Basil, evidently an only child, has been hopelessly "spoiled" by his doting mother, whose understandable desire to indulge her son leaves him completely unprepared for dealing with the people he meets in the neighborhood, at St. Regis, or on school vacations. Apparently assuming that intelligent guidance and reasonable restrictions would stifle her son's love for her, Mrs. Lee "had given him no habits of work and this was almost beyond the power of anything but life itself to remedy" ("The Freshest Boy," 51). Typical of her parenting is the statement which concludes her letter to Basil offering him the chance to finish prep school in Europe: "So, as usual, I want you to do just as you like" ("The Freshest Boy," 43). To his credit, Basil decides to remain in the United States and endure the miseries of St. Regis; for even at this early stage he seems to recognize instinctively that the woman who speaks and acts with such seeming protectiveness ("If you eat so fast you'll have indigestion and then you won't be able to act well" ["The Captured Shadow," 95])[76] is partly just playing the role of an attentive mother and partly indulging an almost unhealthy desire to live through her son: "She hesitated, *covetously* watching his alert and eager face, holding him there" ("The Captured Shadow," 79, emphasis added). The Basil stories in fact seem to trace not simply the process of his transformation from "fresh" child to sentient adult, but concomitantly his growing sense that he can—indeed, must—withdraw from the influence of his mother if he is to grow properly.

Mrs. Lee is perhaps an extreme case. But repeatedly in the Basil stories and indeed throughout the stories of *Taps at Reveille*, Fitzgerald posits parents as liabilities for growing children. For one thing, they prevent their children from developing their own unique identities. Part of Bill Tulliver's problem in "One Interne" is that he initially derives his personal and professional identity from his identically named male ancestors, and especially his father. During his early spiritual crisis at the base of the statue of Christ, the first step in the process of disillusionment that will make him a doctor, Bill clings to the fact that he is defined by his father and his father's ancestors. "Doctor Norton hailed him":

> "I believe I'm addressing William Tulliver the fifth—"
> Bill was glad to be reminded who he was. (353)

Perhaps more dramatically, the children of *Taps at Reveille* repeatedly internalize their parents' (and especially their mothers') fears. Lewis Crum in "The Freshest Boy" is characterized perfectly by "his" attitude toward prep school football:

"I don't like football. I don't like to go out and get a crack in the eye." Lewis spoke aggressively, for his mother had canonized all his timidities as common sense. (28)

Effectively castrated by the internalization of his mother's terror of football injuries, poor Lewis will never outgrow his timidity and will spend his life on the symbolic sidelines of the St. Regis playing fields. Other mothers of *Taps at Reveille* also impose insidious pressure on their children to parrot their statements and to act so as to please them. For example, *The Captured Shadow* is a production of the neighborhood children, and much of its appeal for them is that it is entirely their project, from the composition of the text, to makeup, to lighting. But even as Basil writes the play, his best friend Riply Buckner announces that they should enlist the aid of a local St. Paul drama buff, Miss Halliburton, in its production: "'She wouldn't interfere,' went on Riply, obviously quoting his mother"; furthermore, "The girls' mothers'll like" having Miss Halliburton as supervisor ("The Captured Shadow," 84). None of the children wants to have her involved in the play, and in fact this mother-figure creates problems for them, being incapable even of applying makeup properly.

Even where mothers do not dictate, consciously or otherwise, the thoughts, words, and actions of young people, parents adversely affect the development of their children. The bullying Hubert Blair, so adored by adults and so resented by other boys, is able to hurt others unchecked by using his parents as an excuse. Hubert agrees to perform the lead in *The Captured Shadow* but at the last moment treacherously bows out, leaving the production in a shambles. He makes his cruel move by refusing to show up for a final rehearsal:

"I've got to drive downtown and get father."
He looked coolly at Basil, as if challenging him to deny the adequacy of this explanation.
"Then why did you come in an hour late?" demanded Basil.
"Because I had to do something for mother."
A group had gathered and he glanced around triumphantly. It was one of those sacred excuses, and only Basil saw that it was disingenuous. (92)

Unable to challenge the "sacred" excuse of acting at the behest of parents, Basil and his friends have no choice but to allow Hubert to all but ruin their play. The weak Ailie Calhoun likewise uses her mother as a convenient excuse. "If mother ever saw anybody like [Earl Schoen] come in the house, she'd just lie down and die." But when Ailie decides to pursue Earl, she brings him to her home and "somehow Mrs. Calhoun didn't expire at his appearance on the threshold. The supposedly ineradicable prejudices of Ailie's parents were a convenient phenomenon that disappeared at her wish" ("The Last of the Belles," 263–64).

Sadly, had Mr. and Mrs. Calhoun been truly able to intervene, Ailie might well have been spared the pain of an abortive affair with the boorish Schoen. This ironic situation illustrates how many of the parents of *Taps at Reveille* hurt their children by being themselves ineffectual, weak, even farcical figures. Some characters never comprehend the ineffectuality of their parents. The seriously ill Bill Tulliver clings frantically to the belief that only his physician-father can make a proper diagnosis of his condition—even though his father, being dead, obviously cannot come to his aid ("One Interne," 369). Other parents in *Taps at Reveille* are presented in cameos that range from gently comic to acid. Hubert Blair's father in "The Scandal Detectives" seems, in the words of Sergio Perosa, a "ridiculous figure, whose satiric portrait gives some substance" to what Perosa perceives as a thin plot.[77] Harold Castleton, Sr., in "Majesty" bemoans his daughter Emily's involvement with a deposed Balkan prince, all the while continuing to honor the bank drafts which finance their escapades across Europe. And Minnie Bibble's Southern father in "He Thinks He's Wonderful" regales Basil with discussions of Creoles and boll weevils (72, 70). Though these fathers are comic figures, they lend a sobering edge to the seriocomic tales in which they appear.

In part because the parents cannot, or will not, help their children grow properly into sensitive, responsible adults, there is a sense of negative energy—of ugliness, pain, violence, even evil—lurking within striking distance of the most comfortable homes in even the most seemingly idyllic or comic stories of *Taps at Reveille*. Unable to help their children, the parents of *Taps at Reveille* seem likewise unable to protect them from the destructive forces which had not been so evident to the young Fitzgerald, but which had become painfully obvious after Zelda's mental well-being began to slip in the late 1920s.

The problem need not always be as dramatic as a freak tornado that turns a "placid countryside . . . into a land of mourning" ("Family in the Wind," 317). Far more frightening are the insidious threats of which the characters of *Taps at Reveille* seem vaguely aware even in childhood. Once again it is significant that Fitzgerald opens his collection with the Basil series, for these stories, which so many critics laud for their idyllic rendering of boyhood and their humor, actually underscore the most unsettling aspects of childhood. It can be something as seemingly benign as the need to behave properly for the parents of one's playmates, answering their endless questions about one's own family "which are so meaningless to the young" ("The Scandal Detectives," 9) or forcing oneself to be pleasant to them: "You ought to be more polite to the older people if you want to be popular. You didn't say how do you do to Mrs. Bissel tonight" ("He Thinks He's Wonderful," 61). The stress engendered by the social graces is a subtle blight on childhood which looms surprisingly large in the Basil stories. So too does a more abstract source of stress, the passage of time. In "The Scandal Detectives" it may seem insignificant that little Imogene Bissel, "having just turned thirteen," spends "a bored and solitary evening inspecting the month's bills which were scattered over her mother's desk" (18–19); but that image, working in concert with others throughout *Taps at Reveille*, suggests that the carpe diem theme is an important source of "real inner unity" in the volume. The encroachment of sorrowful adult realities is evident, for example, in "A Short Trip Home." Eighteen-year-old Ellen Baker is blessed with "one of those exquisite rose skins frequent in our part of the country" (i.e., Minnesota). Her complexion is "beautiful"—"until the little veins begin to break at about forty" (335). This is not a late manifestation of the young Fitzgerald's obsession with growing old, but rather his mature awareness that the seeds of adult disappointment are evident in even the most attractive childhoods.

The inevitability of aging, though sobering, is admittedly not something of which the young characters themselves are conscious. But they are conscious of threatening forces along the peripheries of their seemingly secure worlds. Max Perkins, for example, greatly admired Fitzgerald's beautiful description of a yard in "The Scandal Detectives":

> The Whartons' own children had long grown up, but their yard was still one of those predestined places where young people gather in the afternoon. It had many advantages. It was large, open to other yards on both sides, and it could be entered upon skates or bicycles from the street. It contained an old seesaw, a swing and a pair of flying rings; but it had been a rendezvous before these were put up, for it had a child's quality—the thing that makes young people huddle inextricably on uncomfortable steps and desert the houses of their friends to herd on the obscure premises of "people nobody knows." The Whartons' yard had long been a happy compromise; there were deep shadows there all day long and ever something vague in bloom, and patient dogs around, and brown spots worn bare by countless circling wheels and dragging feet. (5–6)[78]

But deliberately excluding any kind of transitional phrase, Fitzgerald continues this description in a totally antithetical vein:

> In sordid poverty, below the bluff two hundred feet away, lived the "micks"—they had merely inherited the name, for they were now largely of Scandinavian descent—and when other amusements palled, a few cries were enough to bring a gang of them swarming up the hill, to be faced if numbers promised well, to be fled from into convenient houses if things went the other way. (6)

This does not reflect simply a history enthusiast's awareness of changing demographics in turn-of-the-century St. Paul. The Whartons' yard is as idyllic as anything in Tarkington's "Penrod" stories—but just beyond it are alien individuals capable of physically harming the youngsters in Basil's crowd.

And yet, it is that very crowd of happy children who make the first move against the "micks," "when other amusements palled." One of the most striking aspects of the Basil stories, and indeed of all the stories in *Taps at Reveille,* is the degree to which seemingly innocent individuals instigate violence against outsiders, against others within their own ranks, or even against themselves. Though it had taken him twenty years to acknowledge this reality and express it in his fiction, Fitzgerald's childhood had been intensely unhappy, in large measure because of the cruelty of other children. One's supposed friends and allies could prove to be one's worst enemies. Even the treacherous Hubert Blair is unsafe in his own yard: he "would not have sprung so gracefully and lithely down the steps [of his house] with his hands in his pockets or whistled the first bar of the Grizzly Bear into the apparently friendly night" had he realized that his supposed playmates, disguised in the adult roles of Southern planter, immigrant, and rabbi, were planning to kidnap him and stuff him into the Blair family garbage can ("The Scandal Detectives," 16). Their actions do not betoken the rationality of justice: though a show-off, Hubert has not hurt Basil and his friends personally and does not deserve this punishment. But their actions likewise do not betoken the shortsighted "innocent" actions with which children are so often credited, and for which they are so often excused. Many of the children in the Basil stories are absolutely vicious, and calculatedly so. One of the Scandal Detectives, Bill Kampf, "had no scruples of any kind":

> It had been decided to put Hubert into a garbage can, and though he had nothing at all against Hubert, the idea had made a pattern on his brain which he intended to follow. He was a natural man—that is to say, a hunter—and once a creature took on the aspect of a quarry, he would pursue it without qualms until it stopped struggling. (17–18)

The naturalistic rhetoric which had seemed so ludicrous and mannered in Fitzgerald's earliest short stories (e.g., "Dalyrimple Goes Wrong") is here chillingly effective in its restraint and appropriateness. Even more chilling, the fundamentally moral Basil is able to rationalize away whatever scruples he might possess about the matter:

> The idea [of putting Hubert into a garbage can] at first horrified them—it would ruin his suit, it was awfully dirty and he might smother. In fact the garbage can, symbol of all that was repulsive, won the day only because it made every other idea seem tame. They disposed of the objections—his suit could be cleaned, it was where he ought to be anyhow, and if they left the lid off he couldn't smother. To be sure of this they had paid a visit of inspection to the Buckners' garbage can and stared into it, fascinated, envisaging Hubert among the rinds and eggshells. (16–17)

That these children could be "fascinated" by the prospect of doing violence to an innocent boy of their circle lends credence to Perosa's argument that the Basil stories illustrate how "the principle of evil is already active in the idyll of youth."[79]

But the capacity of young people to do evil to others pales beside a situation which recurs frequently in the stories of *Taps at Reveille:* an innocent (usually young) person's active complicity in his own immersion in evil.[80] Consider a little-known late story in Fitzgerald's second manner, "A Short Trip Home" (written in October 1927). The opening at first glance seems to be a reversion to the chatty essayistic openings which so marred Fitzgerald's early tales:

> I was near her, for I had lingered behind in order to get the short walk with her from the living room to the front door. That was a lot, for she had flowered suddenly and I, being a man and only a year older, hadn't flowered at all, had scarcely dared to come near her in the week we'd been home. Nor was I going to say anything in that walk of ten feet, or touch her; but I had a vague hope she'd do something, give a gay little performance of some sort, personal only in so far as we were alone together.
>
> She had bewitchment suddenly in the twinkle of short hairs on her neck, in the sure, clear confidence that at about eighteen begins to deepen and sing in attractive American girls. The lamp light shopped in the yellow strands of her hair.
>
> Already she was sliding into another world—the world of Joe Jelke and Jim Cathcart waiting for us now in the car. In another year she would pass beyond me forever. (323)

It quickly becomes apparent that the rather long, complex sentences, the repeated words ("flowered"), the social observations about "attractive American girls," the interested but rather distant narrator, and the odd juxtaposition of nonspecific words ("anything," "something," "of some sort") and minute details ("the twinkle of short hairs on her neck") have been patterned on the fiction of Henry James[81]—an ideal model for a story which, like "The Turn of the Screw," probes the encroachment of evil on a seemingly secure world: the "home" of the story's title. And certainly Ellen Baker at first glance seems secure, back at her parents' house in St. Paul over Christmas break and enjoying her leisure time with attractive friends. Almost immediately, however, our initial favorable impression of Ellen clouds into something sinister, as she abandons her friends, slips out of a back door at a party, and arrives later at a dance in a car driven by a demonic stranger of the kind that had always lurked along the border of the narrator's experiences: "I had always from earliest boyhood thrown a nervous glance toward the dim borderland where he stood, and seen him watching me and despising me" (326–27). Why Ellen would associate with a man who would attack her friend Joe Jelke with brass knuckles is a mystery, but even less clear is the source of her eerie lack of responsiveness to the normal world. She has a "faintly distracted look" (326) which soon devolves into a kind of tunnel vision: when she is with the mysterious stranger, "her eyelids fell a little, shutting other things—everyone else—out of view" (329). There is, further, a growing discrepancy between her fresh and innocent appearance and her less than ladylike actions. The narrator, Eddie Stinson, asks where she met the stranger:

> "On the train," she answered. Immediately she seemed to regret this admission. "You'd better stay out of things that aren't your business, Eddie. You see what happened to Joe."
>
> Literally I gasped. To watch her, seated beside me, immaculately glowing, her body giving off wave after wave of freshness and delicacy—and to hear her talk like that. (328)

Ellen seems increasingly unable to think and speak appropriately, a situation which culminates in a bold-faced lie to her trusting mother. Mrs. Baker believes her daughter unquestioningly when Ellen assures her that she will be stopping in Chicago to visit the Brokaws on her way back to school in the East. The lie and its seemingly innocent source are so convincing that even the narrator, a Yale sophomore who has known Ellen since childhood, does not see what is happening, though on a visceral level he senses something is amiss. While bathing, however, Eddie has an epiphany: since the Brokaws are vacationing in Palm Beach, Ellen's train trip can mean only one thing—a Chicago reunion with the mysterious stranger.

Eddie Stinson's instincts are correct, and he spends the rest of the story attempting to rescue Ellen from a man who rapidly has become the embodiment of evil. What complicates the situation, however, is that Ellen does not want to be rescued. When she sees Stinson at the telegraph counter in the Chicago railroad station, her look is one of "terror mixed up with . . . surprise," but more importantly "there was cunning in it too" (337). The evil already within her is evident in the "terrible expression" on her face and the "snarl" with which she verbally fends off her would-be rescuer (338). So insidious is the "contagion of evil in the air" (339) that Stinson himself begins to feel its effect; but he successfully resists it, and with a declaration of love he begins to reach the still-human core of Ellen. He then challenges the mysterious stranger, who threatens to kill Stinson if he does not get off the train in Fort Wayne and leave Ellen to her fate. But the demonic stranger's threats are ineffectual, as he visibly loses the life force that had enabled him to function. For the mysterious stranger, Stinson suddenly discovers, is in fact dead: "I saw what I had not seen before—that his forehead was drilled with a small round hole like a larger picture nail leaves when it's pulled from a plaster wall" (345). In life the stranger was one Joe Varland, a scoundrel who "used to work the girls travelling alone on the trains" (347); in death, he was essentially an incubus[82] preying on innocent women. With his final disappearance, Ellen is recovered: "What had possessed her had gone out of her, leaving her exhausted but her own dear self again" (346). "A Short Trip Home" is probably Fitzgerald's most emphatic mature statement regarding the attractiveness of evil, and in particular the allure of its self-destructive edge. But at the same time Fitzgerald is insistent that there is a close connection between home and evil. It was while traveling home to St. Paul on the train for Christmas vacation that Ellen initially had been subjected to the incubus. Further, her family's house, far from providing protection, offers back doors that facilitate escape from help, while the family servants act as go-betweens delivering obscure messages between the incubus and his victim (334). Even the well-meaning Mrs. Baker, unable to see what is happening to her daughter and hence unable to help her, blithely believes Ellen's lie and sends her off to Chicago, and the incubus, with her blessing. Not surprisingly, even

St. Paul itself seems to be in mysterious collusion with the forces of evil. Stinson provides a lengthy description of St. Paul at the beginning of Part II of "A Short Trip Home," one which depicts not the Summit Avenue neighborhood familiar to prominent families, but its less attractive districts, beginning with "a vague part of town, broken by its climb into triangles and odd shapes" and ending with its seedy underbelly of "pawnshops, cheap jewellers, . . . and somewhat too blatantly run-down saloons" (330). It is in "that halfway section" of town (331) that Stinson again sees the incubus. And during their final encounter on the train the incubus reveals what neither Eddie nor the reader has wanted to face: that he too is from St. Paul. It is this creature's "home" (343).

The idea that "home" (which, whether in fact or imagination, is the most secure and stable element in anyone's life) can permit evil to thrive, can actually be its source, is a chilling statement of disorder akin to the very notion of hearing "taps at reveille." Likewise, the notion of a home-bred, innocent young woman turning into a sneering, coldly calculating liar and helping to ensure her own destruction is as horrifying, as unnatural, as the walking dead man who preys on her. That an attractive, intelligent individual would engage in deliberate self-destruction may suggest an emotional connection between Ellen and her hard-drinking creator; but far more tenable is Kenneth Eble's surmise that "A Short Trip Home" reflects Fitzgerald's response to Zelda's bizarre behavior at the time of its composition: "Zelda's increasing obsessions help to explain the intensity with which Fitzgerald wrote this story of a woman literally possessed," and in particular the situation in which a man tries to help but is "unable to enlist her feelings or gain her concurrence in his attempt to save her."[83] Fitzgerald has resurrected the ancient literary motif of possession by a demonic force to explain the unnatural appearance of schizophrenic behavior, and has grafted onto it a fairy-tale ending: an avowal of love saves the beautiful victim from destruction—a scenario which unfortunately did not materialize in the Fitzgeralds' case, as over the next months Scott's devotions did not result in his wife's permanent recovery. Further, the very text of the story appropriately conveys a noncommittal, almost slippery quality as the reader, with a willing suspension of disbelief, joins Eddie Stinson in trying to deconstruct his sentimental ideas of "home" and to piece together Ellen's words and actions as in a kind of horrible puzzle. Like a good Henry James ghost story, "A Short Trip Home" is a challenging, intense, and ultimately disturbing tale, and one that Fitzgerald could not possibly have written before Zelda's decline.

Fitzgerald's obvious doubts about the notion of home in "A Short Trip Home" in 1927 might lead one to expect that it would be the target for either vicious satire or neglect once Zelda had her first breakdown in April 1930. After all, none of the Fitzgeralds had ever been receptive to the Norman Rockwellian ideal of happy nuclear families in cozy bungalows in pleasant Midwestern towns; even after little Scottie was born, they simply wandered between a succession of rented apartments, villas, and estates. And certainly after Zelda's breakdown, the idea of home would seen to be almost grotesquely irrelevant, as sadly contrary to the Fitzgeralds' own experience as the magnificent doll-house Zelda had built at Ellerslie.[84] But in fact the stories written after that crisis show Fitzgerald carefully reconsidering the notion of home and, ultimately, positing it as a desirable, even essential aspect of personal and familial survival.

There is nothing sentimental about the positive presentation of homes in the post-breakdown stories of *Taps at Reveille*, largely because the positivism implies a rejection of popularly accepted notions of what constitutes a happy home. One of the securest households in these stories is that of Miles and Stella Calman in "Crazy Sunday," who as a Hollywood couple live, appropriately enough, in a house that resembles a theater: "Miles Calman's house was built for great emotional moments—there was an air of listening, as if the far silences of its vistas hid an audience" (202). Unlike a good nuclear family, the Calmans have no children. Stella, indeed, may have been "fathered" by Miles in an abstract way, having been transformed from a "little gamin" into a sophisticated movie star, "a sort of masterpiece" (222). Further, their domestic troubles, far from being concealed within the family circle, are public matters which, ironically, have seemed to cement their marriage. Even Joel has to admit that Stella obviously loves Miles (212), loves him enough to want to have an affair so as to prolong the illusion that he did not die in a plane crash. Unhealthy? Perhaps. But the fact remains that, Miles's philandering notwithstanding, the Calmans had a household admirably well-suited to their emotional and professional needs. Theirs had been a creative response to the need for a home, and for them it worked.

The home of preference in the post-breakdown stories, however, is the one-parent household, whether in practice or theory. In "Family in the Wind," Dr. Janney will create a one-parent household in Montgomery with an adoptive daughter, much as Charlie Wales in "Babylon Revisited" will try to create a home for himself and his child in Prague. That proposed household serves as a foil for the home which we do see in the story, that of Lincoln and Marion Peters in Paris. It certainly seems like a serene home, what with the "three children mov[ing] intimately about, playing through the yellow oblongs that led to other rooms; the cheer of six o'clock spoke in the eager smacks of the fire and the sounds of French activity in the kitchen" (385). But the domicile of the Peterses is only superficially homey: Lincoln is not doing well financially; Honoria is less than delighted to be there (she is visibly cool about Aunt Marion and Cousin Elsie [390]); and the family is dominated by a jealous and vindictive woman whose moods and imaginary ailments can checkmate instantly the hopes of both Charlie and Honoria. As with "Family in the Wind," the most positive representation of home in "Babylon Revisited" is one that does not yet exist and which may never materialize: a father/daughter one-parent household in a distant town.

Perhaps the most creative home in the post-breakdown stories of *Taps at Reveille* is one that, at first glance, would seem to be no home at all: that involving Crenshaw Engels and "The Fiend" in the story of the same name (written in September 1934). "The Fiend" was written for *Esquire,* but the magazine's editorial policies do not explain why Fitzgerald handled the material as he did, or, more importantly, why he decided to focus upon something which seems alien to the Fitzgerald canon: mass murder and vengeance. But once again the key to this story would appear to be events in Fitzgerald's personal life. Typical of the post-breakdown stories in *Taps at Reveille,* there is little plot and virtually no exposition. Perhaps because no explanations were forthcoming in his own life, the late Fitzgerald explains nothing in this story. All we know are the essential facts, as set forth in the stark opening:

> On June 3, 1895, on a country road near Stillwater, Minnesota, Mrs. Crenshaw Engels and her seven year old son, Mark, were waylaid and murdered by a fiend, under circumstances so atrocious that, fortunately, it is not necessary to set them down here. (374)

Like the facts on Zelda's medical charts, this information tells us virtually nothing. Fitzgerald instead prefers to go beyond the facts about the victims to focus on the impact of the family's destruction on the sole survivor, the husband/father. Like Fitzgerald, Crenshaw Engels is a creative Minnesotan, a photographer; also like Fitzgerald, he is "a great reader" and "considered 'a little unsafe,'" for he had spoken his mind frankly about the railroad-agrarian struggles of the time" (374), much as Fitzgerald dabbled in socialism during the troubled 1930s. But more importantly, Crenshaw is "a devoted family man," and thus when his family is destroyed, he is profoundly affected, both emotionally and professionally. His career as a photographer fails, as "high school students, newly married couples, [and] mothers of new babies" find it difficult to pose for portraits in his studio (374). The townspeople become convinced that Crenshaw is "a man ruined by adversity, a man *manqué,* a man emptied," but in fact he is empty "of all save one thing" (375): the desire for revenge. At the Fiend's first trial, Crenshaw nearly strangles him; at the second trial he "cried aloud once," and then tried to pressure the state legislature to reinstate the death penalty, retroactive to criminals who, like the Fiend, had been sentenced to life imprisonment. When the bill fails, Crenshaw enters the state prison on a ruse and tries to shoot the Fiend. But still determined to exact vengeance on the nameless evil force that destroyed his family and his life, Crenshaw pretends to have a change of heart and convinces the prison warden to let him visit the Fiend in his cell on a regular basis.

Since Crenshaw is convinced that the cruelest punishment involves mental torment, and in particular frustration, over a prolonged period, he establishes a routine of fortnightly visits in which he brings the Fiend reading materials calculated to upset him: "a German doctor's thousand case histories of sexual abnormality—cases with no cures, no hopes, no prognoses, cases listed cold"; "a volume of erotic pieces from each of which the last two pages, containing the consummations, had been torn out; a volume of detective stories mutilated in the same manner" (377). Once Crenshaw even brought him "four inspiringly titled books—that proved to have nothing but blank paper inside" (377). Crenshaw also periodically threatens the Fiend with physical violence, even throwing a dummy bomb into the cell and listening with glee to his victim's screams for help (378).

Fitzgerald makes virtually no reference to Crenshaw's life away from the prison, aside from a brief mention of his job at a local store and the purchase of new grave markers for his wife and son. He is so careful to keep the focus squarely on Crenshaw and the Fiend that even in so short a story (just eight pages) it is easy to believe that thirty years pass. The device of foreshortened time which Fitzgerald had handled so poorly in early stories like "The Cut-Glass Bowl" is startlingly effective in this late tale, as he makes us feel the obsessiveness of Crenshaw's prolonged orgy of revenge.

But ultimately revenge is not at issue. After all, Crenshaw has ample opportunity to throw real bombs into the Fiend's cell, but he chooses not to. His restraint suggests not simply a Hawthornesque or Poesque understanding of the obsessive nature of revenge, the impulse to prolong the process for as long as possible, but rather the fact that the Fiend fills an important emotional gap in Crenshaw's life: the Fiend is Crenshaw's only "family," much as the prison is his only real "home." With no friends and his loved ones dead, Crenshaw achieves his only human contact with the Fiend, and he directs his whole life toward him with the same completeness that other men direct their whole lives toward their spouses and children. The thirty years that Crenshaw faithfully devotes to the Fiend is longer than most marriages, and Fitzgerald further underscores their relationship as a bizarre family circle by depicting the Fiend not as a maniac, but as a harmless soul, "a roly-poly man, who somehow made his convict's uniform resemble a business suit, a man with thick brown-rimmed glasses and the trim air of an insurance salesman" (376). In fact the Fiend has real human emotions, being grateful for the gifts of mutilated books and even agreeing with Crenshaw that he probably should be executed for his crime. He even has "great respect for Crenshaw," whose hair, like his, turns white as they age together (378). So totally in tune are they emotionally, so completely does their relationship constitute a home, that after thirty years Crenshaw finally decides to kill the Fiend, not out of vengeance, but so as "to avoid any mischance by which the other would survive him" (379). In keeping with their emotional sympathy, the Fiend immediately develops acute abdominal pain precisely where Crenshaw's bullet is destined to "ride ragged" through his bowels (379). And when the Fiend dies shortly thereafter of a burst appendix, Crenshaw evinces as much emotion as he did when his biological family died:

> When the Warden had gone Crenshaw still stood there a long time, the tears running out down his face. He could not collect his thoughts and he began by trying to remember what day it was; Saturday, the day, every other week, on which he came to see the Fiend.
> He would not see the Fiend two weeks from now.
> In a misery of solitude and despair he muttered aloud: "So he is dead. He has left me." And then with a long sigh of mingled grief and fear, "So I have lost him—my only friend—now I am alone." (381)

The friend/Fiend play on words anticipates the name of the demonic Arnold Friend in Joyce Carol Oates's short story "Where Are You Going, Where Have You Been?" (1966). It also points to a possible literary precedent for "The Fiend," Stephen Crane's novella "The Monster" (1899), in which the true "monster" is not the faceless victim of a laboratory fire but the small town that cannot look beyond his appearance to the courageous human being within. Crenshaw Engels has in fact become the true "fiend" of the story, much as the Fiend has become his dearest friend, and the emotional blurring of their identities makes bereavement all but unbearable for Crenshaw. He returns to the prison weeks later, claiming to have forgotten that the Fiend is dead. Finally he simply walks away, "his boots sinking deep into the white diamond surface of the flats" (381; cf. the ending of yet another Crane story, "The Bride Comes to Yellow Sky"). Now he truly is "a man *manqué*."

What Dr. Janney, Charlie Wales, and Crenshaw Engels recognize is that home in the purest (and not necessarily the most conventional) sense of the word has many elements to offer that are vital for the quality of life, including mutual tolerance, love, and respect in a context of stability. When Charlie Wales says, "I'm awfully anxious to have a home. . . . And I'm awfully anxious to have Honoria in it" (393), he is confirming the mature Fitzgerald's belief that home and honor go hand in hand. Under the pressure of his deteriorating life Fitzgerald seems instinctively to have reaffirmed the importance of abstract values and the capacity of a home to nurture their growth. Like Charlie Wales, desperate for a home, Fitzgerald "believed in character"; like Wales, "he wanted to jump back a whole generation and trust in character again as the eternally valuable element"; and also like Wales, he had come to the sobering realization that "everything [else] wore out" (387). The longing for home which is so palpable in the stories of *Taps at Reveille* reflects these convictions.

The impulse to "jump back a whole generation" does not mean, however, that Fitzgerald in the late 1920s and early 1930s felt a reactionary, even escapist impulse to return to the historical past. Certainly he still harbored, and would always indulge, an antiquarian's interest in the past; likewise, he would always possess a Spenglerian conviction that the historical process was ongoing, that the national and global crises occurring in his lifetime could be understood within the broad paradigm of social, cultural, political, and economic forces interacting over several centuries. But as his understanding of these elements became deeper and more complex under the impact of personal and professional crises, his fictional treatment of them changed noticeably.

Consider his antiquarian's interest in the past. A story such as "The Night of Chancellorsville" (written in November 1934) is generally dismissed as yet another experimental exercise for *Esquire* magazine, one which reflects his lifelong fascination with the Civil War. But the story is noteworthy for Fitzgerald's refusal to depict the participants in that conflict as all heroes, the battles as all glorious. Indeed, the story is told not from the point of view of a combatant, but from that of a prostitute traveling to Baltimore from Philadelphia to join Hooker's Army—a dark side of the Civil War which did not find its way into the idealized history books so dear to the young Fitzgerald. The story is presented with surprising effectiveness as a dramatic monologue spoken by Nora, an ill-educated, dull, and rather shrill young woman—a technique that would be used with comparable skill by Eudora Welty in "Petrified Man" (1939). Nora is aware of only what is occurring in her immediate vicinity in the train car traveling to Baltimore ("The lights were terrible in that car, smoky and full of bugs, so everything looked sort of yella" [249]). The Civil War means nothing to her except as an opportunity to do a great deal of business and as a source of personal discomfort. When the train arrives at Chancellorsville and suddenly encounters one of the worst battles of the war, Nora's only response is to be annoyed by the delay: "Well, after *this* ride I don't care who wins" (250). And except for a broken window in her train compartment and some noise ("I heard a whole bunch of horses gallop by our windows, but I still couldn't see anything" [251]), the details of the battle itself are beyond her comprehension. Though she is literally in the middle of it, the Battle of Chancellorsville has no meaning for her. Even the wounded soldiers who have been placed on the commandeered train for the trip back to Philadelphia are perceived only as sources of noise that prevent her from getting a good night's sleep (253). That they are suffering seems not to have occurred to her.

To a certain extent "The Night of Chancellorsville" is indeed a literary tour de force, an experiment in point of view, and a sardonic commentary on the people whom the soldiers had died trying to protect. But more importantly it shows the mature Fitzgerald facing certain realities: that we exist on a continuum of historical time which we simply cannot grasp; that the ramifications of what is happening in our immediate vicinity, historically and personally, are often unrealized simply because we lack the necessary objectivity; and that the histori-cal past frankly has been no more idyllic than our own personal pasts. (Witness the Basil stories, whose frequent bitterness places them far closer to Crane's Whilomville stores than to the Penrod tales of Booth Tarkington.) Each of these three realities seems to have offered a modicum of comfort to the mature Fitzgerald, who found strength and hope in the fact that the crises of the present would someday blur into the past; that he had to be as objective as possible if he were to understand and accept the personal and global tragedies of the early 1930s; and that there was no point in yearning for an idyllic past that had never really existed. "The Night of Chancellorsville" thus offers a very personal message to a man whose own life and times had often seemed intolerable.

Other late stories likewise offer both personal and national history lessons to Fitzgerald and his readers. The much-analyzed "Last of the Belles," for example, shows Fitzgerald revisiting the past time and place where he had first met Zelda Sayre, but there is nothing nostalgic about this trip down memory lane. As Scott Donaldson points out, "As the decade wore on, the fascination that Zelda and the South held for Fitzgerald wore off," and he conveyed this by transforming "the charming and vulnerable Sally Carrol [of] 1920 . . . into the vicious and cruelly aristocratic Ailie Calhoun" of 1929.[85] The transformation of belle to jaded flapper is particularly dramatic in that Fitzgerald does not show the process itself: Andy provides us with "before" and "after" shots of Ailie that let us surmise what happened to charmers like Sally Carrol Happer.

Appropriately enough, in 1929, about a year after he finished the last of his Tarleton stories, Fitzgerald was asked by *McCall's* magazine to write an essay on the "present day status of the Flapper." *McCall's* in fact rejected the commissioned essay entitled "Girls Believe in Girls," which its editors felt was too serious.[86] But between his serious examination of the flapper as a feature of the American scene and his earlier probing of flapperdom from a personal perspective, Fitzgerald seems to have derived the immediate inspiration to write the Josephine stories beginning in January 1930. Josephine is an individual from Fitzgerald's private past, leavened (as suggested earlier) by his own sense of encroaching emotional bankruptcy; but she is also emphatically the embodiment of a national historical phenomenon.[87] Her stories begin in 1914, when she is sixteen years old, and end in the midst of World War I, ideal cut-off points for a girl who "was an unconscious pioneer of the generation that was destined to 'get out of hand'" ("First Blood," 134) and who ends up emotionally bankrupt in early adulthood. Where there had been an overriding sense of regret and muted irony in "The Last of the Belles," the Josephine stories are bitter; it is emotionally draining to read about an attractive, intelligent girl whose life Fitzgerald so carefully depicts as purposeless, hopeless. As records of the dete-rioration of American values, reflected in the career of the flapper, the Josephine stories are anything but amusing, though critics inexplicably persist in regarding them as such.[88] To assume that the Josephine stories were meant to be delightfully entertaining is to misread them.

The misinterpretation of the Josephine stories as good-natured nostalgic portraits of Ginevra King is rivaled only by the misreading of "Majesty" (written in May 1929). Where "The Offshore Pirate" of the 1920s offered a light-hearted parody of flapperdom at its birth, "Majesty" offers a correspondingly sober record of its demise. It is a quite serious story in that it fictionally represents a once superficially attractive phenomenon spun out to its historical dissolution in 1929; but the seriousness of its purpose should not obscure the mockery at its core. "Majesty" is as biting a satire as Fitzgerald ever wrote.

From the very beginning Fitzgerald's satiric impulse had not been understood, perhaps because it was too readily obscured by his undergraduate silliness. As early as 1921 Max Perkins had declared that "the time ought to come when whatever you write will go through and where its irony and satire will be understood,"[89] but in fact most readers and critics have never been attuned to it, and their lack of understanding has resulted in striking misreadings of Fitzgerald, usually to his detriment. For example, Lawrence Buell points out that in "The Diamond as Big as the Ritz," the final conversation between John Unger and the Washington sisters "has struck many readers as mawkish," whereas in fact it is "a piece of calculated mock-sentimentalism" which lampoons such pretensions to intellectuality as "his was a great sin who first invented consciousness."[90] John O'Hara likewise offers the observation that Fitzgerald's satire was "implicit" for the sensitive reader, "just as a writer's politics are there for anyone to see who has the curiosity and intelligence to wonder."[91] Satire is certainly apparent in "Majesty," though a close examination of the text suggests that it is far from simply implicit.

Not unlike Josephine Perry, Emily Castleton is both a character and a representation of an historical phenomenon. Her personal career, rising from humble beginnings to global prominence, is encapsulated in the overview of her life: "Emily Castleton was born in Harrisburg in a medium-sized house, moved to New York at sixteen to a big house, went to the Briarly School, moved to an enormous house, moved to a mansion at Tuxedo Park, moved abroad, where she did various fashionable things and was in all the papers" (275). The breathless catalogue of Emily's existence lacks detail and amplitude, not because Fitzgerald lacks the inclination to pursue them but because her case is so typically American, at least in the popular imagination. As the throwaway phrase "various fashionable things" suggests, anyone familiar with the liberated woman of the 1920s knows well what activities fall under that heading. Likewise the subsequent statement that "she became involved in various situations and some of the first bloom wore off" (275) is appropriately vague. It was, in short, the usual stuff: "There were engagements and semi-engagements, short passionate attractions, and then a big affair at twenty-two that embittered her and sent her wandering the continents looking for happiness. She became 'artistic' as most wealthy unmarried girls do at that age (276)—a familiar story, so unoriginal that Fitzgerald deliberately makes no attempt at an original presentation. Finally, at age twenty-four, the much-traveled and somewhat shopworn Emily agrees to marry, in good Whartonesque fashion, Mr. William Brevoort Blair of Newport; but like Ardita Farnum before her, Emily would really rather marry a man with flair, someone for whom she can feel Genuine Passion. Poor doltish Blair is a pale copy of her previous amours:

> "Getting into [Blair's] plane the other day I could only remember Captain Marchbanks and the little two-seater we flew over the Channel in, just breaking our hearts for each other and never saying a word about it because of his wife." (277)

What's a girl to do? Well, where a less spirited woman might go ahead with the wedding, spunky Emily leaves Blair literally at the altar: she flees to Europe to find her True Love.

She finds him rather quickly. After a series of rumors that Emily is "in Cairo, in Constantinople, or the less frequented Riviera" (287), her father receives word from an employee in Europe that she is living with Prince Gabriel Petrocobesco. It initially sounds dazzling, except that the Paris *Matin* reports that His Highness "was invited by the police to leave Paris," for, his title notwithstanding, he is a "dissipated ne'er-do-well" (288), yet another of those European crowned heads deposed after World War I. Emily's father dispatches Emily's long-suffering, old-fashioned cousin, the aptly named Olive Mercy, to Europe to bring her to her senses and fetch her home.

Any resemblance to Lambert Strether ends there. Olive is disgusted rather than enthralled by Emily, whom she finally tracks down in a seedy inn in Czjeck-Hansa: "They were in a large dirty room which might have belonged to a poor boarding house in any quarter of the Western world—faded walls, split upholstery, a shapeless bed and an air, despite its bareness, of being overcrowded by the ghostly furniture, indicated by dust rings and worn spots, of the last decade" (291). The room is clearly an emblem of historical change, and at its center is the equally sorry-looking prince, "a small stout man with hammock eyes and a peering nose over a sweet, spoiled little mouth" (291). His Highness, known as "Tutu" to his American mistress, is much given to mood swings and hypochondria:

> Petrocobesco came back, threw himself into his chair and buried his face in his hands.
> "I can't stand it," he whispered. "Would you mind taking my pulse? I think it's bad. Have you got the thermometer in your purse?"
> She held his wrist in silence for a moment.
> "It's all right, Tutu." Her voice was soft now, almost crooning. "Sit up. Be a man."

"All right."

He crossed his legs as if nothing had happened and turned abruptly to Brevoort [Blair, now Olive Mercy's husband]:

"How are financial conditions in New York?" he demanded. (295)

If Emily had seemed like a fool for choosing this person over $250,000 worth of wedding presents, not to mention the "series of five-thousand-dollar pavilions" which Daddy had set up on the "small, priceless patch of grass on Sixtieth Street" for her and Blair's wedding reception (276, 279), it rapidly becomes clear that Tutu has a charm of his own: Emily dominates him with ridiculous ease. She reprimands him publicly for calling a visitor a "filthy, dirty spy": "'Now that's just the kind of remark you're not to make!' said Emily sharply" (293). Further, Emily commandeers Olive's rental car to use as the Czjeck-Hansa state limousine ("We can have the arms painted on the side of that" [293]). For no sooner does Olive arrive than the "peasant party" of Czjeck-Hansa overturns the new republic and reinstates Tutu as ruler—or, more precisely, as king; for as Emily crows, "I wouldn't marry him unless he insisted on being king instead of prince" (296). We last see Queen Emily and her Tutu riding in a royal procession in London (all those magnesium deposits recently discovered in Czjeck-Hansa lend respectability even to this dubious couple [297]), a sight which brings tears to the eyes of Olive Mercy:

"I wonder if she likes it, Brevoort. I wonder if she's really happy with that terrible little man."

"Well, she got what she wanted, didn't she? And that's something." (298)

Malcolm Cowley's assertion that "Majesty" is "Fitzgerald's coronation of the Jazz Age flapper"[92] is accurate only as far as it goes, for the element of open mockery in the presentation of the jaded-but-plucky Emily and her king, the pudgy milquetoast ruler of a vest-pocket Balkan principality, hardly sounds like a heartfelt toast to the American girl. To a man who, like Charlie Wales, had felt that those in his circle in the early 1920s had been "a sort of royalty, almost infallible, with a sort of magic around us" (386), the events of 1929 and thereafter made the whole notion of American royalty seem like a sick joke. "Majesty" could not have been written before 1929.

That the most attractive aspects of both American life and his own existence could be so tarnished by 1929 was obviously unsettling for Fitzgerald. He seems to have felt that at some point matters had slipped out of control, that like Joel Coles he had taken one drink too many, or like Charlie Wales he had turned a key in a lock in a moment of "wild anger" (399) and in doing so had shut himself away from all that ever mattered. But ultimately what is most striking about the late Fitzgerald is not the impulse to determine what had gone wrong with the country or his own life, or to satirize the old dreams and ideals gone awry, but to learn to deal with the present—and, more importantly, to face his personal future. His sense of history, that is to say, was increasingly personal rather than national; and it focused far more on the present and future than on the past. And what emerged from his new attitude toward history was a keen appreciation of the act of atonement.

Fitzgerald's understanding of atonement is not specifically Catholic, though it does share some features of the Christian mode of action. The first step in the Fitzgeraldian process of atonement is to acknowledge freely the errors in one's personal past. When Charlie Wales revisits his personal Babylon,[93] he is partly motivated by a desire to relive a magic time in his life, one that still so appeals to him that he acknowledges it with one drink every day. And he is also, of course, bidding a reluctant farewell to that wondrous time.[94] But primarily he is returning to the proverbial scene of the crime to confess openly his past mistakes to his sister-in-law, that distant figure draped in the black of priests and judges; to assert that he is, in effect, spiritually cleansed; and to announce his desire to begin life anew. An integral part of that announcement is the implied denial of self. Charlie is emphatic that his primary motivation is to care for little Honoria, much as Dr. Janney is motivated by his desire to care for little Helen. In each case she is an almost preternaturally mature child, a situation which suggests that she is less the concrete motivation behind the desire for a new life (Fitzgerald is careful to avoid the sentimental angel-child of nineteenth-century American fiction) than she is the confirmation of the atoned man's willingness to deny himself, to eschew alcoholism (the ultimate selfish condition) and to work on behalf of others. And work was a key word for the late Fitzgerald. Dr. Janney is of course a trained physician, so by refusing to practice—by not doing his work—he has let down not only himself, but those who depend on him. And by not revealing what kind of business Charlie pursued in the United States or what he has begun to do in Czechoslovakia, Fitzgerald has underscored the importance of the abstract notion of work in "Babylon Revisited." The final step in the process of atonement is to remove oneself from the locus of one's past misdeeds. Dr. Janney leaves his rural home town to live in one of the few urban centers of the South, while Charlie Wales exiles himself to exotic Prague. The act of exile is not a running away, nor is it a kind of punishment: it provides an opportunity to move from a place marred by the memory of selfish, wasteful acts, and to be immersed in a fresh world where work and the caring for others can be facilitated. This fresh world ultimately allows the atoning individual to become part of something far greater than himself, to enter into a vast system the limits of which are unknown even to him—to become, literally, "at one" with something immense. Far from being intimidating, this process is a source of great serenity. It even allows Charlie to tolerate the torments of Marion Peters, so focused is he on those "larger plans" (386).

Ultimately the concept of atonement is something that Fitzgerald had to evolve over time, and under the immense pressure of personal crises. Interestingly, one can see it in mid-evolution in one of the least-known stories of *Taps at Reveille,* "Two Wrongs." Written in October and November of 1929—that is, just a few months before Zelda's nervous breakdown in April 1930—"Two Wrongs" shows Fitzgerald apparently writing an open-ended parable to work through the problems he was experiencing in marriage, including his own role in its deterioration, and the possible solutions to the crisis. "Two Wrongs" is blatantly autobiographical, but Fitzgerald is far more objective in his presentation of himself than one might expect. True, there is a large measure of self-flattery in his portrait of Bill McChesney, "a fresh-faced young Irishman" who attended an Ivy League college and whose immense talent has garnered him both popular and critical acclaim as a producer for the New York stage (223). But the self-portrait is also self-condemnatory: Bill "exud[ed] aggressiveness and self-confidence until the air of his office was thick with it" (223). He still has a chip on his shoulder because Harvard "had me down for a hick" (226). And his New York career suddenly collapses, sending him to Europe to cash in on his Broadway successes with the fresh London audiences. He lives well in Europe, even hobnobbing with English aristocrats, but he makes a fool of himself at Lady Sybil Combrink's party, showing up in tweeds instead of evening dress and effectively flaunting their affair in front of Sybil's husband. Most damning of all, he neglects his wife, Emmy, formerly the star ballet student of Miss Georgia Berriman Campbell in a tiny South Carolina town. Emmy is beautiful, loving, and full of that vital Fitzgeraldian virtue, character: "You're always beautiful. I don't know why. Perhaps because you've got character, and that's always in your face" (235). Emmy also has genuine talent as a ballerina; and so when she miscarries a nearly full-term baby, she responds with a newly focused life. Her "incessant idea was to learn to dance," for she "wanted to use herself on something she could believe in, and it seemed to her that the dance was woman's interpretation of music; instead of strong fingers, one had limbs with which to render Tschaikowsky and Stravinski; and feet could be as eloquent in Chopiniana as voices in 'The Ring'" (240–41). Though being twenty-six years old "she had ten years to make up" (241), Emmy's dedication bears fruit: she wins the opportunity to dance with Paul Makova at the Metropolitan. Bill decides not to stand in her way. While Emmy remains behind in Europe to pursue her ballet career, Bill moves to Denver in the hope of curing his newly active tuberculosis. So the story ends.

For various reasons, "Two Wrongs" is not quite successful, but the primary one is that Fitzgerald tries too desperately to build a case for the rightness, the selflessness of Bill's final act and, concomitantly, for the wrongness, the selfishness of Emmy's. True, the unappealing aspects of the self-portrait as Bill McChesney betoken Fitzgerald's growing awareness of his role in the problems of his marriage, but as the very title of the story suggests, he refuses to believe that it is all his fault. Bill clearly feels that he should have been with Emmy when she slipped getting out of a taxi at the hospital and lost their baby, but he also clearly feels that she should have decided to abandon her ballet career when Bill's tuberculosis recurred: their two wrongs do not make a right, in the opinion of Fitzgerald/McChesney. And the final statement of the story—"He was sure that Emmy would come at the end, no matter what she was doing or how good an engagement she had" (247)—further suggests that it is up to Zelda/Emmy to rectify the situation. What Fitzgerald could not yet admit freely, what would require Zelda's actual breakdown to drive home, was that he truly was at least partly to blame for her tragedy. Further, neither of the Fitzgeralds could begin to get on with their lives until he atoned for his past actions. "Two Wrongs" illustrates Fitzgerald groping toward a conscious understanding of the need for atonement, but at this stage he is aware of only fragments of the process—the need to acknowledge past error, the impulse toward selflessness, the necessity of exile—without understanding either the rest of the procedure, the rationale underlying each step, or, most importantly, its ultimate goal: a sense of peace. If "Two Wrongs" fails as a story, if it is too transparently a wallowing in self-pity or an exercise in self-justification, it is precisely because Fitzgerald was not yet understanding his personal situation in 1929 and, consequently, incapable of formulating a strategy of atonement for dealing with it. Once he did so, under the pressure of Zelda's breakdowns beginning in 1930, he was able to create some of his finest late stories, including "Family in the Wind" and "Babylon Revisited."

The process of atonement which so infuses his late short fiction was both spiritually healthy and artistically enriching for Fitzgerald. Atonement enabled him to face his failed dreams and disappointments, to probe their sources (including his own role in them), and to accept the fact that other disappointments were inevitable. It enabled him to rethink his notions regarding "home," finally coming to perceive it as a potential source of redemption and contentment. And it enabled him to endure the mistakes of the past and the crises of the present with something resembling faith in the "larger" world of the future. Whereas in the previous three collections he had been too young, too inexperienced, or too self-absorbed to comprehend these matters and to apply them to his own life and work, in *Taps at Reveille* we finally see Fitzgerald at a high spiritual and artistic plateau. Though they often had been difficult, the emotional and artistic lessons of the previous fifteen years had finally led to the creation of what is arguably the most revealing and ultimately serene of F. Scott Fitzgerald's four authorized collections of short fiction.

Five years after the publication of *Taps at Reveille,* F. Scott Fitzgerald was dead of a heart attack in Hollywood. It is one of the more futile critical exercises to speculate as to what might have been, but it is clear that Fitzgerald was simply not able to maintain the hard-won sense of personal serenity or the high level of artistic achievement that are evident in his fourth story collection. After *Taps at Reveille* was published in the spring of 1935, Fitzgerald had only a handful of first-rate short stories left in him: "Three Hours Between Planes," "The Lost Decade," and "An Alcoholic Case." Even if combined with the fine pre-1935 stories that had not been included in the four collections—"The Rough Crossing," "Outside the Cabinet Maker's," "Jacob's Ladder," "One Trip Abroad," "The Swimmers"—it is obvious that he would not have had enough quality short fiction to constitute a companion volume to *The Last Tycoon* had he lived to complete it.

But neither the shockingly uneven quality of the post-1935 stories, nor the immensity of the entire short-story canon, nor the much-publicized excesses of Fitzgerald's life should blind us to the fact that he approached his work as a writer of short fiction with dead seriousness. Nor do they gainsay the fact that Fitzgerald's artistic growth from 1920 to 1935 was concurrent with his responses to troubles and challenges in his marriage and professional career—among them crises which would have prevented most individuals from continuing to function as creative writers, let alone developing into one of the most important figures in American literary history. In the final analysis, *Flappers and Philosophers, Tales of the Jazz Age, All the Sad Young Men,* and *Taps at Reveille* are the permanent records of F. Scott Fitzgerald's growth as a man and an artist. They warrant our attention and ultimately our respect.

Notes

Introduction

1. Fitzgerald bibliographer and critic Jackson R. Bryer notes that as of 1979, only twenty-two of Fitzgerald's one hundred eighty stories had been dealt with in scholarly essays or book chapters. But since many of those items are actually "brief notes or bibliographical pieces with little or no critical content," Bryer feels it would be most accurate to say that no more than twenty serious critical essays have been devoted to the entire Fitzgerald short-story canon. As a matter of comparison, during the period studied by Bryer there were more essays written on only two stories by Ernest Hemingway ("The Snows of Kilimanjaro" and "The Short Happy Life of Francis Macomber") than on all the Fitzgerald stories combined ("Introduction," *New Approaches*, p. xii).

    The situation has not improved in the intervening decade. In a good year, two or perhaps three essays are written on individual Fitzgerald short stories—usually "Babylon Revisited" or "The Rich Boy."

2. Malcolm Cowley points out that Fitzgerald "hoped and planned" to create "a uniform edition of his writings, and in it the stories would occupy almost as much space as the novels." See *The Bodley Head Scott Fitzgerald*, vol. 5: *Short Stories* (London: The Bodley Head, 1963), p. 27.

    As early as 1921 Fitzgerald was thinking in terms of a uniform collection of his life's work in the style of Henry James's New York Edition. He wrote to Maxwell Perkins, "Having books scattered around with different publishers, like James + Edith Wharton for instance, stands in the way of ever having collected editions if I ever get to that stage which I of course hope" (letter dated sometime before 28 October 1921, in Bruccoli, *Correspondence*, p. 86).

3. See the letter to Maxwell Perkins, dated 29 April 1920, in *Dear Scott/Dear Max*, p. 30. Perkins wisely declined to include in *Flappers and Philosophers* the six poems proffered by Fitzgerald.

4. Turnbull, *Scott Fitzgerald*, p. 75.

5. Richard Foster, "Fitzgerald's Imagination: A Parable for Criticism," *Minnesota Review* 7 (1967), 154.

6. For example, critic John Peale Bishop, a fellow Princetonian, "was keenly aware of the connection between Fitzgerald's fiction and his life." Wrote Bishop of *The Beautiful and Damned* , "The most interesting thing about Mr. Fitzgerald's book is Mr. Fitzgerald. . . . The true stories about Fitzgerald are always published under his own name" (quoted in Milford, *Zelda*, pp. 119–20). Sergio Perosa sees the same problem with the novel: "He sympathized with his characters and shared some of their illusions and not a few of their attitudes, with the

result that he felt like justifying, incongruously, the greatness of their attempt. . . . He wanted to do [this while passing "a moral judgment on them"], and the thematic unity of the book was seriously compromised" (Perosa, *The Art of F. Scott Fitzgerald*, p. 46).

7. "I devoted . . . much more care myself to the *detail* of the book than I did to thinking out the *general* scheme" (letter to John Peale Bishop, dated late February or early March 1922, in Turnbull, *Letters*, p. 353).

8. Stern argues that the achievement of *The Great Gatsby* can be explained only by the merging of Fitzgerald's personal experience and his imagination. See *The Golden Moment*, chap. 3.

9. Letter to Edmund Wilson, tentatively dated January 1922, in Turnbull, *Letters*, p. 331.

Chapter 1

1. Bruccoli comments on the book's "surprisingly" strong sales in *Epic Grandeur*, p. 147.

2. LeVot, *F. Scott Fitzgerald*, p. 90.

3. H. L. Mencken, "Two Years Too Late," in *H. L. Mencken's Smart Set Criticism*, ed. William H. Nolte (Ithaca, New York: Cornell University Press, 1968), p. 286. Fitzgerald had unwittingly set himself up for this harsh appraisal by evaluating the eight stories in the copy of *Flappers and Philosophers* he had inscribed for Mencken. "The Offshore Pirate" is termed "amusing"; "Head and Shoulders," "The Four Fists," and "Bernice Bobs Her Hair" are dismissed as "trash." (See the photocopy of the inscription in Bruccoli, *Correspondence*, p. 68.) Bruccoli surmises that the ranking of "Benediction" and "Dalyrimple Goes Wrong" as "worth reading" was "no doubt influenced by the circumstance that they had been published in [Mencken's] *The Smart Set*" (Bruccoli, *Epic Grandeur*, pp. 147–48).

4. Letter from John Grier Hibben, dated 27 May 1920, in Bruccoli, *Correspondence*, p. 58; letter from Maxwell Perkins, tentatively dated December 1919, in *Dear Scott/Dear Max*, p. 23. To his credit, Fitzgerald recognized that "The Four Fists" was weak: "I'm sorry to say that I like 'The Four Fists' less than any story I've written save one. It's so priggish + righteous. But many people think its the best" (letter to Phyllis Duganne Parker, tentatively dated Fall 1920, in Bruccoli, *Correspondence*, p. 71).

5. "Sic Transit," *The Nation* 111 (18 September 1920): 329–30, in Bryer, *Critical Reception*, p. 36.

6. Letter to Maxwell Perkins, tentatively dated 11 August 1922, in Turnbull, *Letters*, p. 160; letter to H. L. Mencken, dated 4 May 1925, in Turnbull, *Letters*, p. 481; letter to Chatto & Windus, dated 26 February 1935, in Bruccoli, *Correspondence*, p. 401.

7. John Kuehl writes, "Of the new sexual values, Scott Fitzgerald disapproved on two counts. Romanticist as he was, he based relations between men and women primarily on spiritual qualities. As a moralist, he felt that monogamy represented 'the simplest solution of the mating instinct' and 'the most completely satisfactory state of being in this somewhat depressing world'" (*Apprentice Fiction*, p. 142).

8. Stavola, *Crisis in an American Identity*, p. 46. The affair was not, however, totally one-sided: Ginevra's letters to Fitzgerald run 227 pages of typescript (Lehan, *Craft of Fiction*, p. 95).

9. There are veiled references to Ginevra King throughout Fitzgerald's early stories. The surname of the heroine of "The Offshore Pirate," Ardita Farnam, echoes the name of Ginevra's father's brokerage firm: King, Farnum, and Co. (Lehan, *Craft of Fiction*, p. 54).

10. Bruccoli, *Epic Grandeur*, pp. 88, 89.

11. Bruccoli, *Epic Grandeur*, p. 55.

12. Quoted in Bruccoli, *Epic Grandeur*, p. 101.

13. Milford, *Zelda*, p. 75.

14. LeVot reports that the watch was purchased with the money Fitzgerald received from the movie rights to "Head and Shoulders" (*F. Scott Fitzgerald*, p. 74), while Bruccoli indicates it was paid for by selling "The Camel's Back" to the *Saturday Evening Post* (*Epic Grandeur*, p. 113). The preface to "The Camel's Back" in *Tales of the Jazz Age* is apparently Bruccoli's source, although the tone of the prefaces would suggest that they should not be taken too seriously. The train incident is recorded in Milford, *Zelda*, p. 165.

15. Bruccoli, *Epic Grandeur*, p. 97.

16. The telegram is in Bruccoli, *Correspondence*, p. 51. The close connection between love and money is explored by Scott Donaldson in "Money and Marriage in Fitzgerald's Stories," in Bryer, *New Approaches*, pp. 75–88. The quotation is from page 75.

17. Milton Stern makes a similar point in discussing the remark "How does little Tommy like the poets?" in *This Side of Paradise*. The "satiric tone of 'little Tommy' comes from Fitzgerald, who is trying to do two things at once. He's trying to show how smart and slangy is the inside talk we literary guys make in our rooms, and he is at the same time uneasily aware that perhaps the reader will not take the 'criticism' as seriously as young Fitzgerald would really like him to. The comment implicit in the tone is a shabby attempt to forestall objections by voicing them before anyone else can. If the reader is gulled, then Amory's talk is inside smart talk. If he's not, Fitzgerald can nod and wink with the reader—a bit uncomfortably." Stern notes, however, that he is not certain that Fitzgerald was fully conscious of his intention (*The Golden Moment*, p. 48).

18. It is, of course, difficult for modern readers to appreciate the shock attendant upon a woman bobbing her hair in the years immediately following World War I. It may be easier to imagine in light of this: "In November 1918 the manager of the Palm Garden in New York rented the place to a lady of fashion who wanted to stage a political rally. The participants turned out to be pro-Bolshevik, and the meeting broke up in a riot. The manager admitted that if he had noticed the woman's short haircut, he would never have rented the hall to her." (LeVot, *F. Scott Fitzgerald*, pp. 78–79).

19. For a provocative analysis of Fitzgerald's alcoholism and its impact on his fiction, see Julie M. Irwin, "F. Scott Fitzgerald's Little Drinking Problem," *The American Scholar* 56 (Summer 1987): 415, 418–20, 422–24, 426–27. In a letter to Maxwell Perkins tentatively dated 10 January 1920, Fitzgerald admits to having returned home in "a thoroughly nervous alcoholic state" (*Dear Scott/Dear Max*, p. 24), and many of his subsequent letters, to Perkins and others, make reference to his drinking.

20. Higgins, *A Study*, p. 19.

21. Riley Hughes, "F. Scott Fitzgerald: The Touch of Disaster," in *Fifty Years of the American Novel: A Christian Appraisal*, ed. Harold C. Gardiner (New York: Gordian Press, 1968), p. 139.

22. Sklar terms "Head and Shoulders" a "clever little story about an intellectual genius and a chorus girl who marry and reverse their roles. It is lightly anti-intellectual and takes for its theme the moral that life plays strange tricks. But there is a suppressed cruelty and despair in the situation;

and the weakness of Fitzgerald's treatment may be suggested by comparing it to the 1930 German film *The Blue Angel" (The Last Laocoön,* p. 67). The story line of an intellectual becoming involved with a chorus girl may owe something to *The Picture of Dorian Gray* by one of Fitzgerald's favorite authors, Oscar Wilde.

23. Letter to John Grier Hibben, tentatively dated 3 June 1920, in Turnbull, *Letters,* p. 462.

24. Milford, *Zelda,* p. 64.

25. Bruccoli, *Epic Grandeur,* pp. 96, 6.

26. Percy Lubbock, *The Craft of Fiction* (New York: The Viking Press, 1957), especially chap. 11.

27. The story may originally have been called "Nest Feathers" (letter to Paul Revere Reynolds, dated 28 October 1919, in Bruccoli, *As Ever,* p. 3). Henry Dan Piper reports that it was also called "Variety," and that George Horace Lorimer, editor of the *Saturday Evening Post,* renamed it "Head and Shoulders" (Piper, *Critical Portrait,* p. 65). Fitzgerald had even considered calling it "The Prodigy" (letter to David Arnold Balch, dated 19 June 1920, in Bruccoli, *Correspondence,* p. 60). Fitzgerald's much-touted cleverness with the titles of his stories should not cloud the fact that he often struggled with them, or used the suggestions of others.

28. Letter to David Arnold Balch, dated 19 June 1920, in Bruccoli, *Correspondence,* pp. 59–60. Fitzgerald informs Balch that "I was always interested in prodigies because I almost became one—that is in the technical sense of going to college young. I finally decided to enter at the conventional age of 17."

29. Zelda Sayre [Fitzgerald], "Friend Husband's Latest," *New York Tribune* (2 April 1922), Sec. 5, p. 11, in Bryer, *Critical Reception,* p. 111.

30. Milford, *Zelda,* p. 80.

31. Letter to Edmund Wilson, dated 10 January [1918], in Turnbull, *Letters,* p. 323.

32. See Bruccoli, *Epic Grandeur,* p. 94.

33. Letter to David Arnold Balch, dated 19 June 1920, in Bruccoli, *Correspondence,* p. 60.

34. Letter to Robert Bridges, tentatively dated November 1919, in Bruccoli, *Correspondence,* p. 48.

35. *Notebooks,* Item 1275, p. 193; also in *The Crack-Up,* p. 200.

36. "Sic Transit," *The Nation* 111 (18 September 1920): 329–30, in Bryer, *Critical Reception,* p. 36.

37. Higgins, *A Study,* p. 19.

38. Her given name, if not her character, was taken from a childhood friend in St. Paul, Ardita Ford. (Bruccoli spells it "Ardietta" [*Epic Grandeur,* p. 26], while LeVot spells it "Arditta" [*F. Scott Fitzgerald,* p. 113].) The name would be used again in Gatsby's guest list ("Ardita Fitz-Peters"). When the movie version of "The Offshore Pirate" reached St. Paul, Miss Ford "gave a locally celebrated theatre party so that everyone could 'see what I am like in the movies'" (Mizener, *Far Side,* p. 373, note 48). For "Farnam," see note 9, above.

39. Piper, *Critical Portrait,* p. 74: "[George Horace] Lorimer [of the *Post*] preferred a light, hastily written story like 'Myra Meets His Family' to a better but more pathetic tale like 'The Jelly-Bean.' Fitzgerald experienced considerable difficulty adjusting himself to this hard reality. But

once he grasped the situation he temporarily put his tongue in his cheek and, in 'The Offshore Pirate,' produced for Lorimer's edification an extravaganza of pure advertising-copy prose."

40. Higgins, *A Study*, p. 26; James E. Miller, Jr., *F. Scott Fitzgerald: His Art and His Technique* (New York: New York University Press, 1967), p. 52.

41. "Fitzgerald—One of the Most Promising American Writers of Fiction of the Present Day" [unidentified clipping], in Bryer, *Critical Reception*, p. 58.

42. "The Offshore Pirate" was written in February 1920. In a letter to Maxwell Perkins dated 3 February [1920], Fitzgerald notes that "I've fallen lately under the influence of an author who's quite changed my point of view. He's a chestnut to you, no doubt, but I've just discovered him—Frank Norris. I think *McTeague* & *Vandover* are both excellent" (*Dear Scott/Dear Max*, p. 28). In a letter to H. L. Mencken tentatively dated "Before 7 October 1920," Fitzgerald includes *Moran of the "Lady Letty"* in a proposed uniform edition of Norris's novels (Bruccoli, *Correspondence*, p. 69).

43. Fitzgerald lived briefly in New Orleans during the winter of 1919–20; according to the return addresses of the letters he wrote to Max Perkins, he was living at 2900 Prytania Street as of 21 January 1920 (*Dear Scott/Dear Max*, p. 27). It is possible that he began to read Cable at this time, and the popular *Madame Delphine* would have been the logical story with which to begin a study of New Orleans' best-known writer. By April 1922 Fitzgerald was suggesting that Scribners reprint Cable's work (Bruccoli, *Epic Grandeur*, p. 154).

44. Alice Payne Hackett, *Fifty Years of Best Sellers: 1895–1945* (New York: R. R. Bowker, 1945), p. 21.

45. Arthur Mizener, not recognizing the burlesque of "The Offshore Pirate," cites the image of Curtis Carlyle and Babe blending "minor keys in African harmonics" on a bassoon and oboe as one of the "startling defects exposed by Fitzgerald's efforts to live beyond his intellectual means" ("Introductory essay," [1959] to *Flappers and Philosophers*, p. 15). No one knew better than Fitzgerald (and Ardita and Toby) how ridiculous it was.

46. Fitzgerald felt that Anatole France was one of the three most admirable living writers, along with Conrad and Galsworthy. He and Zelda had attempted unsuccessfully to meet him during their trip to Europe in the summer of 1921 (Eble, *F. Scott Fitzgerald*, p. 70).

47. "Recent Fiction," *Los Angeles Sunday Times* (9 January 1921), Part 3, pp. 38–39, in Bryer, *Critical Reception*, p. 51.

48. Quoted in Milford, *Zelda*, p. 104.

49. William Goldhurst, *F. Scott Fitzgerald and His Contemporaries* (Cleveland: World, 1963), pp. 121, 120.

50. Ruth Prigozy, "'Poor Butterfly': F. Scott Fitzgerald and Popular Music," *Prospects* 2 (1976): 56; Robert Forrey, "Negroes in the Fiction of F. Scott Fitzgerald," *Phylon* 28 (Fall 1967): 295.

51. "Echoes of the Jazz Age," *The Crack-Up*, p. 18.

52. "Handle With Care," *The Crack-Up*, p. 84.

53. "A rich boy might charm his girl by pretending to have been poor, like Toby Moreland, and like George Van Tyne in 'The Unspeakable Egg,' who wins his Fifi by playing the role of a bearded and disheveled roustabout. It did not, of course, work the other way around" (Scott Donaldson, *Fool for Love*, p. 102).

54. Higgins remarks that "consciously or unconsciously, Fitzgerald is close to a parody of the *Post* formula story" (*A Study*, p. 26), and certainly he seems to be acknowledging the *Post*'s heavy use of illustrations. In the original ending of "The Offshore Pirate," it is revealed that Ardita had dreamed the whole encounter. See Jennifer McCabe Atkinson, "The Discarded Ending of 'The Offshore Pirate,'" *Fitzgerald/Hemingway Annual* 6 (1974): 47–49.

55. Lehan, "The Romantic Self and the Uses of Place in the Stories of F. Scott Fitzgerald," in Bryer, *New Approaches*, p. 5; "The Everlasting No," in Thomas Carlyle, *Sartor Resartus* (Philadelphia: Henry Altemus, [1902]), p. 177.

56. Unlike Bernice, Zelda was not of American Indian ancestry, but her appearance suggested otherwise. Her friend Gerald Murphy was struck particularly by Zelda's eyes: "They were strange eyes, brooding but not sad, severe, almost masculine in their directness. She possessed an astounding gaze, one doesn't find it often in women, perfectly level and head-on. If she looked like anything it was an American Indian" (quoted in Milford, *Zelda*, p. 158).

57. For an excellent Spenglerian interpretation of Fitzgerald's fiction, see Richard Lehan, "F. Scott Fitzgerald and Romantic Destiny," *Twentieth Century Literature* 26 (Summer 1980): 137–56.

58. Edwin Moses offers an interpretation of the water/ice imagery in "F. Scott Fitzgerald and The Quest To The Ice Palace." *CEA Critic* 36 (January 1974): 11–14.

59. Zelda had not yet visited the North when Fitzgerald wrote "The Ice Palace." Notes James R. Mellow, "Ironically, before their marriage, Fitzgerald had written one of his more poetic and artful stories, 'The Ice Palace,' which dealt with a Southern belle who experienced the bleakness of a Midwestern winter on a visit to her fiancé and returns home for good—an unusual theme, the effect of geography on love. Considering that the heroine, Sally Carrol Happer, was based on Zelda, Fitzgerald seems to have had a premonition of that alienation of the spirit which Zelda would feel in frigid St. Paul" (*Invented Lives*, p. 144).

60. Patricia Kane notes the element of Babbittry in Harry as well. See "F. Scott Fitzgerald's St. Paul: A Writer's Use of Material," *Minnesota History* 45 (Winter 1976): 143.

61. Allen, *Candles and Carnival Lights*, pp. 38–39.

62. Fitzgerald is, of course, referring to Henry James, Sr. (1811–1882), the noted philosopher who wrote several books on theology, rather than to his son the novelist.

63. Joan M. Allen argues that "Benediction" "manifestly represents the religious sensibility which never left him, even after he publicly denounced the Church. The physical setting is the same as that of 'The Ordeal,' but the seminary in 'Benediction' is an intellectually attractive place, for the students carry volumes of Aquinas, Henry James, Cardinal Mercier, and Kant" (*Candles and Carnival Lights*, p. 43). In her determination to prove that Fitzgerald's Catholicism never really left him, Allen has failed to notice the bitter criticism of the lives of seminarians and priests which is so powerful in "Benediction." By the same token, Eble is not quite correct in arguing that "how little [Fitzgerald] knew of or felt for the religious life may explain the essential weakness of 'Benediction'" (*F. Scott Fitzgerald*, p. 58). Fitzgerald knew enough about the downside of the monastic life to be able to expose its shortcomings, as he does in this story.

64. See the letter to his sister (dated circa 1915) in Bruccoli, *Correspondence*, pp. 15–18.

65. Monroe Stahr, for example, allowed himself to love Minna only when he knew she was about to die. For a provocative discussion of this pattern, see Jan Hunt and John M. Saurez, "The Evasion of Adult Love in Fitzgerald's Fiction," *Centennial Review* 17 (Spring 1973): 152–69.

66. Fitzgerald could not be more explicit: "The problem of evil had solidified for Amory into the problem of sex" (*This Side of Paradise*, p. 280).

67. Heywood Broun, "Paradise and Princeton," *New York Tribune* (11 April 1920), Sec. 7, p. 9, in Bryer, *Critical Reception*, p. 10.

68. "In both 'The Ordeal' and 'Benediction' Fitzgerald's unusual use of light imagery anticipates its importance in 'Absolution' and *The Great Gatsby*. In each story, light, which is symbolic of grace, blessed knowledge or, in short, the essence of all that is good, represents the essence of evil. In these early stories, then, we find the Augustinian antitheses of sacred and secular, spirit and flesh, the City of God and the City of Man, candle and carnival light which would become a central element of the later stories and novels. Perhaps Fitzgerald's unorthodox use of symbolism in these stories as well as his growing apostasy caused some uneasiness in him which he projected onto Catholic commentators, for he claimed that in the critical reception of 'Benediction' and 'Absolution' there was much hostility. In fact, they received favorable reaction from Catholic publications" (*Candles and Carnival Lights*, pp. 44–45).

69. Perosa, *The Art of F. Scott Fitzgerald*, pp. 30–31. Perosa also states incorrectly that Lois will marry Howard. If that were the case, there would be no crisis—and no "Benediction."

70. Mizener, Introduction to *Flappers and Philosophers*, p. 15 .

71. Higgins, *A Study*, p. 18.

72. Quoted in Bruccoli, *Epic Grandeur*, p. 89.

73. Among those he asked was Ernest Hemingway. See *A Moveable Feast* (New York: Charles Scribner's Sons, 1964), p. 151.

74. Fitzgerald had sent his fiancée pills apparently intended to induce menstruation, but Zelda had refused to take them. She is reported to have had three abortions during the marriage, and Fitzgerald feared that they might have contributed to her eventual mental illness (Bruccoli, *Epic Grandeur*, pp. 114, 163n). Item 1564 in Fitzgerald's *Notebooks* reads, "His son went down the toilet of the XXXX hotel after Dr. X—Pills" (p. 244).

75. "Fitzgerald's expression for sexual intercourse with a whore—'I hunted down the spectre of womanhood'—is noteworthy. As late as 1936 fornication would still carry connotations of supernatural corruption in his fiction" (Bruccoli, *Epic Grandeur*, p. 60). The passage Bruccoli refers to is from "Pasting It Together" in *The Crack-Up*, p. 76.

76. For all his implied criticism of seminarians and priests during the years following World War I, Fitzgerald retained his admiration for Thomas Delihant precisely because he was "the old-fashioned Jesuit—the kind they got continually when the best men in the priesthood were all Jesuits" (letter to Cecilia Delihant Taylor, dated 10 June 1917, in Turnbull, *Letters*, p. 415).

77. Harold Piper tries to explain to his wife the actions of his competitor, Clarence Ahearn: "Well, Evie, Ahearn had been fooling around with Marx. If those two had combined we'd have been the little fellow, struggling along, picking up smaller orders, hanging back on risks. It's a question of capital, Evie . . ." (p. 103). As it turns out, Mr. Marx is another local hardware wholesaler with whom Ahearn had considered going into business. Fitzgerald had always been very interested in Marxism, despite his apparent obsession with material wealth. See the remarks on "May Day" in the next chapter.

78. Even the name "Dalyrimple" may owe something to Dreiser. In *The Financier*, the neighborhood grocer to whom thirteen-year-old Frank Cowperwood sells seven cases of Castile soap, thereby beginning his phenomenal business career, is Mr. Dalrymple (chap 3).

79. Stern, *The Golden Moment*, p. 44.

80. Edwin Moses recognizes the importance of Mrs. Bellamy dropping half of Sally Carrol's name, although I feel that the use of just "Sally" signifies a confirmation of the canine more than an "attack on the child-like in Sally Carrol—that is, essentially, on her Southernness." See note 58 above, p. 12.

81. Edwin Moses seems to emphasize too much the apparent negativism in Sally Carrol's return to the South: "At the end of the story she has not grown: the concluding scene is a carefully fashioned recapitulation of the opening one. And the people of Tarleton, Georgia continue to be failures, who stay in Tarleton and 'like it and never want to change things or think or go ahead.' These are important shortcomings, awareness of which sent Sally Carrol off on her abortive pilgrimage, and the virtues that go along with them—'the living in the past, the lazy days and nights you have, and all your carelessness and generosity'—cannot entirely obviate them. Although the South is the wiser choice if one has to choose, what is really needed is a synthesis of the feminine qualities of the South and the masculine ones of the North. But Sally Carrol is hardly the girl to achieve such a synthesis. It is an idea, after all, which better Fitzgerald characters than she never achieved" (see note 58 above, pp. 13–14). Though Moses speaks of the North as masculine and the South as feminine (as do most commentators), he does not recognize the androgyny of Sally Carrol's psychic self and its implications for the story.

82. John Kuehl, "Psychic Geography in 'The Ice Palace,'" in Bryer, *New Approaches*, p. 173. Kuehl's idea of "psychic geography" posits the North as masculine and the South as feminine. He does not address the fact that Sally Carrol has both orientations in herself, and that the story traces her attempts to come to grips with this psychic androgyny.

83. Gallo, *F. Scott Fitzgerald*, p. 86.

84. K. G. W. Cross, *F. Scott Fitzgerald* (New York: Capricorn Books, 1971), p. 33.

85. The supernatural punch bowl may call to mind the end of *The Financier:* "If you had been a mystic or a soothsayer or a member of that mysterious world which divines by incantations, dreams, the mystic bowl, or the crystal sphere, you might have looked into their mysterious depths at this time and foreseen a world of happenings which concerned these two, who were now apparently so fortunately placed. In the fumes of the witches' pot, or the depths of the radiant crystal, might have been revealed cities, cities, cities; a world of mansions, carriages, jewels, beauty; . . . And sorrow, sorrow, sorrow" (*The Financier* [New York: New American Library, 1967], p. 448, ellipses added).

86. "The development of the story . . . tends to recreate a typically Hawthornian atmosphere of fatal gloom. The family at the center of the story undergoes a series of frightful adventures, which are all in direct relationship with the fatal bowl. . . . As one can see from his *Notebooks* Hawthorne was very fond of identifying ideas with concrete things, abstract concepts with everyday objects, and this same preoccupation is present in Fitzgerald's story. But in his case, the symbolism is open and obvious, the style jumbled and forced, and we conclude that once again he followed models that he had imperfectly understood" (Perosa, *The Art of F. Scott Fitzgerald*, p. 35).

87. Lehan, "The Romantic Self and the Uses of Place," p. 50 (see note 55, above).

88. Alan Casty, "'I and It' in the Stories of F. Scott Fitzgerald," *Studies in Short Fiction* 9 (Winter 1972): 54. Casty's interpretation seems doubtful, since Evylyn is not responsible for the acts of destruction in the story.

89. Untermeyer, "F. Scott Fitzgerald," *Makers of the Modern World* (New York: Simon and Schuster, 1955), p. 695.

90. Sklar, *The Last Laocoön*, p. 64.

Chapter 2

1. Letter to Maxwell Perkins, tentatively dated 12 August 1922, in *Dear Scott/Dear Max*, p. 62.

2. The critical consensus is that "May Day" is an interweaving of the "three little character stories" that Fitzgerald had hoped to salvage from "Darling Heart." See letter to Maxwell Perkins, dated 3 February [1920], in *Dear Scott/Dear Max*, p. 28. Arthur Mizener dissents, claiming that "May Day" was "certainly never part of 'Darling Heart'" (*The Far Side of Paradise*, p. 367, note 62).

3. Perkins felt that "Tarquin of Cheapside" would "shock many people not because of the particular crime recorded, but because of the identity of the man accused of it. The crime is a peculiarly repugnant one for it involves violence, generally requires unconsciousness, is associated with negroes." Fitzgerald defended it on the grounds that Katherine Fullerton Gerrould had reviewed it favorably when it appeared in the *Nassau Literary Magazine* and that "it drew letters of praise" when it was published in *The Smart Set*. Perkins capitulated, clarifying that his objections had arisen simply "from the fact that people have a sort of reverence for Shakespeare." See letters dated 2 August 1922, circa 12 August 1922, and 15 August 1922, in *Dear Scott/Dear Max*, pp. 61–63.

4. See letter to Maxwell Perkins, tentatively dated 18 January 1922, in *Dear Scott/Dear Max*, p. 51.

5. Letter to Maxwell Perkins, dated 11 May [1922], in *Dear Scott/Dear Max*, p. 58 (Fitzgerald's emphasis).

6. Sklar, *The Last Laocoön*, p. 130.

7. See letters to Maxwell Perkins, dated circa 10 January 1920 and 3 February 1920, in *Dear Scott/Dear Max*, pp. 25, 28.

8. The matter-of-fact treatment of violence in "Jemina" is reminiscent of Vonnegut's presentation of the Dresden bombing in *Slaughterhouse-Five:*

> The whiskey in the bathtub caught fire. The walls began to fall in.
> Jemina and the man from the settlements looked at each other.
> "Jemina," he whispered.
> "Stranger," she answered.
> "We will die together," he said. "If we had lived I would have taken you to the city and married you. With your ability to hold liquor, your social success would have been assured."
> She caressed him idly for a moment, counting her toes softly to herself. The smoke grew thicker. Her left leg was on fire.
> She was a human alcohol lamp.
> Their lips met in one long kiss and then a wall fell on them and blotted them out. (316).

Likewise, the stage directions of the playlet "Mr. Icky" are reminiscent of those of Ionesco: "Several hours pass. . . . Several songs can be introduced here or some card tricks by [Rodney] Divine or a tumbling act, as desired" (304); "Some risqué joke can be introduced here" (305); "Any other cue may be inserted here" (309); "He picks up a handful of soil passionately and rubs it on his bald head. Hair sprouts" (308); "The play can end at this point or can go on indefinitely" (310).

9. Letters to Maxwell Perkins, dated 6 February 1922 and circa 5 March 1922, in *Dear Scott/Dear Max*, pp. 54, 58; Robert A. Martin, "Hollywood in Fitzgerald: After Paradise," in Bryer, *New Approaches*, p. 132.

10. See letters dated circa late June 1922 and 16 October 1921, in Bruccoli, *As Ever*, pp. 45, 28.

11. See Alan Margolies, "'The Camel's Back' and *Conductor 1492*," *Fitzgerald/Hemingway Annual* 6 (1974): 87–88.

12. Letter to Maxwell Perkins, dated 11 May [1922], in *Dear Scott/Dear Max*, p. 59.

13. Letter to Maxwell Perkins, dated 11 May [1922], in *Dear Scott/Dear Max*, p. 59; Sklar, *The Last Laocoön*, p. 151.

14. Letter to Edmund Wilson, dated 25 June 1922, in Turnbull, *Letters*, p. 336.

15. Letter to Maxwell Perkins, dated 11 May [1922], in *Dear Scott/Dear Max*, pp. 58–59.

16. Letter to Maxwell Perkins, dated circa 20 June 1922, in *Dear Scott/Dear Max*, p. 60.

17. Letter to Maxwell Perkins, dated circa 20 June 1922, in *Dear Scott/Dear Max*, p. 60.

18. Letter to Maxwell Perkins, dated 9 January [1922], in *Dear Scott/Dear Max*, p. 51.

19. Letter to Maxwell Perkins, dated 11 May [1922], in *Dear Scott/Dear Max*, p. 59.

20. The account he gave Max Perkins was slightly different. He indicated that it was begun at "eight o'clock one morning and finished at seven at night & then copied between seven and half past four & mailed at 5 in the morning" (letter dated 10 November 1920, in *Dear Scott/Dear Max*, p. 32).

21. Quoted in Mellow, *Invented Lives*, p. 116.

22. "Too Much Fire Water," *Minneapolis Journal*, 10 December 1922, Women's Section, p. 12, in Bryer, *Critical Reception*, pp. 162–63.

23. "Scott Fitzgerald Scores One More," *Washington* [D.C.] *Herald*, 21 October 1922, p. 7, in Bryer, *Critical Reception*, p. 148.

24. LeVot, *F. Scott Fitzgerald*, p. 117.

25. James E. Miller, Jr., *F. Scott Fitzgerald: His Art and His Technique* (New York: New York University Press, 1967), pp. 52–53.

26. Sklar, *The Last Laocoön*, p. 140.

27. Letter to Maxwell Perkins, dated July 1922, in Bruccoli, *Correspondence*, p. 111; letter to Harold Ober, dated October/November 1922, in Bruccoli, *As Ever*, p. 49; Bruccoli, *As Ever*, p. xviii, note.

28. A. A. White, "The Jazz Age in Story," [*Long Island Press* (?)], no date, in Bryer, *Critical Reception*, p. 164.

29. "Tales of the Jazz Age," *Rochester* [N.Y.] *Democrat and Chronicle*, 10 December 1922, Sec. 3, p. 6, in Bryer, *Critical Reception*, p. 162. John Gunther, "Fitzgerald 'Collects,'" *Chicago Daily News*, 8 November 1922, p. 13, in Bryer, *Critical Reception*, p. 155.

30. John T. Wallace, "Short Stories by Fitzgerald," *Detroit Free Press*, 8 October 1922, magazine, p. 6, in Bryer, *Critical Reception*, p.143.

31. Hildegarde Hawthorne, *New York Times Book Review*, 29 October 1922, p. 12, in Bryer, *Critical Reception*, p. 150. "Tales of the Jazz Age," *Springfield* [Mass.] *Sunday Republican*, 29 October 1922, p. 7A, in Bryer, *Critical Reception*, p. 151.

32. Letter to Maxwell Perkins, dated 6 February 1922, in *Dear Scott/Dear Max*, p. 55.

33. "Too Much Fire Water," *Minneapolis Journal*, 10 December 1922, Women's Section, p. 12, in Bryer, *Critical Reception*, p. 162. "F. Scott Fitzgerald Puffs as Jazz Age Outpaces Him," *Philadelphia Evening Public Ledger*, 28 November 1922, p. 30, in Bryer, *Critical Reception*, p. 157. Stephen Vincent Benét, "Plotting an Author's Curve," *New York Evening Post Literary Review*, 18 November 1922, p. 219, in Bryer, *Critical Reception*, p. 156.

34. "Too Much Fire Water," *Minneapolis Journal*, 10 December 1922, Women's Section, p. 12, in Bryer, *Critical Reception*, pp. 162–63.

35. John Gunther, "Fitzgerald 'Collects,'" *Chicago Daily News*, 8 November 1922, p. 13, in Bryer, *Critical Reception*, pp. 154–55.

36. Letter to Maxwell Perkins, dated July 1922, in Bruccoli, *Correspondence*, p. 111.

37. Hildegarde Hawthorne, *New York Times Book Review*, 29 October 1922, p. 12, in Bryer, *Critical Reception*, p. 150.

38. Margaret Culkin Banning, "Uneven Work of a Genius," *Duluth Herald*, 13 October 1922, Sec. 1, p. 21, in Bryer, *Critical Reception*, pp. 148, 147.

39. "Too Much Fire Water," *Minneapolis Journal*, 10 December 1922, Women's Section, p. 12, in Bryer, *Critical Reception*, p. 162.

40. John Farrar, *New York Herald*, 8 October 1922, Sec. 7, pp. 12, 13 in Breyer, *Critical Reception*, p. 141.

41. Stephen Vincent Benét, "Plotting an Author's Curve," *New York Evening Post Literary Review*, 18 November 1922, p. 219, in Bryer, *Critical Reception*, p. 156.

42. *The Crack-Up*, pp. 77, 86.

43. Letter to Edmund Wilson, dated [Fall 1917], Turnbull, *Letters*, p. 320.

44. "Sleeping and Waking," *The Crack-Up*, pp. 66–67.

45. Glenway Wescott, "The Moral of F. Scott Fitzgerald," in Kazin, ed., *F. Scott Fitzgerald*, pp. 120–21.

46. Letter to Maxwell Perkins, dated 18 September 1919, in *Dear Scott/Dear Max*, p. 22.

47. Letter to Maxwell Perkins, dated 3 February 1920, in *Dear Scott/Dear Max*, p. 28.

48. Letter to Charles Scribner II, dated 12 August 1920, in Turnbull, *Letters*, p. 145.

49. Letter to Harold Ober, dated 5 February 1922, in Bruccoli, *As Ever*, p. 36.

50. For a discussion of the pulsating structure of "May Day," see Anthony J. Mazzella, "The Tension of Opposites in Fitzgerald's 'May Day,'" *Studies in Short Fiction* 14 (Fall 1977): 379–85.

51. James W. Tuttleton, "Seeing Slightly Red: Fitzgerald's 'May Day,'" in Bryer, *New Approaches*, p. 182. Fitzgerald recalls this period in "My Lost City" in *The Crack-Up*, especially pp. 25–26.

52. Robert Emmet Long, *The Achieving of* The Great Gatsby: *F. Scott Fitzgerald, 1920–1925* (Lewisburg, Pennsylvania: Bucknell University Press, 1979), p. 32.

53. Turnbull, *Scott Fitzgerald*, p. 95.

54. Charles R. Anderson, "Scott Fitzgerald: 1896–1940," in Charles R. Anderson, ed., *American Literary Masters*, vol. 2 (New York: Holt, Rinehart and Winston, 1975), p. 959. Lehan, *Craft of Fiction*, pp. 84–85. Tuttleton, "Seeing Slightly Red," p. 184.

55. Interesting, but ultimately unconvincing, is Robert K. Martin's argument that in the presentation of Gordon "Fitzgerald was treating, albeit covertly and perhaps unconsciously, the problems faced by the repressed homosexual when he is forced to leave a place of relative happiness and security, such as the military or a men's college, and to take up a place in a heterosexual world which he fears. Gordon's reaction against the physical nature of Jewel seems to me Fitzgerald's way of expressing Gordon's repulsion at the thought of a woman." See "Sexual and Group Relationship in 'May Day': Fear and Longing," *Studies in Short Fiction* 15 (Winter 1978): 99–101. I quote from page 101.

56. Letter to Carl Hovey, dated 27 October 1920, in Bruccoli, *Correspondence*, p. 71.

57. Michael Paul Gruber, "Fitzgerald's 'May Day': A Prelude to Triumph," *Essays in Literature* (University of Denver) 2 (1973): 33.

58. As Kenneth Eble points out, "The kingdom of Braddock Washington . . . is the vision of Heaven that the undernourished American imagination most often envisions" (*F. Scott Fitzgerald*, p. 80). Robert Sklar suggests that the idea of "life in a provincial Mississippi river village" being "no better than life in hell" is taken from Van Wyck Brooks' *The Ordeal of Mark Twain* (*The Last Laocoön*, pp. 141–42).

59. Frances Fitzgerald Lanahan, "Introduction," *Six Tales of the Jazz Age and Other Stories* (New York: Charles Scribner's Sons, 1960), p. 11.

60. Letter to Edmund Wilson, dated 10 January [1918], in Turnbull, *Letters*, p. 324.

61. Leland S. Person, Jr., "Fitzgerald's 'O Russet Witch!': Dangerous Women, Dangerous Art," *Studies in Short Fiction* 23 (Fall 1986): 444. Person anticipates several of my arguments; however, I am not convinced that the story probes "the self-destructive power of [Fitzgerald's] art" (443).

62. Person, "Dangerous Women, Dangerous Art," 446.

63. Richard Lehan, "The Romantic Self and the Uses of Place in the Stories of F. Scott Fitzgerald," in Bryer, *New Approaches*, p. 9.

64. Higgins, *A Study*, p. 36.

65. The fantasy about a bizarre birth may reflect Fitzgerald's family situation at the time of the story's composition. "The Curious Case of Benjamin Button" was finished in February 1922; a few months earlier, on 26 October 1921, the Fitzgeralds' daughter Scottie had been born, and so the story may reflect her first-time father's natural apprehension about what the new baby would be like. But one may surmise that the story also reflects Fitzgerald's negative imaginative response to Zelda's second pregnancy, which was apparent as of late January or early February 1922. Neither Fitzgerald wanted the second baby, particularly so soon after the

birth of Scottie, and the abortion was performed in March (Milford, *Zelda*, p. 117). The composition of "The Curious Case of Benjamin Button" thus was concurrent with an unwanted pregnancy, and the grotesqueness of the seventy-year-old baby may reflect Fitzgerald's guilty attempt to justify the impending abortion. Fitzgerald's emotional state may also explain the apparently unconscious redirection of the story. As of December 1921—that is, when Scottie was a few weeks old—Fitzgerald called it "the funniest story ever written" and indicated it was so near completion that he would send it to his agent Harold Ober later that week. But by 24 January 1922, it had turned into what Fitzgerald termed "a weird thing," and so it remained. (See letters to Harold Ober, dated circa 1 December 1921 and 24 January [1922] in Bruccoli, *As Ever*, pp. 32,33).

On a less personal note, Fitzgerald indicates in the preface to the story that it was inspired by "a remark of Mark Twain's to the effect that it was a pity that the best part of life came at the beginning and the worst part at the end. . . . Several weeks after completing it, I discovered an almost identical plot in Samuel Butler's 'Note-books'" (ix). Andrew Crosland examines the Twain and Butler connections in "Sources for Fitzgerald's 'The Curious Case of Benjamin Button,'" *Fitzgerald/Hemingway Annual* 11 (1979): 135–39.

Finally, it is possible that "The Curious Case of Benjamin Button" influenced stanza 5 of William Butler Yeats' "Among School Children," written 14 January 1926:

> What youthful mother, a shape upon her lap
> Honey of generation had betrayed,
> And that must sleep, shriek, struggle to escape
> As recollection or the drug decide,
> Would think her son, did she see that shape
> With sixty or more winters on its head,
> A compensation for the pang of his birth,
> Or the uncertainty of his setting forth?

66. Higgins, *A Study*, p. 59.

67. Milton Hindus argues that, for all its fantasy, "The Curious Case of Benjamin Button" is ultimately realistic: "Turning time upside down in this way is not only amusing in its consequences but revealing and instructive in many respects as well. In fact, what began as a wild fantasy ends almost on a note of realism, for in the ordinary course of things old age paradoxically reaches the stage of 'second childhood' also" (*F. Scott Fitzgerald: An Introduction and Interpretation* [New York: Holt, Rinehart and Winston, 1968], p. 106).

68. Edwin Fussell argues that "Fitzgerald is measuring the attitudes and behavior of the Lost Generation by means of a symbol of romantic wonder that is extensive enough to comprehend all American experience. The contrast amounts to the ironic rejection of all that this generation believes in, the immaturity and irresponsibility of its quest for 'experience,' when such a quest is juxtaposed with one (Columbus') that suggests the fullest possibilities for romantic wonder. There is the added implication that some kind of conscious search for experience is at the heart of American cultural history, but that the quest had never taken so childish a form" ("Fitzgerald's Brave New World," *ELH* 19 [December 1952]: 294). Robert Sklar is even more emphatic on this point: "such 'magical, breathless' dawns are false and sentimental dawns. . . . Nature plays many cruel jokes on men, and an appeal to romantic sentiment is chief among them. This passage is not an evocation of romantic wonder, but a heavily ironic deflation of it" (*The Last Laocoön*, p. 78). Sklar seems to be overstating the irony of the situation. Fitzgerald's sense of history and optimism at this early stage of his life were such that he would have responded more to the romantic wonder brought forth by the dawn than to the childishness of those observing it.

69. Ronald J. Gervais, "The Socialist and the Silk Stockings: Fitzgerald's Double Allegiance," *Mosiac* 15 (June 1982): 82.

70. Brian Way, "Scott Fitzgerald," *New Left Review*, No. 21 (October 1963): 43.

71. *The Crack-Up,* p. 69.

72. "I am half black Irish and half old American stock with the usual exaggerated ancestral pretensions. The black Irish half of the family had the money and looked down upon the Maryland side of the family who had, and really had, that certain series of reticences and obligations that go under the poor old shattered word 'breeding' (modern form 'inhibitions'). So being born in that atmosphere of crack, wisecrack and countercrack I developed a two-cylinder inferiority complex. . . . I spent my youth in alternately crawling in front of the kitchen maids and insulting the great" (letter to John O'Hara, dated 18 July 1933, in Turnbull, *Letters,* p. 503).

73. Sklar, *The Last Laocoön,* pp. 169–70.

74. Robert Emmet Long argues that the story opens with the quality of a fairy tale (*The Achieving of* The Great Gatsby, p. 33). Bruccoli terms the preamble "quasi-Biblical" in mood (*Epic Grandeur,* p. 142). Michael Paul Gruber speaks of a "grandiloquent style reserved for court historians and epic poets" ("A Prelude to Triumph," 21).

75. Robert Emmet Long, *The Achieving of* The Great Gatsby, p. 33.

76. *The Crack-Up,* p. 87.

77. The reference to "incurable evils" would at first glance seem to run counter to Fitzgerald's socialist sympathies, but in fact his espousal of socialism always had coexisted with a romantic faith in the preeminence of the individual. For an excellent discussion of Fitzgerald's ambivalence regarding socialism, see Gervais, "The Socialist and the Silk Stockings" (note 69, above).

78. John Gery, "The Curious Grace of Benjimin [sic] Button," *Studies in Short Fiction* 17 (Fall 1980): 496.

79. John Gery, "Curious Grace," 496.

80. William Troy, "Scott Fitzgerald: The Authority of Failure," in Kazin, ed., *F. Scott Fitzgerald,* p. 189. Troy is speaking specifically of *The Beautiful and Damned,* though his words apply as well to "The Curious Case of Benjamin Button."

81. *The Crack-Up,* p. 13. Writes Brian Way, "From the very beginning, Fitzgerald believed that the American adventure of the 1920s, through its lack of restraint and its absence of style, was bound to end in disaster. As early as 1920, in his short story 'May Day,' Fitzgerald had tried to use the suicide of Gordon Sterrett as a way of expressing his sense of this tendency. One of the most urgent problems he faced as a historian of manners was that of finding the right image of disaster. It is this difficulty—far more than his drinking, Zelda's illness, or the need to write magazine stories for money—which explains why it took him nine years to write *Tender Is the Night.* At first, he thought he had found what he was looking for in one of the celebrated murders of the decade—either the Leopold and Loeb case of 1924, or the Dorothy Ellingson case of 1925. Both murders were the result of an irresponsible following-through of impulse—one of the distinguishing faults of the age" (*F. Scott Fitzgerald and the Art of Social Fiction* [New York: St. Martin's, 1980], p. 141).

82. Brian Way, *The Art of Social Fiction,* p. 68.

83. Brian Way, *The Art of Social Fiction,* p. 68; Long, *The Achieving of* The Great Gatsby, p. 63.

84. Long, *The Achieving of* The Great Gatsby, p. 63.

85. Sklar, *The Last Laocoön*, p. 145. Leonard A. Podis is surely correct that Braddock's situation illustrates "the danger in carrying a potential good to its evil inverse" in precisely the way that Dr. Rappaccini's desire to achieve a noble dream created a literally monstrous situation. See "Fitzgerald's 'The Diamond as Big as the Ritz' and Hawthorne's 'Rappaccini's Daughter,'" *Studies in Short Fiction* 21 (Summer 1984): 243–50. I quote from page 245.

86. Sklar maintains that "Fitzgerald was torn between punishing Braddock Washington and exalting him." This ambivalence reflects his continuing affection for the genteel romantic hero at war with his realization that this hero "was a victim of the First World War" (*The Last Laocoön*, p. 168).

87. Erling Larsen, "The Geography of Fitzgerald's Saint Paul," *Carleton Miscellany* 13 (Spring-Summer 1973): 18.

88. "There is little documentation for young Scott's relationship with his parents. Nearly all of their correspondence has been lost, and Scott rarely spoke about them. His sister Annabel has no vivid memories of them, either; it is as if they scarcely existed" (Bruccoli, *Epic Grandeur,* p. 24). (It may be germane to this matter that the family apparently could not decide how to spell the name of Fitzgerald's sister. In family letters she is variously referred to as "Annabel" or "Annabelle.") For a fascinating discussion of Scott and Zelda's relationships with their parents, see Thomas J. Stavola, *Scott Fitzgerald: Crisis in an American Identity* (New York: Barnes & Noble, 1979), especially chap. 2, "Scott and Zelda Fitzgerald: A Joint Psychohistorical Study."

89. Milford, *Zelda*, pp. 24, 23, 52.

90. Eble, *F. Scott Fitzgerald*, p. 78.

91. Compare Fitzgerald's frieze of rejection slips in his New York apartment in 1919 (Bruccoli, *Epic Grandeur*, p. 96). Higgins argues that "the symbol of the biscuits degenerates into bathos as Harry, in a ridiculous scene, signifies the end of past happiness by eating them!" (*A Study*, p. 50, note 141). It is possible, however, that Fitzgerald is drawing upon his knowledge of Irish wakes in this scene. Harry begins to pull the biscuits off the wall and eat them when he realizes that Jeffrey is, for all intents and purposes, dead: the doctors were performing "a living inquest" on his soul (290). In the Irish ceremony of "sin-eating," a friend or relative of the deceased is expected to eat during the wake, with the food representing the sins of the dead person. The more one eats, the more likely it is that the deceased will enter heaven.

92. Edmund Wilson, Jr., "The Jazz King Again," *Vanity Fair* 19 (November 1922): 24, in Bryer, *Critical Reception*, pp. 152–53. Wilson reports that he read the story "with ever increasing admiration at Fitzgerald's mastery of the nuances of the ridiculous. I had never before realized that he was capable of such restrained and ingenious satire," and the passage in which Roxanne teaches herself to ice skate "amused me most." "What was my astonishment when I had finished the story to discover that it was intended to be serious."

93. Bruccoli, *Epic Grandeur*, p. 146; Milford, *Zelda*, p. 168.

94. Bruccoli, *Epic Grandeur*, p. 141.

95. For the popularity of Sir Walter Scott in the South, see Jay B. Hubbell, *The South in American Literature: 1607–1900* (Durham, North Carolina: Duke University Press, 1954), pp. 188–93.

96. Piper, *Critical Portrait*, p. 68. Kenneth Eble seems to have misunderstood the story in declaring that "Fitzgerald need not have provided his central character" with a "good Southern"

ancestry, and that "at the end, [Jim] is planning to buy up a piece of land with the small inheritance he has received" (*F. Scott Fitzgerald*, p. 76). Jim's background is essential for an understanding of his situation, and he abandons his dream of buying and improving some land when he learns that Nancy has married Merritt.

Chapter 3

1. See Mizener, *The Far Side of Paradise*, p. 377, note 40. Fitzgerald recalls this phase of his life in "How to Live on $36,000 a Year," in *Afternoon of an Author*, pp. 87–99.

2. For an account of the Jozan affair, see Milford, *Zelda*, pp. 138–45.

3. Quoted from a letter to Ludlow Fowler, dated Summer 1926, in Bruccoli, *Correspondence*, p. 200.

4. Letter to Ludlow Fowler, dated August 1924, in Bruccoli, *Correspondence*, p. 145.

5. Milford reports that Scott and Zelda had made a suicide pact in the early days of their marriage, promising "that at thirty-five they'd call it quits." Milford also quoted a letter written by Zelda during her engagement: "We will just *have* to die when we're thirty." See Milford, *Zelda*, pp. 236, 71.

6. Letter to Maxwell Perkins, dated circa 25 August 1924, in *Dear Scott/Dear Max*, p. 76.

7. Fitzgerald made a conscious decision to improve the quality of his fiction. He wrote Thomas Boyd in March 1923, "I have decided to be a pure artist + experiment in form and emotion" (Bruccoli, *Correspondence*, p. 126). Though this passage is usually quoted in reference to *Gatsby*, it is also revelant to his work as a writer of short fiction. For example, "Absolution" (written in June 1923) is clearly an attempt to write impressionistically about psychological trauma.

8. Letter from John Peale Bishop, dated 9 June 1925, in Bruccoli, *Correspondence*, p. 169.

9. Fitzgerald wrote Maxwell Perkins on 28 August 1925, "You will notice that one story I included in my dummy Table of Contents that I sent you in July has been withdrawn, and another better one substituted (*Dear Scott/Dear Max*, p. 119). Alan Margolies surmises that Fitzgerald dropped "Dice, Brass Knuckles, & Guitar" because he was unable to revise it satisfactorily ("'Kissing, Shooting, and Sacrificing': F. Scott Fitzgerald and the Hollywood Market," in Bryer, *New Approaches*, p. 70). Fitzgerald was an almost fussy reviser, treating the magazine versions of his stories as working drafts of the texts used in the authorized collections.

10. Though the publication of *All the Sad Young Men* was originally projected for the fall of 1925, it was delayed so that "The Rich Boy" could be serialized in the January and February 1926 issues of *Redbook*. See Fitzgerald's letter to Maxwell Perkins, dated circa 10 September 1925, in *Dear Scott/Dear Max*, p. 121.

11. Letter to Maxwell Perkins, dated 31 March 1925, in *Dear Scott/Dear Max*, p. 99.

12. Letter to Maxwell Perkins, dated circa 25 April 1926, in *Dear Scott/Dear Max*, p. 138.

13. Letter to Maxwell Perkins, dated 27 October 1924, in *Dear Scott/Dear Max*, p. 80.

14. Letter to Maxwell Perkins, dated 1 June 1925, in *Dear Scott/Dear Max*, p. 113.

15. Letter to Maxwell Perkins, dated 1 December [1925] in Bruccoli, *Correspondence*, p. 182.

16. Letters to Maxwell Perkins, dated 31 March 1925 and 1 May 1925, in *Dear Scott/Dear Max*, pp. 99, 103.

17. Letter to Edmund Wilson, postmarked 7 October 1924, in Turnbull, *Letters*, p. 341.

18. Letter to Maxwell Perkins, dated [1 June 1925], in *Dear Scott/Dear Max*, p. 112.

19. Letters to Maxwell Perkins, dated circa 20 October 1925, circa 27 December 1925, and 20 February 1926, in *Dear Scott/Dear Max*, pp. 122, 126, 134.

20. The sales figures are from Bruccoli, *Epic Grandeur*, p. 235. Typical of a Fitzgerald story collection, sales dropped dramatically after 1926. As of 1931, *All the Sad Young Men* had earned just $4,012 (Bruccoli, *As Ever*, p. xviii, note).

21. E. C. Beckwith, "Volume of F. Scott Fitzgerald Stories in Which 'Absolution' Reigns Supreme," *Literary Review of the New York Evening Post*, 13 March 1926, p. 4, in Bryer, *Critical Reception*, p. 260.

22. William Rose Benét, "Art's Bread and Butter," *Saturday Review of Literature*, 3 April 1926, p. 682, in Bryer, *Critical Reception*, p. 268.

23. Henry F. Pringle, "F. Scott Fitzgerald Grows Older and Serene In His Book of Stories," *New York World*, 28 February 1926, p. 6M, in Bryer, *Critical Reception*, p. 253.

24. Malcolm Cowley, *Charm*, May 1926, pp. 80–81, in Bryer, *Critical Reception*, p. 272.

25. Though the stories of *All the Sad Young Men* mention alcohol even less than those of *Tales of the Jazz Age*, some critics continued to regard Fitzgerald as a chronicler of the inebriate. Leon Whipple terms "The Rich Boy" a "good straight tale of one who gets his kick out of liquor," while in the other eight stories "too much of the sentiment is of the alcoholic variety" (*The Survey*, 1 June 1926, p. 331, in Bryer, *Critical Reception*, p. 275).

26. Brooks Cottle, "Books and Their Authors" [unidentified clipping in Fitzgerald's Scrapbook #3], in Bryer, *Critical Reception*, p. 276.

27. [Anonymous Reviewer], *The Dial*, June 1926, p. 521, in Bryer, *Critical Reception*, pp. 274–75. In point of fact, there is only one roadster in the entire collection (it is mentioned briefly in "Hot and Cold Blood"), and the only dance floor is in "Rags Martin-Jones"—a story in which Fitzgerald satirizes the Jazz Age perception of love as a commodity. The world of *All the Sad Young Men* is emphatically one of business offices, trolley cars, and commuter trains.

28. William Rose Benét comments briefly on the "winnowing" [see note 22, p. 267].

29. Letter to Scottie Fitzgerald, dated 7 July 1938, in Turnbull, *Letters*, p. 32.

30. Stern, *The Golden Moment*, p. 171.

31. Donaldson, *Fool for Love*, p. 111.

32. Donaldson observes that Fitzgerald's female protagonists are still "intensely self-centered. And yet if his readers condemn these women, they do so without any warrant from Fitzgerald himself, who seems to have admired them despite their failings" (*Fool for Love*, p. 67). Donaldson's point, though somewhat overstated, is worth noting.

33. James R. Mellow records that when Fitzgerald was at work on *The Great Gatsby*, Zelda wrote a letter of complaint to her friends, Xandra ("Sandy") and Oscar Kalman: "'Scott has started a new novel and retired into strict seclusion and celibacy. He's horribly intent on it and has built up a beautiful legend about himself which corresponds somewhat to the old fable about

the ant and the grasshopper. *Me* being the grasshopper.' The strange feature of the letter is not the familiar complaint about her laziness, but her remark about Fitzgerald's self-imposed 'celibacy.' It puts an odd emphasis on Edmund Wilson's earlier letter to John Bishop about Fitzgerald's having hit on a 'modus vivendi for preventing Zelda from absorbing all his time, emotion, and seminal juice.' But the truth is that for some years past Fitzgerald seems to have had rather subterranean thoughts on the subject of sex and celibacy, ambition and the lure of the flesh, and the role of the priesthood.

"In the unpublished preface to *This Side of Paradise,* written four years earlier, Fitzgerald admitted to having deleted some 'awe-inspiring half-lines' from the earlier versions of his first novel. One of these romantic phrases, 'the dark celibacy of greatness,' gives a sinister cast to his own drives toward becoming one of the great writers of his time. If Fitzgerald thought the phrase too purple, he evidently considered it too important for the wastebasket and used it in his preface" (*Invented Lives,* p. 193).

34. Fitzgerald's contemporaries and modern critics alike consistently deem "Gretchen's Forty Winks" a "domestic comedy." Louise Maunsell Field speaks for most in terming it "amusing and very clever" ("Three Exhibits of Drifting Americans," *Literary Digest International Book Review,* April 1926, pp. 315–16, in Bryer, *Critical Reception,* p. 266). Robert Sklar does not identify the story as comic, but acknowledges that its resolution is typical of the Fitzgerald marriage stories of that period: "Marriage problems, and adultery, had been muted but not insignificant subjects in Fitzgerald's earlier fiction. So long as he aspired to realism he could not have overlooked them; but still his genteel formulas provided a cloak of innocence and inevitably a happy ending." In stories like "Gretchen's Forty Winks," "real or potential marital difficulties were raised and then glossed over, here by a twist of plot, there by a retreat to conventions" (*The Last Laocoön,* p. 235).

Fitzgerald took fairy tales seriously: "The two basic stories of all times are Cinderella and Jack the Giant Killer—the charm of women and the courage of men" (*Notebooks,* #1071, p. 163).

35. Bruccoli, *Epic Grandeur,* p. 141.

36. Hemingway, *A Moveable Feast* (New York: Charles Scribner's Sons, 1964), p. 180.

37. Christiane Johnson, "Freedom, Contingency, and Ethics in 'The Adjuster,'" in Bryer, *New Approaches,* p. 228. Johnson's perceptive analysis is the only essay devoted to this story. For the texts of the three articles by Fitzgerald, see Bruccoli and Bryer, *A Miscellany,* pp. 186,192, 202.

38. Milford, *Zelda,* pp. 201, 245.

39. Clyde B. Davis [unidentified clipping in Fitzgerald's Scrapbook #3], in Bryer, *Critical Reception,* p. 278; Frances Newman, "One of the Wistful Young Men," *New York Herald Tribune Books,* 25 April 1926, p. 4, in Bryer, *Critical Reception,* p. 271. Sergio Perosa likewise sees the story as slight, arguing that it develops "along the slender thread of an argument between two old friends after a quarrel among their children" (*The Art of F. Scott Fitzgerald,* p. 57). In marked contrast, Kenneth Eble sees "The Baby Party" and "The Adjuster" as coming "closest to the best stories in this collection"—however, "neither is very close" (*F. Scott Fitzgerald,* p.104).

40. Sanford Pinsker, "Fitzgerald's 'The Baby Party,'" *Explicator* 45 (Winter 1987): 54.

41. Quoted in Kuehl, *Apprentice Fiction,* p. 142.

42. "My Lost City" (July 1932), in *The Crack-Up,* p. 28.

43. Erik H. Erikson's ideas regarding psychosocial stages were first presented in "Identity and the Life Cycle," *Psychological Issues* 1 (1959), and expanded in *Identity and the Life Cycle* (New York: W. W. Norton, 1980).

44. Higgins, *A Study*, p. 72.

45. H. W. Häusermann, "Fitzgerald's Religious Sense: Note and Query," *Modern Fiction Studies* 2 (May 1956): 82.

46. "Pierrot Penseroso," *Time*, 29 March 1926, p. 39, in Bryer, *Critical Reception*, p. 265.

47. Malcolm Cowley terms "The Baby Party" Fitzgerald's "one excursion into the field of domestic comedy" ("Editor's Note," *The Bodley Head Scott Fitzgerald*, Vol. 5: *The Short Stories* [London: The Bodley Head, 1963], p. 284).

48. To his credit, Higgins recognizes that Fitzgerald is ridiculing "with comic hyperbole the fabulously rich and those who fawn on them, as well as the *femme fatale* and the *homme manqué*" (*A Study*, p. 70). The insistent childishness of Rags may suggest a possible prototype for her: Woolworth heiress Barbara Hutton (1912–1979), the "poor little rich girl" who inherited $42,000,000 at the age of six. Fitzgerald mentions Hutton in a letter to his daughter, dated [July 1938], in Turnbull, *Letters*, p. 36.

49. For an excellent analysis of the snoopopathic style of the story's opening, see Ralph Curry and Janet Lewis, "Stephen Leacock: An Early Influence on F. Scott Fitzgerald," *Canadian Review of American Studies* 7 (Spring 1976): 11. The only full-length essay devoted to the story is Victor Doyno's fine "'No Americans Have Any Imagination': 'Rags Martin-Jones and the Pr–nce of W–les,'" in Bryer, *New Approaches*, pp. 217–25.

50. "His female mirror-image, Dolly resembles Anson Hunter as strikingly as Paula . . . differs from him. . . . So close is she in spirit and purpose to Hunter that they write each other identical letters at precisely the same time on the same subject—the wisdom of ending their relationship" (Peter Wolfe, "Faces in a Dream: Innocence Perpetuated in 'The Rich Boy,'" in Bryer, *New Approaches*, p. 246.

51. Milton Hindus, *F. Scott Fitzgerald: An Introduction and Interpretation* (New York: Holt, Rinehart and Winston, 1968), p. 102.

52. H. Alan Wycherley points out the alliteration in "Fitzgerald Revisited," *Texas Studies in Literature and Language* 8 (Summer 1966): 283. Neil D. Isaacs remarks that "more than a minimum daily dosage of irony is supplied by the story. Some is conscious, as when the glamorous creature, the object and symbol of all Dexter's craving for 'the glittering things themselves' . . . is given the sublimely prosaic name of Judy Jones" ("'Winter Dreams' and Summer Sports," in Bryer, *New Approaches*, p. 200).

53. Not unlike the situation in "The Curious Case of Benjamin Button," there is a time discrepancy in "Winter Dreams." J. R. Boggan points out that at the beginning of the story, Dexter is "not more than fourteen" and Judy is eleven; at the end, Dexter is thirty-two and Judy is twenty-seven. Boggan surmises that Fitzgerald "may have deliberately allowed Dexter to think of Judy as being two years younger than she in fact was. Since Dexter does not want Judy's beauty or desirability ever to fade and can scarcely believe his own words that she is already twenty-seven, F may be trying to show by the calculated age drop how completely Dexter has been unconsciously dictated to by his winter dreams" ("A Note on 'Winter Dreams,'" *Fitzgerald Newsletter*, No. 13 [Spring 1961]: 54).

    The given name of Judy's reprobate husband may be an inside joke: "Lud" was Fitzgerald's nickname for his friend Ludlow Fowler, the prototype for Anson Hunter in "The Rich Boy."

See, for example, Fitzgerald's letter to Fowler, dated November 1919, in Bruccoli, *Correspondence*, p. 49.

54. Fitzgerald was quite frank that "Absolution" was salvaged from a discarded early version of *The Great Gatsby*. He wrote to Maxwell Perkins, "I'm glad you liked *Absolution*. As you know it was to have been the prologue of the novel but it interfered with the neatness of the plan" (letter dated 18 June 1924, in *Dear Scott/Dear Max*, p. 72). Eight years later, he wrote to John Jamieson that the story "was intended to be a picture of [Gatsby's] early life, but . . . I cut it because I preferred to preserve the sense of mystery" (letter dated 15 April 1934, in Turnbull, *Letters*, p. 509). Most commentaries on "Absolution" stress its connections to *Gatsby*, although a few—most notably that of Lawrence D. Stewart—argue that too much has been made of those connections: "It takes uncommon faith to believe that Rudolph could have evolved into the man who gave his name to Fitzgerald's most polished novel" ("'Absolution' and *The Great Gatsby*," *Fitzgerald/Hemingway Annual* 5 [1973]: 185).

The name "Blatchford" may have been taken from Elsie Blatchford, the girlfriend of Ludlow Fowler. They married on 21 October 1926. See letter to Ludlow Fowler, dated Summer 1926, in Bruccoli, *Correspondence*, p. 200, note 1.

55. Higgins points out that *Winesburg, Ohio*, having appeared in 1919, was "too late to influence Fitzgerald's earliest writing, although such influence is visible in some later pieces like 'Absolution'" (*A Study*, p. 1). By March 1923 ("Absolution" was written in June) Fitzgerald was declaring that he could write experimental fiction "much better than Anderson" (letter to Thomas Boyd, dated March 1923, in Bruccoli, *Correspondence*, p. 126). Contemporary reviewers of *All the Sad Young Men* commented on Fitzgerald's attempt to out-Anderson Anderson in "Absolution": "Despite the shadow of Sherwood Anderson in the background, 'Absolution' is almost first-rate. Three-quarters of it, at least, is masterly. Then the author falters. He doesn't know quite what to do with his absorbing juxtaposition of Father Schwartz and Rudolph Miller; and while he doesn't exactly throw his story away, he seems to us to fall back on Anderson" (William Rose Benét, "Art's Bread and Butter," *Saturday Review of Literature*, 3 April 1926, p. 682, in Bryer, *Critical Reception*, p. 268). Other contemporary reviewers detected other influences on the story. Clyde B. Davis remarked that "Ambrose Bierce need not have been ashamed of 'Absolution' had it come from his pen" ([unidentified clipping in Fitzgerald's Scrapbook #3], in Bryer, *Critical Reception*, p. 277), while an anonymous reviewer for *Time* magazine noted that it could have been written by Booth Tarkington—were he "suddenly endowed with a real sense of beauty and a Slavic flair for psychology" ("Pierrot Penseroso," *Time*, 29 March 1926, p. 39, in Bryer, *Critical Reception*, p. 265). Modern commentators are more likely to draw parallels between the Fitzgerald of "Absolution" and the James Joyce of "The Sisters." See note 57.

One other possible influence on "Absolution" has not yet been recognized: Willa Cather. The beautiful but almost malevolent Midwestern landscape of "Absolution" seems to owe far more to, say, "The Sculptor's Funeral" than to *Winesburg, Ohio*. Fitzgerald had been an admirer of Cather since the beginning of his career, and asked Maxwell Perkins to send a copy of *The Great Gatsby* to her (letter dated 31 March 1925, in Turnbull, *Letters*, p. 178).

56. Piper, *Critical Portrait*, p. 105.

57. The image of the confessional as a coffin set on end is apparently drawn from James Joyce's "The Sisters." There are two provocative analyses of the Fitzgerald/Joyce connection in "Absolution": Keith Cushman, "Scott Fitzgerald's Scrupulous Meanness: 'Absolution' and 'The Sisters,'" *Fitzgerald/Hemingway Annual* 11 (1979): 115–21; and John Kuehl, "A la Joyce: The Sisters Fitzgerald's Absolution," *James Joyce Quarterly* 2 (Fall 1964): 2–6.

58. Various critics have perceived Father Schwartz's problem in purely sexual terms. Joan M. Allen argues that he is "driven totally mad by the course his repressed sexuality has taken" (*Candles and Carnival Lights*, p. 100). Rose Adrienne Gallo apparently agrees, indicating that Father Schwartz "has forfeited his innate romanticism and sexual being to live according to a code of perfection which, in denying the body, often constricts the soul" (*F. Scott Fitzgerald*, p. 94). John Kuehl believes there are Joycean "vestiges of homosexuality appearing in 'Absolution,'" but that "except for a few equivocal references, homosexuality has been replaced by heterosexuality, priest and boy becoming secret sharers" ("A la Joyce" [see note 57], 6). Henry Dan Piper asserts that "it is pretty clear that Schwartz's treatment of Rudolph is connected in some way with Schwartz's latent homosexuality" (*Critical Portrait*, p. 107). I see no evidence of homosexuality, latent or otherwise, in Fitzgerald's presentation of Father Schwartz, and feel it is counterproductive to perceive his emotional difficulties as being primarily sexual in nature. My position is well stated by Lawrence D. Stewart: "The priest's disappointed desire for a 'complete mystical union with our Lord' balances with his awareness of the physical unions which are presumably everywhere possible. Living in a world where all is ripeness, he finds denied him the one union he desires. Sexual frustration probably does contribute to the involutions in his behavior, but surely it is an oversimplification to dismiss Father Schwartz's problem as 'the incoherent frustrations of the old Catholic priest, celibate by profession.' Certainly Fitzgerald's treatment of the man encourages another interpretation." That is, "Was it not Fitzgerald's intention to use the language of physical fulfillment in a mystical sense to suggest the priest's permanent three o'clock in the morning?" ("'Absolution' and *The Great Gatsby*" [see note 54], 184–85).

59. "Without question there is a believable change in [Rudolph], Church rituals notwithstanding. In effect, he has granted himself Absolution and released himself from the consequences of his sins. Using less heightened words, he has said what Psalm 90 says to the virtuous: God is my protector and my shelter" (E. R.Hagemann, "Should Scott Fitzgerald be Absolved for the Sins of 'Absolution'?," *Journal of Modern Literature* 12 [March 1985]: 172).

60. *The Outlook*, 5 May 1926, p. 33, in Bryer, *Critical Reception*, p. 274.

61. Hagemann [see note 59], 174, note 14. Hagemann seems especially dismayed by the description of Rudolph's eyes: "'Staccato'? I haven't the faintest idea [what it means] nor did [Fitzgerald]. It intrudes a discordant, musical motif alien to the story." In addition, "What color is 'cobalt'? Blue, green-blue, violet, yellow?" (169). Actually, all it takes is a little imagination to realize that "staccato" eyes would be eyes blinking rapidly; and although it is true that chemistry texts list the many possible colors of cobalt, it is almost always used by non-chemists to mean one thing: 'cobalt blue.'

    For analyses of Fitzgerald's garbled Latin, see E. R. Hagemann, "'Small *Latine*' in the Three Printings of F. Scott Fitzgerald's 'Absolution,'" *NMAL: Notes on Modern American Literature* 4 (Spring 1980): Item 7; and J. I. Morse, "Fitzgerald's *Sagitta Volante in Dei*: An Emendation and a Possible Source," *Fitzgerald/Hemingway Annual* 4 (1972): 321–22.

62. Stern, *The Golden Moment*, pp. 166–68.

63. This point is also made by Robert Emmet Long, *The Achieving of* The Great Gatsby: *F. Scott Fitzgerald, 1920–1925* (Lewisburg, Pennsylvania: Bucknell University Press, 1979), p. 69.

64. Most critics, of course, do not perceive "that thing" as referring to Dexter's true selfhood. Writes Clinton S. Burhans, Jr., Dexter's "love for Judy is no more Platonic than his other winter dreams; it is sensuous and emotional, and 'thing' suggests this tangible reality as well as the nature of what he has lost. Moreover, Fitzgerald's conscious use of the term for these purposes is reflected in his repetition of it nine times in the final passage of the story"

("'Magnificently Attune to Life': The Value of 'Winter Dreams,'" *Studies in Short Fiction* 6 [Summer 1969]: 406). James E. Miller, Jr., sees the phrase "that thing" as indicative of major problems in the story: "The style contains a basic falseness that renders it unconvincing, improbable, and, in Dexter, incongruous ('that thing' is a particularly inept phrase to receive so much emphasis)" (*F. Scott Fitzgerald: His Art and His Technique* [New York: New York University Press, 1967], p.102). The very incongruity of "that thing," however, renders it the ideal phrase to be used by a young man who cannot quite articulate what he has lost. Were he referring to his winter dreams or the tarnished "glittering things," he would mention them by name—or refer to them in the plural ("those things").

65. The implications of the narrator's implied identification with the reader are explored in two articles: Joseph Katz, "The Narrator and 'The Rich Boy,'" *Fitzgerald Newsletter* 32 (Winter 1966): 208–10; and James L. W. West, III and J. Barclay Inge, "F. Scott Fitzgerald's Revision of 'The Rich Boy,'" *Proof* 5 (1977): 127–46.

66. "Fitzgerald's narrative style . . . is remarkably close to Mrs Wharton's—indeed this seems to me a case where one can reasonably speak of a direct influence upon his work. As a rule, the most distinctive quality in his writing is the constant delicate play of atmospheric and poetic suggestion, but what impresses one particularly in 'The Rich Boy' is the sustained pressure of a fine moral intelligence. The tone is dispassionate, sober, analytical; it does not rise to high points of climactic intensity or wit, and so, unlike most of Fitzgerald's writing, it is not especially quotable" (Brian Way, *F. Scott Fitzgerald and the Art of Social Fiction* [New York: St. Martin's, 1980], p. 85).

67. "If we test the narrator's generalization, that the rich are different from us and that because Anson was rich he was as he was, we ask ourselves these questions about the story. How did Anson's parents escape the curse of wealth? . . . Also we find that, although they made mistakes in the process of finding mates, both Paula and Dolly found husbands, and we know that finally Paula believed she found love. Yet both Paula and Dolly were rich girls" (Aerol Arnold, "Why Structure in Fiction: A Note to Social Scientists," *American Quarterly* 10 [Fall 1958]: 335).

68. Letter to Frances Scott ("Scottie") Fitzgerald, dated 12 June 1940, in Turnbull, *Letters,* p. 79.

69. Johnson [see note 37], p. 235.

70. "Story about Zelda & me. All true" (letter to Maxwell Perkins, dated [1 June 1925], in *Dear Scott/Dear Max,* p. 113).

71. Geismar, *Last of the Provincials,* p. 323, note.

Chapter 4

1. Milford, *Zelda,* pp. 195–96.

2. So reads the return address of Fitzgerald's letter to Edmund Wilson, tentatively dated March 1933, in Turnbull, *Letters,* p. 345.

3. Bruccoli, *Epic Grandeur,* pp. 365, 332.

4. Bruccoli, *Epic Grandeur,* pp. 308, 364.

5. Bruccoli, *Epic Grandeur,* p. 24n.

6. For an exhaustive analysis of the evolution of *Tender Is the Night,* see Matthew J. Bruccoli, *The*

Composition of Tender Is the Night: *A Study of the Manuscripts* (Pittsburgh: University of Pittsburgh Press, 1963).

7. Turnbull, *Letters*, pp. 300, 301.

8. Letter circa 1 July 1928, in Turnbull, *Letters*, p. 210; letter dated 1 September [1929], in Bruccoli, *Correspondence*, p. 230.

9. Letter circa 1 May 1930, in *Dear Scott/Dear Max*, p. 166. Fitzgerald was deriving justification for the delay of his novel from the example of James Joyce, who had said in 1928 that his own novel would require "three or four years more"—"& he works 11 hrs a day to my intermittent 8" (letter to Maxwell Perkins, dated circa 21 July 1928, in *Dear Scott/Dear Max*, p. 152).

10. Several of Fitzgerald's most defensive statements to Zelda's doctors appear in Milford, *Zelda*, especially Part Three, "Breaking Down."

11. Wrote Fitzgerald to Perkins, "If you like [*Save Me the Waltz*] please *don't* wire her congratulations, and please keep whatever praise you may see fit to give *on the staid side*—I mean, *as you naturally would*, rather than yield to a tendency one has with invalids to be extra nice to cheer them up. This seems a nuance but it is rather important at present to the doctors that Zelda does not feel that the acceptance (always granted you like it) means immediate fame and money. . . . If she has a success coming she must associate it with work done in a workmanlike manner for its own sake, & part of it done fatigued and uninspired, and part of it done when even to remember the original inspiration and impetus is a psychological trick. She is not twenty-one and she is not strong, and she must not try to follow the pattern of my trail which is of course blazed distinctly on her mind" (letter to Maxwell Perkins, dated circa 30 April 1932, in *Dear Scott/Dear Max*, p. 174).

12. Letter to Dr. Oscar Forel, dated 18 April 1932, in Bruccoli, *Correspondence*, p. 292.

13. Letter from Zelda to Scott Fitzgerald, dated March 1932, in Bruccoli, *Correspondence*, p. 289; passage probably underlined by FSF. Letter from Fitzgerald to Dr. Harry M. Murdock, dated 28 August 1934, in Bruccoli, *Correspondence*, p. 381.

14. Letter from Zelda to Scott Fitzgerald, dated April 1932, in Bruccoli, *Correspondence*, p. 291; passage probably underlined by FSF.

15. "So far the depression hadn't hurt Fitzgerald's income. Indeed, Zelda's illness had stimulated his production, and with his story price at its zenith of $4,000, he earned a record $37,599 in 1931" (Turnbull, *Scott Fitzgerald*, p. 205).

16. Allen, *Candles and Carnival Lights*, p. 119. See letter to Harold Ober, received 2 January 1931, in Bruccoli, *As Ever*, p. 175.

17. A literary precedent for this modernization of dialogue may have been Ernest Hemingway's short story "Today is Friday," written in 1926. Fitzgerald mentions the story in a letter to Hemingway, dated Fall 1926, in Turnbull, *Letters*, pp. 296–97.

18. See the long letter to Maxwell Perkins, dated 15 May 1934, in *Dear Scott/Dear Max*, pp. 195–98.

19. Letter to Harold Ober, received 13 May 1930, in Bruccoli, *As Ever*, p. 168. Despite his early enthusiasm for Hollywood, by 1930 he seems to have felt that the film industry was not worthy of a talented professional novelist. He would be forced to change his position, however, when the still-considerable financial allure of Hollywood made it impossible to ignore in the mid-1930s.

20. Letter from Maxwell Perkins, dated 20 August 1934, in *Dear Scott/Dear Max*, p. 205.

21. Letter to Maxwell Perkins, dated 17 December 1934, in *Dear Scott/Dear Max*, p. 215.

22. Letter to Maxwell Perkins, dated 17 December 1934, in *Dear Scott/Dear Max*, p. 215.

23. Letter to Lois Moran, dated 8 March 1935, in Bruccoli, *Correspondence*, p. 403.

24. Letter to Maxwell Perkins, dated 26 June 1934, in *Dear Scott/Dear Max*, p. 202.

25. Letter to Maxwell Perkins, dated 24 August 1934, in *Dear Scott/Dear Max*, p. 207.

26. Letter to Maxwell Perkins, dated [23 August 1934], in *Dear Scott/Dear Max*, p. 206.

27. Bruccoli surmises that this is the description of a news vendor in *Tender Is the Night*. See Bruccoli, *Composition* [see note 6], p. 70.

28. Letter to Maxwell Perkins, dated 15 May 1934, in *Dear Scott/Dear Max*, p. 195.

29. Letter to Maxwell Perkins, dated 17 December 1934, in *Dear Scott/Dear Max*, p. 396.

30. Maxwell Geismar, *The Last of the Provincials* (Boston: Houghton Mifflin, 1947), p. 338.

31. Constance Drake, "Josephine And Emotional Bankruptcy," *Fitzgerald/Hemingway Annual* 1 (1969): 10.

32. Letter to Maxwell Perkins, dated 9 March 1935, in *Dear Scott/Dear Max*, p. 217.

33. Letter to Maxwell Perkins, dated 26 December 1934, in *Dear Scott/Dear Max*, p. 396.

34. Letter to Maxwell Perkins, dated 8 June 1934, in *Dear Scott/Dear Max*, p. 201, plus p. 276, note 65.

35. See *Dear Scott/Dear Max*, p. 276, note 67.

36. Letter from Zelda to Scott Fitzgerald, after 13 June 1934, in Bruccoli, *Corrospondence*, p. 371. In the same letter Zelda suggested he call the volume simply *Words*, but then declared that it sounded too "experimental."

37. Fitzgerald initially did not like Seldes' title, which he felt "has a faint knell of [Ring Lardner's] funeral bells in it. It is just a bit literary and even sentimental" (letter to Gilbert Seldes, dated 2 February 1934, in Bruccoli, *Correspondence*, p. 327).

38. Richard L. Schoenwald, "F. Scott Fitzgerald as John Keats," *Boston University Studies in English* 3 (Spring 1957): 12. Malcolm Cowley has observed that Fitzgerald was "haunted by time, as if he wrote in a room full of clocks and calendars" (*The Bodley Head Scott Fitzgerald*, vol. 5: *Short Stories* [London: The Bodley Head, 1963], p. 18).

39. Wire to Maxwell Perkins, dated 12 February 1935, in Bruccoli, *Correspondence*, p. 400; letter from Perkins to Fitzgerald, dated 18 February 1935, in *Dear Scott/Dear Max*, p. 216.

40. Letter to Ernest Hemingway, dated 10 May 1934, in Turnbull, *Letters*, p. 307.

41. "I wired you today rather discouragingly in the matter of the sales [of *Gatsby*] and I could send no qualifications in a cable. A great many of the trade have been very skeptical. I cannot make out just why. But one point is the small number of pages in the book,—an old stock objection which I thought we had got beyond. To attempt to explain to them that the way of writing which you have chosen and which is bound to come more and more into practice is one where a vast amount is said by implication, and that therefore the book is as full as it would have been if written to much greater length by another method, is of course utterly futile. The small

number of pages, however, did in the end lead a couple of big distributors to reduce their orders immensely at the very last minute. The sale is up to the public and that has not yet had time to reveal itself fully" (letter from Maxwell Perkins, dated 20 April 1925, in *Dear Scott/ Dear Max*, pp. 100–101).

42. Letter to Bennett Cerf, dated 23 July 1936, in Turnbull, *Letters*, p. 537.

43. Arthur Coleman, "Stories by F. Scott Fitzgerald Are Merely Entertaining," *Dallas Morning News*, 24 March 1935, Sec. 3, p. 8, in Bryer, *Critical Reception*, p. 338.

44. T. S. Matthews, *New Republic* 82 (10 April 1935): 262, in Bryer, *Critical Reception*, p. 347.

45. Eble, *F. Scott Fitzgerald*, p. 115; Cross, *F. Scott Fitzgerald*, p. 92; Geismar [see note 30], p. 337; Cowley [see note 38], p. 34.

46. Writes Louise Tanner, "Fitzgerald to the end was a child of a simpler society, guided by the ethics of yesteryear. . . . His puritanism never quite deserted him. When he tries to horrify us with tales of tricycling around the Etoile . . . he confuses the sinister with the silly" (*Here Today* . . . [New York: Thomas Y. Crowell, 1959], p. 34). In fact, Fitzgerald did not confuse the two. What shocks him (and Charlie) about the tricycling incident is not that it was "sinister" or immoral—it wasn't—but that something so blatantly childish could ever have been perceived as daring and fun by a grown man.

    John V. Hagopian speaks of Wales as a "good time Charlie" ("A Prince in Babylon," *Fitzgerald Newsletter* [Fall 1962]: 100). For an interpretation of the surname "Wales," see William Osborne, "The Wounds of Charlie Wales in Fitzgerald's 'Babylon Revisited,'" *Studies in Short Fiction* 2 (Fall 1964): 86–87. For an imaginative, if sometimes strained, analysis of all the charactonyms in the story, see Ira Johnson, "Roundheads and Royalty in 'Babylon,'" *English Record* 14 (October 1963): 32–35.

47. Gallo, *F. Scott Fitzgerald*, p. 104.

48. Seymour L. Gross makes this point in "Fitzgerald's 'Babylon Revisited,'" *College English* 25 (November 1963): 134.

49. Scott Donaldson, "Scott Fitzgerald's Romance with the South," *Southern Literary Journal* 5 (Spring 1973): 7.

50. Ruth Prigozy, "'Poor Butterfly': F. Scott Fitzgerald and Popular Music," *Prospects* 2 (1976): 52.

51. Tom D'Invilliers speaks for the early Fitzgerald. Bruccoli points out that Fitzgerald "did not volunteer immediately" for service during World War I, "although the aviation service attracted him as the romantic equivalent of the Civil War cavalry" (*Epic Grandeur*, p. 74). He never, of course, made it into aviation, though he dressed for the part: at the time he met Zelda, Fitzgerald wore "dashing yellow boots and spurs (other officers wore the puttees issued to them)" (Milford, *Zelda*, p. 43).

52. Letter to Scottie Fitzgerald, dated 8 August 1933, in Turnbull, *Letters*, p. 3.

53. Eble notes the textual revision in *F. Scott Fitzgerald*, p. 27.

54. Writes Fiedler, "From the beginnings of Western literature, there has been a tradition of the flaw as essential to the writer, but at various times there have been various notions of the ideal charismatic weakness: blindness in the most ancient days, incest in the Byronic period, homosexuality in the *fin de siècle*. But in America the flaw has been pre-eminently drunkenness,

from Griswold's Poe dead in the gutters of Baltimore to Schulberg's Halliday-Fitzgerald dying among the undergraduates at Dartmouth." Fitzgerald seems to have embraced the notion with a vengeance: "Every writer in Fitzgerald makes his first staggering entrance loaded: McKiscoe in *Tender Is the Night,* 'Four-eyes' in *Gatsby,* Wylie in *The Last Tycoon;* the profession is inseparable from the vice." Further, "it is surely no accident that the protagonist of Fitzgerald's best book has, like his author, grown wealthy on Prohibition, the sensitive bootlegger as the last Romantic—the 'great' Gatsby, for whom only the drunken writer turns out to mourn after his inevitable defeat" (*An End to Innocence: Essays on Culture and Politics* [Boston: The Beacon Press, 1955], pp. 176–77.

55. Draft of letter to Zelda Fitzgerald, dated sometime after 1932, in Bruccoli, *Correspondence,* p. 301.

56. Malcolm Cowley notes that Fitzgerald "relived his boyhood in the stories and made little effort to disguise the fact that he was writing autobiography. Almost every incident happened in life and almost every character can be identified." Basil, of course, was based on Fitzgerald; Riply Buckner, Bill Kampf, and Hubert Blair were inspired by Cecil Reid, Paul Ballion, and Reuben Warner, respectively, while St. Regis was based on The Newman School (Cowley, *The Stories of F. Scott Fitzgerald* [New York: Charles Scribner's Sons, 1951], p. 307). Imogene Bissell and Margaret Torrence were based on Margaret Armstrong and Marie Hersey (Bruccoli, *Epic Grandeur,* p. 26). Observes Kenneth Eble, " 'The Captured Shadow,' the play Fitzgerald wrote and produced in 1912, is the same play Basil writes and produces the same year" (*F. Scott Fitzgerald,* p. 23).

57. "Handle With Care," *The Crack-Up,* p. 84.

58. See her comments in Mizener, *The Far Side of Paradise,* pp. 368–69, note 15.

59. Sklar, *The Last Laocoön,* p. 240.

60. Bruccoli, *Epic Grandeur,* p. 292.

61. From the very beginning of his career there has been a critical tendency to argue that Fitzgerald was incapable of creating believable female characters. In 1935 Arthur Coleman [see note 43] commented that the Josephine stories, as well as "The Night of Chancellorsville," "Majesty," and "A Short Trip Home" all prove "that men writers should leave women characters alone, as much as possible; they can not create satisfactory feminine portraits, and the better ones do not even try." More recently, Kenneth Eble has suggested that Fitzgerald stopped writing about Josephine Perry because he "did not, could not, fully understand her or be as privy to her youthful feelings and experiences as he could with Basil" (*F. Scott Fitzgerald,* p. 115). However, Fitzgerald himself felt that "I am half feminine—at least my mind is," and as a result "even my feminine characters are feminine Scott Fitzgeralds" (quoted in Turnbull, *Scott Fitzgerald,* p. 259). André LeVot seems justified in maintaining that Fitzgerald "could understand women with an intuition generally reserved to other women" (*F. Scott Fitzgerald,* p. 19).

62. Eble makes this point in *F. Scott Fitzgerald,* p. 30.

63. Bruccoli, *Epic Grandeur,* p. 23.

64. See Fitzgerald's note in Zelda's letter to him, dated March 1932, in Bruccoli, *Correspondence,* p. 288–89.

65. Henry Dan Piper writes that "the story is spoiled by two rather melodramatic hurricanes" (*A Critical Portrait,* p. 168). Since hurricanes are rather commonplace in Gulf Coast states, since there is usually ample warning before their arrival, and since their destruction is widespread

and oddly systematic (a great deal in towns near their centers, but increasingly less in more distant communities), they would not be the ideal storms for this particular story. Fitzgerald is definitely writing about tornadoes.

66. Letter to Rosalind Sayre Smith, dated sometime after 8 June 1930, in Bruccoli, *Correspondence,* p. 236.

67. Notes Nancy Milford in *Zelda,* another of the Sayre daughters, Marjorie, "was never well": "There was hushed talk of a nervous breakdown." Zelda's maternal grandmother had committed suicide, as did Zelda's brother Anthony after a bout of "that ominous euphemism 'nervous prostration'" (pp. 36, 335–36).

68. Letter to Dr. Adolf Meyer, dated 10 April 1933, in Bruccoli, *Correspondence,* p. 309.

69. John A. Higgins writes that "the second tornado seems particularly superfluous." He suspects, however, that Fitzgerald "attached a symbolic significance to it": "I believe that the second tornado, which hits the recovering town several days later, may be Fitzgerald's symbolic look into Janney's future, showing that he can expect more blows and struggles on his way to reclamation" (*A Study,* p. 144, note 177). Perhaps, though it seems far more tenable to regard the two tornadoes as emblems of Zelda's two breakdowns.

70. Julie M. Irwin, "F. Scott Fitzgerald's Little Drinking Problem," *The American Scholar* 56 (Summer 1987): 424.

71. The only family member Fitzgerald would have trusted enough to raise his daughter was his beloved cousin, Cecilia "Ceci" Delihant Taylor: "I have always wanted, if anything happened to me while Zelda is still sick, to get you to take care of Scottie" (letter to Mrs. Richard Taylor, dated 23 February 1931, in Turnbull, *Letters,* p. 416).

72. Thomas J. Stavola, *Scott Fitzgerald: Crisis in an American Identity* (New York: Barnes & Noble, 1979), p. 24.

73. Letter to Maxwell Perkins, dated 20 February 1926, in *Dear Scott/Dear Max,* pp. 134–35.

74. *Notebooks,* #1610, p. 268.

75. Eble, *F. Scott Fitzgerald,* p. 20.

76. Joseph Mancini, Jr., offers a Jungian interpretation of the Basil series: "Reflecting the nurturing dimension of the Self, Mrs. Lee constantly feeds Basil—most of their discussions take place over one or another of the daily meals. According to his mother, unless Basil eats the special dinner she has prepared for his debut as a playwright, he 'won't be able to act,' both in the theatrical and existential senses" ("To Be Both Light and Dark: The Jungian Process of Individuation in Fitzgerald's Basil Duke Lee Stories," in Bryer, *New Approaches,* p. 94).

77. Perosa, *The Art of F. Scott Fitzgerald,* p. 89.

78. Wrote Perkins to Fitzgerald, "I thought the best part of any of [the Basil stories] was that account of how the boys and girls met in a certain yard at dusk. That was beautifully done. That magical quality of summer dusk for young boys I have never before seen evoked" (Letter dated 28 June 1928, in *Dear Scott/Dear Max,* p. 151). The prototype for the Whartons' yard was that of Betty Ames. Wrote Fitzgerald to her husband, Norris D. Jackson, "I've tried to pay some tribute to that celebrated children's meeting place, the Ames' backyard. Please clip it [the story] and save it for your children, for sooner or later time will wipe out that pleasant spot" (letter postmarked 23 March 1928, in Bruccoli, *Correspondence,* p. 217).

79. Perosa, *The Art of F. Scott Fitzgerald*, p. 88.

80. I find completely untenable Sergio Perosa's argument that this situation occurs in "One Interne." There is nothing to support the idea that Dr. Durfee, a brilliant surgeon, is a "disquieting figure" who "hides a dubious soul" and represents "that mysterious and wicked element which seems to be inherent in life." Likewise, there is nothing to suggest that Thea must "disengage herself from his influence" (*The Art of F. Scott Fitzgerald*, p. 86). If anything, Thea has facilitated the emergence of Dr. Durfee's skills as a surgeon, much as she engineers Bill Tulliver's development into a humane diagnostician.

81. Perosa sees a provocative connection between the incubus of "A Short Trip Home" and "the devilish figure that haunted Miriam in *The Marble Faun*." See *The Art of F. Scott Fitzgerald*, p. 86.

82. Eble identifies this character as an incubus (*F. Scott Fitzgerald*, p. 128). Malcolm Cowley sees the story as "curiously Japanese in spirit; there are many Japanese legends of re-embodied spirits who try to seduce the living and carry them off to a shadow world. In this case, however, the ghost has a social meaning. The living-dead man in high button shoes represents the lower order of humanity that offers a mysterious threat to the standards and the daughters of the rich people whose mansions rise above them on the hill" (*The Bodley Head* [see note 38], pp. 284–85).

83. Eble, *F. Scott Fitzgerald*, p. 129.

84. See Milford, *Zelda*, p. 172, or Bruccoli, *Epic Grandeur*, pp. 261–62.

85. Scott Donaldson, "Scott Fitzgerald's Romance with the South," *Southern Literary Journal* 5 (Spring 1973): 8.

86. See the letter from Harold Ober, dated 24 September 1929, in Bruccoli, *As Ever*, p. 147. "Girls Believe in Girls" was eventually published in *Liberty* magazine, 7 (8 February 1930), pp. 22–24.

87. Two excellent studies of the Josephine series are Constance Drake, "Josephine and Emotional Bankruptcy," *Fitzgerald/Hemingway Annual* 1 (1969): 5–13; and Rochelle S. Elstein, "Fitzgerald's Josephine Stories: The End of the Romantic Illusion," *American Literature* 51 (March 1979): 69–83.

88. Henry Dan Piper, for example, writes that in the Josephine stories "Fitzgerald dissected his heroine with a humor and insight that had been missing when he had known her original some ten years before." Further, Josephine is "an amusing example of that 'finishing school' type that was to be one of the lesser casualties of the Depression and World War II." During the 1930s, Piper continues, Fitzgerald replaced her, "in his more serious fiction," with characters such as Rosemary Hoyt and Cecilia Brady (*A Critical Portrait*, p. 174). Even Fitzgerald's contemporaries found her hilarious. Edith H. Walton, for example, states that Josephine's "wiles and adventures are undeniably comic" ("Scott Fitzgerald's Tales," *New York Times Book Review*, 31 March 1935, p. 7, in Bryer, *Critical Reception*, p. 344).

89. Letter from Maxwell Perkins, dated 31 December 1921, in *Dear Scott/Dear Max*, p. 50.

90. Lawrence Buell, "The Significance of Fantasy in Fitzgerald's Short Fiction," in Bryer, *New Approaches*, p. 33.

91. John O'Hara, Introduction to *The Portable F. Scott Fitzgerald* (New York: Viking Press, 1949), p. xvi.

92. Malcolm Cowley, *The Bodley Head* [see note 38], p. 285.

93. Roy R. Male surmises that the "Babylon" of the story's title was inspired by a statement in William Rose Benét's 1925 review of *The Great Gatsby:* "For the first time Fitzgerald surveys the Babylonian captivity of this era unblinded by the bright lights." See "'Babylon Revisited': A Story of the Exile's Return," *Studies in Short Fiction* 2 (Spring 1965): 270–77. Much less convincing is D. S. Savage's theory that "'Babylon' is most probably an elided form of 'Baby-land.' Certainly there is a marked infantile quality in the escapades of which the returned reveler is reminded by his former fellows." See "The Significance of F. Scott Fitzgerald," *Arizona Quarterly* 8 (Autumn 1952): 208–9.

94. Ronald J. Gervais sees "Babylon Revisited" as one of a series of literary works structured around a farewell to an attractive past. See "The Snow of Twenty-Nine: 'Babylon Revisited' as *Ubi Sunt* Lament," *College Literature* 7 (Winter 1980): 47–52.

Bibliography

Primary Sources

Flappers and Philosophers. New York: Charles Scribner's Sons, 1920.
Tales of the Jazz Age. New York: Charles Scribner's Sons, 1922.
All the Sad Young Men. New York: Charles Scribner's Sons, 1926.
Taps at Reveille. New York: Charles Scribner's Sons, 1935.

Secondary Sources

Aiken, Conrad. "Fitzgerald, F. Scott." In *A Reviewer's abc.* New York: Meridian, 1958.
Allen, Joan M. *Candles and Carnival Lights: The Catholic Sensibility of F. Scott Fitzgerald.* New York: New York University Press, 1978.
Allen, Walter. *The Short Story in English.* New York: Oxford University Press, 1981.
Anderson, Charles R. "Scott Fitzgerald: 1896–1940." In *American Literary Masters,* vol. 2. New York: Holt, Rinehart and Winston, 1975.
Anderson, Margaret. *My Thirty Years' War: An Autobiography.* New York: Covici, Friede, 1930.
Anderson, W. R. "Rivalry and Partnership: The Short Fiction of Zelda Sayre Fitzgerald." *Fitzgerald/Hemingway Annual* 9 (1977): 19–42.
Anderson, William R. "Fitzgerald After *Tender Is the Night:* A Literary Strategy for the 1930s." *Fitzgerald/Hemingway Annual* 11(1979): 39–63.
Arnold, Aerol. "Why Structure in Fiction: A Note to Social Scientists." *American Quarterly* 10 (Fall 1958): 325–37.
Arnold, Edwin T. "The Motion Picture as Metaphor in the Works of F. Scott Fitzgerald." *Fitzgerald/Hemingway Annual* 9 (1977): 43–60.
Atkinson, Jennifer McCabe. "The Discarded Ending of 'The Offshore Pirate.'" *Fitzgerald/Hemingway Annual* 6 (1974): 47–49.
———. "Lost and Unpublished Stories by F. Scott Fitzgerald." *Fitzgerald/Hemingway Annual* 3 (1971): 32–63.
Baker, Carlos. "When the Story Ends: 'Babylon Revisited.'" Pp. 269–77 in *The Short Stories of F. Scott Fitzgerald: New Approaches in Criticism.* Ed. Jackson R. Bryer. Madison: University of Wisconsin Press, 1982.
Bennett, Warren. "Prefigurations of Gatsby, Eckleburg, Owl Eyes, and Klipspringer." *Fitzgerald/Hemingway Annual* 11 (1979): 207–23.
Berg, A. Scott. *Max Perkins: Editor of Genius.* New York: Pocket Books, 1978.
Berryman, John. "F. Scott Fitzgerald." *Kenyon Review* 8 (Winter 1946): 103–12.

Bewley, Marius. "Scott Fitzgerald and the Collapse of the American Dream." In *The Eccentric Design: Form in the Classic American Novel*. New York: Columbia University Press, 1963.

Bicknell, John W. "The Waste Land of F. Scott Fitzgerald." *Virginia Quarterly Review* 30 (Autumn 1954): 556–72.

Bigsby, C. W. E. "The Two Identities of F. Scott Fitzgerald." In *The American Novel and the Nineteen Twenties*. Stratford-upon-Avon Studies, No. 13. London: Edward Arnold, 1971.

Blake, Nelson Manfred. "The Pleasure Domes of West Egg and Tarmes." In *Novelists' America: Fiction as History, 1910–1940*. Syracuse, New York: Syracuse University Press, 1969.

Blankenship, Russell. "F. Scott Fitzgerald (1896–1940)." In *American Literature as an Expression of the National Mind*. New York: Henry Holt and Company, 1949.

Bloom, Nancy. "Coincidence: *21 Balloons* & 'Diamond.'" *Fitzgerald Newsletter* 28 (Winter 1965): 3.

Bodeen, DeWitt. "F. Scott Fitzgerald and Films." *Films in Review* 28 (May 1977): 285–94.

Boggan, J. R. "A Note on 'Winter Dreams.'" *Fitzgerald Newsletter* 13 (Spring 1961): 1–2.

Brondell, William J. "Structural Metaphors in Fitzgerald's Short Fiction." *Kansas Quarterly* 14 (Spring 1982): 95–112.

Bruccoli, Matthew J. *The Composition of* Tender Is the Night: *A Study of the Manuscripts*. Pittsburgh: University of Pittsburgh Press, 1963.

[————.] "Misinformation." *Fitzgerald Newsletter* 24 (Winter 1964): 6.

————, ed. *The Notebooks of F. Scott Fitzgerald*. New York: Harcourt Brace Jovanovich/Bruccoli Clark, 1978.

————. *Scott and Ernest: The Authority of Failure and the Authority of Success*. New York: Random House, 1978.

————. *Some Sort of Epic Grandeur: The Life of F. Scott Fitzgerald*. New York: Harcourt Brace Jovanovich, 1981.

[————.] "Two Issues of TAR." *Fitzgerald Newsletter* 27 (Fall 1964): 1.

————, ed., assisted by Jennifer McCabe Atkinson. *As Ever, Scott Fitz—: Letters Between F. Scott Fitzgerald and His Literary Agent Harold Ober, 1919–1940*. Philadelphia and New York: J. B. Lippincott, 1972.

———— and Jackson R. Bryer, eds. *F. Scott Fitzgerald in His Own Time: A Miscellany*. Kent, Ohio: Kent State University Press, 1971.

———— and Margaret M. Duggan, eds., with the assistance of Susan Walker. *Correspondence of F. Scott Fitzgerald*. New York: Random House, 1980.

Bryer, Jackson R., ed. *F. Scott Fitzgerald: The Critical Reception*. New York: Burt Franklin, 1978.

————, ed. *The Short Stories of F. Scott Fitzgerald: New Approaches in Criticism*. Madison: University of Wisconsin Press, 1982.

———— and John Kuehl. Introduction. Pp. vii–xxvi in *The Basil and Josephine Stories*. New York: Charles Scribner's, 1973.

Buell, Lawrence. "The Significance of Fantasy in Fitzgerald's Short Fiction." Pp. 23–38 in *The Short Stories of F. Scott Fitzgerald: New Approaches in Criticism*. Ed. Jackson R. Bryer. Madison: University of Wisconsin Press, 1982.

Burhans, Clinton S., Jr. "'Magnificently Attune to Life': The Value of 'Winter Dreams.'" *Studies in Short Fiction* 6 (Summer 1969): 401–12.

Butwin, David. "In the Days of the Ice Palace." *Saturday Review* 55 (29 January 1972): 55–56.

Cardwell, Guy A. "The Lyric World of Scott Fitzgerald." *Virginia Quarterly Review* 38 (Spring 1962): 299–323.

Carlyle, Thomas. *Sartor Resartus*. Philadelphia: Henry Altemus, [1902].

Cass, Colin S. "Fitzgerald's Second Thoughts About 'May Day': A Collation and Study." *Fitzgerald/Hemingway Annual* 2 (1970): 69–95.

Casty, Alan. "'I and It' in the Stories of F. Scott Fitzgerald." *Studies in Short Fiction* 9 (Winter 1972): 47–58.

Cifelli, Edward. "Bernice's Liberation: Fitzgerald's 'Bernice Bobs Her Hair.'" *NMAL: Notes on Modern American Literature* 8 (Winter 1984): Item 19.

Collins, Angus P. "F. Scott Fitzgerald: Homosexuality and the Genesis of *Tender Is the Night.*" *Journal of Modern Literature* 13 (March 1986): 167–71.

Cowley, Malcolm. Introduction and Notes. Pp. vii-xxv, et passim in *The Stories of F. Scott Fitzgerald.* New York: Charles Scribner's, 1951.

———. Introduction and Editor's Note[s]. *The Bodley Head Scott Fitzgerald,* vol. 5: *Short Stories.* London: The Bodley Head, 1963.

———. "Third Act and Epilogue." *New Yorker* 21 (30 June 1945): 53, 54, 57, 58.

Crosland, Andrew. "Sources for Fitzgerald's 'The Curious Case of Benjamin Button.'" *Fitzgerald/Hemingway Annual* 11 (1979): 135–39.

Cross, K. G. W. *F. Scott Fitzgerald.* New York. Capricorn Books, 1971.

Curry, Ralph and Janet Lewis. "Stephen Leacock: An Early Influence on F. Scott Fitzgerald." *Canadian Review of American Studies* 7 (Spring 1976): 5–14.

Cushman, Keith. "Scott Fitzgerald's Scrupulous Meanness: 'Absolution' and 'The Sisters.'" *Fitzgerald/Hemingway Annual* 11 (1979): 115–21.

Daniels, Thomas E. "English Periodical Publications of Fitzgerald's Short Stories: A Correction of the Record." *Fitzgerald/Hemingway Annual* 8 (1976): 124–29.

———. "The Texts of 'Winter Dreams.'" *Fitzgerald/Hemingway Annual* 9 (1977): 77–100.

———. "Toward a Definitive Edition of F. Scott Fitzgerald's Short Stories." *Papers of the Bibliographical Society of America* 71 (Third Quarter 1977): 295–310.

Dardis, Tom. "F. Scott Fitzgerald: What Do You Do When There's Nothing to Do?" In *Some Time in the Sun.* New York: Charles Scribner's Sons, 1976.

Davison, Richard Allan. "F. Scott Fitzgerald and Charles G. Norris." *Journal of Modern Literature* 10 (March 1983): 40–54.

Donaldson, Scott. *Fool for Love: F. Scott Fitzgerald.* New York: Congdon & Weed, 1983.

———. "Money and Marriage in Fitzgerald's Stories." Pp. 75–88 in *The Short Stories of F. Scott Fitzgerald: New Approaches in Criticism.* Ed. Jackson R. Bryer. Madison: University of Wisconsin Press, 1982.

———. "Scott Fitzgerald's Romance with the South." *Southern Literary Journal* 5 (Spring 1973): 3–17.

Dos Passos, John. "Fitzgerald and the Press." *New Republic* 104 (17 February 1941): 213.

Doyno, Victor. "'No Americans Have Any Imagination': 'Rag Martin-Jones and the Pr–nce of W–les.'" Pp. 217–25 in *The Short Stories of F. Scott Fitzgerald: New Approaches in Criticism.* Ed. Jackson R. Bryer. Madison: University of Wisconsin Press, 1982.

Drake, Constance. "Josephine and Emotional Bankruptcy." *Fitzgerald/Hemingway Annual* 1 (1969): 5–13.

Eble, Kenneth E. *F. Scott Fitzgerald.* Rev. ed. Boston: Twayne, 1977.

———, ed. *F. Scott Fitzgerald: A Collection of Criticism.* New York: McGraw-Hill, 1973.

———. "Touches of Disaster: Alcoholism and Mental Illness in Fitzgerald's Short Stories." Pp. 39–52 in *The Short Stories of F. Scott Fitzgerald: New Approaches in Criticism.* Ed. Jackson R. Bryer. Madison: University of Wisconsin Press, 1982.

Edenbaum, Robert I. "'Babylon Revisited': A Psychological Note on F. Scott Fitzgerald." *Literature and Psychology* 18 (1968): 27–29.

Elstein, Rochelle S. "Fitzgerald's Josephine Stories: The End of the Romantic Illusion." *American Literature* 51 (March 1979): 69–83.

Embler, Weller. "F. Scott Fitzgerald and the Future." Pp. 214–21 in *F. Scott Fitzgerald: The Man and His Work.* Ed. Alfred Kazin. New York: Collier, 1962.

Fiedler, Leslie A. "Some Notes on F. Scott Fitzgerald." In *An End to Innocence: Essays on Culture and Politics.* Boston: Beacon Press, 1955.

Fitzgerald, F. Scott. *Afternoon of an Author: A Selection of Uncollected Stories and Essays.* Ed. Arthur Mizener. New York: Charles Scribner's Sons, n.d.

———. *The Beautiful and Damned.* New York: Charles Scribner's Sons, 1922.

———. *The Crack-Up.* Ed. Edmund Wilson. New York: New Directions, 1956.

———. "Fitzgerald on 'The Ice Palace': A Newly Discovered Letter." *Fitzgerald/Hemingway Annual* 4 (1972): 59–60.

———. *The Great Gatsby.* New York: Charles Scribner's Sons, 1925.

———. *The Last Tycoon.* New York: Charles Scribner's Sons, 1941.

———. *Tender Is the Night.* New York: Charles Scribner's Sons, 1934.

———. *This Side of Paradise.* New York: Charles Scribner's Sons, 1920.

Forrey, Robert. "Negroes in the Fiction of F. Scott Fitzgerald." *Phylon* 28 (Fall 1967): 293–98.

Foster, Richard. "Fitzgerald's Imagination: A Parable for Criticism." *Minnesota Review* 7 (1967): 144–56.

Fulkerson, Tahita N. "Ibsen in 'The Ice Palace.'" *Fitzgerald/Hemingway Annual* 11 (1979): 169–71.

Fussell, Edwin S. "Fitzgerald's Brave New World." *ELH* 19 (December 1952): 291–306.

"The Future of Fitzgerald." *Minneapolis Journal* (31 December 1922), editorial section, p. 6. Rpt. pp. 413–14 of *F. Scott Fitzgerald in His Own Time: A Miscellany.* Ed. Matthew J. Bruccoli and Jackson R. Bryer. Kent, Ohio: Kent State University Press, 1971.

Gallo, Rose Adrienne. *F. Scott Fitzgerald.* New York: Frederick Ungar, 1978.

Geismar, Maxwell. "F. Scott Fitzgerald: Orestes at the Ritz." In *The Last of the Provincials: The American Novel, 1915–1925.* Boston: Houghton Mifflin, 1947.

[Gerould, Katherine Fullerton.] "April Lit Successful Because of Grim Note." *Daily Princetonian* (24 April 1917), 1, 3. Rpt. p. 303 of *F. Scott Fitzgerald in His Own Time: A Miscellany.* Ed. Matthew J. Bruccoli and Jackson R. Bryer. Kent, Ohio: Kent State University Press, 1971.

Gervais, Ronald J. "A Miracle of Rare Device: Fitzgerald's 'The Ice Palace.'" *NMAL: Notes on Modern American Literature* 5 (Summer 1981): Item 21.

———. "The Snow of Twenty-Nine: 'Babylon Revisited' as *Ubi Sunt* Lament." *College Literature* 7 (Winter 1980): 47–52.

———. "The Socialist and the Silk Stockings: Fitzgerald's Double Allegiance." *Mosaic* 15 (June 1982): 79–92.

Gery, John. "The Curious Grace of Benjimin [*sic*] Button." *Studies in Short Fiction* 17 (Fall 1980): 495–97.

Gessner, Robert. *The Moving Image: A Guide to Cinematic Literacy.* New York: E. P. Dutton, 1968.

Gingrich, Arnold. Introduction. Pp. ix-xxiii in *The Pat Hobby Stories.* New York: Charles Scribner's Sons, 1962.

Goldhurst, William. *F. Scott Fitzgerald and His Contemporaries.* Cleveland, Ohio: World, 1963.

Grebstein, Sheldon. "The Sane Method of 'Crazy Sunday.'" Pp. 279–89 in *The Short Stories of F. Scott Fitzgerald: New Approaches in Criticism.* Ed. Jackson R. Bryer. Madison: University of Wisconsin Press, 1982.

Griffith, Richard R. "A Note on Fitzgerald's 'Babylon Revisited.'" *American Literature* 35 (May 1963): 236–39.

Gross, Seymour L. "Fitzgerald's 'Babylon Revisited.'" *College English* 25 (November 1963): 128–35.

Gruber, Michael Paul. "Fitzgerald's 'May Day': A Prelude to Triumph." *Essays in Literature* (University of Denver) 2 (1973): 20–35.

Hackett, Alice Payne. *Fifty Years of Best Sellers: 1895–1945.* New York: R. R. Bowker, 1945.

Hagemann, E. R. "Should Scott Fitzgerald be Absolved for the Sins of 'Absolution'?" *Journal of Modern Literature* 12 (March 1985): 169–74.

_____. "'Small *Latine*' in the Three Printings of F. Scott Fitzgerald's 'Absolution.'" *NMAL: Notes on Modern American Literature* 4 (Spring 1980): Item 7.

Hagopian, John V. "A Prince in Babylon." *Fitzgerald Newsletter* 19 (Fall 1962): 1–3.

Harrison, James M. "Fitzgerald's 'Babylon Revisited.'" *Explicator* 16 (January 1958): Item 20.

Häusermann, H. W. "Fitzgerald's Religious Sense: Note and Query." *Modern Fiction Studies* 2 (May 1956): 81–82.

Hemingway, Ernest. *A Moveable Feast.* New York: Charles Scribner's Sons, 1964.

Higgins, John A. *F. Scott Fitzgerald: A Study of the Stories.* Jamaica, New York: St. John's University Press, 1971.

Hindus, Milton. *F. Scott Fitzgerald: An Introduction and Interpretation.* New York: Holt, Rinehart and Winston, 1968.

Hoffman, Frederick J. "*The Great Gatsby* and Its World." In The Great Gatsby: *A Study.* New York: Charles Scribner's Sons, 1962.

_____. *The Twenties: American Writing in the Postwar Decade.* Rev. ed. New York: The Free Press, 1965.

Holman, C. Hugh. "Fitzgerald's Changes on the Southern Belle: The Tarleton Trilogy." Pp. 53–64 in *The Short Stories of F. Scott Fitzgerald: New Approaches in Criticism.* Ed. Jackson R. Bryer. Madison: University of Wisconsin Press, 1982.

Houston, Penelope. "Visits to Babylon: F. Scott Fitzgerald and Hollywood." *Sight and Sound* 21 (April-June 1952): 153–56.

Hughes, Riley. "F. Scott Fitzgerald: The Touch of Disaster." Pp. 135–49 in *Fifty Years of the American Novel: A Christian Appraisal.* Ed. Harold C. Gardiner. New York: Gordian Press, 1968.

Hunt, Jan and John M. Saurez. "The Evasion of Adult Love in Fitzgerald's Fiction." *Centennial Review* 17 (Spring 1973): 152–69.

Irwin, Julie M. "F. Scott Fitzgerald's Little Drinking Problem." *The American Scholar* 56 (Summer 1987): 415, 418–20, 422–24, 426–27.

Isaacs, Neil D. "'Winter Dreams' and Summer Sports." Pp. 199–207 in *The Short Stories of F. Scott Fitzgerald: New Approaches in Criticism.* Ed. Jackson R. Bryer. Madison: University of Wisconsin Press, 1982.

Johnson, Christiane. "Freedom, Contingency, and Ethics in 'The Adjuster.'" Pp. 227–40 in *The Short Stories of F. Scott Fitzgerald: New Approaches in Criticism.* Ed. Jackson R. Bryer. Madison: University of Wisconsin Press, 1982.

Johnson, Ira. "Roundheads and Royalty in 'Babylon.'" *English Record* 14 (October 1963): 32–35.

Johnston, Kenneth G. "Fitzgerald's 'Crazy Sunday': Cinderella in Hollywood." *Literature/Film Quarterly* 6 (Summer 1978): 214–21.

Kane, Patricia. "F. Scott Fitzgerald's St. Paul: A Writer's Use of Material." *Minnesota History* 45 (Winter 1976): 141–48.

Katz, Joseph. "The Narrator and 'The Rich Boy.'" *Fitzgerald Newsletter,* No. 32 (Winter 1966): 2–3.

Kazin, Alfred. "Fitzgerald: An American Confession." In *The Inmost Leaf: A Selection of Essays.* New York: Harcourt Brace, 1955.

_____, ed. *F. Scott Fitzgerald: The Man and His Work.* New York: Collier, 1962.

_____. *On Native Grounds: An Interpretation of Modern American Prose Literature.* New York: Harcourt Brace Jovanovich, 1970.

Kelley, David J. F. "The Polishing of 'Diamond.'" *Fitzgerald Newsletter* 40 (Winter 1968): 1–2.

Kreuter, Kent and Gretchen Kreuter. "The Moralism of the Later Fitzgerald." *Modern Fiction Studies* 7 (Spring 1961): 71–81.

Kuehl, John. "A la Joyce: The Sisters Fitzgerald's Absolution." *James Joyce Quarterly* 2 (Fall 1964): 2–6.

————, ed. *The Apprentice Fiction of F. Scott Fitzgerald: 1909–1917.* New Brunswick, New Jersey: Rutgers University Press, 1965.

————. "Psychic Geography in 'The Ice Palace.'" Pp. 169–79 in *The Short Stories of F. Scott Fitzgerald: New Approaches in Criticism.* Ed. Jackson R. Bryer. Madison: University of Wisconsin Press, 1982.

————. "Scott Fitzgerald's Reading." *Princeton University Library Chronicle* 22 (Winter 1961): 58–89.

———— and Jackson R. Bryer, eds. *Dear Scott/Dear Max: The Fitzgerald-Perkins Correspondence.* New York: Charles Scribner's Sons, 1971.

LaHurd, Ryan. "'Absolution': *Gatsby*'s Forgotten Front Door." *College Literature* 3 (Spring 1976): 113–23.

Lanahan, Frances Fitzgerald. Introduction. Pp. 5–11 in *Six Tales of the Jazz Age and Other Stories.* New York: Charles Scribner's Sons, 1960.

Larsen, Erling. "The Geography of Fitzgerald's Saint Paul." *Carleton Miscellany* 13 (Spring-Summer 1973): 3–30.

Latham, Aaron. *Crazy Sundays: F. Scott Fitzgerald in Hollywood.* New York: Viking Press, 1971.

LeGates, Charlotte. "Dual-Perspective Irony and the Fitzgerald Short Story." *Iowa English Yearbook* 26 (1977): 18–20.

Lehan, Richard D. *F. Scott Fitzgerald and the Craft of Fiction.* Carbondale: Southern Illinois University Press, 1966.

————. "F. Scott Fitzgerald and Romantic Destiny." *Twentieth Century Literature* 26 (Summer 1980): 137–56.

————. "The Romantic Self and the Uses of Place in the Stories of F. Scott Fitzgerald." Pp. 3–21 in *The Short Stories of F. Scott Fitzgerald: New Approaches in Criticism.* Ed. Jackson R. Bryer. Madison: University of Wisconsin Press, 1982.

LeVot, André. *F. Scott Fitzgerald: A Biography.* Trans. William Byron. Garden City, New York: Doubleday, 1983.

Lewis, Janet. "'The Cruise of the Rolling Junk': The Fictionalized Joys of Motoring." *Fitzgerald/Hemingway Annual* 10 (1978): 69–81.

Lindfors, Bernth. "Paris Revisited." *Fitzgerald Newsletter* 16 (Winter 1962): 4.

Long, Robert Emmet. *The Achieving of* The Great Gatsby: *F. Scott Fitzgerald, 1920–1925.* Lewisburg, Pennsylvania: Bucknell University Press, 1979.

Lubell, Albert J. "The Fitzgerald Revival." *South Atlantic Quarterly* 54 (January 1955): 95–106.

Lueders, Edward. "Revisiting Babylon: Fitzgerald and the 1920s." *Western Humanities Review* 29 (Summer 1975): 285–91.

McCollum, Kenneth. "'Babylon Revisited' Revisited." *Fitzgerald/Hemingway Annual* 3 (1971): 314–16.

Male, Roy R. "'Babylon Revisited': A Story of the Exile's Return." *Studies in Short Fiction* 2 (Spring 1965): 270–77.

Malin, Irving. "'Absolution': Absolving Lies." Pp. 209–16 in *The Short Stories of F. Scott Fitzgerald: New Approaches in Criticism.* Ed. Jackson R. Bryer. Madison: University of Wisconsin Press, 1982.

Mancini, Joseph, Jr. "To Be Both Light and Dark: The Jungian Process of Individuation in Fitzgerald's Basil Duke Lee Stories." Pp. 89–110 in *The Short Stories of F. Scott Fitzgerald: New Approaches in Criticism.* Ed. Jackson R. Bryer. Madison: University of Wisconsin Press, 1982.

Margolies, Alan. "'The Camel's Back' and *Conductor 1492.*" *Fitzgerald/Hemingway Annual* 6 (1974): 87–88.

————. "'Kissing, Shooting, and Sacrificing': F. Scott Fitzgerald and the Hollywood Market." Pp. 65–73 in *The Short Stories of F. Scott Fitzgerald: New Approaches in Criticism.* Ed. Jackson R. Bryer. Madison: University of Wisconsin Press, 1982.

————. "A Note on Fitzgerald's Lost and Unpublished Stories." *Fitzgerald/Hemingway Annual* 4 (1972): 335–36.

Marshall, Margaret. "Notes By the Way." *Nation* 152 (8 February 1941): 159–60.

Martin, Robert A. "Hollywood in Fitzgerald: After Paradise." Pp. 127–48 in *The Short Stories of F. Scott Fitzgerald: New Approaches in Criticism*. Ed. Jackson R. Bryer. Madison: University of Wisconsin Press, 1982.

————. "The Hot Madness of Four O'Clock in Fitzgerald's 'Absolution' and *Gatsby*." *Studies in American Fiction* 2 (Autumn 1974): 230–38.

Martin, Robert K. "Sexual and Group Relationship [*sic*] in 'May Day': Fear and Longing." *Studies in Short Fiction* 15 (Winter 1978): 99–101.

Matthews, T. S. *"Taps at Reveille."* P. 107 in *F. Scott Fitzgerald: The Man and His Work*. Ed. Alfred Kazin. New York: Collier, 1962.

Mazzella, Anthony J. "The Tension of Opposites in Fitzgerald's 'May Day.'" *Studies in Short Fiction* 14 (Fall 1977): 379–85.

Mellow, James R. *Invented Lives: F. Scott & Zelda Fitzgerald*. New York: Ballantine Books, 1984.

Mencken, H. L. "Two Years Too Late." P. 286 in *H. L. Mencken's Smart Set Criticism*. Ed. William H. Nolte. Ithaca, New York: Cornell University Press, 1968.

Messenger, Christian K. *Sport and the Spirit of Play in American Fiction: Hawthorne to Faulkner*. New York: Columbia University Press, 1981.

Milford, Nancy. *Zelda*. New York: Avon, 1970.

Miller, James E., Jr. *F. Scott Fitzgerald: His Art and His Technique*. New York: New York University Press, 1967.

Mizener, Arthur. *The Far Side of Paradise: A Biography of F. Scott Fitzgerald*. 2d ed. Boston: Houghton Mifflin, 1965.

————, ed. *F. Scott Fitzgerald: A Collection of Critical Essays*. Englewood Cliffs, New Jersey: Prentice-Hall, 1963.

————. Introduction. Pp. xv-xxvii in *The Fitzgerald Reader*. New York: Charles Scribner's Sons, 1963.

————. Introduction and Notes. Pp. 3–12, et passim in *Afternoon of an Author*. New York: Charles Scribner's Sons, 1957.

————. Introductory Essay. Pp. 11–16 in *Flappers and Philosophers*. New York: Charles Scribner's Sons, 1959.

————. "The Maturity of Scott Fitzgerald." *Sewanee Review* 67 (October-December 1959): 658–75.

————. "The Voice of Scott Fitzgerald's Prose." *Essays and Studies* [English Association] N. S. 16 (1963): 56–67.

Monk, Donald. "Fitzgerald: The Tissue of Style." *Journal of American Studies* 17 (April 1983): 77–94.

Morris, Wright. "The Function of Nostalgia: F. Scott Fitzgerald." Pp. 25–31 in *F. Scott Fitzgerald: A Collection of Critical Essays*. Ed. Arthur Mizener. Englewood Cliffs, New Jersey: Prentice Hall, 1963.

Morrison, Gail Moore. "Faulkner's Priests and Fitzgerald's 'Absolution.'" *Mississippi Quarterly* 32 (Summer 1979): 461–65.

Morse, J. I. "Fitzgerald's *Sagitta Volante in Dei:* An Emendation and a Possible Source." *Fitzgerald/Hemingway Annual* 4 (1972): 321–22.

Moses, Edwin. "F. Scott Fitzgerald and The Quest To The Ice Palace." *CEA Critic* 36 (January 1974): 11–14.

Mosher, John Chapin. "That Sad Young Man." Pp. 67–71 in *F. Scott Fitzgerald: The Man and His Work*. Ed. Alfred Kazin. New York: Collier, 1962.

Moyer, Kermit W. "Fitzgerald's Two Unfinished Novels: The Count and the Tycoon in Spenglerian Perspective." *Contemporary Literature* 15 (Spring 1974): 238–56.

Murphy, Garry N. and William C. Slattery. "The Flawed Text of 'Babylon Revisited': A Challenge to Editors, A Warning to Readers." *Studies in Short Fiction* 18 (Summer 1981): 315–18.

Nettels, Elsa. "Howell's 'A Circle in the Water' and Fitzgerald's 'Babylon Revisited.'" *Studies in Short Fiction* 19 (Summer 1982): 261–67.

O'Hara, John. Introduction. Pp. vii-xix in *The Portable F. Scott Fitzgerald*. Ed. Dorothy Parker. New York: Viking Press, 1949.

Osborne, William R. "The Wounds of Charlie Wales in Fitzgerald's 'Babylon Revisited.'" *Studies in Short Fiction* 2 (Fall 1964): 86–87.

Perlis, Alan. "The Narrative Is All: A Study of F. Scott Fitzgerald's *May Day*." *Western Humanities Review* 33 (Winter 1979): 65–72.

Perosa, Sergio. *The Art of F. Scott Fitzgerald*. Trans. Charles Matz and Sergio Perosa. Ann Arbor: University of Michigan Press, 1965.

Person, Leland S., Jr. "Fitzgerald's 'O Russet Witch!': Dangerous Women, Dangerous Art." *Studies in Short Fiction* 23 (Fall 1986): 443–48.

Petry, Alice Hall. "Love Story: Mock Courtship in F. Scott Fitzgerald's 'The Jelly-Bean.'" *Arizona Quarterly* 39 (Fall 1983): 251–60.

―――. "The Picture(s) of Paula Legendre: Fitzgerald's 'The Rich Boy.'"*Studies in Short Fiction* 22 (Spring 1985): 232–34.

Phillips, Larry W. *F. Scott Fitzgerald on Writing*. New York: Charles Scribner's Sons, 1985.

Pike, Gerald. "Four Voices in 'Winter Dreams.'" *Studies in Short Fiction* 23 (Summer 1986): 315–20.

Pinsker, Sanford. "Fitzgerald's 'The Baby Party.'" *Explicator* 45 (Winter 1987): 52–55.

Piper, Henry Dan. *F. Scott Fitzgerald: A Critical Portrait*. New York: Holt, Rinehart and Winston, 1965.

―――. "Frank Norris and Scott Fitzgerald." *Huntington Library Quarterly* 19 (August 1956): 393–400.

―――. "Scott Fitzgerald's Prep-School Writings: Several Newly-Discovered Additions to the Canon of His Published Works." *Princeton University Library Chronicle* 17 (Autumn 1955): 1–10.

―――. "The Untrimmed Christmas Tree: The Religious Background of *The Great Gatsby*." Pp. 321–34 in The Great Gatsby: A Study. Ed. Frederick J. Hoffman. New York: Charles Scribner's Sons, 1962.

Podis, Leonard A. "Fitzgerald's 'The Diamond as Big as the Ritz' and Hawthorne's 'Rappaccini's Daughter.'" *Studies in Short Fiction* 21 (Summer 1984): 243–50.

Posnock, Ross. "'A New World, Material Without Being Real': Fitzgerald's Critique of Capitalism in *The Great Gatsby*." Pp. 201–13 in *Critical Essays on F. Scott Fitzgerald's The Great Gatsby*. Ed. Scott Donaldson. Boston: G. K. Hall, 1984.

Powers, J. F. "Cross Country: St. Paul, Home of the Saints." *Partisan Review* 16 (July 1949): 714–21.

―――. "Dealer in Diamonds and Rhinestones." *Commonweal* 42 (10 August 1945): 408–10.

Prigozy, Ruth. "Fitzgerald's Short Stories and the Depression: An Artistic Crisis." Pp. 111–26 in *The Short Stories of F. Scott Fitzgerald: New Approaches in Criticism*. Ed. Jackson R. Bryer. Madison: University of Wisconsin Press, 1982.

―――. "Gatsby's Guest List and Fitzgerald's Technique of Naming." *Fitzgerald/Hemingway Annual* 4 (1972): 99–112.

―――. "'Poor Butterfly': F. Scott Fitzgerald and Popular Music." *Prospects* 2 (1976): 40–67.

―――. "The Unpublished Stories: Fitzgerald in His Final Stage." *Twentieth Century Literature* 20 (April 1974): 69–90.

[Review of *All the Sad Young Men*]. "The Gossip Shop." *Bookman* [New York] 63 (May 1926): 374–75.

Robbins, J. Albert. "Fitzgerald and the Simple, Inarticulate Farmer." *Modern Fiction Studies* 7 (Winter 1961–1962): 365–69.

Robillard, Douglas. "The Paradises of Scott Fitzgerald." *Essays in Arts and Sciences* 4 (May 1975): 64–73.

Rosenfeld, Paul. "F. Scott Fitzgerald." In *Men Seen: Twenty-Four Modern Authors*. New York: Dial Press, 1925.

Roulston, Robert. "Whistling 'Dixie' in Encino: *The Last Tycoon* and F. Scott Fitzgerald's Two Souths." *South Atlantic Quarterly* 79 (Autumn 1980): 355–63.

Savage, D. S. "The Significance of F. Scott Fitzgerald." *Arizona Quarterly* 8 (Autumn 1952): 197–210.

Scharnhorst, Gary. "Scribbling Upward: Fitzgerald's Debt of Honor to Horatio Alger, Jr." *Fitzgerald/Hemingway Annual* 10 (1978): 161–69.

Schoenwald, Richard L. "F. Scott Fitzgerald as John Keats." *Boston University Studies in English* 3 (Spring 1957): 12–21.

Schrader, Richard J. "F [*sic*] and Charles G. Norris." *Fitzgerald Newsletter* 26 (Summer 1964): 3–4.

Shain, Charles E. *F. Scott Fitzgerald*. Minneapolis: University of Minnesota Press, 1961.

Sklar, Robert. *F. Scott Fitzgerald: The Last Laocoön*. New York: Oxford University Press, 1967.

Slattery, Sister Margaret Patrice. "The Function of Time in GG [*sic*] and 'Babylon.'" *Fitzgerald Newsletter* 39 (Fall 1967): 1–4.

Spatz, Jonas. "Fitzgerald, Hollywood, and the Myth of Success." Pp. 31–37 in *The Thirties: Fiction, Poetry, Drama*. Ed. Warren French. 2d ed., rev. Deland, Florida: Everett/Edwards, 1976.

Speer, Roderick S. "*The Great Gatsby*'s 'Romance of Motoring' and 'The Cruise of the Rolling Junk.'" *Modern Fiction Studies* 20 (Winter 1975): 540–43.

Spencer, Benjamin T. "Fitzgerald and the American Ambivalence." *South Atlantic Quarterly* 66 (Summer 1967): 367–81.

Staley, Thomas F. "Time and Structure in Fitzgerald's 'Babylon Revisited.'" *Modern Fiction Studies* 10 (Winter 1964–1965): 386–88.

Stanley, Linda C. *The Foreign Critical Reputation of F. Scott Fitzgerald: An Analysis and Annotated Bibliography*. Westport, Connecticut: The Greenwood Press, 1980.

Stavola, Thomas J. *Scott Fitzgerald: Crisis in an American Identity*. New York: Barnes & Noble, 1979.

Stein, William Bysshe. "Two Notes on 'The Rich Boy.'" *Fitzgerald Newsletter* 14 (Summer 1961): 1–3.

Stern, Milton R. *The Golden Moment: The Novels of F. Scott Fitzgerald*. Urbana: University of Illinois Press, 1970.

Stewart, Lawrence D. "'Absolution' and *The Great Gatsby*." *Fitzgerald/Hemingway Annual* 5 (1973): 181–87.

Swinnerton, A. C. "In Other Colleges: *Nassau Literary Magazine*." *Williams [College] Literary Monthly* 33 (May 1917): 411–12.

Tanner, Louise. "Babylon Revisited: F. Scott Fitzgerald." In *Here Today* . . . New York: Thomas Y. Crowell, 1959.

Tanner, Stephen L. "Fitzgerald: 'What to Make of a Diminished Thing.'" *Arizona Quarterly* 34 (Summer 1978): 153–61.

Taylor, Dwight. "Scott Fitzgerald in Hollywood." *Harper's* 218 (March 1959): 67–71.

Toor, David. "Guilt and Retribution in 'Babylon Revisited.'" *Fitzgerald/Hemingway Annual* 5 (1973): 155–64.

Tressin, Deanna. "Toward Understanding." *English Journal* 55 (December 1966): 1170–74.

Trilling, Lionel. "F. Scott Fitzgerald." In *The Liberal Imagination: Essays on Literature and Society*. New York: Charles Scribner's Sons, 1950.

Troy, William. "Scott Fitzgerald: The Authority of Failure." Pp. 188–94 in *F. Scott Fitzgerald: The Man and His Work*. Ed. Alfred Kazin. New York: Collier, 1962.

Turnbull, Andrew, ed. *The Letters of F. Scott Fitzgerald*. New York: Dell, 1963.

———. *Scott Fitzgerald*. New York: Charles Scribner's Sons, 1962.

Tuttleton, James W. "Seeing Slightly Red: Fitzgerald's 'May Day.'" Pp. 181–97 in *The Short Stories of F. Scott Fitzgerald: New Approaches in Criticism*. Ed. Jackson R. Bryer. Madison: University of Wisconsin Press, 1982.

Twitchell, James B. "'Babylon Revisited': Chronology and Characters." *Fitzgerald/Hemingway Annual* 10 (1978): 155–60.

Untermeyer, Louis. "F. Scott Fitzgerald." *Makers of the Modern World*. New York: Simon and Schuster, 1955.

Van Winkle, Cortlandt. "Prose Surpasses Verse in June Number of Lit." *Daily Princetonian* (9 June 1915): 1, 4. Rpt. p. 301 of *F. Scott Fitzgerald in His Own Time: A Miscellany*. Ed. Matthew J. Bruccoli and Jackson R. Bryer. Kent, Ohio: Kent State University Press, 1971.

Voss, Arthur. *The American Short Story: A Critical Survey*. Norman: University of Oklahoma Press, 1973.

Wanning, Andrews. "Fitzgerald and His Brethren." Pp. 57–63 in *F. Scott Fitzgerald: A Collection of Critical Essays*. Ed. Arthur Mizener. Englewood Cliffs, New Jersey: Prentice-Hall, 1963.

Way, Brian. *F. Scott Fitzgerald and the Art of Social Fiction*. New York: St. Martin's, 1980.

———. "Scott Fitzgerald." *New Left Review* 21 (October 1963): 36–51.

Weir, Charles, Jr. "'An Invite with Gilded Edges': A Study of F. Scott Fitzgerald." *Virginia Quarterly Review* 20 (Winter 1944): 100–13.

Wells, Elizabeth. "A Comparative Statistical Analysis of the Prose Styles of F. Scott Fitzgerald and Ernest Hemingway." *Fitzgerald/Hemingway Annual* 1 (1969): 47–67.

Wells, Walter. "The Hero and the Hack." In *Tycoons and Locusts: A Regional Look at Hollywood Fiction of the 1930s*. Carbondale: Southern Illinois University Press, 1973.

Wescott, Glenway. "The Moral of Scott Fitzgerald." Pp. 115–29 in *F. Scott Fitzgerald: The Man and His Work*. Ed. Alfred Kazin. New York: Collier, 1962.

West, James L. W., III. "Fitzgerald and *Esquire*." Pp. 149–66 in *The Short Stories of F. Scott Fitzgerald: New Approaches in Criticism*. Ed. Jackson R. Bryer. Madison: University of Wisconsin Press, 1982.

———. *The Making of* This Side of Paradise. Philadelphia: University of Pennsylvania Press, 1983.

——— and J. Barclay Inge. "F. Scott Fitzgerald's Revision of 'The Rich Boy.'" *Proof* 5 (1977): 127–46.

West, Ray B., Jr. *The Short Story in America*. Chicago: Henry Regnery, 1952.

White, William. "Mr. North, Mr. Bruccoli, and Fitzgerald." *American Book Collector* 15 (November 1964): 25–26.

———. "The Text of 'Babylon Revisited.'" *Fitzgerald Newsletter* 28 (Winter 1965): 4–7.

———. "Two Versions of F. Scott Fitzgerald's 'Babylon Revisited': A Textual and Bibliographical Study." *Papers of the Bibliographical Society of America* 60 (Fourth Quarter 1966): 439–52.

Wilson, Edmund, ed. *The Crack-Up*. New York: New Directions, 1956.

———. "Fitzgerald Before *The Great Gatsby*." Pp. 78–84 in *F. Scott Fitzgerald: The Man and His Work*. New York: Collier, 1962.

Wolfe, Peter. "Faces in a Dream: Innocence Perpetuated in 'The Rich Boy.'" Pp. 241–49 in *The Short Stories of F. Scott Fitzgerald: New Approaches in Criticism*. Ed. Jackson R. Bryer. Madison: University of Wisconsin Press, 1982.

Wright, Austin McGiffert. *The American Short Story in the Twenties*. Chicago: University of Chicago Press, 1961.

Wycherley, H. Alan. "Fitzgerald Revisited." *Texas Studies in Literature and Language* 8 (Summer 1966): 277–83.

Index